ON

Pragmatics & Beyond
New Series

16

William C. Mann and Sandra A. Thompson (eds)

Discourse Description

DISCOURSE DESCRIPTION

DIVERSE LINGUISTIC ANALYSES OF A FUND-RAISING TEXT

edited by

WILLIAM C. MANN and SANDRA A. THOMPSON

JOHN BENJAMINS PUBLISHING COMPANY
AMSTERDAM/PHILADELPHIA

1992

Library of Congress Cataloging-in-Publication Data

Discourse description : diverse linguistic analyses of a fund-raising text / edited by William C. Mann and Sandra A. Thompson.
p. cm. -- (Pragmatics & beyond, ISSN 0922-842X ; new ser. 16)
Includes index.
1. Discourse analysis. 2. Fund-raising. I. Mann, William C. II. Thompson, Sandra A. III. Series.
P302.D5487 1992
401'.41--dc20 91-46957
ISBN 90 272 5026 X (Eur.)/1-55619-282-7 (US) (Hb) (alk. paper) CIP
ISBN 90 272 5031 6 (Eur.)/1-55619-288-6 (US) (Pb) (alk. paper)

John Benjamins Publishing Co. · P.O. Box 75577 · 1070 AN Amsterdam · Netherlands
John Benjamins North America · 821 Bethlehem Pike · Philadelphia, PA 19118 · USA

Table of Contents

Zero Population Growth

November 22, 1985

Dear Friend of ZPG:

At 7:00 a.m. on October 25, our phones started to ring. Calls jammed our switchboard all day. Staffers stayed late into the night, answering questions and talking with reporters from newspapers, radio stations, wire services and TV stations in every part of the country.

When we released the results of ZPG's 1985 Urban Stress Test, we had no idea we'd get such an overwhelming response. Media and public reaction has been nothing short of incredible!

At first, the deluge of calls came mostly from reporters eager to tell the public about Urban Stress Test results and from outraged public officials who were furious that we had "blown the whistle" on conditions in their cities.

Now we are hearing from concerned citizens in all parts of the country who want to know what they can do to hold local officials accountable for tackling population-related problems that threaten public health and well-being.

ZPG's 1985 Urban Stress Test, created after months of persistent and exhaustive research, is the nation's first survey of how population-linked pressures affect U.S. cities. It ranks 184 urban areas on 11 different criteria ranging from crowding and birth rates to air quality and toxic wastes.

The Urban Stress Test translates complex, technical data into an easy-to-use action tool for concerned citizens, elected officials and opinion leaders. But to use it well, we urgently need your help.

> Our small staff is being swamped with requests for more information and our modest resources are being stretched to the limit.

Your support now is critical. ZPG's 1985 Urban Stress Test may be our best opportunity ever to get the population message heard.

1601 CONNECTICUT AVENUE, NW ■ WASHINGTON, DC 20009 ■ (202) 332-2200

With your contribution, ZPG can arm our growing network of local activists with the materials they need to warn community leaders about emerging population-linked stresses before they reach the crisis stage.

Even though our national government continues to ignore the consequences of uncontrolled population growth, we can act to take positive action at the local level.

Every day decisions are being made by local officials in our communities that could drastically affect the quality of our lives. To make sound choices in planning for people, both elected officials and the American public need the population-stress data revealed by our study.

Please make a special contribution to Zero Population Growth today. Whatever you give -- $25, $50, $100 or as much as you can -- will be used immediately to put the Urban Stress Test in the hands of those who need it most.

Sincerely,

Susan Weber

Susan Weber
Executive Director

P.S. The results of ZPG's 1985 Urban Stress Test were reported as a top news story by hundreds of newspapers and TV and radio stations from coast to coast. I hope you'll help us monitor this remarkable media coverage by completing the enclosed reply form.

Introduction

Discourse linguistics is a rewarding area of study, but it presents some unnecessary, avoidable difficulties. One difficulty comes not from the subject matter, but in discovering and comprehending various approaches. This book is designed to help reduce that difficulty.

This is a book for students — both the degree-seekers and the researchers. There are many different ways to analyze texts; we have tried to make various approaches accessible and comparable, by inviting several analysts to study and report on the same text, by asking them to meet certain criteria of comparability, and by putting the resulting papers in one volume.

We selected a text that shows language working in ways that go beyond the common preconceptions. Rather than choose, say, an encyclopedia entry as the text for analysis, we have picked a text in which the author is not simply trying to inform the reader. It is a letter, mailed in bulk by an organization that is supported by contributions from donors, primarily donors who receive letters such as this one. Zero Population Growth, the organization, is based in Washington, D.C. The letter is used by permission. The organization, ZPG, seeks to represent people who are concerned about overpopulation, in particular about population growth in the United States. It seeks to influence public officials and public opinion so that overpopulation and related problems are mitigated. The organization is independent, not part of any government. It engages in lobbying and publicity campaigns, using money donated by interested individuals or organizations.

The text therefore must be constructed to have many different communication effects: informing about the organization, producing approval of the organization and its activities, producing a desire to contribute, and so forth. These, especially the desire to contribute, require special treatment in the text and so can potentially expose its methods as well as its structure.

The letter is shown next. We have segmented it so that our authors could refer to its parts in a consistent way; the segmentation is given at the end of this introduction. The segmentation is intended to be as superficial and theory-neutral as possible, simply reflecting visible subdivisions. We have left it to the authors to discern what is significant.

The book has been divided into two sections, the first on text organization, and the second on lexical and grammatical concerns. Each section has its own introduction. This collection represents a wide range of perspectives and viewpoints on discourse analysis, and we are grateful to our authors, who have worked hard to contribute to this book; there are others whom we wish could have contributed, but who, regrettably, could not.

Segment 1
ZERO
POPULATION
GROWTH

Segment 2 November 22, 1985

Segment 3 Dear Friend of ZPG:

Segment 4 At 7:00 a.m. on October 25, our phones started to ring.

Segment 5 Calls jammed our switchboard all day.

Segment 6 Staffers stayed late into the night, answering questions and talking with reporters from newspapers, radio stations, wire services and TV stations in every part of the country.

(para)

Segment 7 When we released the results of ZPG's 1985 Urban Stress Test, we had no idea we'd get such an overwhelming response.

Segment 8 Media and public reaction has been nothing short of incredible!

(para)

Segment 9 At first, the deluge of calls came mostly from reporters eager to tell the public about Urban Stress Test results and from outraged public officials who were furious that we had "blown the whistle" on conditions in their cities.

(para)

Segment 10 Now we are hearing from concerned citizens in all parts of the country who want to know what they can do to hold local officials accountable for tackling population-related problems that threaten public health and well-being.

(para)

Segment 11 ZPG's 1985 Urban Stress Test, created after months of persistent and exhaustive research, is the nation's first survey of how population-linked pressures affect U.S. cities.

Segment 12 It ranks 184 urban areas on 11 different criteria ranging from crowding and birth rates to air quality and toxic wastes.

(para)

Segment 13 The Urban Stress Test translates complex, technical data into an easy-to-use action tool for concerned citizens, elected officials and opinion leaders.

Segment 14 But to use it well, we urgently need your help.

(para)

> Segment 15 Our small staff is being swamped with requests for more information and our modest resources are being stretched to the limit.

(para)

Segment 16 Your support now is critical.

Segment 17 ZPG's 1985 Urban Stress Test may be our best opportunity ever to get the population message heard.

(page, para)

Segment 18 With your contribution, ZPG can arm our growing network of local activists with the materials they need to warn community leaders about emerging population-linked stresses before they reach crisis stage.

(para)

Segment 19 Even though our national government continues to ignore the consequences of uncontrolled population growth, we can act to take positive action at the local level.

(para)

Segment 20 Every day decisions are being made by local officials in our communities that could drastically affect the quality of our lives.

Segment 21. To make sound choices in planning for people, both elected officials and the American public need the population-stress data revealed by our study.

(para)

Segment 22 Please make a special contribution to Zero Population Growth today.

Segment 23. Whatever you give -- $25, $50, $100 or as much as you can -- will be used immediately to put the Urban Stress Test in the hands of those who need it most.

Segment 24 Sincerely,

Segment 25(handwritten signature)

Segment 26 Susan Weber
Segment 27 Executive Director

Segment 28 P.S.

Segment 29 The results of ZPG's 1985 Urban Stress Test were reported as a top news story by hundreds of newspapers and TV and radio stations from coast to coast.

Segment 30 I hope you'll help us monitor this remarkable media coverage by completing the enclosed reply form.

I. TEXT ORGANIZATION

Following our plan of helping the student, we raise a few of the questions we see as most important. We expect that readers can read these papers, find the authors' answers to most of these questions, and then to go on to find their own answers.

1. What is the nature of text organization? Some might see it as a matter of arbitrary convention, a collection of layout diagrams that have come into use with no particular merit. Others might see text organization as a set of patterns employed to achieve particular effects, always chosen for the purpose at hand, with re-invention rather than re-use of particular patterns. There are other assumptions besides these extremes. Why do we find that texts are organized?

2. How is form related to function? How do the words, syntactic structures, and other structural elements create particular effects as the text is read? Is there a way to describe texts in an abstract way so that this relationship become simple? Perhaps with proper description each form — a class of conjunctions for example — is always used to create a specific effect. Or is it the case that for any particular communicative purpose, every kind of linguistic resource is available to the speaker?

The papers in this volume tend toward the latter answer, but the answers are neither as extreme as they might be nor in full agreement. The problem is made more complex by the fact that there is no consensus on what the relevant set of functions is, and also by the fact that the terminology of "function" is itself used in a diverse and somewhat equivocal way in the field. This leads to the next question.

3. What are the functions of text organization? Are they outcomes, such as wanting to contribute? Are they experiences, such as recognition of the speaker's wisdom? Are they processes, such as thinking about the concepts chosen by the speaker for the hearer to think about?

There is a widely shared assumption in our culture that the principal function of language is to inform. Under this assumption the speaker knows something that the hearer does not, but the hearer comes to know it by being told; a text has a collection of messages to deliver, and if it delivers them then it is a successful text.

This assumption is found not only in popular culture, as Michael Reddy's conduit metaphor, but also in linguistics. Many linguists seem to either believe it or else are willing to take it as a working assumption while attending to other matters. Linguists who examine it directly seem to almost universally reject it, taking instead a stance that language is pluralistic in function, and that informing is merely one of the functions of language use, the primary function in some texts but not others. Unfortunately, the group who have carefully examined this particular assumption seem to be in the minority, and their view does not prevail over cultural bias in the rest of the field.

The papers collected here give a good opportunity to examine a diversity of language functions, and to see whether the message exchange model can be rescued by generalization, as the Callows attempt to do, or whether it is better to try to replace it, as others attempt to do.

4. Does each paper convey a particular method of analyzing text? Could I apply each of these methods to the fund-raising letters that I receive in tomorrow's mail?

As we indicated, we have asked each author to be explicit about essential definitions and methods. They have only partially succeeded. For the text organization papers, employing the authors' methods requires practice as well as good definitions, and so the papers cannot possibly convey the skill of analysis itself.

But the methods are also not fully specified, and it is worthwhile to try to determine what additional help would be needed in order to make each analysis method fully explicit. There is a real possibility that some or all of the methods rely on social experience of an unspecifiable kind, and that without such informal aid, text analysis methods will lack most of their insightfulness.

It was particularly interesting to find that while we, as editors, valued explicitness and definiteness very highly, some of our colleagues did not. We have seen instances in which important-looking theoretical issues were left open in a paper, although they were not in fact open issues to the author. Authors sometimes made deliberate choices against explicitness and definiteness. We find such choices particularly interesting, since in our own work we make progress by making our expectations into definite, testable positions, which then fail in interesting and repairable ways. For us, to avoid definiteness is to avoid progress. Yet for some of our colleagues, there are more dominant goals. All of this suggests that it would be worthwhile to try to develop a greater consensus on what the goals and central tasks of text linguistics really are.

5. What is the object of study of each paper? How does it relate to the notion of realization? The Mann, Matthiessen, and Thompson paper focuses on pre-realizational description of text structure.

6. What are the research goals of each paper? Why does the author value the knowledge of text organization? For some, it is a fresh source of evidence and insight for understanding details of text such as lexical and syntactic choices. For others, it is a move toward a more comprehensive understanding, perhaps of interpersonal communication or social organization.

7. How do the authors' assumptions disagree? Using the list of assumptions in Mann, Matthiessen and Thompson's paper as a benchmark, there seems to be general agreement on several, such as the notion that texts are organized. But there is disagreement on others, such as the homogeneity of text-organizing devices. Several papers, in different ways, present three kinds of text-organizing patterns, one found only spanning whole texts, one found repeatedly within texts, and a third that prevails only for units that are the size of sentences or smaller. Do these threefold patterns represent agreement or superficial similarity?

***

The papers in this section share an assumption that a major part of text structure has to do with relations among component parts. These have been given various names in the literature, but their significance in understanding text organization is recognized by all the authors in this section.

The Callows, assuming that text structure follows from intended meanings, propose 'coherence relations' to hold between units of the text, and show how these relations convey the functions of informing, expressing attitudes and emotions, and bringing about changes.

Mann et al.'s Rhetorical Structure Theory views the text in terms of the relations among its component parts. The same relations are assumed to hold at all levels of text structure, so that a specification of these relations from roughly clause level to overall text level yields a hierarchical analysis of the entire text, which captures the ways in which the parts are related to each other.

Like Mann et al., Meyer's approach is specifically hierarchical. Basing her analysis on earlier work of Grimes, her method also reveals the relationships among the component parts from the sentence level up through the higher levels of logical organization and argumentation to the overall organization of the text.

Longacre's analysis begins with the assumption that the ZPG letter is an instance of hortatory discourse, that is, discourse which is intended to influence the behavior of its readers. Assuming that certain schemas characterize each discourse type, Longacre's paper shows how the letter is organized by applying the hortatory schema to it, and by showing how the schema predicts the natural groupings found in the text.

Winter's paper addresses the question of the organization of the text in terms of answers to questions which readers might ask of the writer. If these questions can reveal the connection between two sentences or clauses, then the questions serve to make explicit those clause relations.

Jordan's analysis, in addition to revealing relations among clauses, is also concerned with lexical cohesion and with the texturing capabilities of what he calls the prevalent 'problem-solution' structure which the writer applies to the themes and arguments of the text.

Pike's paper views text in a structured way related to the way sentences are seen in the tagmemic framework. Insights from multiple sentences are thus made available for refining one's understanding of each sentence.

Text as Purposive Communication: A Meaning-based Analysis

Kathleen Callow and John C. Callow
Summer Institute of Linguistics[1]

1. Foundational Assumptions[2]

1.1 *A Discourse Conveys Meaning*

A discourse is not simply an organised collection of words, it is the distillation in verbal form of the thoughts and outlook of the communicator. If we view a discourse simply as the realisation of lexical and syntactic rules or patterns, we are missing the whole point. Of course verbal forms do realise language systems, but no one outside the classroom uses verbal forms *for this purpose.* People use verbal forms to *communicate meaning*, and the exploiting of the verbal forms of the language is simply a means to this end.

In our view, therefore, discourses primarily realise meanings, and only secondarily realise language-structures: to reverse this order is to let the tail wag the dog. It is important not to view the verbal forms of a discourse as independent and self-subsistent. Rather, verbal forms are signals, signals of the meaning which the speaker or writer wishes to convey. It is the intended meaning of the speaker which controls the selection of specific verbal forms, and any analysis of the resultant discourse which does not give due weight to that intended meaning will be inherently incomplete and defective.

1.2 *Meaning is Distinct from Form*

J'ai faim and *I'm hungry* both mean the same: the two forms convey one meaning. If we are asking our family to be quiet, we may say, *Please be quiet*, or *Less noise, there!* or *Could you reduce the decibels a bit, you lot?*

Whichever form we employ, the meaning is essentially the same. But when such diverse verbal forms can convey one meaning, it is obvious that we do not generate verbal communications from a lexical base. If we did, the three ways of requesting quietness would require three bases. We are claiming that there is only one meaning-base and that the underlying meaning is the same whichever form is expressing it, and in whatever language. Meaning must be considered as distinct from the verbal forms which express it.

The meaning expressed in verbal communication is a universal, i.e. it is capable of multiple realisations in words, but is independent of those realisations, which are specifics. Alternatively, the meaning may be viewed as a constant, and the various forms available for expressing it as the variables. In analysing discourse we are analysing a specific realisation of an underlying meaning which is a universal; it is capable in principle of realisation in any language.

We will call the meaning being expressed in a verbal communication the *message*, and any given set of verbal forms encoding it, the *discourse*. One message may be encoded in several different discourses (either in different languages, or in paraphrases). A message combined with one such realisation in discourse is what we are calling a *text*.

1.3 *The Communicator is Central*

In making a sharp distinction between meaning and form we have in effect denied that meaning is inherent in words, as if it were some vague Platonic essence attached to each verbal form. But if meaning is not inherent in words, then where is it to be found? The kind of meaning with which we are concerned here is *the meaning the speaker intends to convey*. As he communicates he is using verbal forms as signals of his inward thoughts, attitudes, emotions, purposes, etc. Words do not *have* meanings, they *signal* meanings.

And the meaning that is thus signalled is not a linguistic abstraction. *Meanings are in people's heads*. The speaker is central. He uses verbal forms as outward signals of his inward thoughts and emotions, and the signalling system he uses is one shared by a whole community of people. Words are culturally-agreed-upon signals, and a whole community uses these signals in similar ways to express a vast range of experience and attitudes. The meaning of a word is its use in the community, and a speaker is well aware of the meaning-value the community will put on his verbal coinage.

1.4 *Meaning is Structured*

In distinguishing meaning from the forms which express it, we are not denying that meaning has structure, but only that it has *language-based* structure. Rather, since meaning is always the meaning of a communicator, meaning itself has a structure which mirrors cognition. Every element claimed to belong to the structure of meaning must have some cognitive counterpart in the mind of the communicator, or else it is without foundation. Meaning must be analysed in terms of cognitive categories, and these cognitive categories can be seen to relate to each other in a structured way.

In approaching discourse analysis, therefore, we assume that the verbal forms of the text were selected by the speaker or writer to convey his meaning, and that those forms can best be analysed in the light of the meaning-structure which they reveal. To give a brief illustration: the verbal form in our text, *Please make a special contribution* could be analysed simply as a transitive clause in imperative mood, and so on. But if we relate it to the underlying meaning-structure, we view it, instead, cognitively, as an event desired by the writer, which she wishes the addressee to carry out. It is in this speaker-related way that we shall approach the analysis of the entire text.

2. The Model

2.1 *The Structure of the Message*

Freeing the study of meaning from a one-to-one correlation with words enables us to develop a model which does not have to start from the bottom, on a one-word-at-a-time basis, and build gradually upwards. Rather, we can establish meaning-units which are not related to a word-count, but to the thoughts and intentions of the speaker. It is the speaker's purpose in communicating which determines both the structural form and the detailed expression of the discourse. We therefore consider the meaning-structure of the message as being determined from the top downwards, the speaker's overall purpose being the controlling factor, while other subsidiary purposes (for speakers may have several simultaneously) similarly control structure and expression at lower levels.

2.1.1 *The Units Comprising the Message*

Whenever human beings communicate verbally, they do so about something, and for some purpose. These two parameters of *reference* and *purposive significance* define all the units in a message, whatever their size.

The largest unit of communication is the message itself. A whole book may be about how to take photographs of birds, for instance. The reference is then to taking photographs, and to birds (both highly generically), and the purpose is to instruct in how to do this well. It is important to realise that these high-level references and purposes do represent cognitive realities: we can think generically as well as specifically.

The smallest unit of communication is the proposition, which is roughly the cognitive counterpart of a clause. This also has reference and purposive significance. The question *Does Jonathan play tennis?* realises references to *Jonathan* and to *playing tennis*. The response *Yes* realises identical references, to Jonathan and to tennis-playing. The two utterances differ in their purposive significance, the first realising the purpose of eliciting information and the second that of providing it: since both utterances express both reference and purposive significance, both realise propositions. What the speaker means by *Yes* is *Jonathan plays tennis*, which is propositional.

Intermediate between propositions and messages is ranged a hierarchy of configurations, which nest in each other and build up into the total message. Each configuration is defined by its reference and its significance. The size of the configuration is immaterial. There is no important difference between the cognitive unit underlying a paragraph, and that underlying a chapter: it is simply a matter of size and complexity.

2.1.2 *The Relations Joining the Units*

The human mind cannot make sense of units unless they are coherently related. As we receive any communication, we can only grasp what relates coherently both to our existing knowledge and to the rest of the message. Thus a message consists not simply of units but of *units-in-relation*.

The relations which thus enable units to cohere are called *coherence relations*, to distinguish them from relations of other kinds which we will consider later. They may hold between units of any level, but are best illustrated at the propositional level, where they can be realised by forms such as *because, after, and, for example,* or zero.

Related propositions constitute a configuration. The clauses *Mary blushed* and *Simon laughed*, do not, as they stand, realise a configuration, because their relationship is not clear. But *Mary blushed because Simon laughed*, does realise a configuration. *When Mary blushed, Simon laughed*, realises a different configuration: the units are the same but the coherence relation is different.

2.1.3 *The Three Imports*

In 2.1.1 we spoke of *purposive significance* as one of the parameters defining a unit. We must now consider this parameter more precisely.

There are an infinite number of purposes with which a human being may communicate, but we are considering all of these to fall into just three broad general categories, which we are defining in terms of the area of human personality and experience which is involved. These categories we are calling *imports*.

Human beings communicate in order to:

(i) exchange knowledge about the world around them;
(ii) relate mutually with their fellows, especially by sharing emotions, attitudes and evaluations;
(iii) bring about changes in the course of events.

We are calling these three imports the *informative*, the *expressive* and the *conative* respectively. The *informative* involves the knowledge-store of speaker and hearer; the *expressive* involves their emotions and values; the *conative* involves their desires, intentions and wills.

2.1.4 *The Purposive Chain*

The three imports, informative, expressive and conative, form a progression. But unlike grammatical categories, which are mutually exclusive and operate as it were in watertight compartments, meaning categories exhibit a considerable degree of intermingling and overlay. This is simply because a speaker means numerous things at one time; he may, for example, be informing and expressing emotion simultaneously. Thus the kind of progression exhibited by the three imports is not that of the addition of units together, but of the overlaying of one purpose upon another. Basic to all communication is the informative import: there has to be a reservoir of known facts before there can be any reaction to those facts, or any direction of the will concerning them. The conative import lies at the end of the progression, for desires, intentions and purposes arise on the basis of evaluated facts, not on the basis of facts alone. It is not necessary for all these purposes to be expressed in the surface structure. The underlying information may be provided by the situation, as when we say *How beautiful!* looking at a sunset. Or we may express an attitude or evaluation when we really want to influence a person's actions. We may say, *The blue one suits you much better than the red*, when we really mean *Wear the blue one*. We know that the hearer's mind will move on from expressed attitude to appropriate action: we do not need to say so.

We are calling this informative-expressive-conative progression *the purposive chain*. Once more a cognitive reality lies behind the technical term: there is an inherent directionality in human thinking. Our thought-processes are not static, but in constant directional flow. *We constantly assume purposiveness,* and our minds very readily move forward from one purpose to the next.

In general, any communication, long or short, is to be analysed as far along the purposive chain as the communication situation warrants. Thus the familiar utterance *Dinner's ready!* is not purely informative; the speaker really means *come and eat!* The hearer is intended to move on from the given information to the required action. If any family member treats the utterance as purely informative, and responds with *Thank you for telling me*, then the utterance has failed of its purpose, and the speaker may well be annoyed: information exchange is inappropriate while the dinner is cooling on the table.

Thus both expressive and conative utterances either contain or assume elements from further down the chain. But the purpose which affects the overall structure of the message, and the one in terms of which hearer-reaction may be assessed as appropriate or inappropriate, is always the one that lies furthest along the purposive chain.

2.1.5 *Schematic Patterning*

Each import imposes its own characteristic patterning on the message as a whole. An informative message will provide information, supported by evidence, illustration, comparison, and so on. An expressive message will present values and attitudes, supported by elements either validating or opposing those values. A conative message will propose some activity, supporting that proposal with elements of persuasion, motivation, etc.

It is the part it plays in the overall patterning which gives each element in the message its distinctive contribution, its significance with respect to the whole. We call the overall patterning of the message its *schema*, and the relations which define each contribution *schematic relations*. Since the text before us carries a conative message, only *conative schema* patterns will be discussed in this paper. In accordance with the principle of the purposive chain (2.1.4.), both informative and expressive elements may be expected to be present in such a message, but their contribution to the message as a whole will be determined by the speaker's conative purpose.

2.1.6 *Natural Prominence*

Every unit in meaning-structure is characterized not only by reference and import, but also by natural prominence: some elements comprising that unit are more prominent than others.

Natural prominence derives from several sources, of which we are now in a position to understand two, *cohesive prominence* and *purposive prominence*.

Cohesive prominence occurs when two units are joined in a coherence relation: unless this is a purely additive relationship, it is normal for one member of the pairing to carry more impact, more cognitive weight, than the other. Thus *result* is more naturally prominent than *reason, response* than *stimulus*, and so on.

Purposive prominence derives from import: conative import carries more natural prominence than expressive, which in turn carries more prominence than informative.

It is the natural prominence of certain elements in a unit which defines its structure. The naturally prominent elements constitute the structural core of the unit, to which the less prominent elements relate. Naturally prominent elements may be reinforced, i.e., given extra prominence, by a variety of devices, but even without such devices prominence is inevitably associated with the element concerned, simply by virtue of its import and relationships.

2.2 *The Orientation of the Message*

2.2.1 *The Source of the Orientational Elements in a Message*

So far we have spoken of messages as consisting of a structured hierarchy of units, each defined in terms of *reference* and *import*. The *reference* is what the speaker chooses to talk about, and the *import* is the reason why he is communicating that content. The addressee, so far, has scarcely come into the picture.

Yet a communicator is constantly aware of the addressee as he conveys his message. Both initially and throughout, he monitors the addressee's state of knowledge, his comprehension, attitudes and reactions — and presents his message accordingly. He orients his message towards the audience.

In so doing, he has two ends in view: first, that his message be correctly understood, and second, that it be well received (i.e. that the addressee believe, agree or comply, as is appropriate). The need to be understood prompts the communicator to be aware of the addressee's initial state of knowledge, and of his continued comprehension. The desire to communicate successfully prompts him to a constant awareness of the addressee's emotions, attitudes and values.

It is those elements in a message which derive from either aspect of this monitoring activity which we are calling the *orientational elements*. They are shaped not by the author's specific purposes in the particular message, which give rise to the schema, but by his general purpose of communicating comprehensibly and successfully with a particular audience. Orientational elements in a message arise from audience-awareness.

2.2.2 *Orientational Elements: Message Support*

The communicator's main communicative purpose gives rise to the structural core of the message, while his audience-awareness gives rise to the orientational elements. Some of these are realised as distinct units, supporting the structural core. This single factor accounts for several well-known facts about discourse. Speaking very generally, the distinction between thematic and non-thematic material, foreground and background, figure and ground, derives from this source, as does, at a lower level, the distinction between main and subordinate clauses — though skewing is more frequent at this level.

To illustrate the orientational elements of a message involves making clear some theoretical assumptions not hitherto mentioned. It is assumed that a human being's entire store of knowledge constitutes a complex but well-ordered mental network, of which only a small part is illuminated by consciousness at any one time. The remaining, unilluminated parts of the network vary greatly in their accessibility, i.e., the ease with which they can be brought into the illuminated area.

A further assumption — part of the theory of the realisation of meaning in surface-structure — is that words do not act as signals of meaning in isolation, but only in a context, a context which, whether situational or verbal, must be shared by communicator and addressee. Thus the real surface-structure signals of meaning are not words as such, but words-in-contextual-matrix.

It follows that if a communicator wishes to convey his message comprehensibly, he has to ensure that adequate context (i.e. the essential components of the context in his own mind) is brought into the illuminated area of the mind of the addressee. Many of the supporting elements in discourse have this function: they provide needed setting, prompt the retrieval of known-but-unilluminated information, and so on.

An illustration may make the point clear. If someone says to a colleague, *When the manager comes in, would you give him this report?*, the initial clause of that utterance does not contribute to the purpose of the message, which is conative. In fact, the same clause could introduce a message of any import: the proposition which it realises is neutral as to import; it is *not import-bearing at all*.

But it does have a contribution to make to the message: it has *orientational function*. The purpose of *When the manager comes in* is to illuminate in the mind of the addressee the appropriate context in terms of which the rest of the message is to be understood. A great deal of orientational material is *context-providing* in this way.

Other orientational elements correct misunderstandings, provide explanations, or appeal to the known values of the addressee in order to validate or increase the acceptability of the core material. Such orientational elements are units in the structure of the message, and have all the same characteristics as core units excepting only that they have some orientational significance instead of import.

It is worth noting that the orientational aspect of messages provides us with a further kind of natural prominence: import-bearing material is naturally more prominent than non-import-bearing. We will be making use of this fact in our analysis.

2.2.3 *Orientational Elements: Message Prosodies*

The orientational material which we have just been discussing tends to occur in identifiable chunks, and hence enters readily into the hierarchical structure of the message in a supporting capacity. There is, however, other orientational material which is not part of message-structure, but occurs throughout the message independently of the structural hierarchy. This pervasive type of orientational material we are calling *prosodies* of the message.

There are two classes of *prosody*, according to whether the material concerned is oriented towards the knowledge or the values of the addressee. The former are called *information prosodies*, the latter *value prosodies*.

Everything relating to the way information is presented to the hearer is handled as an information prosody. The constant relating of new to familiar material carries on throughout the message, and 'new' and 'familiar' are estimated with respect to the addressee and his current state of knowledge: information is not presented in vacuo, but as oriented to a particular audience.

Similarly, the communicator's awareness of the attitudes and values of the addressee may colour the discourse from beginning to end. If the addressee is known to hold extreme political views, or to dislike the communicator, or to be conceited, any of these attitudes may well influence both the content and the presentation of the message. Elements in the message which trace their origin to such a source are value prosodies.

2.2.4 *Orientational Prominence*

Natural prominence forms an important factor in the structuring of a message. Orientational prominence, by contrast, belongs to the orientation of the message to the hearer. Whether relating to the addressee's knowledge (e.g., presenting information as surprising) or to his attitudes (e.g. presenting some contingency as desirable), the prominence involved is independent of the structural hierarchy. It may pervade the message as a whole, or occur intermittently, or occur only once in the message. Such prominence is conveyed either by departure from established patterns (e.g., by unusual word order) or by forms carrying inherent prominence, such as emotive vocabulary, exclamations and many figures of speech. This surface-structure phenomenon we are calling *marked prominence*.

2.3 The Realisation of the Message

The realisation of the message in surface-structure is not strictly part of the theory of meaning, since it has to be worked out separately for every language. Nevertheless, there are one or two points relevant to discourse analysis which should be mentioned here.

First, and most importantly, meaning and surface structure do not always exhibit exact matching. Since language basically expresses the contours of our minds, congruence between the two is the norm. Nevertheless events, normally expressed by verbs, may be realised instead by nouns. Or the boundaries of units such as paragraphs, which normally coincide with meaning-units, may fail to do so. Language is flexible, and mismatch is possible. Whenever mismatch occurs it has significance, and this must be assessed.

The fact that there are several ways of saying the same thing means that the communicator is always choosing between options to best express his meaning. The analyst most clearly discerns the communicator's purpose when he compares what the communicator did say with what he might have said: the study of grammatical and lexical alternatives has a significant part to play in analysis.

Finally, in written material, the visual representation of the message may also be the realisation of underlying meaning-categories.

3. The Analysis of the Message: Approach and Method

To analyse a discourse in terms of the message it conveys obviously involves analysing that message. But in the model of meaning presented here, this would involve analysis at all levels — every proposition, every configuration, and the relations between these, as well as the message viewed as a whole. Since such an analysis is impossible in this paper, we will omit propositional analysis (on the grounds that most meaning-studies so far have involved material at clause-level or lower) and will select only one intermediate-sized configuration for study, which will have to be taken as representative of the rest. We will then concentrate our attention on the analysis of the message as a whole.

Since different aspects of the analysis involve different methods, we will try to make these clear as we progress. One preliminary comment seems appropriate here. Although in meaning-structure, higher-level units and relations control the lower (in the sense that the communicator's overall purpose determines his detailed presentation), nevertheless in practice analysis at all levels goes on simultaneously. Good low-level decisions can only be made with the total context in mind, but low-level clues can have high-level significance: it is impossible to restrict oneself to one level at a time methodologically, whatever one does theoretically. The main proviso to be borne in mind is that at all levels good surface-structure evidence should be available to support every analytical decision concerning the message.

4. The Analysis of a Configuration, Paragraph 14-15

4.0 *Model and Method*

The configuration selected for analysis is that realised in segments 14 and 15. It will be referred to as (cognitive) *paragraph 14-15*. (Where visual (printed) paragraphs are referred to, this will be stated explicitly.)

In the analysis of any configuration, our procedure is first to exhibit its referential and purposive unity, contrasting it with adjacent units by defending its boundaries; secondly, to display its relational structure and prominence patterns; and thirdly, to describe orientational factors.

A configuration consists structurally of propositions joined in cohesive relations, and this will be presented in the form of a chart (see Fig.1, section 4.2). Since it is not possible here to present the theory of propositions and relations in detail, the reader will to some extent have to take this chart on trust. Some preliminary observations on propositions, however, may be helpful.

(i) A proposition represents a meaning-entity. Since it is cognitive and not linguistic, it should ideally be represented by some non-linguistic symbolism. For the sake of comprehensibility, however, a strictly formalised version of English is employed instead.

(ii) A proposition spells out the exact referential content of the surface-structure forms. These forms are invariably a sort of shorthand: much is always meant which is not signalled explicitly. For example, no agent is mentioned in *to use it well*, but using cannot occur without an agent, hence the proposition must state the agent overtly; it has to fill in the gap in the surface-structure shorthand, using evidence from elsewhere in the text. Similarly, exact reference must be provided for figures of speech, deictics and proforms — *swamped with requests* does not mean that anyone got wet; the word *we* does not have the same reference throughout the text. The proposition must make the referential meaning clear.

(iii) Every event-concept in the message, however realised, forms the central element in a proposition, and is represented in the propositional display by a verb. Thus *your help* realises an event, not a thing, so is represented in the display by a verb (*that you help us*). Thing-concepts are represented by nouns, or by pronouns with reference specified.

(iv) Propositions vary in prominence. Prominence derives from a variety of sources, which are discussed in 2.1.6 and 2.2.2. See also 4.3 14a(iii).

4.1 *The Unity and Initial Boundary of Cognitive Paragraph 14-15*

Why, then, is a cognitive paragraph considered to start at 14, when the visual paragraph ends with it?

Each configuration should be distinguishable from adjacent configurations by being about something different (i.e. having distinct referential content) and by having a distinct communicative (import-related) purpose. Paragraph 14-15 is about ZPG's need of help: the preceding material is about the Urban Stress Test. Hence a referential break between 13 and 14 is clear.

With respect to communicative purpose, segments 11 and 12 are informative, segment 13 is evaluative. It is only in segment 14 that the real purpose of the letter emerges, i.e. the solicitation of funds. Segment 14 onwards is conative in import.

Hence, both referentially and purposively there is a break between 13 and 14: indeed, 14 is the pivotal segment in the letter, where the thrust of the message changes. We will now present detailed evidence to support this.

(i) Segment 14 contains the first reference to *you* in the letter, apart from the salutation. From this point on, the addressees are constantly a part of the referential content.

(ii) It also contains the first mention of *we (ZPG)* since 10a.

(iii) It contains the first mention in the letter of any kind of need or lack, the previous material having been extremely positive. This signals a change of purpose.

(iv) It contains the first indication of conative import in the letter. (*We need your help* is not informative, but a mitigated conative.)

(v) It begins with the connective *But*. Connectives are rare in this letter and *but* occurs nowhere else. It marks the turning-point in the letter between the informative/expressive material preceding and the conative material following.

(vi) It contains, in the initial purpose clause, the first overt statement of purpose with ZPG as agent — a further indication that the conative element has begun.

(vii) It contains present time references representing event propositions, whereas 11-13 use timeless present tenses to realise attributive propositions.

With clear evidence before us that segment 14 starts a new cognitive unit, we are left with the question, why is this conspicuously new material represented as the end of a visual paragraph (13-14) containing material quite different from it in reference and import? Why this mismatch between message and surface-structure representation?

One can only conclude that the lack of visual representation for the cognitive boundary must be in order to blur or disguise that boundary. In other words, the reader is meant to remain unaware of the change in content and thrust: the first hint that contributions are being sought is slipped into the text in a way that is visually unobtrusive. For evidence that it is also verbally unobtrusive, see 4.3., 14a(iii).

4.2 *The Structure of Paragraph 14-15*

Structurally, any configuration has a head element, which the rest of the unit supports. Here the head element is realised by *we urgently need your help*. The preceding clause makes clear the purpose for which that help is wanted (to use the Stress Test well) and the following segment (15) makes clear the reason why such help is necessary (staff and funds are both inadequate).

The structure of the configuration is presented here in the form of a chart. Each proposition is on a separate line, with the corresponding text written above. Successive propositions relating to one segment are labelled (15a), (15b) and so on.

All propositions are joined to adjacent propositions and propositional groupings by coherence relations. These are doubly represented in the chart: a relational label is to be found to the left of each proposition, and a verbal label in standardised English occurs at the beginning of all propositions other than head (naturally prominent) ones (e.g. 'because', 'who', etc.).

Any naturally prominent proposition has its relational label capitalised. The chart therefore provides a display of the natural prominence patterns of the paragraph. Orientational prominence will be discussed in 4.3.

The initial *But* is taken as relating to a unit at a higher level than that in which it has its overt realisation. It is therefore omitted from this chart.

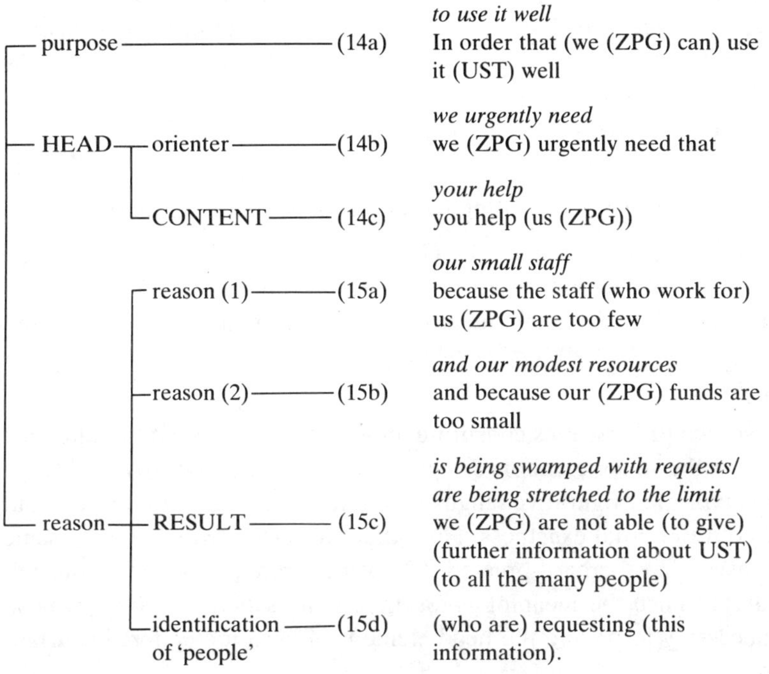

Figure 1: Chart of the relational structure of cognitive paragraph 14-15

Notes on the structure of paragraph 14-15:

14a (we(ZPG))

The parentheses round *we* indicate that it has no overt realisation in the surface structure. The parentheses round *ZPG* indicate that this is the specific reference intended. *We* is here taken to refer to ZPG as an organisation, and not to Susan Weber and the other officers personally.

14a it(UST)

UST is the specific referent of the pronoun *it*. The pronominal usage is particularly interesting here, since the Urban Stress Test is normally (seven times) referred to by its full title. The only exceptions are two pronominal usages (here and in 12) and one synonymous reference (*our study* (21)). The use of the pronoun here therefore indicates a considerable degree of backgrounding: the Stress Test is no longer topical in this new unit.

14c (us(ZPG))

Parentheses are used because there is no overt realisation in the text. The event *help* requires that someone be helped; referential exactness requires that this someone be made explicit. As frequently happens, the realisation of an event by a noun instead of a verb either allows or requires the omission of related concepts from surface-structure realisation.

15a because

Formalised English indicating the coherence relation of reason.

15a the staff (who work for) us (ZPG)

The possessive pronoun *our* does not here indicate a relationship of actual possession, hence the intended relationship has to be spelt out exactly.

15c and 15d

These two propositions constitute an attempt to spell out the intended reference of the two metaphors *swamped with requests* and *stretched to the limit*. It is typical of figurative language that it provides extra vividness, but with loss of referential exactness. Here the reference seems to be the same in both cases, that the hard-pressed ZPG staff could not handle the incoming requests. Since the meaning is essentially the same, only one proposition is necessary to handle the head element of both metaphors in surface structure.

4.3 *Orientational Elements in Paragraph 14-15*

The configuration will be considered in its surface-structure order, comments being made, wherever relevant, which relate to supporting functions, message prosodies (both informational and value prosodies) and special prominence.

14a to use it well

(i) This subordinate clause has dual function. It realises the purpose for the adumbrated appeal *we need your help*, but by being forefronted it acquires higher level significance also, and provides the context within which the whole of the rest of the letter is to be understood.

(ii) *use well* initiates a value-prosody here. One who presents an appeal must not only present that appeal in a favourable light: he must also counteract any negative reaction on the part of the addressee, and allay his fears. The strong emphasis, from this point onwards, on how the money will be used, indicates that the writer is taking steps to allay fears that the money would not be used properly. Thus, immediately before the need for money is mentioned, the reassuring collocation *use well* is presented.

(iii) The word *use* does not here convey new information, but refers back to *easy-to-use* in 13. The word *it* also conveys known information, referring to the Stress Test, as already discussed (4.2., notes on 14a). A new cognitive unit carries much more referential prominence if it starts with new information, but here the first clause carries mostly old information, and the boundary of the new unit is thus referentially blurred. Moreover, the initial clause realises non-import-bearing material, a further prominence-diminishing factor. The impact on the reader of the conative *we need your help* is therefore considerably cushioned.

The analysis of this one clause makes clear that it is quite inadequate to say simply that a clause does or does not convey prominence. *To use it well*, by virtue of being forefronted, provides high-level context. It also carries a positive value which recurs as a value-prosody of the letter. For both these reasons it is prominent. Yet with respect to reference and import, it is not prominent. It serves to highlight positive values and to down-play the start of the solicitation simultaneously.

14b,c we urgently need your help

This first mention of the need for funds is highly generic, with the main event realised by a noun. Successive references are increasingly specific: *your support* (16); *your contribution* (18); *special contribution* (22); *$25, $50, $100 or as much as you can* (25). The distribution of generic and specific references is of considerable significance in this letter, and expounds value-prosodies and prominence factors. Here, the generic form is used to introduce a concept of probable negative value, and to minimise the natural prominence it would have as the conative head of the configuration.

15a-d The reference intended by these two metaphors has already been discussed. Their orientational significance is considerable. They are presented in parallel contexts in the surface structure (*our + adj. + noun subject + is/ are being + metaphor*), yet in spite of the formal parallelism they are not parallel at all informationally: the reference to the staff contains largely old information, with positive overtones carried over from 6,7 and 10, while the reference to *modest resources* contains new information carrying potentially negative value. The cadence of the parallelism is intended to carry over positive connotation from the busyness of the staff to the inadequacy of the funds.

There is a further mismatch which has orientational significance. Segment 15 is both indented and underlined, making it visually the most prominent segment on the page. Yet structurally it realises simply the reasons for the request for funds adumbrated in 14, so carries much less natural prominence than 14. The providing of special visual prominence has the effect, yet once more, of down-grading the prominence of 14 by comparison.

A further possible reason for the visual prominence given to 15 is that this is the last mention in the letter of the reason that funds are required. This is surprising, in a letter which is characterised by references repeated throughout. But references to *need* carry negative value, and the emphasis here shifts from the need to the purpose for which the funds will be used, which is much more positive.

We thus conclude that paragraph 14-15 demonstrates a subtle and unusual interplay of factors. Boundary phenomena, informational prosodies, value prosodies and graphic devices all combine to diminish the prominence of the request for funds, and to diminish the negative value that such a request would otherwise carry.

5. The Analysis of the Total Message

5.0 *Method of Analysis*

Since the message consists of configurations, and since configurations are defined by reference and import, the method of analysis consists of seeking spans exhibiting unity in these two respects. Where referential and purposive spans coincide, this is strong evidence both for the existence of a configuration, and for its defining characteristics. If the evidence clashes, priority is normally given to factors revealing the communicator's purpose. (For an example of this, see 5.1.1.3.)

5.0.1 *Referential Evidence*

Referential spans should be marked on a working copy as follows:

(i) All references to the same Thing or Event should be marked in the same way. Thus *our study* (21) should be marked in the same way as all *Urban Stress Test* references.

(ii) All references within one semantic domain should be marked similarly. Note that we are not looking for exact verbal repetition, but for references to closely-related concepts, as *reporters, media, reported, news story*, and so on.

(iii) The spans marked by references to each human participant should be clearly indicated. This will involve assigning accurate reference to all pronouns and deictics. Thus, repetitions of *you/your* in this text should all be considered as singular (='you, the addressee'). (Evidence for this: the singular salutation, *Friend* (3); the singular (*your*) *contribution* (18) — a plural 'you' would have required 'contributions'.)

5.0.2 *Evidence Relating to Import*

Ideally, the three imports should be separately and clearly indicated on the text. If these are not initially clear to the analyst, the following kinds of evidence should be sought and marked.

(i) stretches employing same verb tense, with same meaning; (Note that the present tense is especially ambiguous in English, being used for description, present action, habitual action, imperative, narration. These must be kept separate.)

(ii) stretches employing same mood, whether realised in the verb or by auxiliaries;

(iii) statements of need, desire, intention; also purpose clauses: especially when occurring with first-person agent, these frequently signal conative import.

Boundaries where import changes may be signalled by any of the following: connectives (especially logical and contrastive connectives); change of person as agent; change of writer's mood (evidenced by strongly positive or negative vocabulary, change from casual to formal style, and so on).

5.1 *The Structural Core of the Message*

The message consists of configurations related to each other by the *schema* relations, that is, by the different contributions which each configuration makes to the overall purpose of the message. We will seek first to establish the units which constitute the message (5.1.1). With these established, we will go on to consider the schema pattern which the message presents (5.1.2). Closely related to the schema is the purposive chain, and we will consider how this operates in the message in 5.1.3

5.1.1 *The Units Comprising the Message*

5.1.1.1 *Evidence for Referential Spans*

The establishing of referential spans reveals the following:

(i) The Urban Stress Test is mentioned, whether by title, pronoun or synonym, in almost every visual paragraph. It can thus be taken as the topic of the whole message.

(ii) Extended reference, at scattered points throughout the message, is a characteristic of this text. For example, references to *community leaders, public officials* occur in 9, 13, 18, 20, 21, and generically in 23. References thus extended throughout the discourse cannot be used for establishing configuration boundaries, but they do have significance in the discourse, since they frequently realise value prosodies of some importance.

(iii) Referential spans would indicate the setting up of the following configurations. (A notional label is attached to each, as an aid to grasping the overall picture. In a full analysis at all levels, this label would be replaced by a theme for each unit, carefully worked out on the basis of prominence and other evidence.)

4-10 *many phone calls*
11-13 *the Urban Stress Test*
14-18 *using the UST well*
19-21 *using the UST locally*
22-23 *special contribution*
29-30 *media coverage of UST*

5.1.1.2 *Evidence from Import Spans*

To a large extent, evidence relating to import confirms the above configurations, and the above listing can therefore simply be expanded by attaching import labels to each configuration. However, one referentially minor boundary (between 18 and 19) acquires extra significance when import is considered. In addition, the inclusion of evidence concerning import makes clear the prominence patterns of the message.

The 18-19 boundary will be considered in the next section (5.1.1.3.). Assuming that conclusion for the moment, we will now present a revised version of the configurations listed above indicating the import of each (Fig.2). Prominence based on import will be represented, with the most prominent configurations to the left. The imports are considered to have prominence in the order: conative, mitigated conative, expressive (emotive), expressive (evaluative), informative. When read from the top downwards, Fig.2 indicates the import of each configuration, and its prominence in relation to the other configurations. A dotted line signals a major structural break.

UNITS	CONATIVE	MITIGATED CONATIVE	EMOTIVE EXPRESSIVE	EVALUATIVE EXPRESSIVE
4-10			*Many phone calls*	
11-13				*Urban Stress Test*
----	----	----	----	----
14-18		*to use UST well, we need help*		
19-21				*local action desirable*
----	----	----	----	----
22-23	*special contribution*			
29-30		*media coverage of UST*		

Figure 2: The prominence structure of the message

Comments:

(i) There is no purely informative configuration in the letter. Segments 11 and 12 are informative, but referentially they form one configuration with 13, which provides an evaluative conclusion to the unit. Obviously this is not an information-conveying text.

(ii) The prominence patterns here shown make clear that a non-prominent configuration precedes each major break, and a prominent one follows it. There is a diminution of prominence before the mitigated conative in 14 and the conative head of the message in 22. The diminution of prominence is shown in the surface structure by lack of emotive vocabulary, lack of figures of speech, and, in the case of 19-21, lack of new information.

(iii) The major break at the end of 13 has already been justified in 4.1. The break at the end of 21 is justified by change of import; change in prominence; direct imperative in 22; full title of *Zero Population Growth* in 22; underlining of 22.

5.1.1.3 Defence of Boundaries

Ideally, all configuration boundaries should be defended from surface-structure evidence relating to reference and import. An example of such a defence has already been given, in 4.1. In that case, referential criteria and import confirmed each other in establishing the boundary.

Here, only one other configuration-boundary will be considered, that between segments 18 and 19. It provides an example of establishing a boundary where criteria clash. There is, of course, no theoretical objection to saying that the boundary is indeterminate, provided that the adjacent units exhibit clearly distinct nuclei. There is a real danger, however, of brushing under the carpet of indeterminacy valuable evidence as to the progression of the writer's thought, which often shows up most clearly at unit boundaries.

The referential evidence in favour of continuity between 18 and 19 is strong. *Local* occurs in 18, 19 and 20, *community/communities* in 18 and 20; *activists* in 18, and *act* and *action* in 19. There is also a continuity of reference to future possibility: *can arm* (18); *can act* (19); *could ...affect* (20).

Other criteria, however, favour a break between 18 and 19.

(i) There is a change in *person as agent*. This is disguised by the fact that in both cases the agent is realised by *we/our* in surface structure. However, up to and including 18, *we* refers to *we (ZPG)*, whereas in 19 and 20, *we* includes the addressee also — as evidenced by *our national government, our communities, our lives*. This inconspicuous change to inclusive *we* marks a change in the writer's approach to the reader. (See 5.1.2.)

(ii) There is strong structural parallelism between 14, 16 and 18: all begin with an adumbrated appeal *we ... need, your support, your contribution*. In 14 and 16, this appeal is followed by supporting material. In 18 the same pattern emerges: the initial adumbrated appeal is followed by an expression of purpose supporting it. But there seems no adequate evidence for extending the supporting role to 19-21.

(iii) The end of 18 is clearly linked to the beginning of 16, forming an inclusio or semantic sandwich structure; *before* (18) (underlined for prominence) links back to *now* (prominent by position) in 16. Similarly, *crisis stage* (end of 18) links back to *critical* (16). This inclusio seems to bind 16-18 together as a unit.

We have considered the above to be adequate evidence for terminating a configuration at the end of 18.

5.1.2 *The Message Schema*

The message schema is the pattern of the purposive thrust of the message, formed by the significant contribution of each configuration to the whole. The main configurations of the message have already been considered in 5.1.1.2. We must now consider the contribution made by each to the purposive thrust of the letter, which we take to be, *Give us (ZPG) money in order that we may circulate the Urban Stress Test.*

(4-10) *many phone calls*

This is a highly prominent and expressive configuration, yet it contains no information which is essential either to the comprehension or to the carrying out of the appeal. The appeal could have been made and supported without any mention of the media at all. Why does the letter begin with the prominent presentation of schematically irrelevant material?

One answer to this question will be found in 5.2.3.2. Another answer is to be found in the nature of conative messages whenever the addressee has the option of *not* complying: the communicator making the appeal has to validate himself, has to defend to the addressee his suitability to make the appeal. The media are here called in as an independent, third-party witness to the great importance of the UST, and indirectly of ZPG itself.

The schematic function of this configuration is therefore third-party *validation of communicator*.

(11-13) *Urban Stress Test*

No-one can comply with an appeal unless they understand it. This configuration provides essential information about the test which is to be circulated, and does so before the appeal itself is launched, in its preliminary form, in 14. The nature of the information, however, is such as to further validate the UST to the reader: it is not only successful in the eyes of the media, but also a thorough and scientific document. This in turn validates ZPG as a responsible organisation. This unit therefore has a dual role schematically, providing (i) *essential information* (ii) *validation by evidence*.

(14-18) *to use UST well, we need help*

At this point the thrust of the message changes: the preliminaries to the actual appeal begin with the expression of need in 14. Before the direct appeal itself, which is not reached until 22, the writer prepares the way by a persuasive build-up. The addressee must not only be persuaded that the person making the appeal has the right to do so: he must also be convinced of the desirability of the action he is being requested to carry out. This configuration provides this persuasive element. It attempts to validate the giving of money as being needed (14-15), urgent (16-17), and for a good purpose (18). Its schematic function is therefore that of *persuasion* concerning the *directed activity*.

(19-21) *local action desirable*

This configuration provides a different kind of persuasion. In the last analysis, the addressee will only perform the directed action (giving) if he wants to. The purpose of this unit, the last before the appeal itself, is to make him want to. Informationally it contains little that is new, but there is a new twist to an old theme: it contains simultaneously a hint of benefits if the addressee complies (sound choices will improve the quality of our (inclusive) lives), a veiled threat of undesirable results of non-compliance (officials cannot make sound choices without our data), and an appeal to the citizen-conscience (our (inclusive) government is failing, our (inclusive) communities are at risk, the American public needs you to act). The schematic role of this configuration is therefore that of *personal motivation to act*.

(22-23) *special contribution*

The main appeal has now been reached — one which the reader must have anticipated since he first opened the envelope. It functions simultaneously as the head and closing configuration of the body of the letter.

(29-30) *media coverage of UST*

This has the function of *ancillary appeal*. Informationally, it serves to remind the reader of the media-as-witness, hence constitutes an *echoed validation*. But its essential schematic function is to provide a different but related appeal which is intended to facilitate the carrying out of the main appeal. Its function is that of *stimulus to immediate action*.

We are now in a position to combine the earlier analysis in terms of reference and import, with the analysis of schema roles which we have just discussed. We will combine reference and import in a summary label.

UNITS	SCHEMA ROLE	REFERENCE AND IMPORT
4-10	VALIDATION of ZPG by third party	*How many phone calls we received!*
11-13	VALIDATION of ZPG by evidence	*The UST is scientific and usable*
14-18	PERSUASION concerning the directed activity	*To use UST to avoid a crisis, we need help*
19-21	MOTIVATION of addressee to perform directed activity	*Local action is to our (inclusive) advantage*
22-23	APPEAL	*Give a special contribution to ZPG*
29-30	STIMULUS to immediate action	*Report to ZPG about media coverage*

Figure 3: Schema roles of the structural units of the message

5.1.3 *The Purposive Chain*

So far, the purposive chain has operated quite normally in the discourse, with information and evaluation preceding the conative element. The letter does, however, use the purposive chain in two other distinctive ways, which will now be discussed.

First, the attempt to validate some desired action usually takes the form of a positive evaluation *of the action itself*. Here, no attempt is made to validate giving as such: giving is assumed throughout to be an acceptable activity — presumably this is a value accepted in the community. But money is a commodity whose value is determined solely by the *use to which it is put*. Hence the persuasion takes the form of validating, not the act of giving, but the activity one step further up the chain, the using of the money.

Second, the purposive chain proves on close inspection to be suddenly, and repeatedly, cut off at different points in the letter. The thrust of the message is, roughly, *Give us money so that we can circulate the UST*. The obvious next step in the chain is, why circulate the UST?

The only reasons given overtly are, (to get) *the population message heard* (17) and *to make sound choices* (21). But these are highly generic reasons. What exactly is the population message? What constitutes a sound choice? We are not told.

We may assume, from the logo, from the content of the letter, and from mentally completing the purposive chain, that the sole purpose of circulating the UST is to reduce population growth in the United States to zero. *But this is never stated overtly*. Possibly even among *friends of ZPG* this might have struck a discordant note. The writer probably bore in mind the high profile of the family in American life, the average citizen's vigorous independence, and his poor tolerance of official interference in personal affairs such as family size. At any rate, it cannot be without significance that the writer, whether for reasons of tact or otherwise, totally omits all mention of what is, in fact, the ultimate purpose of the letter.

5.2 *The Orientational Aspects of the Message*

Here we handle all aspects of the message which do not arise directly from the writer's purpose, but from his audience-awareness. As a rough rule of thumb, we may consider these as elements in the message which the writer would probably have conveyed differently if he had had the same purpose but a different audience. (A letter requesting funds for ZPG but addressed to a British audience would have had to be different in several respects.)

5.2.1 *Orientational Support*

We said earlier that no message can be understood without a context. Since each audience brings to a message a different store of existing knowledge, some part of the message has to be devoted to bringing into ready accessibility those parts of the addressee's memory-store which are needed for the comprehension of the message.

In any communication where the parties are previously unknown to each other, or when the identity of the communicator is unknown (as at the start of a telephone communication) the first necessity is to *identify the participants*. In this letter, this function is performed by the salutations at the beginning and end of the letter, by the list of officers and sponsors, and by the ZPG logo. (The graphic element in this presentation will be considered in 5.3) These elements, therefore, constitute part of the orientational support of the letter, comparable to introductions in conversation, or to the setting in a narrative. They are *context-providing*.

5.2.2 *Orientational Prosodies*

5.2.2.1 *Information Prosodies*

The writer faces a problem with respect to the addressees. Some will already know about the UST, through the media or previous correspondence: others may know a little about ZPG, but nothing about the Stress Test. The problem is to supply information about the UST for the latter, without irritating the former by telling them what they already know.

The solution is to present the information first, and briefly, as already known, and thereafter in considerably more detail as new. This device is frequently resorted to by radio news presenters, who face a similarly non-homogeneous audience. Here the first mention of UST is as assumed information, in a *When* ... clause (7). Hints are given as to its content, but still as assumed information, in 9 (*conditions in their cities*) and 10 (*problems that threaten public health and well-being*). Detailed information, presented as new, does not start until 11.

The other factor which should be noted is how reference is made to the Urban Stress Test itself. It has already been pointed out (4.2, note on 14a) that the test is almost always given its full title in the text, even when normal English usage would have allowed a pronoun, or an abbreviated reference such as *our test*. There is obviously deliberate use of the full title well beyond what is linguistically necessary. Since the title is also frequently underlined, full discussion will be postponed to 5.3. where graphic devices are discussed. In terms of purely informational effect, however, it should be noted here that the writer is making sure that whatever else may be soon forgotten, the reader will have the words *Urban Stress Test* indelibly printed on his mind, and in a very positive context.

5.2.2.2. *Value Prosodies*

The value prosody *using well* has already been discussed in 4.3., in connection with paragraph 14-15. Two others, which did not occur in that unit, will be discussed here, as they have a wide distribution in the text.

The referential area covered by the terms *citizen* and *community* is represented in 10, 13, 18, 19 and 20. Positive terms used, collocating closely with these, are *concerned, all parts of the country, action-tool, positive action*. The positive associations which are assumed to surround *community* and *citizen* in the minds of the readers are thus strengthened.

The other value prosody is a negative one, that surrounding the word *population*. We said in 5.1.3. that ZPG's purpose of reducing population growth is never stated overtly, and this is true. But the writer goes to considerable pains to ensure that the word *population* is given unpleasant associations in the mind. The word is used six times in the body of the letter, excluding use in the ZPG logo, and only one of these occurrences is in a neutral context (*get the population message heard* (17)). The other five uses collocate it with *problems that threaten public health and well-being* (10); *pressures* (11); *stresses/stress* (18,20); and *uncontrolled...growth* (19). Clearly, although the question of *how* to reduce population growth is avoided, the message is intended to come through clearly that *population* is a threat and a hazard, and has highly undesirable associations.

5.2.3 *Marked Prominence*

5.2.3.1 *Prominence Marked by Special Devices*

There is frequent use of prominence devices, including:

(i) inherently 'prominent' vocabulary: *overwhelming, incredible, furious, urgently, critical, drastically, special, immediately,* and others;
(ii) 'superlative' terminology: *in every part of the country, in all parts of the country, first survey, best ... ever, need it most, top news story, from coast to coast;*
(iii) figures of speech: *nothing short of incredible* (litotes and hyperbole), *deluge of calls, blown the whistle, action tool* (metaphors) and others already mentioned elsewhere.

It is noticeable that these devices are not distributed evenly throughout the letter, there being a much heavier concentration in the first half of the letter — obviously, feelings are engaged first, and reasoning later. It has already been noted (5.1.1.2.) that there is a 'lull' in the prominence immediately preceding the start of the conative section, in 10-13, and also preceding the appeal itself, in 19-21 — the pause before the pressure.

5.2.3.2 *Prominence Marked by Departure from Norms*

Two configurations exhibit unusual prominence patterns.

We will consider first the schematic configuration 14-18, of which the constituent configuration, paragraph 14-15, has already been analysed in detail. In that analysis it became clear that the naturally-prominent conative element was diminished in prominence by other factors. The same happens in 16 and 18, where *support* and *contribution* signal propositions *that you support us* and *which you will contribute to us*. Both of these are essentially conative, but mitigated by being nominalized. In addition, *contribution* is diminished by being in a non-prominent coherence relation (means).

It is probable that this diminution in the impact of the conative is deliberate, and for two reasons:

(i) The writer is not ready to make the actual appeal at this point, yet giving has to be mentioned in order to be urged and validated. Hence the solution, to mention it with prominence diminished as much as possible.

(ii) To express these mitigated conatives more fully would involve being more explicit. *Give!* would be premature, *when you give* presumptuous, and *if you give* unthinkable.

The other configuration exhibiting unusual prominence patterns is the opening one, 4-8. Among the coherence relations, stimulus normally precedes response. With respect to import, informative material normally precedes expressive. This configuration departs from both these norms simultaneously. The response (*all the phone calls*) is mentioned first, and highly expressively: the stimulus (*the release of the test*) is mentioned later, and is purely informational. This double inversion puts marked prominence on the beginning of the letter.

The reason for this lies in the nature of human cognition: anything involving knowledge and facts is much less gripping than anything involving emotions and action — unless the addressee eagerly wants those facts. The writer assumed, almost certainly rightly, that very few of the addressees were awaiting news of the UST with bated breath: an informative start, therefore, would rank very low on the interest-scale.

But it was essential to the writer's purpose to gain the addressee's attention at the very beginning, for the addressee was not a captive audience, and might quite well never read the letter at all. The writer's task, then, was to make the reader want to read on, and to want it more than he wanted anything else at the moment when he first glanced at it. The solution was to make him eager to find out about the UST, to put him into a state of suspense over what constituted the stimulus to which the phone calls were such a dramatic response. Hence the double inversion we have noted, with strongly marked prominence on the response resulting.

5.3 *The Visual Representation of the Message*

The model presented here is normally concerned with the way meaning is presented *verbally* in the surface-structure. However, since it covers varied aspects of meaning at all levels, there is no difficulty in relating graphic devices in the surface structure to the aspect of meaning which they represent. (See the reproduction of the letter in the Introduction.)

(i) The logo, list of officers and sponsors, and salutations, have already been mentioned in 5.2.1. Each of these has a formalized graphic representation in terms of position on the page, size of print, etc. None of this is at all unusual, so it carries virtually zero prominence, and is probably passed over by most readers. It is context-providing, bringing to the fore the appropriate area of the reader's past experience (i.e. ZPG as an organisation) before he starts reading, and identifying the sender with the already-familiar ZPG.

(ii) Visual paragraphing

Normally visual paragraphs correlate quite closely with cognitive and/or grammatical ones, however defined. Here they do not. The skewing of boundaries at 13-14, with the purpose of diminishing prominence, has already been discussed.

The other visual device used here is to present many more visual units than there are underlying cognitive ones. Configurations 9 and 10, for example, constitute specifics of 8, so would normally be considered as in the same cognitive unit. Similarly, 18 is specific in relation to 16-17, yet it is made a separate visual unit.

Undoubtedly the purpose of this device is to provide an adequate amount of white space on each page, and make reading as easy as possible.

(iii) Underlining

Much of this is conventional. Underlining of the main appeal is normal. Underlining of *action-tool* and *we can act to take action at the local level* are to give prominence to an important value-prosody in the letter, in the latter case contrastively with (inactive) *national government*. Both topical and contrastive underlining are normal.

A further normal use of underlining is with *before* in 18, here representing a prominent intonation pattern.

The underlining in 15, and its purpose, have already been discussed in 4.3.

The most interesting use of underlining in the letter is its presence or absence with the title *(ZPG's) 1985 Urban Stress Test*. This is underlined when it is presented as new information in 7, and when it is used to reactivate the concept of the test after a gap (11, 17, 29). At points where a pronoun, deictic or synonym would have served equally well, the title is given in full but without underlining (9, 13, 23).

ZPG is only underlined once preceding the UST title, and that is in 17. This could be because it is sentence-initial, contrasting in this respect with all other occurrences except 11. The fact that 'ZPG' is not underlined initially in 11, and is in 17, could be due to any one of three factors:

a. a typist's oversight;
b. the contrast between an informative context (11) and an expressive one (17);
c. because referentially, the test itself is more prominent than ZPG in 11, whereas by the time we reach 17, ZPG is beginning to come to the fore referentially (cf. reference to *ZPG* in 18, and *we* in 18-21).

We prefer the latter explanation.

6. Conclusion

6.1 *Significant Insights of this Approach*

Perhaps the greatest achievement we would claim for this approach is that it sees the text as a whole, and that the analysis of the minutiae — the selection of nominal as against pronominal forms, the exact reference of "we", the use of subordinate clauses — does not obscure the overall picture with a mass of detail, but rather builds up those details into a richly-faceted and coherent whole.

Thus as we approach the text in the light of the writer's purposes, we become aware of the constant ebb and flow of prominence, the switch from metaphorical to literal forms of expression, the guarded approach to an unpopular topic. Moreover, we can pinpoint in all these cases not only what the writer is doing, but also why. The emotive prominence of the opening sentences is attention-creating, but contributes almost nothing to the main purpose of the letter; the steady build-up of purposive prominence, from the deliberately down-played *We need help* to the underlined and overt appeal at the end, provides the structural thrust of the whole letter. The metaphors in the first half of the letter are vividly emotive, whereas the metaphor which expands on 'our modest resources' is introduced into the letter in a way calculated to present ZPG's impecunious state to the reader in the best possible light. In these instances, and many others, we are able to trace obviously similar purposes. This enhanced awareness of the significance of low-level elements leads to a much greater appreciation of the complex strands which motivate the message as a whole.

Some insights in the analysis presented here can be traced back to one specific part of the theoretical model used. The total absence from the text of any mention of the reduction of population growth — the main purpose of the organization — became apparent to us only when we applied to the text the theoretical principle of the purposive chain. We doubt very much if a casual reader would have noticed this omission, but it is unquestionably deliberate.

Reducing the phrases and clauses of the text to propositions seems at times almost brutal. What possible purpose can be served by representing *to use it well* as 'in order that (we (ZPG) can) use it (UST) well' or *our modest resources* as 'our (ZPG) funds are too small'? Yet it is precisely the effort to pinpoint the actual reference intended which shows up the difference between *we/our* in these examples, which exclude the reader, and *we/our* forms which do not. Similarly, comparing all references to UST in the text reveals that the instance quoted here, with realization by the pronoun *it*, is quite untypical and needs explanation. And comparison of the generic and positive surface form *modest resources* with the meaning being expressed (lack of funds) contributes to our awareness of this text as one which consciously attempts to foresee and control readers' reactions to unpleasant facts, and which does so by devices such as those used here, i.e. genericness and metaphor.

Recollections of freshman English classes are that they succeeded in killing, for us, literary texts which had previously been vibrant and meaningful. But analysis does not inevitably brush the bloom off the butterfly. When approached from the writer's viewpoint, as here, texts resemble not butterflies pinned in the display cabinet, but butterflies on the wing.

We wish to conclude by pointing out also several theoretical advantages of the model which we have here outlined.

First, it spans the uncomfortable gap that has long existed in meaning-studies, between word-semantics at the lowest level, and discourse analysis at the highest. We have here a structured and consistent approach which is equally applicable at all levels, and which thus unites the two extremes.

In addition, the model employed here points the way forward to a genuine and high-level generativeness. We do not generate discourses from lexemes upwards but from purposes downwards. This model provides a structural framework for such a high-level approach to the generation of discourses.

Finally, it provides a basis for cross-language comparison. Since the meaning-base is a universal, the discourses generated from it may be in any language. A discourse in one language may thus be directly compared with its counterpart in another language, no matter how different their surface structure forms. The need for such an objective basis of comparison has long been apparent in translation practice and theory.

Notes

1. We are indebted to two colleagues in S.I.L., Ellis Deibler and John Tuggy, for numerous fruitful discussions on the nature of meaning, and for outlines of the propositional analysis of this text; also to the editors, for helpful comments on an earlier version of this paper. We are grateful to Miss Margaret Carter for typing the manuscript.

2. These and other assumptions are spelt out in more detail in *Meaning-based Text Analysis, by Kathleen Callow. (To be published by University Press of America.)*

Rhetorical Structure Theory and Text Analysis

William C. Mann
University of Southern California
Information Sciences Institute
and
Summer Institute of Linguistics

Christian M.I.M. Matthiessen
University of Sydney

Sandra A. Thompson
University of California at Santa Barbara

1. Aims of Discourse Analysis

> from Advanced Learner's Dictionary (Hornby et al).
> **language n. 1.** human and non-instinctive method of communicating ideas, feelings, and desires by means of a system of sound symbols. **2.** ...

The key distinguishing attribute in defining "language" is that it is a method of communicating. When people get together and interact, especially in frequently recurring kinds of encounters, our usual experience is that the interaction is purposeful for one or more participants. They can achieve particular ends by using language. If speaker and hearer are using a shared language then frequently they can achieve their purposes, but if they do not have a shared language then they fail. Communication is effective if it creates the potential for a successful outcome, achievement of the participants' purposes. Invitations to social events, negotiations to buy things and requests for gifts of money are a few of these kinds of encounters.

All this would be tediously obvious, except that this capacity of languages to enable success in such interactions has not been accounted for by linguistics. In our research in discourse analysis, we aim to contribute to an account of how language can be used to communicate, i.e. a detailed description of how it contributes to the outcomes of interactions.

Pleading for money has a particularly long social history. It is a most representative class of language use encounters. The form we study here (a letter to a large set of people from a corporation organized for a narrow social cause) is contemporary. An essential part of success in this encounter is of course having a suitable number of addressees give money. To create the potential for such an outcome, the addressees must:

*know that money has been requested,
*know how to comply with the request,
*be motivated and willing to respond.

So to account for the ZPG letter as communication requires that we account for how it can produce at least these effects.

To use language as in the ZPG letter is not merely performing in some role or ritual as an institutional beggar; playing out a role can be done as an activity without consequences, and a view of language simply in terms of social roles would miss the point. Rather, the attempt to induce people to choose to give money is a characteristic, if not defining, attribute of this class of encounters. It is the attempt to get money by symbolic means that is the communicative essence of this class of encounters.

More generally, we want our discourse theories to provide paths or mappings both from situation to language, explaining how or why particular uses of language were chosen, and from language and situation to effect, explaining why particular uses of language succeeded or failed. For the latter, the most obvious fulfillment in the theory presented here is that it imputes to the speaker desires for particular effects. This element distinguishes it from many other approaches to discourse description. Most often, discourse descriptive methods have no place for intended effects, although frequently the developers of the methods will acknowledge them.

Certain kinds of presentations, texts, have a kind of wholeness or integrity that others lack. We recognize that they "hang together" and are understandable as single objects. They are coherent. Every element has some role in the whole text; otherwise the text contains a nonsequitur. This is the sense in which we see magazine articles as texts, but magazines, news broadcasts, and some dialogues as structured collections of texts.

A theory of textual communication should account for this coherence; if it is an *organizational* theory then it should account for the presence or absence of nonsequiturs. To account for nonsequiturs, the theory must assign (or appropriately fail to assign) a status to every part of the text. One of our aims in creating a theory of communication is this kind of comprehensive assignment of status. This is not to say that there is anything wrong with selective commentary or partial theories, except that they cannot by their nature account for the impression of unity or integrity that is one of the identifying marks of texthood.

2. Varieties of Structure

The term "structure" in this paper is used in an organizational sense.[1] The name of the theory, Rhetorical Structure Theory (RST), employs this sense. A theory of text structure describes what sorts of parts texts have, and the principles of combination of parts into entire texts. Since the term is widely used in many senses, we attempt to sketch here the various kinds of structure that RST recognizes, and within those the scope of the theory itself.

Even in our narrow sense of the term, RST does not attempt to describe all of the kinds of structure that a text may have. It recognizes three principal kinds:

1. Holistic Structure — structure deriving from the properties of the genre or variety of text, used in this case to describe the form of letters and account for expressions such as *Sincerely*.
2. Relational Structure — structure expressing the organization of coherent contiguous text, used in this case to describe the internal composition of the body and P.S. of the letter.
3. Syntactic Structure — as the term is commonly used.[2]

As will be seen below, RST is a theory of relational structure. It acknowledges other kinds, interacting strongly with holistic and syntactic structure, but it does not attempt to incorporate accounts of either genre or syntax. In the interaction, there are alignments of the various sorts of structure, so that often a particular arrangement, such as a combination of clauses, can be described in more than one way. The varieties of structure interpenetrate and illuminate each other, making descriptions in terms of these perspectives particularly interesting. One of the consequences of this interpenetration is that there is no sharp boundary, either in principle or in practice, between the different varieties.[3]

3. Introduction to Rhetorical Structure Theory

For several years there has been a research effort at USC Information Sciences Institute (ISI) aimed at describing written discourse. The original motivation for this research was that its results might be useful as a theoretical basis in designing computer programs with some of the capabilities of authors. The effort has ranged beyond this limited goal, and resulted in an understanding of discourse that has had many other uses, including several applications in linguistics. The effort has involved a study of the nature of text as a medium of communication, with an interest in developing a theory of text structure that could serve both as an analytical tool and as a tool for text generation. We call this theory Rhetorical Structure Theory (RST), since it provides a framework for describing rhetorical relations among parts of a text.[4]

In the construction of this theory we have analyzed more than 400 texts, from one paragraph to several pages in length, of the following types: administrative memos, personal letters, letters to the editor, advertisements, *Scientific American* articles and abstracts, newspaper articles and editorials, organizational newsletter articles and appeals (as exemplified in the Zero Population Growth letter that is the focal text of this book), public notices in magazines, travel brochures, and recipes.

In the course of examining these texts, we observed that many phenomena of text structure involved pairs of regions of the text. The mutual relevance of the two parts, and sometimes their position and form, could be identified with recurrent relations holding between the parts. These relations, sometimes but not always indicated by conjunctions, could hold between text parts of a wide range of sizes, from clauses to groups of paragraphs. These observations led to the formation of a testable set of assumptions (described below) and to the realization of these assumptions in the mechanisms of RST.

RST describes texts in a rich and highly constrained way and thus predicts much about their character and effects. It describes functions and structures that make texts effective and comprehensible tools for human communication.

3.1 *Underlying Assumptions*

Our observations about text structure have led to a number of basic assumptions underlying RST:

1. Organization — Texts consist of functionally significant parts; the parts are elements of patterns in which parts are combined to create larger parts and whole texts. The assumption that text is organized is not controversial; the opposite — that texts do not commonly have an internal organization — is not defended seriously in the linguistic literature.
2. Unity and Coherence — To be recognized as a text, the writing must create a sense of overall unity to which every part contributes. The presence of this unity and coherence is uncontroversial, but there are diverse views of its source.
3. Unity and Coherence Arise From Imputed Function — A (region of) text is perceived as having unity and coherence because all of its parts are seen as contributing to a single purpose of the writer, i.e. as created to achieve a single effect. As an alternative, some have assumed that unity and coherence come from conformity to a familiar pattern in the subject matter, such as a temporal sequence or repeated reference to a character. Others find it in more abstract semantic patterns, such as hyponomy and metonymy.
4. Hierarchy — Texts are organized such that elementary parts are composed into larger parts, which in turn are composed into yet larger parts up to the scale of the whole text. Without specifying the nature of the parts or the principles of composition, the assumption of hierarchy contrasts with other assumptions about the patterns of text structure. For example, one could assume that text structure is formed by adjacency patterns or by linearly related chains of clauses or semantic propositions.
5. Homogeneity of Hierarchy — As indicated above, RST describes relational structure and its interaction with holistic and syntactic structure. Within relational structure, RST assumes homogeneity:

there is one set of structural patterns available for organizing the text at every scale, from the largest, an element of holistic structure (e.g. letter body, magazine article body, possibly the whole text...) down to the smallest scale (possibly a two-clause combination). This set of patterns is identified as RST **schemas** (to be further discussed below). The potential for relational organization does not vary with scale; frequencies will vary with scale, genre and other influences. There are no conventional patterns at scales between the RST schema and the element of holistic structure. An alternative assumption might be that there is a rank-scale or size-scale of objects, e.g. sections and paragraphs, which each have their own distinct functional descriptions and principles of relational composition.

4. Relational Composition — The principal structural pattern in multisentential text is relational: a small set of highly recurrent relations holding between pairs of parts is used to link parts together to form larger parts. There are several kinds of alternative assumptions used by various researchers. In one, structural patterns are patterns of constituent categories (analogous to the mechanisms of certain grammars). In another, structural patterns are by nature semantic; they are necessarily patterns of subject matter, e.g. temporal or causal chains. Note that RST does not assume that all structuring is relational, nor that relational structure excludes semantic structuring, nor that all patterns are based on simple pairs. The RST assumption is that relational patterns are strongly dominant.

7. Asymmetry of Relations — The most common type of text structuring relation is an asymmetric class, called nucleus-satellite relations in RST. This class is asymmetric because one member of a pair of text spans is more central (the **nucleus**) and one more peripheral (the **satellite**). Further, a text part that is the nucleus for some text-structuring relation will have functional similarities with other nuclei. There are other theories of text structure that also recognize this asymmetry (cf. Grimes (1975), van Dijk (1985), van Dijk (1981) and the Longacre, Meyer and Pike papers in this volume, as well as the references that they cite.)

8. Nature of Relations — Text structuring relations are functional; the character that they all share can be stated in terms of the categories

of effects that they produce. They can be described in terms of the purposes of the writer, the writer's assumptions about the reader, and certain propositional patterns in the subject matter of the text. The text structuring relations reflect the writer's options of organization and presentation; it is in this sense that an RST structure is "rhetorical."

In contrast, one could assume that text structuring relations simply represent relations in the subject matter (e.g. of succession, cause or conditionality.)

Strictly speaking, the relations of a text do not hold between the various word sequences of which the text consists. Rather, the word sequences are realizations of more abstract entities: meanings and intentions that are represented by those word sequences. In this sense *all of RST is pre-realizational, since it makes statements about how such meanings and intentions are structured and combined, but not about how they are realized.* It is inconvenient to acknowledge the abstraction on every mention, so we will generally say that relations hold between spans of text, but the distinction between the abstract entity and its realization always remains.

Although RST identifies the nature of text structuring relations as functional, it does not presume any particular function. Discovery of the relations and their functions is however an empirical matter. In research, a great deal of misunderstanding and misrepresentation of language has come from assuming that the sole or principal function of language is *informing*, and that it therefore operates as a message passing medium, a code. This agrees with the outlook and metaphors of our culture (*content*, *convey*, *message*, language as a conduit (Reddy 1979)), but it does not stand up to careful examination; see for example the abundant exceptions to that view in Larkin & O'Malley (1973). The relations in fact perform a diversity of functions; some are involved with informing, but many perform presentational and social functions with little informative value. If one sees the function of text as predominantly informing or message-passing, then one is led to a view that text structure performs predominantly a representational function. This can be mitigated by a broad definition of "message," but not corrected.

Another alternative is to assume that the knowledge of text structuring relations is a variety of lexical knowledge, e.g., of conjunctions. This assumption would be most reasonable if the relations were always signalled explicitly. (Something close to this assumption can be arrived at by beginning one's investigation with the conjunctions and discovering relations from them.) In RST the relations are not identified with any particular ways in which they are represented. Most of them, but not all, can be made accessible to the reader by conjunctions, often a variety of conjunctions, and all of them can be conveyed in other ways, including being fully implicit. The assumption that text structuring relations are lexical is an alternative, not compatible with RST.

9. The Number of Relations — The set of text structuring relations is in principle open, so that additional previously unused relations can arise. However, the frequency of creation of new relations is extremely low, and for all but a kernel set the frequency of use of rare or unknown relations is also extremely low, so that text in a culture can be analyzed virtually entirely in terms of a small set of highly recurrent relations, the knowledge of which is shared in the culture. The relations can be arranged in a taxonomy, with the particular number of relations reflecting definitional splitting and joining of taxonomic categories. An alternative assumption might be that the set of relations used in a particular culture and situation is drawn from a fixed universal set, possibly not yet fully documented, but in principle not expandable.[5]

In this paper, we use these assumptions to help characterize RST and to clarify the analysis at points where the assumptions become crucial. The assumptions are in fact built into the mechanisms of RST. Many correspondences of these assumptions to RST's mechanisms will be evident as the latter are described below. Space limits prevent explaining the correspondence here. For a more detailed treatment of RST's mechanisms, see Mann & Thompson (1988) and Mann & Thompson (1989).

The use of RST to investigate a number of linguistic issues serves to validate RST's assumptions. Some of the relevant studies are described below.

First, RST provides a general way to describe the relations among organizational elements in a text, whether or not those relations are grammatically or lexically signalled. Thus, RST is a useful framework for relating the meanings of conjunctions, the grammar of clause combining, and non-signalled parataxis (i.e. asyndeton; for discussion, see Matthiessen & Thompson (1989), Thompson & Mann (1986) and Thompson & Mann (1987).)

Second, descriptive RST has been used as an analytical tool for a wide range of text types. Noel (1986) shows how it can be used to characterize news broadcasts. Fox (1987) demonstrates how explanations of the choice between pronoun and full NP in expository English texts can be derived from the organizational structure revealed by RST.

Third, descriptive RST lays a foundation for studies in contrastive rhetoric. Cui's analysis of Mandarin and English essays (Cui 1985) is an example.

Fourth, RST has proven to be useful in analyzing narrative discourse as well. Kumpf (1986) is a study of the interlanguage of Japanese and Spanish speakers. The author shows that RST is valuable in describing the grammatical and rhetorical properties of the narratives produced by these speakers.

Finally, RST provides a framework for investigating Relational Propositions, Which are unstated but inferred propositions that arise from the text structure in the process of interpreting texts (see Section 7.1 and Mann & Thompson (1986)). Since the coherence of a text depends in part on these Relational Propositions, RST has been useful in the study of text coherence.

3.2 *Terminology and mechanisms of RST*

The key elements of RST are **relations** and **spans**.[6] Essentially, the relation definitions identify particular relationships that can hold between two text spans.

A **text span** is any portion of text that has an RST structure (and thus has a functional integrity, from a text-organizational point of view), or that is realized by a **unit**. Units, defined in Section 3.3, are typically clauses. (For convenience we also speak informally of the region of text that realizes a text span as being a text span.) In general, a text span will not be interrupted by another text span, but defining text spans in functional terms rather than strictly orthographic terms allows for interrupted text spans. Section 6 discusses an instance of an interrupted text span in the analysis of the ZPG letter.

The notion of the structure of a text is defined in terms of the network of relations among successively larger text spans.

Relations are defined to hold between two non-overlapping text spans called the **nucleus** and the **satellite**. A relation definition consists of two fields:

1. **Constraints:** including a set of constraints on the nucleus, a set of constraints on the satellite, and a set of constraints on the combination of nucleus and satellite.
2. **Effect:** including a statement of the effect that plausibly the writer was attempting to produce in employing the relation, and (derived from that statement) the locus of effect, identified as either the nucleus alone or the nucleus-satellite combination.

We can see how these fields function to specify a relation definition by taking as an example the definition of the **Evidence** relation, shown in Figure 1.

---

1. *Constraints:*
   a. Constraints on the Nucleus: The reader might not believe the nucleus to a degree satisfactory to the writer.
   b. Constraints on the Satellite: The reader believes the satellite or will find it credible.
   c. Constraints on the combination of Nucleus and Satellite: The reader's comprehending the satellite increases his or her belief of the nucleus.

2. *Effect:*
   a. The reader's belief of the nucleus is increased.
   b. Locus of the Effect: Nucleus.

Figure 1: Definition of the Evidence Relation

The **Evidence** relation is appropriate to relate two text spans one of which (the evidence satellite) provides evidence for the claim put forth in the other (the nucleus). As an example we can consider this extract from a letter to the editor of BYTE magazine; the writer is praising a federal income tax program published in a previous issue. Here Unit 2 provides evidence for the claim in Unit 1, as diagrammed in Figure 2.

1. The program as published for calendar year 1980 really works.
2. In only a few minutes, I entered all the figures from my 1980 tax returns and got a result which agreed with my hand calculations to the penny.

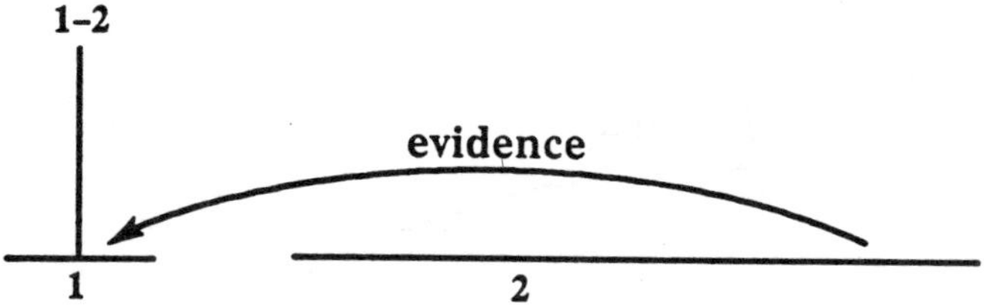

Figure 2: RST Diagram of the Tax Program Letter

The Effect field in a relation definition specifies the intended effect on the reader of that particular relation. In the case of the **Evidence** relation, for example, part a. of the Effect field stipulates that the writer intends that the effect of using the Evidence relation is to increase the reader's belief in the nucleus. Thus in the case of the BYTE magazine example, the analysis reflects the judgment that the writer's purpose in including the satellite Unit 2 was to increase the reader's belief in the claim that *the program really works*. Since every definition has an Effect field, the analyst can thus provide a plausible reason the writer might have had for including each part of the whole text.

The relation definition does not constrain the order of spans, and for virtually every relation, both of the possible orders nucleus-satellite and satellite-nucleus are found.

Closely related to the functionality of the Effect field is the functionality of nuclearity. Informally, we speculate that nuclearity influences the way the reader assigns different roles to different parts of the text. If the satellite gains its significance through the nucleus, the writer can indicate, by the inherent nuclearity of the relation used, that the nucleus is more deserving of response, including attention, deliberation, and reaction.

The Locus of Effect field thus allows us to distinguish between those relations whose locus of effect is the nucleus from those whose locus of effect is both the nucleus and the satellite.

When the locus of effect is the nucleus, as in the **Evidence** relation, nuclearity represents the qualitative differences between the essential and the inessential. The satellite supports the nucleus, but does not contribute to it. When the locus of effect is both nucleus and satellite, a different sort of function is performed: the relation is expressing particular characteristics of the subject matter.

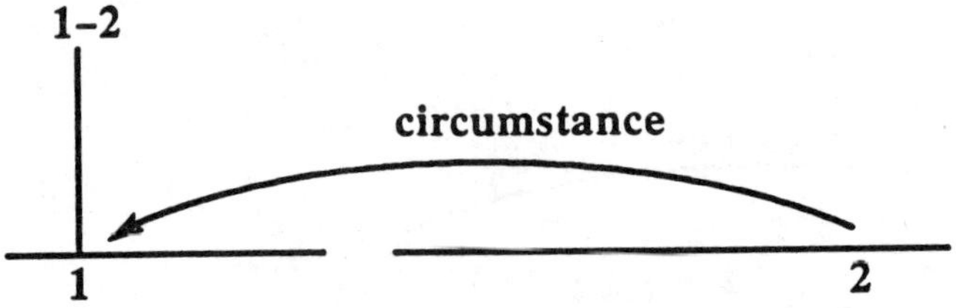

Figure 3: RST Diagram Showing the Circumstance Relation

For example, a relation whose locus of effect is both nucleus and satellite is the **Circumstance** relation. The definition of the **Circumstance** relation specifies that the satellite sets a subject matter framework within which the nucleus can be interpreted. The intended effect is simply that the reader should recognize that the situation presented in the satellite provides the framework for interpreting the nucleus; its locus is thus both the nucleus and the satellite.

As an example of the **Circumstance** relation, consider this extract from an ad for computer disks, as diagrammed in Figure 3.

1. Cleaning agents on the burnished surface of the Ectype coating actually remove build-up from the head,
2. while lubricating it at the same time.

The locus of the effect of the **Circumstance** relation is both nucleus and satellite: the intended effect is that the reader recognize that the satellite (*while lubricating it at the same time*) provides a framework within which to interpret the nucleus (*Cleaning agents ... actually remove build-up*).

The nuclearity of the **Circumstance** relation, where the locus of effect is both the nucleus and the satellite, is thus quite different from the nuclearity of the **Evidence** relation, where the locus of effect is just the nucleus. Where the locus of effect is just the nucleus, nuclearity reflects the *supporting* role of the satellite; where the locus of effect is both the nucleus and the satellite, nuclearity reflects the symbiotic role of the nucleus and the satellite in the reader's recognition of subject-matter relationships.

Each field of a relation definition specifies particular judgments that the text analyst must make in building the RST structure. Since the analyst has access to the text, has knowledge of the context in which it was written, and shares the cultural conventions of the writer and the expected readers, but has no direct access to either the writer or other readers, judgments about the writer or readers must be plausibility judgments rather than judgments of certainty. That is, every judgment of the completed analysis is of the form, *It is plausible to the analyst that ...*". In the case of the Effect field, for example, the analyst is judging whether it is plausible that the writer desires the specified effect on the reader.

3.3 *Steps in performing an RST analysis*

The first step in analyzing a text is to divide it into **units**. Unit size is arbitrary in RST; in principle the units can be of any size from typical lexical items to entire paragraphs or larger. In our work on RST, however, we have found it useful to use units that have some relatively theory-neutral functional integrity. We have derived interesting results from considering the units to be roughly clauses, except that clausal subjects and objects and restrictive relative clauses are considered parts of their host clauses rather than separate units.[7,8] The units we are working with here, then, are typically located at the boundary region shared by relational structure and syntactic structure. Larger units may be useful for various other purposes, such as describing the overall structure of larger texts.

The next step is to identify spans and relations, working either from the top down (progressive refinement) or from the bottom up (aggregation), or both, as deemed convenient. Again, in determining what relation should be said to hold between two given text spans, the analyst is asking at each point whether the relation definition plausibly applies. Notationally, we represent nuclei under vertical lines and satellites at the ends of arcs, as shown in Figure 4, which shows the schema representing the top level organization of the body of the ZPG letter. While the schema is a technical

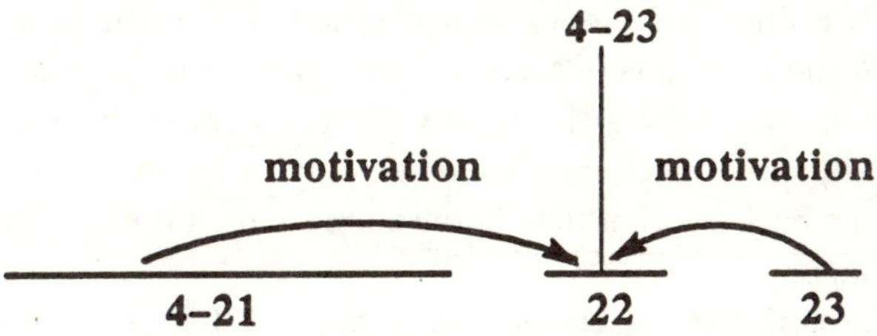

Figure 4: Highest Level RST Schema Diagram for the ZPG Letter

device in the more elaborate definition of RST, here we can think of it simply as an iconic convention, showing how units and relations are grouped. In the case of nucleus-satellite relations, the grouping consists of one nucleus and all of its satellites.

As in other kinds of analysis of linguistic structure, RST sometimes yields *multiple analyses* for a text. There are various sources of this multiplicity, one of which is ambiguity of discourse structure. We present a single analysis below; there are comments on alternate analyses of the text in Section 5.

The set of relations in RST is not a closed set. Among those which we have found useful are the following:

Nucleus-Satellite Relations

Evidence	Justify	Antithesis
Concession	Circumstance	Solutionhood
Elaboration	Background	Enablement
Motivation	Volitional Cause	Non-volitional Cause
Volitional Result	Non-volitional Result	Purpose
Condition	Otherwise	Interpretation
Evaluation	Restatement	Summary

Multi-nuclear Relations

Sequence	Contrast	Joint

Precise definitions for all these relations, and of the conditions under which they can be applied, can be found in (Mann & Thompson 1989). Here we will be concerned only with those relations that figure in our analysis of the ZPG letter, whose definitions can be found in the Appendix.

The role of *subjective judgment* in the theory should be made clear. To account for communication as one of the principal functions of language, a linguistic theory must be functional, in the sense that it must provide representations and draw conclusions about what the functions of particular uses of language are. If a linguistic theory of text structure is to be functional, judgments about the functions of texts and text parts must be made in the process of creating and testing the theory. In practice, such judgments are necessarily subjective, since they are made only by human beings who communicate, on the basis of what they know about their culture, their society, and their language.

This kind of judgment has of course been applied frequently in developing RST (and every other account of language function). In addition, RST employs subjective judgments in another, more controversial role. They are used not only in evaluating an analysis, but in producing it. We use this approach in RST because it is an effective way to develop functional descriptions of text, as a step toward ultimately coming to understand communication. Texts are complex objects, with correspondingly complex functional descriptions. To arrive at such descriptions, as our general goals require, it is necessary to develop and combine many smaller functional descriptions.[9]

The specific representation of this kind of judgment in RST is that, as mentioned above, the analyst affirms certain statements about the text and the writer as *plausible* rather than factual. Related to this approach is the fact that RST relations are defined without referring to particular textual patterns; the **Purpose** relation is defined without reference to *in order to*. This intentional lack of explicit hooks makes such judgments essential.

4. RST Analysis of the ZPG Letter

The original ZPG letter, used with permission, is shown in the introduction to this book. The integer segment numbers are based on visual subdivision; the finer segmentation used in our analysis is explained below.

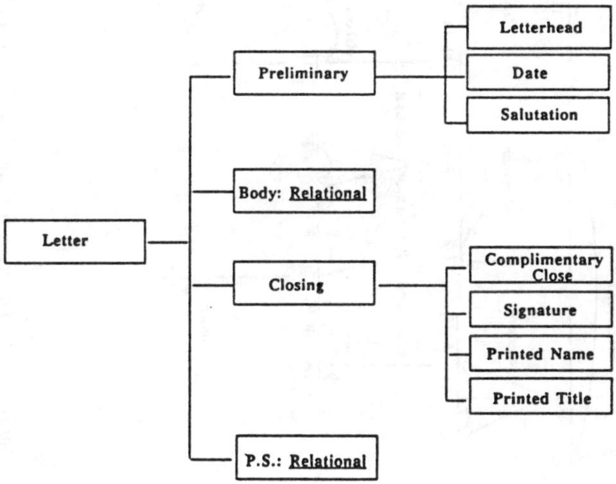

Figure 5: Holistic Structure Sequence for the ZPG Letter

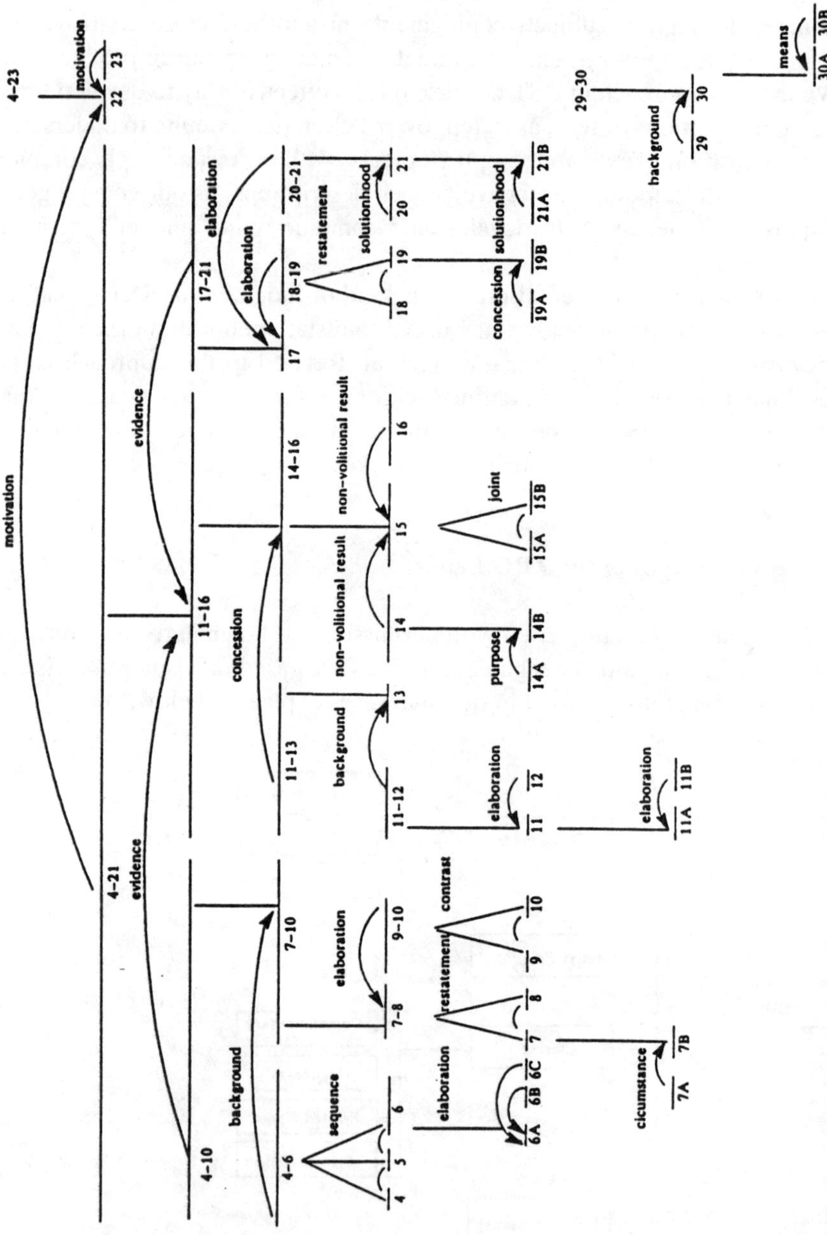

Figure 6: RST Diagram for the Body of the ZPG Letter

We expect that the holistic structure of letters is specified so that one of the alternatives is the sequence shown in Figure 5, possibly with more or less substructure or grouping than is shown. The body and P.S. elements of this sequence are specified as potentially having relational structure.

The RST analysis of the ZPG letter is given in Figure 6. In this section, we will discuss the analysis and the rationale for the judgments we have made.[10] All numbers refer to units.

The topmost level of our analysis recognizes certain conventional properties of a letter which we consider not to be part of its relational structure, since, as pointed out in Section 2, they are part of the holistic structure; they are included as part of what we know about the form of letters of this kind in our culture. Thus 1 is a letterhead logo, 2 is the date, and 3 is the greeting. The body of the letter is 4-23, which has an RST analysis, to be discussed below. Units 24-27 constitute the closing, and 28-30 comprise the P.S., whose internal structure can also be described by an RST analysis.

Before discussing the body of the letter, let us briefly discuss the RST analysis of the P.S., 28-30. The analysis reflects the afterthought nature of a P.S. by attributing it to the holistic structure associated with letters, and not taking it as a discontinuous element of the body of the letter. Internally, we have considered it to consist of a **Background** satellite (29) to the nuclear 30, which itself is composed of a nucleus (30A) and a **Means** satellite (30B). According to its definition, the **Background** relation is appropriate for 29-30: the satellite 29 increases the reader's ability to comprehend an element in the nuclear 30 (namely *this remarkable media coverage*).

We will have no more to say here about the opening 1-3, the closing 24-27, or the P.S.. Further reference to *the text* will be to the body of the letter, 4-23.

Let us now turn to the RST analysis of the body of the letter. The diagram in Figure 6 reflects the intuition that the nuclear unit of the entire text (that reached by tracing from the top of the RST structure (here the node labeled 4-23) through vertical lines) is 22. This is appropriate because the purpose of the letter is blatantly to seek contributions, and it is in 22 that the appeal is stated in its most directive fashion: *Please make a special contribution to Zero Population Growth today*.

Supporting the nuclear appeal in 22 are two **Motivation** satellites, which together constitute the remainder of the text. Thus, the RST analysis reveals the functional structure of this letter to consist of a nuclear request accompanied by several paragraphs motivating the reader to comply with the request.

Taking the smaller **Motivation** portion first, we note simply that 23, assuring readers that their contribution will be put to good use, is the final sentence in the letter — a last-ditch effort at motivating readers to give money.

The larger **Motivation** chunk is the entire body of the letter preceding the request, comprising 4-21. According to the RST diagram, this text span consists of a nuclear claim 11-16, which tells readers how badly their help is needed, flanked by two pieces of evidence for that claim, 4-10 and 17-21. Let us now consider the internal structure of each of these pieces of evidence.

The first piece of evidence, consisting of 4-10, is thematically unified around the public reaction to the release of the results of the Urban Stress Test. That is, this span provides evidence for the claim that readers' help is needed by detailing how ready the public is for the ZPG message that the Urban Stress Test provides.

The nucleus of this segment is 7-10, which describes the unexpected public response to the Test results. As **Background** to this nuclear claim, we find the narrative sequence in 4-6, describing the events of the day the Test results were released. These narrative Units 4-6 are related to each other by the multi-nuclear relation **Sequence**. Note that within this sequence, 6 can be subdivided into a nuclear 6A plus two **Elaboration** satellites, 6B and 6C.

Looking more closely now at the nuclear span of this first **Evidence** satellite, 7-10, we see that this span consists of the nuclear pair 7-8, and an **Elaboration** satellite. Units 7-8 are related to each other by the bi-nuclear relation **Restatement**. That is, 8 restates the content of 7, the idea that the public response has been *overwhelming* and *incredible*. (Note that 7 itself consists of a nuclear 7B preceded by a *when*-clause in a **Circumstance** relation.)

Finally, 9-10, the elaboration of 7-8, generalizing the reactions during the first month after the release of the Test results, are related to each other by the bi-nuclear relation **Contrast**. That is, 9 contrasts with 10 in that 9 gives the initial reactions, coming from *reporters* and *outraged public officials*, while 10 gives the less immediate and more moderate reactions from *concerned citizens in all parts of the country*.

The first piece of evidence, then, for the claim that readers' help is needed, is the portion of the text describing the positive reactions to the results of the Urban Stress Test.

The second piece of evidence for this assertion that help is needed is the span 17-21, thematically discussing the role that the Test can play in raising public consciousness about population-related problems in cities.

The nucleus of this span is 17, which claims that the Urban Stress Test may be the best way to disseminate the *population message*; it is followed by two **Elaboration** satellites.

The first of these **Elaboration** satellites, 18-19, consists of two spans in a **Restatement** relation: 19 restates (*we can take positive action at the local level*) what 18 conveys (*warn community leaders about population-related stresses*). Unit 19 itself consists of a **Concession** satellite 19A and a nuclear 19B.

The second of the **Elaboration** satellites is 20-21. Unit 20 is in a **Solutionhood** relation with 21, and 21A is in a **Solutionhood** relation with 21B. Thus, the problem in 20, that local officials are faced with decisions that affect us, is solved by 21, providing them with the data from the Test to enable them to make sound choices. But 21 also consists of a problem and its solution: 21A presents the problem of making sound choices, and 21B presents the solution, which is to get the data to elected officials and the American public.

We have now described both of the **Elaboration** satellites in the **Motivation** span 4-21.

Before going on to the nucleus of this **Motivation** satellite, let us pause briefly to comment on a feature of Unit 21, namely its indirectness. As we have just suggested, the RST analysis claims that it is plausible to analyze 21 as presenting a solution to the problem in 20 of local officials making decisions that affect our daily lives. But a careful reading of 21 shows that it does not literally present such a solution, since all it says is that elected officials and the American public need the population-stress data. However it is clear in understanding 21 that the writer is suggesting that when the officials *have* the data it helps in solving their problem of making sound decisions. Analysis must take many kinds of indirect and metaphorical modes of expression into account, including indirect speech acts, various kinds of hedging, metonymy and many other ploys.

Now let's turn to the nucleus (11-16) of the **Motivation** satellite whose two **Evidence** satellites we have just considered. Units 11-16 are related by the **Concession** relation: 11-13 form a **Concession** satellite to the nuclear 14-16.

Since this example of **Concession** is not as straightforward as that seen in 19A-19B, let's pause briefly to justify it. As discussed in Thompson & Mann (1986) and Mann & Thompson (1989), the **Concession** relation can be fruitfully thought of as involving apparent incompatibility but actual compatibility. The definition of **Concession** (see Appendix) includes the provision that the writer intends the actual compatibility of the satellite and the nuclear spans to increase the reader's positive regard for the nucleus.

In these terms, the span 11-16 can be seen as contrasting 11-13, describing the positive attributes of the Urban Stress Test, with 14-16, which point out the desperate financial straits of ZPG. These two situations are potentially incompatible, since a lack of funds decreases the value of the Urban Stress Test. However, the writer views the two situations as compatible; they are compatible if readers respond with the needed funds. And she hopes to increase the reader's positive regard for the nuclear span describing the desperate financial straits by getting the reader to recognize the compatibility as well.

We hope to have convinced you that 11-13 are plausibly analyzed as constituting a **Concession** satellite to 14-16. Within this **Concession** satellite itself, 11-13, 13 is the nucleus, with 11-12 as an **Background** satellite. That is, 11-12 provide a basis for understanding the statement about "translation" in 13. Units 11-12, in turn, are in an **Elaboration** relation, with 12 providing details of 11, and 11B, the participial clause, is a further elaboration for 11A.

The nucleus of the **Concession** relation in 11-16 is 14-16. Within this span, 15 is the nucleus and 14 and 16 are satellites, each in a **Non-volitional Result** relation. That is, 14 *we need your help* and 16 *your support is critical* are plausibly intended by the writer as results of the situation described in 15. Units 14A-B can be further analyzed in terms of the relation **Purpose**.

Finally, 15A and 15B together form a **Joint** Schema; that is, they jointly perform the double role described for 15, and none of the other RST relations holds between them, as specified by the definition of **Joint**.[11]

Our description of the RST analysis for the ZPG text is now complete. The analysis shows that the body of the ZPG letter can be understood as a request for donations (22), preceded by a lengthy portion (11 paragraphs) motivating readers to comply with this request. Within this motivation section, we have seen that a nuclear claim that help is urgently needed is flanked by two pieces of evidence for this claim. One of these pieces of evidence asserts that the Urban Stress Test has been very well received, and the other claims that the Urban Stress Test can be useful for ZPG action at the local level.

Now we can review the ways in which this particular analysis represents the general assumptions identified in Section 3.1.

The assumption of Organization (#1) is obviously represented by the structural analysis. The assumption of Unity and Coherence (#2) is represented by the fact that for each of the relational parts (the body and the P.S.) every part is incorporated into a single connected analysis. That unity and coherence arise from imputed function (#3) is represented by the requirement that the analyst confirms the fit of the relation definitions used in the analysis, including the Effect field, according to which the analyst imputes to the writer an intention of effect for each relation employed. Roles in terms of intended effects are thus assigned to every part of the text. (The assumption that the nature of text structuring relations is functional (#8) is fulfilled in the same way.)

The assumptions of hierarchy (#4) and homogeneity of hierarchy (#5) are represented in RST's mechanisms, which produce a hierarchy by using the same mechanism at every level.

The assumptions on relational composition (#6) and the dominance of asymmetry (#7) are fulfilled in the analysis, since of the 31 terminal units, 23 stand in a nucleus-satellite relation, 6 in a multinuclear relation and only 2 in a Joint structure. In addition, there are 10 nonterminal nucleus-satellite relations and no multinuclear ones.

Finally, the assumption that in practice the number of relations is small (#9) is seen in this analysis, which uses 14 different relations to accomplish 30 links. A list of these relations is in Figure 7.

5. Alternative Analyses

It often happens that a text has more than one analysis; it is a normal and predictable outcome, given the way that RST is defined. We and others

Background	Means	Motivation
Evidence	Concession	Elaboration
Non-volitional Result	Sequence	Circumstance
Contrast	Solutionhood	Joint
Restatement	Purpose	

Figure 7: The Relations of the ZPG Letter

have had the experience of giving the same text to several analysts, who then created differing analyses, sometimes more than one from an individual analyst. There are several qualitatively different causes of this multiplicity:

1. Boundary Judgments — results of forcing borderline cases into categories.
2. Text Structure Ambiguity — comparable to many other varieties of linguistic ambiguity.
3. Simultaneous Analyses — multiple compatible analyses (see Ford 1987 for some discussion).
4. Differences Between Analysts — especially, differing plausibility judgments.
5. Analytical Error — especially by inexperienced analysts.

There is a well-known phenomenon associated with grammatical ambiguity, in which people initially regard a construct as unambiguous, and only later recognize that there are other analyses. This fixation on particular analyses arises in RST as well. This is seen when several analysts analyze the same text and then accept each other's analyses.

With experienced analysts, multiplicity of analyses represents primarily simultaneous analyses and text structure ambiguities. The particular role of the analyst causes bizarre analyses to be legitimately rejected, and so the actual levels of ambiguity are much lower than experience with formal grammatical analyses would lead one to expect.

Multiplicity of RST analyses is normal, consistent with linguistic experience as a whole, and is one of the kinds of pattern by which the analyses are informative.

By way of illustration, we take one such case from the ZPG letter; it concerns the appropriate analysis of the relation of 11-13 to 14-16. In Section 6 we justified labeling this relation **Concession**, acknowledging that this analysis might need justification. Indeed, this relation could be thought to be an instance of **Background**. However, we argue that **Concession** is more plausible.

Recall that 11-13 characterize the Urban Stress Test, while 14-16 bemoan the lack of resources and issue the first plea for financial support.

Before we consider the multiple analysis for these two spans, we briefly note that there are two analyses for the relation between 11-13 and 14-16 that, although initially attractive, are not real options. These are **Con-**

trast and **Antithesis**, since the two spans do not serve to compare two situations and contrast them on one or more points of difference, as required by the definitions of these two relations.

However, it is certainly plausible that 11-13 be analyzed as providing background to 14-16, according to our definition of **Background**, since it could be seen as containing information necessary for the interpretation of 14-16. See Figure 8 for a diagram of this alternative. Although this is a plausible analysis, we do not take backgrounding to be the primary function of 11-13 in this highly manipulative text. Rather, as suggested above, we claim that 11-13 are serving to highlight the appeal for funds in 14-16 by pointing out all the virtues of the Urban Stress Test as potentially incompatible with *using* it — incompatible unless the needed funds are donated.

This case of multiple analyses seems to be a genuine case of what we call "Simultaneous Analyses"; that is, there are two compatible analyses, but one of them appears, to the three of us at least, to be more plausible in terms of the perceived overall goals of the writer.[12]

6. Consequences and Inferences from the Analysis: Rhetorical Patterns

6.1 *Centrality at the Whole-Text Level*

One of the outcomes of an RST analysis is identification of a portion of the text that represents the essence of the text as a whole. It is called the **Comprehensive Locus of Effect**. It is arrived at by pruning the structure diagram as follows: Starting at the top (whole-text) node, trace down to each nucleus. For each relation linking nucleus to satellite, if the relation is

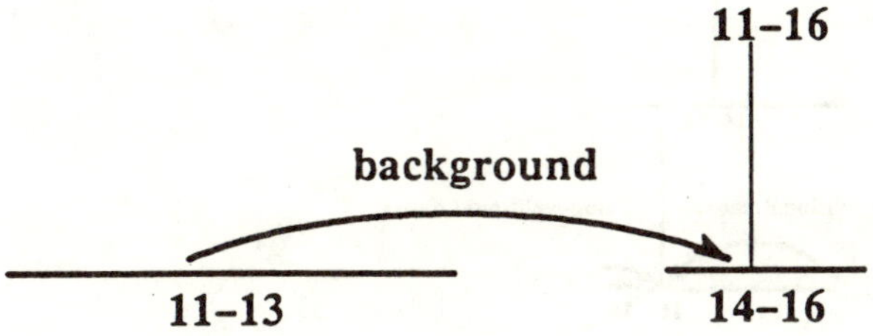

Figure 8: An Alternate Analysis of Units 11 through 16

defined to have a locus of effect that is the nucleus only, remove the satellite. Trace down repeatedly in the same way to all terminal units. The resulting “text” with some satellites deleted, is the comprehensive locus of effect.

In our experience this resulting ”text” remains coherent and represents a kind of ideational essence of the larger text. It is formally representative in the sense that the whole text is considered in deriving it.

For the ZPG letter body, the comprehensive locus of effect is simply segment 22: *Please make a special contribution to Zero Population Growth today.*, which certainly reflects the judgment that this letter is in essence an appeal for funds.

For the P.S. the comprehensive locus of effect is the second sentence: *I hope you'll help us monitor this remarkable media coverage by completing the enclosed reply form.*, which reflects the separate appeal being made in the P.S.

As one of the outcomes of a whole-text analysis, we can have some confidence that the comprehensive locus of effect does not misrepresent the text as an informal summary might, for example by focusing on only one portion.

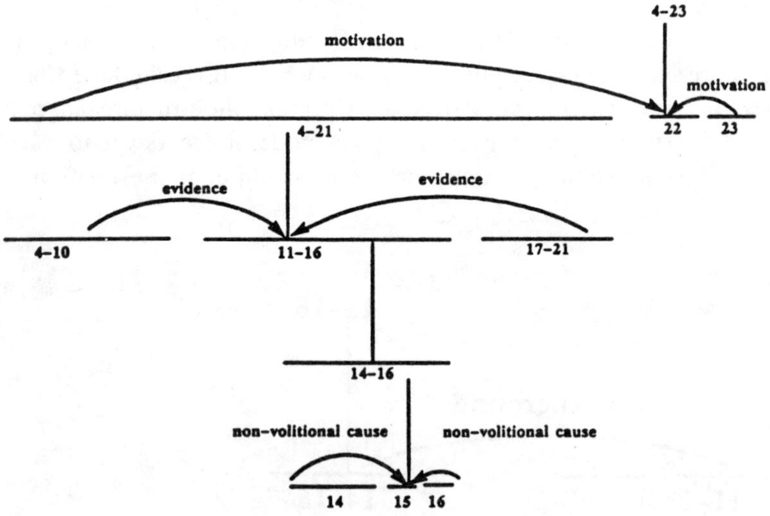

Figure 9: Satellite-Nucleus-Satellite Patterns in the ZPG Text

6.2 *A Presentational Pattern*

The RST analysis brings out an interesting pattern in the organization of the ZPG text. As Figure 6 shows, there are three places in the analysis where a nucleus is flanked by two satellites of the same relation; these are reproduced in Figure 9.

This pattern is readily visible only with an analytical tool such as RST offers, in which there is a distinction between nuclear and satellite portions of the text. This pattern is somewhat unusual among the more than 400 texts we have analyzed. Without many more examples of this Satellite-Nucleus-Satellite pattern, we cannot be sure whether it reflects properties of the appeal-letter genre or habits of the author of this particular letter, but in either case it seems to reveal the repetitive mode in which this appeal letter is written. That is, this Satellite-Nucleus-Satellite pattern highlights our feeling as readers that the letter is strongly organized around a mode of leading up to the point, stating the point, and driving it home.

7. Consequences and Inferences from the Analysis: Relations, Grammar and Lexis

7.1 *Relations, Relational Propositions and Explicit Signals*

Another kind of consequences of the text structure, labeled "relational propositions" in Mann & Thompson (1986), involves communication of information in the relational structure itself. The relations can communicate for the writer, just as clause structure or words can. Sometimes this communication is entirely implicit; sometimes it is signalled in various ways.

(By a **signal** of a relation we mean any single lexical, morphological or syntactic construct that regularly occurs in conjunction with the relation, and that can be taken to represent (perhaps ambiguously) the presence of the relation. There are some complex patterns that are outside of this definition, and some possibilities for inferential recognition of relations that are outside of both of the above.)

For example, segment 20 talks about decisions by local officials *that could drastically affect the quality of our lives*. Segment 21 talks about these officials having the results of the study. In the analysis there is a **Solution-**

hood relation between these two. The satellite (20) presents a problem of decision-making (or our living with the results), for which having the data is a (partial) solution. Mediating between these is the implicit idea that the quality of the decisions may be improved if they are informed decisions. A plausible inferential path would say that if the officials have the data, then they may use it in making decisions, and that if they use it, the quality of the decisions may increase, and that if the quality of the decisions increases then the quality of our lives may increase.

Having the data is thus a (partial and uncertain) solution to the problem of quality presented in segment 20. This claim of solutionhood is the relational proposition; it is conveyed by the solutionhood relation itself, and is not explicitly signalled. It is this solutionhood that makes the satellite relevant; even though the claim is obviously quite tenuous, if it were denied (say, elsewhere in the text) then segment 20 would become a nonsequitur and the coherence of the text as a whole would thus be broken.

Relational propositions have a status comparable to that of the explicit assertions of the text. The writer is responsible for their veracity, and can be quoted as claiming their truth, though to a lesser extent than is the case with explicit assertions. However, they obviously differ from the explicit assertions in that they are interpretively imposed on a text.

Relational propositions affect our interpretation of texts in two ways. They help explain the significance of various kinds of structure-indicating signals when they are present. In the absence of signals, they indicate the basis of coherence of texts and specify part of what the text communicates. For some texts, recognizing this kind of implicit communication is crucial to explaining the text as a means of communication.

A corollary to this is that RST predicts that although some relations may be signalled by conjunctions or connectives of various sorts, the relations will be recognized even if they are unsignalled. Strikingly, most of the relations in the ZPG text are unsignalled. This is strong confirmation of the assumptions of RST: a text is understood to cohere in the ways that it does largely by virtue of its relational structure rather than by virtue of overt markers signalling relations among its parts. In other words, connectives are better thought of as guiding the interpretation of a text than as necessary signals of relations (cf. Martin (1983) on the role of explicit conjunctions in marking rather than creating conjunctive relations).

Thus there are only eight relational signals in the text. Let's briefly consider each of them. The first is the *when* at the beginning of 7A, marking the relation between 7A and 7B as one of **Circumstance**.

Next is a pair of adverbs that together signal the **Contrast** relation between 9 and 10. As we pointed out in the analysis, 9 gives the initial and stronger reactions, while 10 gives the less immediate and more moderate reactions to the Urban Stress Test news. As signals, we find *At first* at the beginning of 9 and *Now* at the beginning of 10.

The next two explicit signals are signals of concession. The first is *But* at the beginning of 14. Recall that 11-13 and 14-16 are in a **Concession** relation, which we justified at some length in Section 4 above. The second signal of concession is the *Even though* in 19A, marking 19A as a **Concession** satellite to 19B. This situation nicely illustrates our assumption that relations are perceived to hold between parts of a text largely independently of the signals used. A relation may be unmarked, or, as in this case, it may be marked by one of a variety of signals. A **Concession** relation is typically either marked on the satellite with a "concessive conjunction" such as *although*, or marked instead on the nucleus with a *but*. The claim made in Thompson & Mann (1986), that concession is a matter of discourse relations rather than a matter of a certain type of "subordinate" clause is supported by the ZPG text.

After the *But* in 14A, there is an infinitive purpose clause, marked with a *to*.

The next relational signal in the text is the *To* in *To make sound choices* in 21A, which signals the **Solutionhood** relation between 21A and 21B. 21A talks about making sound choices and 21B talks about getting the population-stress data to those who make these choices. Thus the satellite 21A presents a problem of decision-making, for which having the data is a (partial) solution. The infinitive *To make sound choices* sets up the problem to which the following main clause presents the solution.

This example provides interesting confirmation of our claim that relations and signals do not correspond in any simple way. Note that in terms of grammatical form the infinitive clause in 14A (*to use it well*) and that in 21A (*to make sound choices ...*) are identical. Yet the first one accompanies a **Purpose** relation, and the second one accompanies a **Solutionhood** relation. That is, analyzing 21A-21B as in a **Solutionhood** relation, rather than as in a **Purpose** relation, is consonant with our perception of the writer's goal to motivate the reader to donate money: it is more plausible that the writer is bringing up the idea of officials making decisions that affect our lives as a **problem**, which dissemination of the test data can help solve, than that she is claiming that officals and the public need the data for the *purpose* of making sound choices. Such an argument cannot readily be made for the relation between 14A-B. We will return to 20A-B shortly, as it illustrates another consequence of RST.

Finally, in the P.S., there is a **Means** satellite signalled by *by* in 30B.

Thus, of all the relations in our analysis, as shown in Figure 6, only eight are explicitly signalled. Most of the interpretation of the coherence of this text, then, is achieved by inference.

The abundance of unsignalled relations highlights the importance of the differences between text understanding, which involves recognition of text structure and relations, and a symbol decoding task. Recognizing relations requires that the reader make judgments about the writer, including judgments of the plausibility of intentions. Symbolic decoding proceeds on the basis of the conventional import of symbols and their compositions, without judging such factors.

This suggests that much ongoing work that seeks to develop a formal compositional semantics of language will be permanently incomplete with respect to coherent texts.

7.2 *"Subordination"*

Another consequence of our analysis of the ZPG text in terms of RST is the insight we can gain into the issue of "subordination". As suggested in Matthiessen & Thompson (1989), one kind of what has been studied as grammatical "subordination" is perhaps better viewed as a clause-level and partially grammaticized reflex of nucleus-satellite patterns found pervasively in text.

Following Halliday (1985), Matthiessen and Thompson propose to abandon the term "subordination" and to make a distinction between **hypotaxis** and **embedding**. Hypotaxis includes the category of "subordinate" causes that are generally thought of as adverbial clauses in English grammar: clauses expressing time, reason, cause, condition, etc. Embedding, on the other hand, includes essentially restrictive relative clauses, subject and object clauses, and clausal complements to verbs and adjectives.

This distinction turns out to have far-reaching consequences as we consider the relationship between "subordination" and text structure, since hypotaxis, but not embedding, seems to play a role at the clause level very similar to that of the relations of RST in text organization in general. In other words, hypotactic clauses seem to be clause-level satellites in the relational structure of the text, no different in function from other satellites encompassing many clauses. To fully support this position is beyond the scope of this paper (for discussion, see Matthiessen & Thompson (1989)); however, in the ZPG text, there are several interesting pieces of support for this view.

First, note that the text contains two **Solutionhood** relations, which happen to be adjacent to each other, the relation between 20-21, and the relation between 21A-21B. We have commented on both of them: the first provided an illustration of relations without signals, while the second provided an illustration of one grammatical form (an infinitive) signalling both a **Purpose** relation (14A-B) and a **Solutionhood** relation (21A-B). Now, in the context of "subordination", we can tie these arguments together to show that the hypotactic clause *To make sound choices...* in 21A is functioning in the relational structure of the ZPG text in precisely the same way as the non-"subordinate" sentence in 20: both are **Solutionhood** satellites to their nuclei.

Second, the text contains a number of examples of embedding. None of these perform text-organizing functions in the same way as do the hypotactic clauses, as just illustrated for the infinitives expressing **Purpose** and **Solutionhood** relations. For example, to continue the discussion in terms of grammatical infinitives, notice that 9 contains the expression *eager to tell the public....* The infinitive in this expression, however, unlike those in 14A and 21A, is not functioning in the text to signal any of the relations of RST (see Appendix); rather it is an element of the grammatical structure of the expression, which itself is embedded as a truncated relative clause modifying *reporters*.

The same can be said for each instance of embedding in this text. To take just one further example, none of the relative clauses in the text play a role in the relational structure of the text. For instance, 9 contains the relative clause *who were furious that we had "blown the whistle"....* Such a relative clause tells us something about the *public officials* calling the ZPG office, but it does not relate portions of text in the same way that the RST relations do.

In other words, when we consider the function that these embedded clauses have — such as forming complements to adjectives and verbs, or serving to modify noun phrases — we find that these types of functions are not needed in the description of relations between larger units.

The RST analysis of the ZPG text, then, supports the general finding that of the two types of "subordination" which have been identified in the literature, only one of them, hypotaxis, can be understood as involving the

7.3 *Concessives*

Finally, the RST analysis confirms earlier findings relating to the **Concession** relation.

Thompson & Mann (1986) point out that, although the literature on concession concerns itself largely with the meanings of certain conjuctions such as *although*, consession can be insightfully viewed in terms of discourse relations rather than simply in terms of the meanings of conjunctions. As noted in Sections 4 and 7.1, the two examples of the **Concession** relation in the ZPG text are signalled in different ways: one with an adverbial clause marked with *even though* and one with a main clause marked with *but*. Viewing concession solely as a meaning of certain types of "subordinate" clause conjunctions would miss the functional similarities between these two situations. So the claim made in Thompson & Mann (1986), that concession is a matter of discourse relations rather than simply a matter of the meaning of certain conjunctions, is supported by the ZPG text.

8. Status of RST

RST is a step in the process of developing theories of communication. Its strengths include the fact that it provides comprehensive analyses rather than selective commentary, illustrated in its assigning a purpose and status to every unit of the relational elements of the ZPG letter. Because RST is applicable to many kinds of texts, enabling a unified description of text structure regardless of genre, it helps to factor the genuinely genre-specific aspects of text from the more genre-independent ones.

There are several aspects of text description that seem particularly important for communication, but which it does not yet address; we hope that these will be addressed, not necessarily by us, in the near future.

RST has not yet been effectively related to dialogue. It must be expanded beyond written monologue to dialogue and multilogue in order to encompass a fully representative range of the functions of language. This will perhaps be the most significant modification of its present form.

RST also has not yet been related to all of the kinds of theories with which it should interact. Theories of holistic structure and syntactic structure are the most obvious cases; elaboration in both directions would be helpful. In these cases the need can only be partly met by augmentation of RST, since one really needs to connect to theories that are functional in the same effects-oriented sense that RST employs.

In the case of holistic structure, there are function-oriented accounts that suggest that a useful functional reconciliation is possible. Although the relationally-structured parts of a text are simply parts of a larger whole, they are the parts that justify and motivate the existence of the text. The whole is thus subordiante to the part, and the functions of the nonrelational parts, such as the signature of a letter, promote the effects that organize the relational parts. This functional whole-under-part organization needs investigation.

RST makes no claims about the order of development of parts of a text, nor about how that order might limit the writer's options. Preliminary studies by Cecilia Ford and colleagues of a large number of short texts indicated that neither progressive refinement (top down) nor aggregation of apriori collections (bottom up) was very credible as a simple explanation of how the texts might have been developed. A complex mixed strategy seems called for; more study is needed.

A systematic description of how reltions are realized is also needed, one that ranges more widely than any study of conjunctions, covering the various kinds of unsignalled cases as well.

Beyond these, linking RST to theories of text properties such as information flow, thematic structure, and lexical relations would also be worthwhile.

9. Conclusion

We have presented RST as a way to account for the functional potential of text, its capacity to achieve the purposes of speakers and produce effects in hearers. The principal assumptions that RST encodes in its methods have been identified. In the course of accounting for potential effects, we have also shown a way to distinguish coherent texts from incoherent ones, and identified a few of the consequences of text structure.

In presenting our analysis of the ZPG letter we hope that the methods have been made explicit enough so that, by using these and the related techniques found in other publications, you will be able to experiment with RST and improve it.

Appendix: Relation Definitions

All of the relations used in the analysis, and a number of others, have been defined in the style described above. In Mann & Thompson (1989), all of the definitions are given, exemplified and discussed. The definition of **Evidence** was discussed at length in Section 3.2 above. In this section we present definitions of the other relations used in the analysis, with only occasional brief discussion. In the definitions, N represents the nucleus and S the satellite. Since for many readers the natural examples have the status of *data* rather than just exposition, the examples used in Mann & Thompson (1989) and Mann & Thompson (1988) to illustrate the relations are also presented, but without unit division or analysis.

We should note that the relation definitions have the status of applications of the theory rahter than elements of the theory. One might want to change or replace the definitions in accounting for other languages, genres, or views of language function than the ones that led to these definitions; such changes are expected and do not cross the definitional boundaries of RST.

The relations are organized as follows:

Motivation, Concession, Background
Circumstance, Solutionhood, Elaboration,
Purpose, Non-volitional Result, Means, Restatement
Sequence, Contrast, Joint

The first group has only the nucleus as its locus of effect, the second group has nucleus + satellite, and the third group is not nucleated.

==

Motivation

constraints on N: presents an action in which R is the actor (including accepting an offer), unrealized with respect to the context of N

constraints on the N + S combination: Comprehending S increases R's desire to perform action presented in N

the effect: R's desire to perform action presented in N is increased

locus of the effect: N

From a personal message on an electronic bulletin board:

Text Example: "The Los Angeles Chamber Ballet (the ballet company I'm dancing with) is giving 4 concerts next week ... Tickets are $7.50 except for the opening night ... The show is made up of new choreography and should be very entertaining. I'm in 3 pieces."

Several relations involve notions of cause. In broadly defining these relations. it is hard to include both situations that are intended outcomes of some action and causation that does not involve intended outcomes, such as physical causation. Because of this difficulty, we have divided the relations into volitional and a non-volitional groups. Similarly we also dvide them on the basis of nuclearity into cause and result groups. Non-Volitional Result, below, is one of the four relations so produced.

==

Concession

constraints on N: W has positive regard for the situation presented in N;
constraints on S: W is not claiming that the situation presented in S doesn't hold;
constraints on the N + S combination:
W acknowledges a potential or apparent incompatibility between the situations presented in N and S; W regards the situations presented in N and S as compatible; recognizing the compatibility between the situations presented in N and S increases R's positive regard for the situation presented in N
the effect: R's positive regard for the situation presented in N is increased
locus of the effect: N and S

Text Example: "Title: Dioxin
Concern that this material is harmful to health or the environment may be misplaced. Although it is toxic to certain animals, evidence is lacking that it has any serious long-term effect on human beings."

Text Example: "Although Jim lists tennis, Chinese food, and travel to exotic locales among his favorite hobbies, one can't help but wonder at the unmentioned interests that help spark Jim's creativity, leading him to concoct an unending stream of imaginative programs."

==

Background

constraints on N: R won't comprehend N sufficiently before reading text of S
constraints on the N + S combination:
S increases the ability of R to comprehend an element in N
the effect: R's ability to comprehend N increases
locus of the effect: N

Text Example: "Home addresses and telephone numbers of public employees will be protected from public disclosure under a new bill approved by Gov. George Deukmejian. Assembly Bill 3100 amends the Government Code, which required that the public record of all state and local agencies, containing home addresses and telephone numbers of staff, be open to public inspection."

==

Circumstance

constraints on S: S presents a situation (not unrealized)
constraints on the N + S combination:
S sets a framework in the subject matter within which R is intended to interpret the situation presented in N

the effect: R recognizes that the situation presented in S provides the framework for interpreting N

locus of the effect: N and S

Text Example: "Probably the most extreme case of Visitors Fever I have ever witnessed was a few summers ago when I visited relatives in the Midwest."

Text Example: "P.M. has been with KUSC longer than any other staff member. While attending Occidental College, where he majored in philosophy, he volunteered to work at the station as a classical music announcer. That was in 1970."

==

Solutionhood

constraints on S: presents a problem

constraints on the N + S combination:

the situation presented in N is a (partial) solution to the problem stated in S;

the effect: R recognizes the situation presented in N as a (partial) solution to the problem presented in S

locus of the effect: N and S

Text Example: "One difficulty ... is with sleeping bags in which down and feather fillers are used as insulation. This insulation has a tendency to slip towards the bottom. You can redistribute the filler. ..."

In the definition of the solutionhood relation, the terms problem and solution are broader than one might expect. The scope of problem includes:

1. questions
2. requests, including requests for information
3. some descriptions of desires, goals, intellectual issues, gaps in knowledge or other expressions of needs
4. conditions that carry negative values, either expressly or culturally, including calamities and frustrations.

It thus compares to Grimes' Response predicate (Grimes 1975).

==

Elaboration

constraints on the N + combination:

S presents additional detail about the situation or some element of subject matter which is presented in N or inferentially accessible in N in one or more of the ways listed below. In the list, if N presents the first member of any pair, then S includes the second:

1. set : member
2. abstract : instance
3. whole : part
4. process : step
5. object : attribute

6. generalization : specific

the effect: R recognizes the situation presented in S as providing additional detail for N. R identifies the element of subject matter for which detail is provided.

locus of the effect: N and S

From a conference announcement brochure:

Text Example: "Sånga-Säby-Kursgård, Sweden, will be the site of the 1969 International Conference on Computational Linguistics, September 1-4. It is expected that some 250 linguists will attend from Asia, West Europe, East Europe including Russia, and the United States. The conference will be concerned with the aplication of mathematical and computer techniques to the study of natural languages, the development of computer programs as tools for linguistic research, and the application of linguistics to the development of man-machine communication systems."

==

Purpose

constraints on N: presents an activity

constraints on S: presents a situation that is unrealized

constraints on the N + S combination:

S presents a situation to be realized through the activity in N

the effect: R recognizes that the activity in N is initiated in order to realize S

locus of the effect: N and S

Text Example: "To see which Syncom diskette will replace the ones you're using now, send for our free "Flexi-Finder" selection guide and the name of the supplier nearest you."

Text Example: "Presumably, there is a competition among trees in certain forest environments to become as tall as possible so as to catch as much of the sun as possible for photosynthesis."

==

Non-Volitional Result

constraints on S: presents a situation that is not a volutional action

constraints on the N + S combination:

N presents a situation that caused the situation presented in S; presentation of N is more central to W's purposes in putting forth the N-S combination that is the presentation of S.

the effect: R recognizes that the situation presented in N could have caused the situation presented in S

locus of the effect: N and S

Text Example: "The blast, the worst industrial accident in Mexico's history, destroyed the plant and most of the surrounding suburbs. Several thousand people were injured, and about 300 are still in hospital."

==

Means

constraints on N: presents an action.
constraints on S: none
constraints on the N + S combination:
presented in S actually tends to make possible or likely the situation presented in N.
the effect: R recognizes that the situation presented in S actually tends to make possible or likely the situation presented in N.
locus of the effect: N and S

Text Example: "By bouncing sound off rock layers under the sea floor and recording the reflections with many detectors, structural images of the crust can be made at the boundaries where plates collide and drift apart."

==

Restatement

constraints on the N + S combination:
S restates N, where S and N are of comparable bulk
the effect: R recognizes S as a restatement of N
locus of the effect: N and S

Text Example: "A WELL-GROOMED CAR REFLECTS ITS OWNER The car you drive says a lot about you."

The last three relations — **Sequence, Contrast** and **Joint** — are non-nucleated.

==

Sequence

constraints on N: multi-nuclear
constraints on the combination of nuclei:
A succession relationship between the situations is presented in the nuclei[13]
the effect: R recognizes the succession relationships among the nuclei.
locus of the effect: multiple nuclei

Text Example: "Peel oranges and slice crosswise. Arrange in a bowl and sprinkle with rum and coconut. Chill until ready to serve."

==

Contrast

constraints on N: multi-nuclear
constraints on the combination of nuclei:
no more than two nuclei; the situations presented in these two nuclei are (a) comprehended as the same in many respects (b) comprehended as differing in a few respects and (c) compared with respect to one or more of these differences
the effect: R recognizes the comparability and the difference(s) yielded by the comparison is being made
locus of the effect: multiple nuclei

Text Example. "Animals heal, but trees compartmentalize. They endure a lifetime of injury and infection by setting boundaries that resist the spread of the invading microorganisms."

==

Joint

The Joint relation is a notational shorthand for the JOINT schema defined elsewhere. Its "relation definition" does not contain any constraints or specify any effects.

Text Example: "Employees are urged to complete new beneficiary designation forms for retirement or life insurance benefits whenever there is a change in marital or family status.

...

Employees who are not sure of who is listed as their beneficiary should complete new forms since the retirement system and the insurance carrier use the most current form to disburse benefits."

Notes

1. This is distinct from some other uses in discourse analysis, e.g. for describing referential recurrence.
2. RST can interface with different theories of syntactic structure. However, the nature of the 'interface' between rethorical structure and syntactic structure may vary quite significantly depending on the nature of the syntactic theory. In general, functional theories of syntactic structure will simplify the interface considerably. The treatment of so-called subordinate clauses is a case in point; see Section 7.2.
3. In RST, the approach to theorizing is to treat theories as components of an account rather than as monolithic. While we do not select any particular theory of holistic structure, the systemic theory of generic structure, Hasan (1978), Halliday & Hasan (1988), or macrostructure theory, van Dijk (1972), van Dijk (1977), van Dijk (1980) offer possibilities. In each case the theory provides much more than just a correlate of holistic structure. RST also has strong interactions with independent theories of Thematic Structure, i.e. the establishment and maintenance of topics, and with Exchange Structure, i.e. dialogue structure, but these interactions are beyond the scope of the paper (see Section 8).
4. We gratefully acknowledge the valuable input provided by Cecilia Ford, Barbara Fox, and Peter Fries in the development of RST. We express special thanks to Peter Fries for his comments on the analysis of the ZPG text.

   RST extends a tradition of research on the relational basis of text structure. The unabridged version of Mann & Thompson (1989), Mann & Thompson (1987a), contains a substantial discussion of the relationships between, and the influence upon, RST and other relational studies of text, including the work of Beekman, Callow, Grimes, Grosz, Halliday, Hasan, Hobbs, Hoey, Jordan, Kopesec, Longacre, Martin, McKeown, Meyer, Pike, Sidner and Winter. Other major papers on RST include Mann & Thompson (1987b) and Mann & Thompson (1988).

This research was sponsored in part by National Science Foundation grant IST-8408726, in part by AFOSR contracts FQ8671-84-01107 and F49620-87-C-0005, and in part by DARPA contract MDA903-87-C-641; the opinions in this report are solely those of the authors.

5. A paper currently in preparation refutes this alternative assumption by showing evidence for a particular mechanism for expanding the set of relations in culture-specific ways. (Mann 1990).

6. For a more formal discussion of the mechanisms of RST, including a set of detailed relation definitions, see Mann & Thompson (1988).

7. The rationale for this is that these clauses are embedded constituent parts in other structures but they do not combine with other clauses in terms of relational structure. Thus, subject and object clauses enter into and are determined by the transitivity structure of the clause they are embedded in. In contrast, non-embedded clauses may be related to one another as wholes and form rhetorically motivated clause combinations.

8. On this basis we have broken down some of the segments of the ZPG letter into parts designated with subscripts A, B, and C as follows. Subscript A always designates the first part of the segment.
   6B: answering questions
   6C: and talking with reporters .... country.
   7B: we had no idea .... response.
   11A: ZPG's *Urban Stress Test*, ... is the nation's first survey ... cities.
   11B: created after months of persistent and exhaustive research,
   14B: we urgently need your help.
   15B: and our modest resources are being stretched to the limit.
   19B: *we can act to take positive action at the local level.*
   21B: both elected officials .... study.
   30B: by completing the enclosed reply form.

9. Of course, there are methodological risks in approaching the problem in this way, risks of circularity, divergence of analysis from actual function, nonrestrictiveness of the theory, vagueness, indefiniteness of analytic outcome, etc., but in today's linguistics, descriptions must be produced through human judgments of function if they are going to be produced at all. These issues have been faced and some progress made, but there are no guarantees.

10. Recall that all of these judgments are plausibility judgments. Thus, though the analysis is presented as if it were "truth", each analytical statement in it should be read as *It is plausible that the writer intended ...*

11. Recall that in a more formal presentation of RST there is another mechanism, called the schema, which is useful for specifying how relations can be combined on a single nucleus, and for handling various exceptional structures. In that treatment there is a Joint schema but no Joint relation.

12. Our thanks to Peter Fries for discussion of this point.

13. Note that the definition does not cover presentational sequence, e.g., "First ...; Second ..."

References

Cui, Songren
1985 *Comparing Structures of Essays in Chinese and English*, Master's thesis, UCLA.

Ford, Cecilia
1987 "Overlapping relations in text structure." In Scott DeLancey and Russel Tomlin (eds.), *Proceedings of the Second Annual Meeting of the Pacific Linguistics Society*. Oregon: University of Oregon, Linguistics Department.

Fox, Barbara A.
1987. *Discourse Structure and Anaphora in Written and Conversational English*. Cambridge: Cambridge University Press.

Grimes, J.E.
1975 *The Thread of Discourse*, The Hague: Mouton.

Halliday, M.A.K.
1985 *An Introduction to Functional Grammar*, London: Edward Arnold.

Halliday, M.A.K. and Ruqaiya Hasan
1989 *Language, Context and Text: a social semiotic perspective*. Oxford: Oxford University Press.

Hasan, R.
1978 "Text in the systemic-functional model." In W. Dressler (ed.), *Current Trends in Text Linguistics*. Berlin: de Gruyter.

Kumpf, Lorraine
1986 *Structuring Narratives in a Second Language: a Description of Rhetoric and Grammar*. Ph.D. thesis, Los Angeles: University of California.

Larkin, Don and Michael H. O'Malley
1973 "Declarative sentences and the rule-of-conversation hypothesis." In *Papers from the Ninth Regional Meeting*. pp. 306-319, Chicago: Linguistic Society.

Mann, William C.
1990 "The origins of text structuring relations." Ms., Information Sciences Institute.

Mann, William C. and Sandra A. Thompson
1986 "Relational propositions in discourse." *Discourse Processes* 9,(1),57-90. Also available as ISI/RR-83-115.

1987a *Rhetorical Structure Theory: A Theory of Text Organization*, USC Information Sciences Institute, Technical Report ISI/RS-87-190.

1987b "Rhetorical structure theory: A framework for the analysis of texts." *IPrA Papers in Pragmatics* 1,79-105. Also available as report ISI/RS-87-185.

1988 "Rhetorical structure theory: Toward a functional theory of text organization." *Text* 8, (3), 1988,243-281. This is an abridged version of Mann & Thompson 1989.

1989 "Rhetorical structure theory: A theory of text organization." In Livia Polanyi (ed.). *The Structure of Discourse*. Norwood N.J.: Ablex. Also available as ISI/RS-87-190 from Document Center, USC/ISI, 4676 Admiralty Way, Marina del Rey, CA 90292.

Martin, James R.

1983 "Conjunction: the logic of English text." In Janos S. Petöfi and Emel Sözer (eds.). *Papers in Text Linguistics*. Volume 45: *Micro and Macro Connexity of Texts*, pp. 1-72, Hamburg: Helmut Buske Verlag.

Matthiessen, Christian and Sandra A. Thompson

1989 "The structure of discourse and "subordination"." In J. Haiman and S. Thompson (eds.). *Clause Combining in Grammar and Discourse*, Amsterdam/Philadelphia: John Benjamins. Also available as ISI/RS-87-183.

Noël, Dirk

1986 *Towards a Functional Characterization of the News of the BBC World News Service. Antwerp Papers in Linguistics*, 49. Antwerp, Belgium.

Reddy, Michael

1979 "The conduit metaphor." In A. Ortony (ed.). *Metaphor and Thought*. Cambridge: Cambridge University Press.

Thompson, Sandra A. and William C. Mann

1986 "A Discourse View of Concession in Written English." In Scott DeLancey & Russell Tomlin (eds.). *Proceedings of the Second Annual Meeting of the Pacific Linguistics Conference*, Pacific Linguistics Conference.

Thompson, Sandra A. and William C. Mann

1987 "Antithesis: A Study in Clause Combining and Discourse Structure." In Ross Steele and Terry Threadgold (eds.). *Language Topics: Essays in Honour of Michael Halliday*, Volume II, Amsterdam/Philadelphia: John Benjamins. Also available as ISI/RS-87-171.

van Dijk, Teun A.

1972 *Some Aspects of Text Grammars*. The Hague: Mouton.

1977 *Text and Context: Explorations in the Semantics and Pragmatics of Discourse*. London: Longman.

1980 *Macrostructures*. Hillsdale, NJ.: Erlbaum.

1981 *Studies in the Pragmatics of Discourse*. The Hague: Mouton.

1985 *Semantic Discourse Analysis*. New York: Academic Press.

An Analysis of a Plea for Money

Bonnie J.F. Meyer
The Pennsylvania State University

1. Introduction

Research on reading comprehension is focusing more and more on the interaction between reader and text in the comprehension process. A text can be written with various types of organizations, and a reader can likewise approach a text with various organizational expectations. The different organizational plans and strategies brought to the text by the reader interact with attributes of text to affect the reader's understanding of the text.

A text is not just a series of sentences or paragraphs. This is because it follows a hierarchy of content, so that some facts (statements, etc.) are superordinate or more important than others. It seems plain that the process of creating such a hierarchy must be governed by writing plans that organize texts.

A topic can be viewed as an array of interrelated ideas. Due to readers' limited capacity to remember everything in text and their need to selectively forget some information, writers must cue readers into viewing some information as more important to remember than other information. The use of writing plans (Meyer 1985) by writers accomplishes this goal. Writing plans cue readers into the writer's perspective by the way they structure topic content and the emphasis they place on certain aspects of this content. More specifically, they explicitly or implicitly suggest the type of overall structure to use in interpreting the topic. In addition, they highlight and superordinate the writer's thesis. They also subordinate major details that support this major thesis and further subordinate, interrelate and sequence the very specific details about the topic.

The readers' task, then, is to construct a cognitive representation of the text which is similar to that intended by the writer. This task will be much easier for readers if writers select appropriate structures to interrelate their ideas and cue the readers into these structures.

This chapter briefly examines why psychologists are interested in specifying the structures of texts, discusses differences in approaches to text analysis, and presents the theory and method for Meyer's approach (1975, 1985) to prose analysis. In addition, the fund-raising letter from Zero Population Growth is analyzed with this approach to discourse analysis.

2. Why Analyze Text?

The structure of discourse is the organization that binds it together, and delivers its overall organization. This structure shows how some ideas are of central importance to the author's message, which is bound by this overall organization, while other ideas are shown to be peripheral. The text structure specifies the logical connections among ideas as well as the subordination of some ideas to others. It is the structure of text that primarily differentiates text from simple lists of words or sentences.

Educators and psychologists interested in reading comprehension have sought to describe and classify the structure of texts. A description is desired in order to examine how readers identify and utilize text structure in the comprehension process. In order to examine what information a learner has processed from a particular text, a researcher needs to know just what information was contained in the text. Procedures for analyzing text structure and content have been put to use as scoring templates to evaluate a reader's memory from a text. Thus, text analysis has been an important methodological tool in conducting research on reading comprehension and memory.

Often researchers hypothesize that the representation of the text in memory is parallel to their analysis of the text structure. Comparisons of structures identified from the text and those identified from recalls given by readers assist investigators in attempts to validate their models of the representation of text in memory. Models of memory representations based on prose analysis procedures are usually posited for certain types of learners under certain types of task conditions. Researchers study variations between the text structure and analyses of recalls when the types of learners and task conditions are varied systematically.

Another reason for specifying text structure deals with the problem of generalizing research findings with a particular passage to other texts. Text structure is a significant dimension along which text selections can be evaluated as to their differences and commonalities.

3. Reasons for Different Approaches in Identifying the Structure of Text

Given the usefulness in reading research for identifying the structure of text, it might be expected that the field would have agreed on a simple, universally accepted method. However, there at least three reasons for the lack of such a method in the study of reading. First, interest in specifying text structure has historically come from a wide variety of disciplines, including rhetorics, folklore, linguistics, education, psychology, and artificial intelligence (cf. Meyer & Rice 1984). These disciplines have had different approaches and goals for analyzing text structure. The multiplicity of disciplines involved serves to diversify the text structures proposed as well as enrich our understanding of text structure.

Another reason for the variety of analysis approaches currently used to study reading comprehension results from the purposes for which they were developed. For example, if the research goal is to ascertain memory of the gist of the texts, then the analysis structure may be quite different than if the goal is memory storage of inferences.

The most difficult problems are those that are inherent in the complexity of the text, the reading process, and the writing process. A portion of the difficulty arises from the complexity of the reading process (Meyer & Rice 1984). Since the text and reader interact in this process, it is hard to isolate entirely textual variables. The structure of the information read from a text may appear differently to readers with different prior knowledge and purposes. A reasonable escape from this obstacle is to analyze the text from the point of view of the author; however, there are some problems with this approach. If a poorly written exposition is selected that fails to logically interrelate ideas either explicility or implicilty (i.e., Flower's 1979, writer-based lists, rather than reader-based conceptual hierarchies), the text analyst may want to identify the potential conceptual structure underlying the topic in order to better score recall of more astute readers.

Even in well-written text, the underlying structure may be implicitly rather than explicitly signaled. In these cases, it is necessary for the text analyst to make inferences about the organization in the text. Individual differences among analysts in making such inferences can produce variablity in the analyses produced. With most texts there is high agreement in the structures produced after using the Meyer approach (1975, 1985) to text analysis; agreement is about 90 to 95% among graduate students on their analyses of a text after taking a short course on prose analysis.

However, with one ambiguous text we have found two very different, but equally plausible structures (Meyer & Rice 1982). This text about railroads can be viewed as a narration or as an exposition. As Brewer (1980) notes, in narration the central mental representation is a series of temporally occurring events, while in exposition the underlying mental processes involve logical and quasi-logical thinking. If this ambiguous text is viewed as a narrative the dates and history are of central importance, while the causal chains of actions taken by businessmen are of minor importance. The importance of these items is reversed if the text is viewed as an exposition. Recall data from subjects reading and remembering the railroad text verify the plausibility of both structural interpretations of the texts, since some subjects recall the text as a narrative and others recall it as an expository text. Such texts with multiple structures have been encountered infrequently.

4. Theory and Method for the Analysis Utilized

The method (Meyer 1975, 1985) that I employ to get from the text to its underlying structure is a procedure based on the work in linguistics of Grimes (1975). The resulting analysis of a text is called the **content structure**. It represents the underlying logic and message of the text from the perspective of the author. The match is assumed to be relatively high between the content structure analysis of a text and the logic and message in the mind of the author and certain types of readers. Such readers are skilled, possess the prior knowledge and perspective assumed by the author, and a desire to understand the author's logic. Their comprehension process will follow the structure strategy (Meyer, Brandt, & Bluth 1980; Meyer, Young, & Bartlett 1989) and involve an active effort to discover the overall relationships among the main ideas of the text.

The relationships that form the logic in the content structure have been discussed as ways or schemata for thinking about ideas at least since Aristotle (trans., 1960). Also, thecontent-based relationships (verb type relations) appear to be schemata used in cognition (Rumelhart & Ortony 1977). The levels in the content structure are dictated by the major logical relations; the hierarchy is hypothesized to relate to allocation of processing time and access to retrieval when reading tasks for prose learning experiments and many similar school tasks (Meyer, Brandt, & Bluth 1980).

Three primary levels of text are identified in this approach to prose analysis and they each appear in the resultant content structure of an analyzed text. The first is the top-level structure or overall organization of the text as a whole. The second is the macropropositional level, which pertains to the issues of logical organization and argumentation. The third is the sentence or micropropositional level, which is concerned with the way ideas are organized within sentences, and the way sentences cohere and are organized within a text. These levels of the content structure are discussed in more detail below.

4.1 *Top-Level Structure*

Drawing upon linguistics and rhetoric, I have (e.g., Meyer & Freedle 1984; Meyer 1985) gathered evidence for five basic top-level structures to organize discourse: comparison, collection, description, causation, and response: problem/solution. The typology is not intend to be exhaustive or definitive, but there is good support that there are significant distinctions among these discourse types. The comparison structure is organized on the basis of similarities and differences and can be particularly memorable (Meyer & Freedle 1984). The description structure has few organizational cues to aid memory; description simply specifies or gives attributes of a superordinate idea. Collection merely groups things together; if used in conjunction with description an enumeration of attributes of an idea are presented. If you read a passage that gives a collection of descriptions about an idea, the best way to utilize the structure is to count and remember the group of attributes described. The sequence type of collection structure gives you more organization in that the ideas presented are ordered in time; this structure appears to be very easy for readers to use (Englert & Hiebert 1984; Raphael, Englert, & Kirschner 1986). The causation structure has the organization of time with the cause preceding the effect in time of occurrence (not necessarily temporal order in the passage) as well as the added organization of the cause and effect relationship. The response: problem/ solution structure has all the organizational components of causation with

Table 1: Basic Organizational Structures and Signals that Cue Readers to these Structures (taken from Meyer, Young, & Bartlett, 1989)

Organization & Definition	Signals
Description	
Descriptive ideas that give attributes, specifics, or setting information about a topic. The main idea is that attributes of a topic are discussed.	for example, which was one, this particular, for instance, specifically, such as, attributes of, that is, namely, properties of, characteristics are, qualities are, marks of, in describing
e.g. newspaper article describing who, where, when and how.	
Sequence	
Ideas grouped on the basis of order or time. The main idea is the procedure or history related.	afterwards, later, finally, last, early, following, to begin with, to start with, then, as time passed, continuing on, to end, years ago, in the first place, before, after, soon, more recently
e.g. recipe procedures, history of Civil War battles, growth from birth to 12.	
Causation	
Presents causal or cause and effect-like relations between ideas. The main idea is organized into cause and effect parts.	as a result, because, since, for the purpose of, caused, led to, consequence, thus, in order to, this is why, if/then, the reason, so, in explanation, therefore
e.g. directions: if you want to take good pictures, then you must ....; explanations: the idea explained is the effect and the explanation is its cause	
Response: Problem/solution	
The main ideas are organized into two parts: a *problem* part and a *solution* part that responds to the problem by trying to eliminate it, or a *question* part and an *answer* part that responds to the question by trying to answer it.	problem: problem, question, puzzle perplexity, enigma, riddle, issue, query, need to prevent, the trouble solution: solution, answer, response, reply, rejoinder, return, comeback, to satisfy the problem, to set the issue at rest, to solve these problems
e.g. scientific articles often first raise a question or problem and then seek to give an answer or solution.	

Organization & Definition	Signals
Comparison Relates ideas on the basis of differences and similarities. The main idea is organized in parts that provide a comparison, contrast, or alternative perspective on a topic.	not everyone, but, in contrast, all, but, instead, act like, however, in comparison, on the other hand, whereas, in opposition, unlike, alike, have in common, share, resemble, the same as, different, difference, differentiate, compared to, while, although
e.g. political speeches particularly where one view is clearly favored over the other.	
Collection can occur with any of the five structures. It simply groups or lists ideas together. Passages are often organized as a listing of descriptions about a topic. A sequence, a special type of collection with more organization (see above), always contains a listing of ideas, but the ideas are ordered sequentially. A collection can occur when groups of causes are presented, groups of effects are listed, groups of solutions are posited, groups of ideas are contrasted to another idea, and so forth.	common signals include: and, in addition, also, include, moreover, besides, first, second, third, etc., subsequent, furthermore, at the same time, another and so forth

the addition of overlapping ideas between the problem and solution where the solution attempts to eliminate the problem. Thus, the response: problem/solution structure provides the most inherent structure of these four latter structures (description, collection, causation, and response: problem/solution) and should provide the greatest aid to memory. However, it also appears to be one of the most difficult structures to learn to adequately use (Meyer, Young, & Bartlett 1989). These types of organization are clarified further in in Table 1, taken from a training manual instructing readers about text structure (Meyer, Young, & Bartlett 1989).

The five basic top-level structures are familiar in various contexts. Political speeches are often of the comparison type, and in particular, its unequally weighted subtype. Newpaper articles are often of the descriptive type, telling us who, where, how and when. Scientific treatises often adhere to the problem/solultion type, first raising a question or problem and then seeking to give an answer or solution (cf., Jordan 1984). History texts often reflect the collection/sequence structure.

Research (e.g., Meyer, Young, & Bartlett 1989) has shown that teaching young and old adults about these top-level structures and how to use them to aid memory can increase reading comprehension. In Meyer *et al.*'s study over 100 adults were randomly assigned to three groups: (1) instruction about top-level structures, (2) instruction focused on practice with the same reading materials, but without instruction about top-level structures, and (3) no instruction. All groups improved their recall from the pretest to posttests, but the young and old adults in the top-level structure group showed substantially more improvement, doubling the information remembered. Young and old adults in the top-level structure group increased their ability to use the structure (up 90 to 100%) and to correctly answer main idea questions. They shifted in the types of information considered important and claimed improved reading strategies, superior memory for their reading in the laboratory and everyday life, and increased interest in and enjoyment of reading. Old and young adults improved equivalently from this instruction and maintained their improvement two weeks after instruction. The study points to the psychological reality of these top-level structures and their practicality for improving memory from everyday reading materials.

4.2 Macropropositions

These five structures that serve as top-level structures also can occur throughout the macroproposition level interrelating sentences and paragraphs. The term macroproposition refers to the level of prose analysis at which the gist of portions of the text is central. At the macroproposition level the focus is with the relationships among ideas represented in complexes of propositions or paragraphs. The relationships at this level tend to be organizational or what have been called "logical" or "rhetorical". A number of classifications of these types of relations that operate in text have been proposed (e.g., Beaugrande 1980; Frederiksen 1975; Graesser 1981;

Grimes 1975; Halliday & Hasan 1976; Mann & Thompson 1987; Meyer 1975, 1985).

The 18 rhetorical relationships presented in Grimes (1975) and also Meyer (1975) can be collapsed into the five distinct groups that were discussed above: comparison, description, collection, causation, and response: problem/solution. The structures not only occur at the overall level for the top-level structure, but also can occur throughout the macroproposition level interrelating paragraphs and sentences. In the final section of this paper examples of these relationships will be given as found in the fund-raising letter.

4.3 *Micropropositions*

The subordinate propositions in the content structure of a text are the micropropositions. The structure of simple sentences is diagrammed with case grammar (after Fillmore 1968 and Grimes 1975). Halliday and Hasan (1976) have identified mechanisms (reference, substitution, ellipsis, conjuction, and lexical cohesion) by which authors tie phrases and sentences together at this microproposition level. The Meyer approach (1975, 1985) used in this chapter provides a classification system for mechanisms of conjunction (e.g., collection, comparison, description).

The format for the case grammar analysis is displayed in Figure 1. The verb (lexical predicate) is one level above the equally weighted role or case related arguments. The role label and the content are at the same level in the structure. The content from the text is in capital letters, while the relationships are in lower case letters.

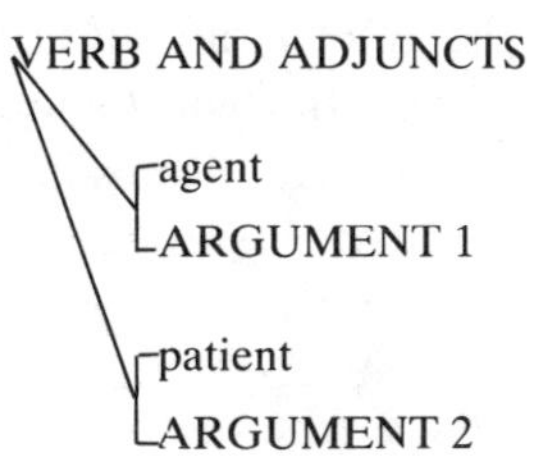

Figure 1: Basic Format for the Analysis at the Microproposition Level.

4.4 *Attributes of the Method*

The Meyer system of prose analysis is applicable to all types of expository prose and has also been applied to story materials (Meyer, Haring, Brandt, & Walker 1980) and everyday memory materials (e.g, bus schedules, prescriptions, tax forms; Meyer, Marsiske & Willis 1990). As shown in the next section of this chapter, the system also can be applied to fund-raising mail. The minimal unit of analysis is the idea unit, which includes both actual content named in the text and relational terms inferred from the text.

The specificity for analyzing the text depends on the purpose of the analysis. For teachers using the approach to teach top-level structure, they may want to stop with the top-level structure and not analyze to more specific details. In studying the logic of exposition in reading and writing instruction, an analysis may be sufficient that includes only the top-level structure and macropropositions and excludes the micropropositions. For prose learning studies, it depend on the research question and resources; the more minute the analysis, the longer the scoring time. Crucial components for scoring will be required if arguments are made up of phrases from the text, rather than individual words. Generous rules are necessary to score for substantive recall, rather than verbatim recall.

The analysis procedure produces a single, hierarchically organized representation of a passage's structure (the content structure). It is a propositional structure with the relationships at the microproposition level held primarily by verbs from the text, whereas at the macropropositional level, they are held by the rhetorical relations. The arguments are individual content units from the text or content units that are parts of other proprositions.

The content structure is best formed by following a top-down procedure. The passage is first examined for its top-level structure. The top-level structure will be the relationship that can subsume the greatest amount of text (see response: problem/solution for the fund raising letter and Figure 2). The content structure is formed by unpeeling layers of relationships in a top-down fashion. Once the top-level structure is identified, then the next most inclusive relations are identified until the case grammar level of analysis is reached.

5. Analysis of the Fund-raising Letter

The fund-raising letter was analyzed with this system. Figure 2 depicts the first two levels of the content structure discussed above, top-level structure and macropropositions.

Figure 3 shows the entire content structure for the text and depicts all three levels of analysis. The numbers in the figures correspond to the numbered segments of the fund-raising letter. All the information in Figure 2 also appears on Figure 3, but the shorter form with deletion of the analysis of the micropropositions makes for an easier grasp of the overall structure. The creation of these structures from the text took about eight hours of analysis time. This is the same procedure and time involvement used to analyze texts used in reading experiments. The analysis is not perfect, but it reasonably well represents the ideas and relationships in the text and can be

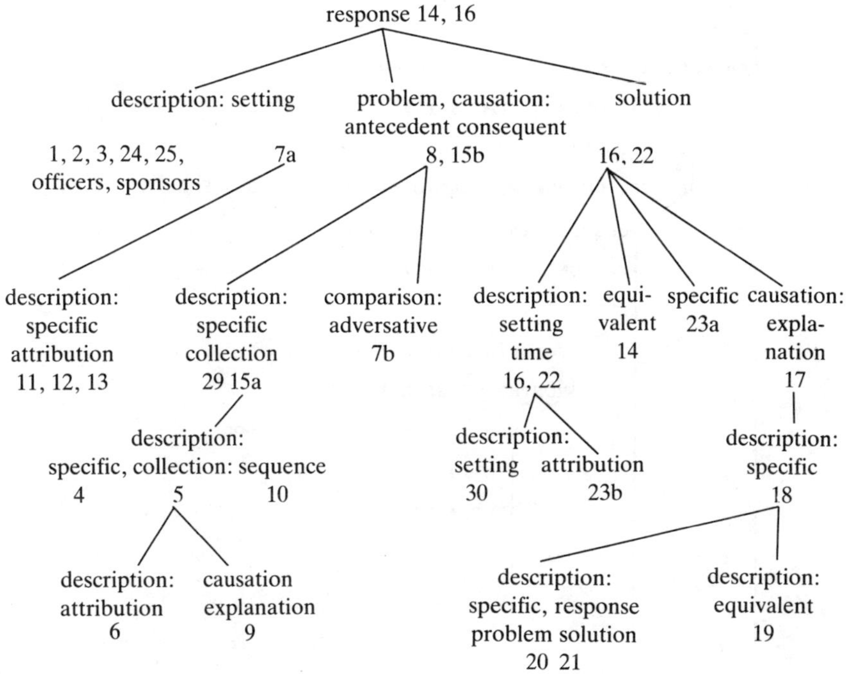

Figure 2: Superordinate Structure of the Zero Population Growth Letter.

```
response (variety = fund raising letter) CRITICAL (16) NEED HELP (14)
    description: setting
    DEAR FRIEND OF ZPG (3)
        description: CONSTITUENCY IDENTIFICATION
        ZERO POPULATION GROWTH (1)
            description: specific
            collection
            LIST OF OFFICERS
            LIST OF SPONSORS
            EXECUTIVE DIRECTOR (27)
                description: specific
                SUSAN WEBER (24, 25, 26)
    description: setting time
    NOVEMBER 22, 1985 (2)
    problem
    causation: covariance, antecedent
    RELEASED RESULTS OF ZPG'S 1985 URBAN STRESS TEST (7a)
        description: specific
        SURVEY OF HOW POPULATION-LINKED PRESSURES AFFECT U.S. CITIES (11)
            description: attribution
            NATION'S FIRST (11)
            CREATED (11)
                description: setting time
                MONTHS OF RESEARCH (11)
                    description: attribution
                    collection
                    PERSISTENT (11)
```

(*continued*)

```
                    EXHAUSTIVE (11)
RANKS (12)
      patient
      URBAN AREAS (12)
            description: specific
            184 (12)
      range
      DIFFERENT CRITERIA (12)
            description: specific
            11 (12)
            collection: sequence
            CROWDING (12)
            BIRTH RATES (12)
            OTHER CRITERIA
            AIR QUALITY (12)
            TOXIC WASTES (12)
TRANSLATES (13)
      patient
      DATA (13)
            description: attribution
            collection
            COMPLEX (13)
            TECHNICAL (13)
      latter
      ACTION TOOL (13)
            description: attribution
            EASY-TO-USE (13)
      benefactive
```

(*continued*)

```
                  collection
                  CONCERNED CITIZENS (13)
                  ELECTED OFFICIALS (13)
                  OPINION LEADERS (13)

causation: covariance, consequent
HAS BEEN NOTHING SHORT OF INCREDIBLE (8) REMARKABLE COVERAGE (30)
     comparison: adversative
     HAD NO IDEA GET OVERWHELMING RESPONSE (7b)
     patient
     collection
     MEDIA REACTION (8)
     PUBLIC REACTION (8)
     description: specific
     collection AND (15)  P.S. (28)
     WERE REPORTED (29)
          patient
          RESULTS OF ZPC'S 1985 URBAN STRESS TEST
          latter
          TOP NEW STORY
          agent
          HUNDREDS OF STATIONS (29)
               description: specific
               collection
               NEWSPAPER (29)
               TV (29)
               RADIO STATIONS (29)
          range
```

(*continued*)

```
            COAST TO COAST
    IS BEING SWAMPED (15)
            patient
            OUR SMALL STAFF (15)
            agent
            REQUESTS FOR MORE INFORMATION (15)
            description: specific
            collection: sequence FIRST NOW
            STARTED TO RING (4)
                    patient
                    OUR PHONES (4)
                    description: setting time
                    7:00 A. M. OCTOBER 25 (4)
            JAMMED (5)
                    agent
                    CALLS (5)
                    patient
                    OUR SWITCHBOARD (5)
                    description: setting time
                    ALL DAY (OCTOBER 25) (5)
                    description: attribution
                    collection
                    STAYED ANSWERING (6)
                    STAYED TALKING (6)
                            agent
                            STAFFERS (6)
                            description: setting time
```

(*continued*)

```
            LATE INTO NIGHT (6)
            benefactive
            REPORTERS (6)
                description: constituency identication
                collection
                NEWSPAPERS (6)
                RADIO STATIONS (6)
                WIRE SERVICES  (6)
                TV STATIONS (6)
                description: setting location
                EVERY PART OF THE COUNTRY (6)
        causation: explanation CALLS CAME MOSTLY FROM (9)
        collection
        EAGER TO TELL (9)
            agent
            REPORTERS (9)
            patient
            PUBLIC (9)
            range
            URBAN STRESS TEST RESULTS (9)
        causation: covariance, consequent
        WERE FURIOUS (9)
            patient
            OUTRAGED PUBLIC OFFICIALS (9)
        causation: covariance, antecedent
        HAD BLOWN THE WHISTLE (9)
            agent
            WE (ZPG) (9)
```

(*continued*)

```
          patient
          CONDITIONS (9)
          range
          THEIR CITIES (9)
ARE HEARING (10)
    description: setting time
    NOW (10)
    agent
    CONCERNED CITIZENS (10)
    description: setting location
    ALL PARTS OF THE COUNTRY (10)
    description: specific
    WANT TO KNOW (10)
        patient
        WHAT THEY CAN DO (10)
        latter
        HOLD ACCOUNTABLE (10)
            patient
            LOCAL OFFICIALS (10)
            range
            TACKLING POPULATION-RELATED PROBLEMS (10)
                description: attribution
                THREATEN (10)
                    patient
                    collection
                    PUBLIC HEALTH (10)
                    WELL-BEING (10)
```

(continued)

```
ARE BEING STRETCHED (15)
    patient
    OUR MODEST RESOURCES (15)
    latter
    LIMIT (15)
solution
YOUR SUPPORT (16) MAKE SPECIAL CONTRIBUTION TO ZPG (22)
    description: setting time
    NOW (16) TODAY (22)
    description: specific
    GIVE (23)
        patient
        comparison: alternative
        $25 (23)
        $50 (23)
        $100 (23)
        AS MUCH AS YOU CAN (23)
        description: setting location
        ENCLOSED REPLY FORM (30)
        description: attribution
        WILL BE USED TO PUT (23)
            description: manner
            IMMEDIATELY (23)
            patient
            URBAN STRESS TEST (23)
            latter
            HANDS OF THOSE WHO NEED IT MOST (23)
    description: equivalent
```

(continued)

```
NEED YOUR HELP (14)
    patient
    WE (ZPG (1, 14))
    description: manner
    URGENTLY (14)
    latter
    USE URBAN STRESS TEST WELL  (14)
causation: explanation
MAY BE OPPORTUNITY TO GET (17)
    description: manner
    BEST EVER (17)
    latter
    POPULATION MESSAGE HEARD (17)
    description: specific
    CAN ARM (18)
        agent
        ZPG (18)
        instrument
        CONTRIBUTION (18)
        patient
        NETWORK OF LOCAL ACTIVISTS (18)
            description: attribution
            GROWING (18)
        latter
        WARN (18)
            agent
            THEY (LOCAL ACTIVISTS) (18)
```

(*continued*)

```
        instrument
        MATERIALS (18)
        patient
        COMMUNITY LEADERS (18)
        latter
        EMERGING POPULATION-LINKED STRESSES (18)
        description: setting time
        BEFORE STRESSES REACH CRISIS STAGE (18)
description: specific
response
problem
AFFECT (20)
    description: manner
    DRASTICALLY (20)
    patient
    QUALITY OF OUR LIVES (20)
    agent
    DECISIONS (20)
        description: attribution
        EVERYDAY (20)
        ARE BEING MADE (20)
            agent
            LOCAL OFFICIALS (20)
            range
            COMMUNITIES (20)
solution MAKE SOUND CHOICES (21)
NEED (21)
```

(continued)

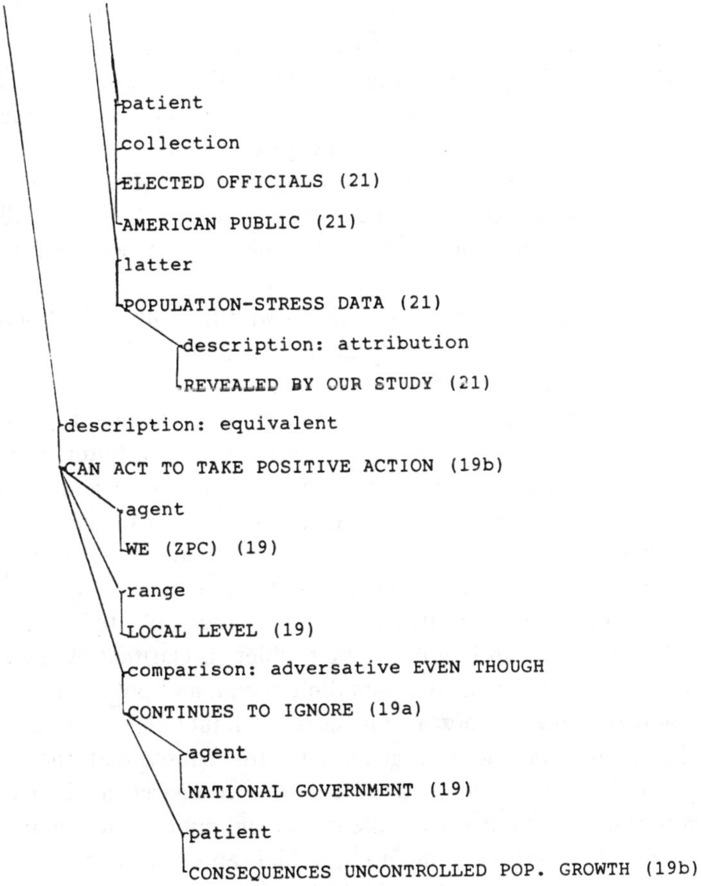

Key
lower case words = relationships among
ideas from the text
CAPITALIZED WORDS = WORDS FROM THE TEXT

Figure 3: Content Structure of the Zero Population Growth Letter.

used reliably in scoring. The remainder of this section of the chapter looks at the three levels of the content structure with examples from the fund-raising letter.

The top-level structure of the text corresponds to its overall organizing principle. The response: problem/solution is the top-level structure that subsumes all the content and relationships in the fund raising letter (see Fig. 2 and Fig. 3).

The response:problem/solution structure is described within the particular setting of the zero population organization as seen in the content structure (Fig. 3). The problem was caused by the release of the *Urban Stress Test* (segment 7) which resulted in incredible media and public reaction (segment 8) and the stretching of the group's modest resources (15b). This is the problem selected by the author of the letter. The solution is for their members to give money (segments 16 and 22) so that they will have the resources to meet the demand for their materials and meet their group's goals (segment 17).

Refer to Figures 2 and 3 in conjunction with the following description of the macroproposition level for the fund raising letter. The response top-level structure characterizing this letter is described within the context of the description: setting information given in Figure 3. It includes segments 1, 2, 3, 24, 25, and 26 and indicates the audience for the letter, friends of ZPG, and the date. The problem portion of the response structure involves two parts of a causation relation. The antecedent part is the release of the results of ZPG's Urban Stress Test (7). The Urban Stress Test is described more specifically as a survey of how population-linked pressures affect U. S. cities (11). Numerous attributes of the survey are presented in segments 11, 12, and 13 as shown in Figure 3. The problem is clarified by the consequences of releasing the test, the incredible media and public reaction (8) and stretching of ZPG's modest resources to the limit (15b). A great deal of space and emphasis in the letter is given to the first consequent, the remarkable media and public reaction; the reaction is compared to their lack of expectation of it (7). The details of the media and public reaction are given in great depth (29, 15a) including a sequential report of the history of the reactions they have received (4, 5, 6, 10).

The solution proposed in the letter is a contribution to ZPG (22); this contribution is to be given now, today (see description: setting time in Figure 3, segments 16 & 22), and is to be given using a prescribed form (see description: setting location in Figure 3, segment 30). The contribution is specified further in segment 23a, where alternative amounts of money are suggested. Segment 23b describes the use of the gift. The plea to solve the problem is stated in an equivalent form in segment 14 (see Figure 3, description: equivalent). The writer also presents rationale for solving the posited problem that would appeal to the audience of this letter. This rationale is conveyed by causation: explanation in Figure 3 (see segment 17). The rationale is described more specifically in segments 18, 19, 20, and 21 of the fund raising letter.

collection: sequence
- segment 4
- segment 5
- segment 10

Figure 4: Format in the Content Structure of the Collection: Sequence Relationship.

Next, examples will be given of the various rhetorical relationships that tie information at the macropropositional level. Each of these relations will be defined with segments from the fund-raising text.

Collection includes a list of elements related in some unspecified manner. The basis for the collection ranges from a group of attributes of the same character, event or idea, to a group related by association, to a group related by simultaneity, to a group related by time sequence. No causal relations exist among the related arguments in the collection relation. The ideas interrelated by collection appear at the same level of the content structure. The following example shows ideas related in this manner in the fund-raising letter; the format of collection: sequence in the content structure is shown in Figure 4.

Example of collection: sequence.

At 7:00 a.m. on October 25, our phones stared to ring (segment 4). Calls jammed our switchboard all day (segment 5). Now we are hearing from concerned citizens in all parts of the country ... (segment 10).

Causation shows a causal relationship between ideas where one idea is the antecedent or cause and the other is the consequent or effect. The relation is often referred to as the condition, result, or purpose with one argument serving as the antecedent and the other as the consequent. The arguments are before and after in time and causally related. There are two types: the covariance with equally weighted arguments and the explanation where the antecedent conditions or principles are subordinate to the consequent, the event or idea explained. The first type is depicted in Figure 5 and the second is shown in Figure 6.

Example of causation: covariance.

When we released the results of ZPG's 1985 Urban Stress Text we had no idea we'd get such an overwhelming response (segment 7). Media and public reaction has been nothing short of incredible! (segment 8).

Causation: explanation is found when previously stated information is explained in a more abstract manner (related to broader context, premises

- causation: covariance
- antecedent
- segment 7
- consequent
- segment 8

Figure 5: Format in the Content Structure of the Causation: Covariance Relationship.

segment 5
- causation: explanation
- segment 9

Figure 6: Format in the Content Structure of the Causation: Explanation Relationship.

- response
- problem
- segment 20
- solution
- segment 21

Figure 7: Format in the Content Structure of the Response: Problem/Solution Relationship

widely accepted in society of which the writer and reader are a part), or explained through more concrete background events.

Example of causation: explanation.

Calls jammed our switchboard all day (segment 5). At first, the deluge of calls came mostly from reporters eager to tell the public about Urban Stress Test results and from outraged public officials who were furious that we had "blown the whistle" on conditions in their cities (segment 9).

Response: problem/solution is similar to the causation in that the problem is before in time and an antecedent for the solution. In addition, there must be some overlap in content between the problem and solution. The arguments are equally weighted and occur at the same level in the content structure as shown in Figure 7.

Example of response: problem/solution.

Every day decisions are being made by local officials in our communities that could drastically affect the quality of our lives (segment 20). To make sound choices in planning for people, both elected officials and the American public need the population-stress data revealed by our study (segment 21).

The format shown in Figure 7 is used except when the response: problem/solution structure is the top-level structure of the text as it is for the fund raising letter. Here, as seen in Figures 2 and 3, response is pulled up a level from problem and solution simply for aesthetic reasons to make a top to the tree structure.

The *comparison* relation points out differences and similarities between two or more topics. There are three subtypes of comparison: alternative, adversative, and analogy. The first two types will be exemplified because they occur in the fund raising letter. The alternative interrelates equally weighted alternative options or equally weighted opposing views; it is depicted in Figure 8. The adversative relates a favored view to a less desirable opposing view or relates what did happen to what did not happen; Figure 9 shows how it is formatted in the content structure.

Example of comparison: alternative.

Whatever you give — $25, $50, $100 or as much as you can — ... (segment 23).

Example of comparison: adversative.

...we had no idea we'd get such an overwhelming response (segment 7b). Media and public reaction has been nothing short of incredible! (segment 8).

comparison: alternative
$25
$50
$100
AS MUCH AS YOU CAN

Figure 8: Format in the Content Structure of Comparison: Alternative.

segment 8
comparison: adversative
segment 7b

Figure 9: Format in the Content Structure of Comparison: Adversative.

Description relates an idea to more information about it. A greater number of distinctions are made among the types of descriptive relations. All descriptive relations have the same format in the content structure. The descriptive argument and descriptive relation are subordinate to the idea described. The types of descriptive relations used in the fund raising letter will be discussed and exemplified.

Description: attribution describes qualities of a proposition; it adds colors, qualities, attributes; we often find collections of attributes describing a person, event, or idea. Figure 10 shows how this relation appears in the content structure.

Example of description: attribution.

Calls jammed our switchboard all day (segment 5). Staffers stayed late into the night, answering questions and talking with reporters from newspapers, radio stations, wire services and TV stations in every part of the country (segment 6).

Description: specific gives more specific information about something that was stated in a general way; statement to examples; abstract to concrete. The superordinate is less precise/more inclusive, while the subordinate is more precise/less inclusive. An example is graphed in Figure 11.

Example of description: specific. As shown in this example where segments 8 and 29 are related, arguments of a rhetorical relation do not have to be adjacent in the surface structure of the text.

Media and public reaction has been nothing short of incredible! (segment 8). The results of ZPG's 1985 Urban Stress Test were reported as a top news story by hundreds of newspapers and TV and radio stations from coast to coast (segment 29).

Description: equivalent restates the same information in a different way. The dominant argument is staged in the foreground by more frequent usage in the text (see Figure 12).

Example of description: equivalent.

With your contribution, ZPG can arm our growing network of local activists with the materials they need to warn community leaders about emerging population-linked stresses before they reach the crisis stage (segment 18). ...we can act to take positive action at the local level (segment 19b).

Description: manner describes the way an event or event complex is performed. Manners describe how much, how often, how difficult, and so forth. There are no relations of this type at the macroproposition level in the fund raising text, but only at the microproposition level as in the following sentence (also see Figure 13).

Example of description: manner.

...we urgently need your help (segment 14).

Description: setting relationships include description: setting time and description: setting location. The first gives the time in which the event or idea occurred and the second gives its location. The description: setting

segment 5
description: attribution
segment 6

Figure 10: Format in the Content Structure of Description: Attribution

segment 8
description: specific
segment 29

Figure 11: Format in the Content Structure of Description: Specific.

segment 18
description: equivalent
segment 19b

Figure 12: Format in the Content Structure of Description: Equivalent.

NEED YOUR HELP
description: manner
URGENTLY

Figure 13: Format in the Content Structure of Description: Manner.

ARE HEARING (10)
description: setting time
NOW (10)
description: setting location
ALL PARTS OF THE COUNTRY (10)

Figure 14: Format in the Content Structure of Description: Setting.

depicted at the top of Figure 2 shows this relation operating at the macropropositional level; the examples given below and in Figure 14 show it working at the microproposition level.

Examples of description: setting time and description: setting location. *Now we are hearing from concerned citizens in all parts of the country... (segment 10a).*

The final descriptive relationship used in the ZPG letter is *description: constituency identification*. This relationship identifies a part in relation to its whole. Segment 3, *Dear Friend of ZPG*, was related to segment 1, *Zero Population Growth*, in this way and is shown at the top of Figure 3.

6. Conclusion

The fund raising letter can be analyzed with the Meyer approach (1975, 1985) to text analysis. This analysis system has been applied primarily to expository text. Many fund raising letters probably conform to the response: problem/solution top-level structure. With the problem the writer can attempt to lure the reader into involvement with an issue and then explain how the reader can help solve the problem by sending money. This is a more subtle approach than just stating that they should immediately send money. However, another variation of the fund raising letter is "send money" followed by causation: explanation, where the rationale for sending money is given.

Fund raising letters may provide interesting stimuli in memory experiments with young and older adults. Letters of this type certainly are typical of a type of everyday reading materials.

References

Aristotle. (L. Cooper, trans.)
1960 *The Rhetoric of Aristotle*. New York: Appleton-Century-Crofts.

Beaugrande, R.
1980 *Text, Discourse, and Process*. Norwood, N.J.: Ablex.

Brewer, W.F.
1980 "Literary Theory, Rhetoric, and Stylistics: Implications for Psychology." In R.J.

Spiro, B.C. Bruce, and W.F. Brewer (eds.), *Theoretical issues in reading comprehension*. Hillsdale, J.J.: Lawrence Erlbaum Associates.

Englert, C.S., and E.H. Hiebert
1984 "Children's developing awareness of text structures in expository materials." *Journal of Educational Psychology* 76.65-74.

Fillmore, C.
1968 "The case for case." In E. Bach and R. Harms (eds.), *Universals in Linguistic Theory*. New York: Holt, Rinehart & Winston.

Flower, L.
1979 "Writer-based prose: A cognitive basis for problems in writing." *College English*. 41.19-37.

Frederiksen, C.H.
1975 "Acquisition of semantic information from discourse: Effects of repeated exposures." *Journal of Verbal Learning and Verbal Behavior*. 14.158-169.

Graesser, A.C.
1981 *Prose Comprehension Beyond the Word*. New York: Springer-Verlag.

Grimes, J.E.
1975 *The Thread of Discourse*. The Hague: Mouton.

Halliday, M.A.K. and R. Hasan
1976 *Cohesion in English*. London: Longman.

Jordan, M.P.
1984 *Prose Structures in Everyday English Texts*, London: George Allen and Unwin.

Mann, W.C., and S.A. Thompson
1987 "Rhetorical structure theory: A theory of text organization." In L. Polanyi (ed.), *The structure of discourse*. Norwood, N.J.: Ablex Publishing Corporation.

Meyer, B.J.F.
1975 *The Organization of Prose and Its Effects on Memory*. Amsterdam: North-Holland.

1985 "Prose analysis: Purposes, procedures, and problems." In Bruce K. Britton and John B. Black (eds.), *Understanding expository text*. Hillsdale, N.J.: Lawrence Erlbaum Associates, 11-64, 269-304.

Meyer, B.J.F., D.M. Brandt, and G.J. Bluth
1980 "Use of the top-level structure in text: Key for reading comprehension of ninth-grade students". *Reading Research Quarterly* 16:1.72-103.

Meyer, B.J.F., and R.O. Freedle
1984 "The effects of different discourse types on recall." *American Educational Research Journal*. 21:1.121-143.

Meyer, B.J.F., M.J. Haring, D.M. Brandt, and C.H. Walker
1980 "Comprehension of stories and expository text." *Poetics: International Review for the Theory of Literature*. 9.203-211.

Meyer, B.J.F., and G.E. Rice
1982 "The interaction of reader strategies and the organization of text." *Text*. 2.155-192.

Meyer, B.J.F., and G.E. Rice
1984 "The structure of text." In P.D. Pearson and M. Kamil (eds.), *Handbook of research in reading*. New York: Longman.

Meyer, B.J.F., M. Marsiske, and S.L. Willis
1990 *Text processing and everyday task performance by the elderly*. Paper presented at the Cognitive Aging Research Conference in Atlanta, GA.

Meyer, B.J.F., C.J. Young, and B.J. Bartlet
1989 *Memory Improved: Reading and Memory Enhancement Across the Life Span Through Strategic Text Structures*. Hillsdale, N.J.: Lawrence Erlbaum Associates.

Raphael, T.E., C.S. Englert, and B.M. Kirschner
1986 *The Impact of Text Structure Instruction and Social Context on Students' Comprehension and Production of Expository Text (Research Series No. 177)*. East Lansing: Michigan State University, Institute for Research on Teaching.

Rumelhart, D. E., and A. Ortony
1977 "The representation of knowledge in memory." In R.C. Anderson, R. Spiro, and W. Montague (eds.), *Schooling and the Acquisition of Knowledge*. Hillsdale, N.J.: Lawrence Erlbaum Associates. 99-136.

The Discourse Strategy of an Appeals Letter

Robert E. Longacre

0. As an appeal for funds, this letter[1] can be considered to be a variety of hortatory discourse, which is, in turn, a subtype of behavioral discourse (the latter can also include such discourses as eulogies and campaign speeches, Longacre 1983). Hortatory discourse aims at influencing conduct, that is, getting the receivers of the text to do something they are not currently doing, to discontinue doing something they are doing, to continue doing something they are already doing, to expend greater effort in an activity already embarked on, to modify the nature of their efforts, and so on. As an appeal for funds, this letter aims to elicit further contribution to a cause that the reader may already have given to and to solicit contributions from those who have not given previously.

A distinction needs to be made between hortatory discourse and persuasive discourse. Unlike hortatory discourse, whose goal is to influence conduct, persuasive discourse is primarily aimed at influencing beliefs and values. The text in hand is not a persuasive discourse as such. No attempt is made to give a careful statement of the goals of ZPG, to state the means whereby they could be attained, or to argue the worthwhileness of those goals. The worthwhileness of the cause is alluded to only obliquely, in terms of "population-related problems." Popular interest and hearty response to a press release is further assumed to vindicate the cause, as is also the imposing list of officers and sponsors on the left hand margin of the letterhead. Above all, it is assumed that the letter is directed to readers who are already friendly to the cause — "Dear Friend of ZPG" (segment 3). Assuming, then, that the writer and the reader have the same or very similar beliefs and values, the letter sets out to influence conduct in a very specific way, that is, to get the reader to send in a *contribution*.

In this article I shall discuss the schema/superstructure which characterizes this type of discourse and which is exemplified by this letter. I shall then attempt to match the schema to the surface structure by (1) inspecting the letter for natural seams which indicate groupings of the segments, and (2) looking for correspondences between moves of the schema and the natural groupings found within the discourse. This should yield a *macrosegmentation* of the discourse, i.e. a meaningful division into big 'chunks' — which can be recursive in more complicated discourses than the relatively simple one found in this letter.[2] Eventually *macrosegmentation* must lead into *microsegmentation*, i.e. the consideration of how the various segments (for the most part, sentences) within a large division of text relate to each other and what part each segment plays in the local and global context. In examining the microstructure of the discourse, attention will be paid to considerations of *dominance* (of one part of the discourse over near or more remote parts)[3] and *mitigation*[4] as a tactical device in composing the letter. *Macrostructures* of parts and of the whole will be formulated in the course of the analysis.

1. The schema/superstructure

A schema is discourse-type specific but it is not discourse specific in terms of the content of a particular text. Comparing the production of a discourse of a given type to a game, we can characterize the schema as a summary of the high-level moves of the game. Thus, a hortatory text, that is a text whose purpose is to modify the conduct of the receivers of the text, has four typical moves:[5] (1) establishment of the authority/credibility of the text producer; (2) presentation of a problem/situation; (3) issuing of one or more commands, which can be mitigated to suggestions of varying urgency; and (4) resort to motivation (essentially threats with predictions of undesirable results, and promises along with predictions of desirable results). In this schema, (3) is minimal and basic, i.e. a hortatory discourse cannot be such without commands/suggestion and it may consist wholely of commands/suggestions. Characteristically such a discourse is brusque and brief. But even in such a minimal hortatory text, the presence of (2) is implied (or present in the context of the situation), i.e. there is necessarily some problem/situation which evokes the command elements. Most hortatory discourse also includes (4), motivation — unless the power of the speaker/writer over the addressee is uncontestable. All of this in turn implies (1) even if not overtly stated.

Notice that this sets apart a hortatory discourse from a persuasive discourse which has essentially the following moves: (1) problem/question; (2) proposed solution/answer; (3) supporting argumentation (logic, experimentation, authority); (4) appeal (often very subtle) to give credence, or to adopt certain values. In this persuasive schema point (4) is minimal and basic. Point (3) includes among other things the authority of the speaker but this factor is perhaps not as prominent as in hortatory discourse. Notice, however, that persuasive and hortatory discourse can co-exist in one text, especially when the same text embeds persuasive discourse as a means of supplying motivation in the hortatory schema. Probably expository discourse is similar to persuasive but it does not have to have any move which corresponds to element 4 of persuasive discourse and is likely to have *evaluation* of the solution as one of its main points (Hoey 1983).

Narrative discourse and various kinds of procedural/instructional discourses are different still. Narrative discourse must have an *inciting incident* (something out of the ordinary has happened; otherwise how can there be a story?). A story also has *mounting tension* culminating in a *climax* of tension/confrontation followed by a *denouement* (Longacre, 1983). In a sense the inciting moment is parallel to the problem/situation of the other discourse types, but it is progressively developed to a climax (the problem is like a wave which comes to crest) in a way not characteristic of other discourse types. The denouement is like a solution in the other schemata. Elements of command and persuasion, if present, are characteristically expressed in a moral at the end. Above all, narrative discourse must have punctiliar sequential happenings — something not demanded in other discourse types, which have either a line of command (hortatory), of persuasion, or of exposition.

As for procedural discourse we expect: problem/need; preparatory procedures; the main, efficient procedures; and concluding (often utilization) procedures (Barnard and Forster 1968).

In applying the hortatory schema to the text at hand, segments 4-10 can be considered to constitute an effort to underscore the worthiness of the ZPG cause — although we observed above that this is also enhanced by the names on the left side of the letter, while the particular authority of the letter writer is established by her being executive director of the organization. Only at the end of the paragraph, in segment 10, are the background problems responsible for the existence of ZPG alluded to: "population-related problems that threaten health and well-being." So in the main, segments 4-10 correspond to move (1) of the hortatory schema with some passing allusion to (2). This paragraph, segments 4-10, is largely narrative in tone.

Segments 11-17 correspond to move (2) of the hortatory schema; here the problem/situation is presented as an opportunity occasioned by the results attained and attainable by ZPG's 1985 Urban Stress Text (henceforth UST). This paragraph, although superficially expository in tone, is covertly hortatory; without (yet!) making an appeal, segments 14-17 state a need.

Segments 18-24 contain a motivated appeal — and thus correspond to moves (3) and (4) of the hortatory schema. Segments 18-21 are largely motivation while segments 22-24 contain the overt appeal (to which the whole letter has led up).

What about segments 28-30, the postscript? Here the letter implements a familiar tactic of an appeal letter. In effect, the strategy is to get you — before you toss the letter into the waste basket — to at least take the letter seriously enough to do *something* with it, that is, fill out an enclosed simple questionnaire or response form. The P.S. contains a motivation (Segment 29) and an appeal (Segment 30).

2. The Macrosegmentation of the Text ('Chunking')

Chunking a text into its gross parts requires that we confront a discourse schema (such as those sketched above) with an examination of the text for surface structure indications of natural segmentation. In juxtaposing these two concerns we save ourselves from perpetrating a sterile dissection of the text; we are able, on the contrary, to immediately make a beginning at attributing *functions* to the various discourse parts. Attributing functions to the parts enables us to view it as a functioning whole rather than as a dissected cadaver.

Looking at the letter we find that we are not initially much helped in our gross segmentation. The writer has gone to an apparent excess of indentation which is of little help as far as discovering the structural paragraphs. Segment 15 is inset and underlined — presumably to point out something crucially significant. The letter, however, is framed and formatted so as to be an effective appeal. Accordingly, in an effort to make the contents more accessible to quick scanning by the average reader, an orthographic paragraph in this letter contains typically one or two sentences — although segments 4-6 containing three sentences in the first orthographic paragraph. The indentation and open lines between the orthographic paragraphs very probably make the letter more readable than could be achieved by more conservative paragraphing. In the balance of this article I will ignore the orthographic indentation and spacing, and will group the sentences which are contained in the body of the letter into the three parts noticed at the end of Section 1. above, i.e. segments 4-10: the worthiness of the ZPG cause (schema, move 1); segments 11-17, the UST presents an opportunity to be exploited (schema, move 2); and segments 18-24, the motivated appeal to send a contribution (schema, moves 3 and 4). I will refer to these three parts as *structural paragraphs* (Longacre 1979).

In justifying this three-fold gross chunking, I submit the following argument. Paragraph I (Segments 4-10) is largely narrative; it tells the story of the public reaction consequent on the release of the results of ZPG's 1985 UST. Paragraph II (Segments 11-17) takes as its topic ZPG's 1985 Urban Stress Test. The references to the topic in Segment 11 and 17 provide a nice *inclusio* for this paragraph (and the phrase is underlined in both sentences). Paragraph III, the motivated appeal, is similarly bracketed with references to the reader's making a contribution (Segment 18: "with your contribution" and Segment 22: "Please make a special contribution..."). This paragraph is overtly hortatory in tone; not only does it contain an imperative in Segment 22 but segments 18-20 contain modals and Segment 21 has "need" as its main verb. In Segment 19 the clause which contains the modal is underlined: "We can act to take positive action at the local level." Thus, in surface structure, we pass from narration (in Paragraph I), and mitigated (covert) exhortation (in Paragraph II) to overt exhortation ("we can do it"..."send in your contribution") in Paragraph III. Furthermore, the topic, i.e. what a stretch of text is about, is plainly marked in all three paragraphs: the story of the public reaction; the effectiveness of ZPG's 1985 UST; and the crucialness of your contribution. Again, as we say above, the segments function in the schema of the hortatory discourse so as to give respectively: the *authority* of the writer and her cause; the *problem* explained (ZPG's 1985 UST is a good instrument but our staff is overwhelmed in trying to get the message out); and the *motivated appeal*.

3. The microsegmentation of the text

No one who works for long and in detail with text analysis can avoid positing a set of relations to explain how the segments of the text relate to each other. This has been obvious for some time in Biblical studies and in translation theory. Beginning with the work of Fuller in 1959 ("Inductive Bible Study") a set of relations was elaborated by John Beekman and colleagues within the Summer Institute of Linguistics (culminating in Beekman and Kopesec 1981). My own somewhat parallel work has gone through a similar series of elaboration and revision (Ballard, Conrad, & Longacre 1971a, 1971b, and Longacre 1972, 1976, 1983b). De Beaugrande and Dressler (1981) give a catalogue, as do Grimes (1975), van Dijk (1977), and Mann and Thompson (1987, 1988). One could wish that all of us could agree on the number and labelling of the relations involved, but the underlying similarities among these lists are more significant than the disagreements.

Along with the elaboration of these interclausal relations (which can be found in both intrasentential and intersentential distribution) I have elaborated surface structure taxonomies for the sentence (Longacre 1970 and 1985) and paragraph (Longacre 1979 and 1980) both as recursive units. While the surface structure of the paragraph depends heavily on the relations which it encodes, I note the following differences and correlations between the encoding of such relations and the surface structure of the paragraph in which they are found.

(1) I take the sentence divisions (at least of written text) quite seriously as encoding options on the part of the text producer. Propositions that could have been represented seriatim as separate sentences are combined into sentences which display internal coordination and/or subordination. Presumably the text producer's discourse strategy is at work here in what he/she decides to 'bundle' together as one sentence as opposed to material encoded as separate bundles.

(2) I take, therefore, the task of paragraph-level microanalysis to be one of relating sentence to sentence with only an occasional excursion into the internal structure of sentences.

(3) A signal exception to the above is the need to account for the cohesive relations of adverbial clauses (Thompson and Longacre 1985, 178-234, Matthiessen and Thompson 1989).

(4) I believe that paragraphs sometimes have multi- functional surface slots such as setting/introduction, terminus/conclusion, and comment. Settings/introductions are like 'ice-breakers', necessary preliminary information which supersedes some of the other notional functions (for example introduction of a participant, a topic, a description of attendant circumstances). Likewise terminus/conclusion occurs to mark the end of the paragraph whatever further notional functions it may have. These openers and closers typically have elements that are off-the-line[6] in their discourse types and are morphosyntactically identifiable. Comment, likewise off-the-line and morphosyntactically identifiable, is often introduced by a word such as *it*, *this*, *that* which is deictic in function relative to the preceding sentence.

(5) I believe that a comparatively small inventory of paragraph types can be posited,[7] provided that we recognize that paragraphs take on chameleon-like the discourse features of the discourses that they occur in. For example, I set up a thesis- reason paragraph that has thesis as its dominant member (by virtue of being on the mainline of the discourse type and having the verb form that dominates its type) but which appends a *reason* as ancillary (i.e. a segment or segments which is not on the main-line of its discourse type and which semantically expresses cause or reason). I abbreviate the name of this paragraph type to *reason* paragraph; it is named for its distinctive ancillary member. This paragraph occurs in narrative to explain why someone acted in a certain way or suffered a given contingency. In such circumstances I call the paragraph type a *narrative reason paragraph*. In a hortatory text, however, the same paragraph type can occur with a thesis which is on-the-line of exhortation (some sort of command/suggestion) and an off-the-line reason unit which presents a motivation to implement the command/suggestion. One could set up here an exhortation- motivation paragraph peculiar to hortatory text. On the other hand, it avoids multiplying paragraph types if we simply say that we have here a hortatory reason paragraph with semantic modification of the reason paragraph occasioned by its occurring in hortatory discourse. We can likewise have other variants of this structure occasioned by other discourse types, for example, a procedural reason paragraph, or an expository reason paragraph (Longacre 1979).

All this means that we are left with the necessity of positing semantic variation in the surface structure slots of the paragraph: a kind of notional versus surface split-level structure. But this seems better than forever multiplying surface structure units occasioned by such semantic variations, or on the other hand ignoring the latter.

(6) The paragraph as thus envisioned is a highly recursive unit — but the recursive layering is resultant on the frequently complex nesting of relations which are implied or marked in the *surface* structure. All these relations must be identified and interrelated. Keeping track of this layering constitutes a reader-burden, whatever particular approach is followed in writing up the analysis. I suggest that the reader, in the balance of this paper, make frequent reference to the constituency display which is appended to this article. In an attempt to partially index the layering of recursive paragraph structure I will reserve the term *main* paragraph for the inclusive units which explain the three points of this letter, i.e. the three major chunks as described in Section 2.

3.1 *The Structure of Main Paragraph I (segments 4-10)*

As we have already stated, this paragraph is largely narrative in tone. What it tries to accomplish is to present ZPG as a worthy cause as judged by the public reaction to publishing the results of the 1985 UST. In this paragraph Segments 4-8 constitute the Thesis and Segments 9-10 the Comment; the whole unit (4-10) constitutes a narrative comment paragraph. Semantically the Thesis is a recountal (in the form of an embedded narrative sequence paragraph) while the Comment is a kind of analysis of what happened and can be considered to be a narrative contrast paragraph which turns on the contrast of "At first..." in Segment 9 and "Now..." in Segment 10.

In the first part of this paragraph, the Thesis (recountal) is structured as a narrative sequence paragraph which has four component slots: three Sequential Theses (ST's) and a Terminus. Segments 4,5, and 6 are on the line of this piece of embedded narrative; the verbs "started to ring," "jammed," and "stayed" portray sequential happenings which are either inherently punctiliar (Segment 4) or are viewed as simple happenings (Segments 5-6) in quite regular narrative fashion. In addition, time adverbs help the narrative movement: "At 7:00 A.M. on Oct. 25...all day....late into the night." The complex of related lexical items, "phones," "switchboards," and "staffers" provides thematic unity. The comparative length and detail which characterize Segment 6 (Sequential Thesis$_n$) in depicting the ZPG's staff working overtime to answer questions and to talk to reporters indicate a development which is locally climactic; by convention I label Segment$_6$

Sequential $Thesis_n$ (ST_n) instead of just Sequential $Thesis_3$ (ST_3) which would not indicate anything climactic.

Segments 7 and 8 constitute a Terminus which is summary in force; all the above is characterized as "an overwhelming response" (Segment 7) and a "reaction" which has been "nothing short of incredible" (Segment 8). The two sentences constitute a narrative concessive paragraph with Segment 7 as Concession and Segment 8 as Thesis. The initial adverbial clause "when we released the results of ZPG's 1985 UST", harks back to a time immediately preceding Oct. 25 and serves to introduce the 1985 UST which is made thematic further on in the second main paragraph of the whole discourse. Neither sentence 7 with its flashback in past tense (of "have") nor sentence 8 with its present perfect tense (of "be") has narrative verbs; the whole unit (7-8) — as a summary — is best considered to be off the main line of development of the narrative paragraph. Within the unit composed of Segments 7 and 8 the latter is dominant and is the thesis which outranks the irrealis negative structure in Segment 7 — which is ancillary and is labelled Concession.

The second half of this paragraph (Segments 9 and 10) is a comment (analysis) on the narrative presented in Segments 4-8. It represents a temporal contrast turning on the time adverbs "at first" and "now." It is, however, somewhat expository in tone and apparently Segment 10 should be considered to be the dominant member (and hence the Thesis) while Segment 9 can be considered to be ancillary and the *antithesis*. We can consider the paragraph (Segments 9-10) to be an expository contrast paragraph where time relations are used not to provide narrative movement but to explain and to analyze happenings which have been previously reported. It is important to note that, although the more inclusive unit, segments 4-10, is a narrative comment paragraph, the internal structure of the comment itself, Segments 9-10, is expository — and as exposition it is clearly off-the-line of the narrative paragraph to which it belongs.

In neither Segment 9 nor Segment 10 do the main verbs represent sequential punctiliar happenings; rather they represent spans of activity. The phrase "deluge of calls" in Segment 9 echoes the references to the unexpectedly large response as mentioned in Segments 7 and 8. The sentences in these segments could be schematized as: "At first...calls came (mostly) from X and Y; now we are hearing from Z", where X symbolizes "reporters"; Y symbolizes "outraged public officials" and Z symbolizes "concerned citizens." The contrastive adverb "now" — presumably referring to elapsed time from Oct. 25 and including the present — can be assumed to mark the more important segment of the paragraph. Here a study of the relative clauses in 9 and 10 is relevant. Thus, Segment 9 has "reporters [who were] eager to tell the public about UST results", and "outraged public officials who were furious that we had blown the whistle on conditions in their cities." Presumably the relevant additional information thus brought into Segment 9 gives a further opportunity to mention favorably the 1985 UST results (important in the rest of the letter), and the wretched conditions in certain U.S. cities. Segment 10 is a sentence which has a long relative clause with a further embedded complement of "know": "(concerned citizens) who want to know what they can do to hold local officials accountable for tackling population-related problems that threaten public health and well-being." Aside from the oblique reference to conditions in certain cities found in Segment 9, the deeply embedded phrase "population-related problems that threaten public health and well-being" is the first clear reference in the letter to the nature of the problems whose existence led to the formation of ZPG. Presumably the "friends of ZPG" referred to in the salutation (Segment 3) agree that conditions in many U.S. cities are deplorable and that unrestrained population growth is central in the development of these deplorable conditions.

The main verbs in Segments 9 and 10 occur in clauses which emphasize *source* and which contrast the calls from reporters and outraged public officials with the presumably more significant response now coming from concerned citizens. As we have already observed, this paragraph is essentially expository in tone even though it centers around a temporal contrast. Simplifying the sentences the contrast can be schematically represented as follows:

S.9	T past	P_m	$S_{x,y}$
S.10	T present	P_m	S_z

T represents time past and present; P_m represents verbs that can broadly be construed as motion, and $S_{x,y}$ represents earlier sources of calls versus Sz the latter and (more gratifying) source of calls. The paragraph (9-10) uses, then, a temporal contrast as a framework for presenting contrasting value judgements regarding earlier and later respondents.

The message is: ZPG is a worthy cause; not only has it had an overwhelming response to its promulgation of the 1985 UST results, but, in the last analysis, it is the more thoughtful and civic-minded portion of our citizenry who have answered — and they want to know what to do about it.

3.2. *The structure of Paragraph II (Segments 11-17)*

Having presented in paragraph I the story of the response to the promulgation of ZPG's 1985 UST results and having analyzed those results in a way to put ZPG in the best possible light, the writer of the letter goes on in main paragraph II to argue that the UST is an effective tool and that realizing its full impact will require the help of the readers of the letter. This paragraph is superficially expository in tone, but the references to "we need your help" (Segment 14) and to "your support...is crucial" (Segment 16) are probably typically pieces of mitigated exhortation which prepare us for the open appeal which is to follow in the last paragraph.

The superficially expository tone of the paragraph is evident from the main verbs which dominate it: "is" (copulative) in Segment 11, "ranks" (static-relational) in Segment 12; "translates" (static in the sense of "shows the equivalence of") in Segment 13; "need" (expression of a lack without a verb of pleading) in Segment 14; "is being swamped" (passive, represents an ongoing situation) in Segment 15a; "are being stretched" (similar) in Segment 15b; "is" (copulative) in Segment 16; and "may be" (modal of the copulative) in Segment 17. Nevertheless, Segment 14 can be interpreted as a mitigated appeal as can likewise Segment 16; this interpretation hinges on the use of the verb 'need.' In keeping with the mitigated hortatory tone of this part of the paragraph, I make Segments 14-17 dominant over the earlier Segments 11-13 in this paragraph, which are simply expository.

In keeping with the dominating role of the included (mitigated) hortatory paragraph (Segments 14-17), the whole paragraph (Segments 11-17) is likewise taken to be mitigated hortatory (symbolized as H?). Looking at the logical relation involved in the whole, we proceed to classify the structure as concessive with Segments 11-13 encoding the Concession and Segments 14-17 (which dominate) the Thesis. The whole paragraph (11-17) can therefore be called a (mitigated) hortatory concessive paragraph. The Concession consists of an expository coordinate paragraph with three Theses, Segments 11-13 respectively. The first Thesis explains that the 1985 UST is the nation's first survey of the effect of population-related pressures on our cities. The second Thesis gives some idea of the criteria used to rank the 184 urban areas thus surveyed. The third Thesis is that "complex technical data" is transformed by the survey into an "easy-to-use action tool for concerned citizens, elected officials and opinion leaders." I have labelled the three theses $Thesis_1$, $Thesis_2$, and $Thesis_n$ to recognize the climactic nature of the third thesis. Precisely because the survey's results translate into an action tool, a need has arisen as sketched in the last part of the paragraph.

The second part of this paragraph, the Thesis (Segments 14- 17) consists of a mitigated hortatory reason paragraph, which I will further characterize as cyclic.[8] I consider that it consists of a Thesis (Segment 14), a Reason (Segment 15), recapitulated Thesis (which I will label, Thesis', Segment 16) and a Terminus (Segment 17) which has an immediate function as closure relative to Segments 14-16, but which is somewhat multi- functional and will necessitate some further discussion. The bond between the Thesis and the Thesis' consists in the fact that Segment 16 is a paraphrase of Segment 14: "...we urgently need your help...Your support now is crucial." The opening words of Segment 14 are a backreference to sentence 13; thus the affirmation that the 1985 UST is an "easy-to-use action tool" is echoed in the next sentence: "But to use it well...". This backreference not only serves a cohesive function but leads into the statement of need[9] on which the overt appeal will eventually be based. In between Thesis and Thesis' comes the Reason (Segment 15), which is a coordinate sentence — the part which is orthographically set in. The staff is too small to answer all the inquiries and "our modest resources are being stretched to the limit." This adds some poignancy to the renewed statement of need in Thesis' (Segment 16) where the word "now" occurs.

But what does Segment 17 accomplish? I have construed it as Terminus of the paragraph which is found in Segments 14-16. It reiterates the phrase "ZPG's 1985 Urban Stress Test" which has not been mentioned since Segment 11; as such it provides a grand *inclusio* for the whole second main paragraph (Segments 11-17). On the other hand, the presentation of ZPG's 1985 UST as an opportunity to get "the population message heard" reaffirms the urgency mentioned in Segment 14 and this seems to more specifically relate Segment 17 to what *immediately* precedes in Segments 14-16. Finally, Segment 17 could well be taken as preliminary to the last main paragraph Segment 18-23. What then? Need any of these functions be ignored? Certainly not, whatever the limitations of tree diagrams in compelling us to make certain methodologically-induced choices. Let Segment 17 be primarily allocated to the paragraph consisting of Segment 14-16 but let us recognize that inclusio, chiasmus, and the like often override groupings based on other considerations, so that the first and last sentences of main paragraph II (with overt mention of ZPG's Urban Stress Test) have this feature regardless of their precise status within the parts of the paragraph. Let us go further and suggest that Segment 17 could be considered to be essentially transitional; i.e. it simultaneously concludes the second main paragraph and introduces the third main paragraph.

This whole paragraph (Segments 11-17) can be summarized as "Although ZPG's 1985 UST is a superb action tool it can't be effectively used without your help."

3.3 *The Structure of Main Paragraph III (Segments 18-23)*

This paragraph structures as a hortatory reason paragraph. The Reason (Motivation) is found in Segments 18-21; the Thesis (Appeal) is found in Segments 22 and 23. Since the latter is clearly hortatory (note "Please make a contribution" in Sentence 22), the whole paragraph is hortatory — since the dominating status of the thesis determines the paragraph's classification. *Moreover, since Paragraph III is overtly hortatory while Paragraph II is only covertly (mitigated) hortatory, and Paragraph I is narrative and expository, then Segment 22, which dominates the dominating paragraph (III) must be considered to dominate the entire discourse.* The reasoning here — as in earlier sections of the paper is simply: In any given discourse type the parts of the discourse that are nearer to the main line of that discourse type dominate over parts that are farther from the main line. In a narrative discourse, narrative elements dominant over non-narrative elements. In a hortatory discourse, hortatory elements dominate over non-hortatory elements. A corollary of the above is: overtly hortatory elements dominate over covertly hortatory elements (where exhortation is mitigated). I therefore in the body of this appeals letter rank main paragraph III, which is overtly hortatory (in segments 22 and 23) over main paragraph II, which is mitigated exhortation, and both over main paragraph I, which is narrative. This reasoning carried to its end makes Segment 22 dominant the entire discourse. And why not? Isn't the letter, stripped of all embellishment an *appeal for contributions*?

First of all, I examine the structure of the Reason (Motivation) in Segments 18-21. These sentences constitute a mitigated hortatory paragraph, in which three motivations are expressed as coordinated Theses. Theses one and two (Segments 18 and 19) have verbs of ability as their main verbs: "can arm", "can act"; while the verb "need" characterizes Segment 21 to which Segment 20 (with a passive present progressive) is attached as ancillary.

Segment 18, $Thesis_1$, begins with the phrase "with your contribution" — thus anticipating the appeal in Segment 22 and echoing the themes of "need" and "opportunity" from previous sentences. This thesis affirms that ZPG "can arm our growing network of local activists with the materials they need." A purpose clause is attached: "to warn community leaders about emerging population-linked stresses before they reach the crisis stage." Note here again the reference to the background problems that are the concern of ZPG (cf. Segment 10); again this reference is buried under several layers of constituent structure within the sentence — but achieves a certain prominence by being sentence final.

Segment 19, $Thesis_2$, is a concessive sentence whose initial concessive clause is critical of the national government's insensitivity to the problems that concern ZPG: "Even though our national government continues to ignore the consequences of uncontrolled population growth...". The main clause affirms that "we can act to take positive action at the local level." The nature of this positive action is not spelled out beyond what was suggested in the previous sentence, viz. seeing to it that "local activists" have the information that they need.[10]

$Thesis_n$ (which I consider the most specific and programmatic of the three) is expressed in an embedded paragraph. It is an Expository Circumstantial paragraph with Segment 20, the Circumstance, clearly ancillary to Segment 21, the Thesis. Segment 20 simply states that every day local officials make decisions "that could drastically affect the quality of our lives." Segment 21, the Thesis, states that such local officials and indeed the American public at large, need information regarding population-induced stresses, if "sound choices" are to be made in our community — and this needed information is precisely what ZPG's "study", that is, the ZPG 1985 UST, has revealed. So Segments 18 and 19 stress the *opportunity* suggested in Segment 17, while Segments 20, 21 revert to presenting a *need*. The presentation of opportunity and need (without overt appeal) is here a characteristic piece of mitigated exhortation.

All that is lacking is the overt appeal — to which the whole letter has been warming up — "Please make a special contribution to Zero Population Growth today" (Segment 22). While an imperative is used — the first in the whole letter — it is lightly mitigated with "please." Segments 22, and 23 together make up a hortatory reason paragraph in which the non-imperative Segment 23 is ancillary to the imperative Segment 22. Here the Reason is that type of motivation that can be called a promise; it also assumes in the opening clause that a contribution will be forthcoming: "Whatever you give — $25, $50, $100, or as much as you can will be used immediately to put the Urban Stress Test in the hands of those who need it most." Here the organization pledges itself to use the contributions sent in for the purpose intended — a necessary pledge in view of the non-too-rare abuse of contributions by such groups.

The whole paragraph (Segments 19-23) could be summarized as: "We have an unparalleled opportunity to use ZPG's 1985 UST to stimulate and guide action on the local level. Please send in your contribution today."

What of the postscript? Again we have a motivated appeal in a hortatory reason paragraph. The Reason (Motivation), Segment 29, reechoes Paragraph I in the body of the letter as to the worthiness of the ZPG cause as evidenced by the news coverage that is occasioned. The Thesis (Appeal) in Segment 30 is more carefully mitigated than the main appeal which is found in Segment 22. So instead of getting: "Please help us monitor this remarkable media coverage..." we read "we hope you'll help us monitor this remarkable media coverage...". The indicated activity desired on the part of the reader is "completing the enclosed reply form." [Any response is better than none; let us at least hear from you even in the absence of a contribution. We may get a contribution from you on the next round.]

4. Conclusion

The macrostructure (van Dijk 1977, and 1980) of this letter can be stated as follows (ignoring the gimmick in the P.S. at the end): "Public response to the promulgation of the results of ZPG's 1985 UST has proven ZPG to be a worthy cause. The 1985 UST is a superb action tool. With your help we can use it to stimulate and guide action on the local level. Please send in your contribution today."

Positing this macrostructure constitutes a hermeneutic of the text by accounting for: (a) what is included in the text and its reason for being included; (b) the relative elaboration of the parts of a text (e.g. the relative elaboration found within main paragraph I is both attention getting and authority establishing; and (c) the thrust, the semantic import of the whole.

Everywhere in the analysis I have been guided by the consideration that this is a hortatory text (not an essay, nor a story) in which commands/suggestions necessarily dominate. The meaning of the letter is found in demonstrating the dominance of elements which express command/suggestion over other elements and in showing how all the other elements of the letter relate to the dominating element(s).

Thus, I have argued that Segment 22, the only one containing an imperative form, can be shown to dominate its own paragraph which in turn dominates the whole letter. This is, I believe, typical of discourses of this type (hortatory). What few command forms there are must be considered to be somehow central to the whole even if they are statistically in a minority. I have further argued that Points I and II (corresponding to the first two main paragraphs) are related to the command element with which Paragraph III terminates as establishing the credibility of the ZPG cause and warming up to the appeal by describing an opportunity and a need growing out of it. Our initial resort to a hortatory schema which includes certain moves considerably facilitated the beginning analysis. Schemata, properly used, have considerable analytic and hermeneutic value.

This appeal letter is a typical piece of hortatory discourse which starts out with narrative and expository material, warms up to an appeal via mitigated command elements, and finally graduates to an outright open appeal at its climax. A very different sort of hortatory discourse, the Greek text of the first epistle of John in Biblical literature, is developed along very similar lines (Longacre 1983a). It is significant that two different texts separated by some 2000 years and belonging to radically different cultural milieus exhibit very similar discourse strategies.

Appendix: Constituent Display of Appeal Letter of Noverber 22, 1985

Epistolary Conventions

S_1 (Identification)

S_2 (Date)

S_3 (Salutation)

Body of Letter (Hortatory Discourse)

POINT$_1$ (Credibility claim):(N) Comment Paragraph

THESIS (Recountal): (N) Sequence Paragraph

S_4 ST$_1$: At 7:00 A.M. on October 25, our phones started to ring.

S_5 ST$_2$: Calls jammed our switchboard all day.

S_6 ST$_n$: Staffers stayed late into the night answering questions and talking with reporters from newspapers, radio stations, wire services, and TV stations in every part of the country.

TERMINUS (summary): (N) Concession Paragraph

S_7 CONCESSION: When we released the results of ZPG's 1985 UST, we had no idea we'd get such an overwhelming response.

S_8 THESIS: Media and public reaction has been nothing short of incredible!

S_9 COMMENT (Analysis): E (temporal) Contrast Paragraph

ANTITHESIS: At first the deluge of calls came mostly from reporters eager to tell the public about UST results and from outraged public officials who were furious that we had "blown the whistle" on conditions in their cities.

S_{10} THESIS: Now we are hearing from concerned citizens in all parts of the country who want to know what they can do to hold local officials accountable for tackling population-related problems that threaten public health and well-being.

$POINT_2$ (the Problem):(H?) Concession Paragraph

CONCESSION:(E) Coordinate Paragraph

S_{11} $THESIS_1$: ZPG's 1985 Urban Stress Test, created after months of persistent research, is the nation's first survey of how population-linked pressures affect U.S. cities.

S_{12} $THESIS_2$: It ranks 184 urban areas on 11 different criteria ranging from crowding and birth rates to air quality and toxic wastes.

S_{13} $THESIS_n$: The Urban Stress Test translates complex technical data into an easy-to-use action tool for concerned citizens, elected officials, and opinion leaders.

THESIS: Cyclic (H?) Reason Paragraph

S_{14} THESIS: But to use it well we urgently need your help.

S_{15} REASON: Our Small staff is being swamped with requests for more information and our modest resources are being stretched to the limit.

S_{16} THESIS': Your support now is crucial.

S_{17} TERMINUS: ZPG's 1985 Urban Stress Test may be our best opportunity ever to get the population message heard

$POINT_n$ (motivated appeal):(H) Reason Paragraph

REASON (Motivation):(H?) Coordinate Paragraph

S_{18} $THESIS_1$: With your contribution, ZPG can arm our growing network of local activists with the materials they need to warn community leaders about emerging population-linked stresses before they reach the crisis stage.

S_{19} $THESIS_2$: Even though our national government continues to ignore the consequence of uncontrolled population growth, we can act to take positive action at the local level.

THESISn: (E) Circumstantial Paragraph

S_{20} CIRCUMSTANCE: Every day decisions are being made by local officials in our communities that could drastically affect the quality of our lives.

S_{21} THESIS: To make sound choices in planning for people, both elected officials and the American public need the population stress data revealed by our study.

THESIS (Appeal):(H) Reason Paragraph

S_{22} THESIS: Please make a special contribution to Zero Population Growth today.

S_{23} REASON (motivating promise): Whatever you give — $25, $50, $100 or as much as you can — will be used immediately to put the Urban Stress Test in the hands of those who need it most.

EPISTOLARY CONVENTIONS

S_{24} Complimentary close

S_{25} Written signature

S_{26-27} Signature printed and title

S_{28} P.S.

The POSTSCRIPT (Appended (mitigated) Hortatory discourse of one paragraph added according to a further epistolary convention): (H?) Reason Paragraph

S_{29} REASON (Motivation): The results of ZPG's 1985 Urban Stress Test were reported as a top news story by hundreds of newspapers and TV and radio stations from coast to coast.

S_{30} THESIS (Appeal): I hope you can help us monitor this remarkable news coverage by completing the enclosed reply form.

Notes

1. Because this is a letter, it is characterized by the customary epistolary conventions appropriate to its time and culture. Thus, the letterhead with the rubric ZPG and the Washington address at the bottom serves to identify the organization that has sent out the letter (Segment 1). The material in the left-hand margin — officers and sponsors of ZPG — serves further to identify the organization and put some substance to what might otherwise carry little weight. Segment 2, the date, Segment 3, the salutation, Segment 24, the complimentary close, Segment 25, the written signature, and Segments 26 and 27, the printed signature and title, as well as segment 28 (P.S.) are further epistolary conventions.

   These conventions primarily serve performative, that is, sender-receiver function, date the time of the appeal, and attempt by the letterhead conventions to identify ZPG and put it in a favorable light.

   That these conventions are used skillfully is seen in the wording of the salutation ['Dear Friends of ZPG'], begging the question of the reader's positive attitude to the cause represented; in the date [less than one month since the alleged storm of response broke on the heads of the ZPG staff]; and the signature wherein it is indicated (via letter head) that Susan Weber is Executive Director of the organization.

2. Recursion in macrosegmentation occurs when a major division of a discourse is itself a discourse, whose big 'chunks' must in turn be isolated and inspected to see if further such recursion must be postulated or if we can pass immediately to considerations of microsegmentation.

3. Dominance is here opposed to ancillary. The pair of terms *dominant* and *ancillary* are offered as the inter-sentential counterparts of the intra-sentential relations, independent

and subordinate. Thus, in "John went downtown because he was bored" we have the independent clause "John went downtown" and the subordinate clause "because he was bored". Notice, however, the following pair of sentences: "John went downtown. He was completely bored with sitting around the house all day". Here I term the first sentence "John went downtown", *dominant* and the second sentence *ancillary*.

4. The term has been used effectively by Labov and Fanshell (1977:84-86) in regard to making requests. An outright bald command may be disguised and softened to make it more socially acceptable to the hearer or reader. Thus, "Write this letter at once" can be mitigated to "Please write this letter as soon as possible" or to "Please give this letter top priority in your work this morning", or to "Would you mind getting this letter to me for my signature before coffee-break?" or even to "This letter should be mailed off this morning".

5. cf. Longacre 1983a. The hortatory schema employed here originated, however, in field workshops conducted in the Philippine branch of the Summer Institute of Linguistics by Austin Hale and Michael Walrod.

6. In any discourse type there is a main line of development and further elements which supplement/support the main line. In narrative text there is a storyline of punctiliar sequential happenings reported in sentences whose main verb(s) are some sort of past tense, completive aspect, or a special narrative tense (Biblical Hebrew, many African languages). In hortatory text there is a line of exhortation carried by imperative or modal forms which command, suggest, or urge some action. Everything else in the hortatory text supplements or support the line of exhortation. Other discourse types also have main line elements and additional elements. All of this can be tersely summarized as on-the-line versus off-the-line elements which are subject to morphosyntactic and/or lexical identification. On-the-line elements dominate off-the-line elements in local-span (paragraph analysis); cf. Longacre 1989b.

7. This is hardly the place to give a complete inventory and description of the paragraph types that are frequently encountered in languages around the world or even only in English (cf. Longacre 1979, 1980). I summarize briefly here; (1) a paragraph must have one or more *theses* which are characterized by having sentences whose main verb(s) is on the mainline in the discourse type in which that paragraph is found. Theses may be related to each other as coordinated (coordinate paragraph), contrasted (antithetical paragraph), or reflecting chronological succession (sequence paragraph). A single thesis may, on the other hand be accompanied by an ancillary segment whose main verb is off-the-line in the discourse type in which the paragraph is found. Besides setting/introduction, terminus/conclusion, and comment mentioned above under (4), further ancillary segments can relate to a thesis as reason, result, concession, paraphrase, amplification and the like. Longacre 1989b, 83-118, contains a more recent and more discursive presentation of paragraph types (relative to Biblical Hebrew) than are found in earlier articles cited above.

8. Paragraph types have (a) basic relational structures as indicated by such terms as coordinate, antithetical, reason, result, etc.; (b) variants determined by the discourse type which the paragraph represents, i.e. narrative, procedural, hortatory, expository, and the like; and (c) further stylistic variants of which *cyclic* (or chiastic) structure is the most common. A cyclic paragraph has a structure such as ABA, ABCBA, and the like — a sort of lexical rhyming. In the text above segments 14, 15, and 16 constitute a *cyclic hortatory reason paragraph* (of ABC structure); cf. Longacre 1979.

9. The placement of sentences which are an expression of need (and may use the actual verb 'need' as in segments 14 and 21), in the dominance pattern of hortatory discourse probably requires further consideration. I have at present decided that an explanation of need is a kind of mitigated exhortation — a covert solicitation for fulfillment of the need. While an expression of need is properly preliminary to an appeal, an appeal may be pragmatically carried out by going no further than expressing a need. Consequently, I have ranked 'need' as higher in dominance than (other) motivations such as threats/unpleasant consequences and promises/good consequences, cf:
   a. We need your help very much.
   b. If you help us, we'll be able to accomplish some significant results.
   c. If you don't help us, we may have to fold up our operation.

   Here, I think quite clearly that (a) outranks (b) and (c) which are given to support (a) and are ancillary to it.

   If, however, we say:
   a. Please help us this month.
   b. Our need is great and urgent.

   just as clearly (a) outranks (b) which is ancillary to (a).

10. The failure to specify ZPG's precise aims and the means proposed to accomplish them leaves the reader who has received no previous ZPG mailings wondering. Will zero population growth be accomplished by extensive use of birth control and sterilization, reducing teen-age pregnancies through a resurgence of continence in this segment of the population, or by extensive use of abortion?

References

Ballard, D. Lee, Robert J. Conrad, and R.E. Longacre

1971a "The deep and surface grammar of interclausal relations." *Foundations of Language*. 7.70-118.

1971b "More on the deep and surface grammar of interclausal relations." *Language Data*. Asian-Pacific Series, No. 1. Ukarumpa (Papua New Guinea): Summer Institute of Linguistics.

de Beaugrande, R., and W. Dressler

1981 *An Introduction to Textlinguistics*. London: Longmans.

Beekman, J., J. Callow, and M. Kopesec

1981 *The Semantic Structure of Written Communication* (private circulation).

Barnard, Myra Lou and Jannette Forster

1968 The Dibabawon Texts in *Discourse, Paragraph, and Sentence Structure in Selected Philippine Languages*, volume III. Final Report Contract No. 0-8-062838-0391. Washington: Office of Education, Institute of International Studies, 269-301.

Dijk, T.A. van

1977 *Text and Context: Explorations in the Semantics and Pragmatics of Discourse*. London: Longman.

1980 *Macrostructures: An Interdisciplinary Study of Global Structures in Discourse, Interaction, and Cognition*. Hillsdale, NJ: Lawrence Erlbaum Associates.

Fuller, Daniel P.
1959 *The Inductive Method of Bible Study*. 3rd edition. Pasadena: Fuller Theological Seminary.

Grimes, J.E.
1975 *The Thread of Discourse*. The Hague: Mouton.

Hoey, Michael
1983 *On the Surface of Discourse*. London: George Allen & Unwin.

Labov, Willam and David Fanshel
1977 *Therapeutic Discourse: Psychotherapy as Conversation*. New York: Academic Press.

Longacre, R.E.
1970 "Sentence structure as a statement calculus." *Language* 46.783-815.

1976 *An Anatomy of Speech Notions*. Lisse: Peter de Ridder Press.

1979 "The paragraph as a grammatical unit." In T. Givón (ed.), *Discourse and Syntax*. New York: Academic Press, 115-134.

1980 "An apparatus for the identification of paragraph types." *Notes on Linguistics*. 15.5-23. Dallas: Summer Institute of Linguistics.

1983a "Exhortation and mitigation in the Greek text of the First Epistle of John." *Selected Technical Articles Related to Translation* 9. Dallas: Summer Institute of Linguistics.

1983b *The Grammar of Discourse*. New York: Plenum Press.

1985 "Sentences as combinations of clauses." In Timothy Shopen (ed.), *Language Typology and Syntactic Description:Complex Constructions*. Cambridge: Cambridge University Press, 235-286.

1989a *Joseph, a Story of Divine Providence*. Winona Lake: Eisenbrauns.

1989b "Two Hypotheses regarding text generation and text analysis." *Discourse Processes* 12.413-460.

Matthiesen, Christian and Sandra A. Thompson.
1989 "The structure of discourse and 'subordination'." In John Haiman and Sandra A. Thompson (eds.), *Clause Combining in Grammar and Discourse*. Amsterdam/ Philadelphia: John Benjamins.

Mann, W.C. and S.A. Thompson
1987 *Rhetorical Structure Theory: A Theory of Text Organization*. Marina del Rey: University of Southern California, Information Sciences Institute. To appear in Livia Polanyi, ed. *Discourse Structures*.

Mann, W.C. and S.A. Thompson
1987 "Rhetorical Structure Theory: toward a functional theory of text organization." *Text* 8:3.243-281.

Thompson, Sandra and Robert E. Longacre
1985 "Adverbial clauses". In Timothy Shopen (ed.), *Language Typology and Syntactic Description: Complex Constructions*. Cambridge: Cambridge University Press.

The Notion of Unspecific versus Specific as one Way of Analysing the Information of a Fund-Raising Letter*

Eugene Winter
University of Birmingham

Analysing the Letter

In analysing the letter, we will be considering the 22 sentences from Segment 4 to Segment 23 and from Segment 28 to Segment 29. We take the letter head logo, Zero Population Growth, as the long-term Solution to be desired for. The date is crucial to the reality of the letter. What exists at one date may no longer exist at a later date. To this extent the 'truth' of the letter is perishable. For the purposes of the analysis, we play the part of intended American readers of a letter written by Susan Weber.

We consider the categories which we are going to use to analyse the letter in three parts, with the analysis of the letter as the fourth part.

PART 1: 1. INTRODUCTION TO METALANGUAGE NOUNS

PART 2: THE STRUCTURE OF DISCOURSE
2. The Unit of Written Sentence
3. Question Criteria
4. The notion of Clause Relations

---

*I am indebted to Michael Hoey and Hieng-Hong Lau for detailed discussions of this paper. Thanks are also due to Jose Luiz Meurer for his helpful suggestions. Not least, I should thank Sandra Thompson and William Mann for Jolting me into action with their criticisms of my original paper.

We begin with the notion of metalanguage nouns.

PART 1: 1. INTRODUCTION TO METALANGUAGE

In our present inadequate state of knowledge, an ideal linguistic analysis is one whose use of categories enhances our understanding of a sentence in the text in its immediate context of adjoining sentences. Taking all grammar of the clause for granted, and using only what grammar we will need, we are going to use a framework of Questions and Clause Relations for the limited purpose of discussing the linguistic relation between *UNSPECIFIC* and *SPECIFIC* elements which bind the meaning *inside* and *outside* the grammatical boundary of the sentence. In our discussion of this basic text relation (Winter 1977:78), we will limit it to unspecific open class of subject matter and closed class nouns which affect the meaning of clauses or sentences.

To do so, we are going to discuss the reference of nouns, using terms from Halliday and Hasan 1976 and showing where we depart from their terms. One difference is that we are concerned with reference to adjoining clauses from a clause-relational point of view; that is, we are concerned with the nature of information signalled by certain nouns for their unique clauses and sentences. Another difference is that, for us, anaphoric or cataphoric reference are simply *directions* from which inherently unspecific nouns are made specific. We treat *unspecificness* as the basic text organiser, noting that both open-class and closed-class nouns can be inherently unspecific.

To explain these differences, let us take such nouns as *results*, *idea*, *response* and *reaction* as found in two of its crucial sentences in Segment 7 below. Of the four, the nouns *idea*, *response* and *reaction* have endophoric reference and the remaining noun *results* is exophoric. Endophoric reference means either anaphoric or cataphoric reference; that is, reference within the letter itself. Exophoric means reference outside the letter.

> SEGMENT 7: When we released the *results* of ZPG's 1985 Urban Stress Test, we had no *idea* we'd get such an overwhelming *response*. Media and public *reaction* has been nothing short of incredible!

The four nouns cited here are candidates for the *metalanguage of the clause*. These are nouns which "talk about" the nature of the clause or sentence as a message in the text itself, and consequently do not refer to concrete things in the outside world; it is our language about our unique clauses and sentences. As usual, Bolinger (1980:27) has anticipated this property of nouns: "..words that point, affirm, deny, conjoin, and relate, words that tell how other words are to be understood." Out of context, only one of the four nouns is made specific *inside* the grammatical boundary of its sentence. Instead of saying that the noun *idea* has immediate cataphoric reference, we say that it is specified as zero noun clause:" (that) we'd get such an overwhelming response" and that its unspecificness has been completed.

Similarly, instead of saying that the nouns *response* and *reaction* have anaphoric and cataphoric reference respectively, we note that their unspecific meaning binds their host sentences directly to immediately adjoining sentences. Simplifying the connections, the noun *response*, signalled by the deictic *such*, is made explicit by the lexical choices of the preceding three sentences of Segments 4 to 6, and the noun *reaction* by the lexical choices of the following two sentences of Segments 9 and 10. Thus, we see Segments 7 and 8 connecting the meaning of the three sentences which *precede* them to the meaning of the two sentences which *follow* them.

Like the nouns *idea* and *results*, the two nouns *response* and *reaction* are inherently *unspecific*, and their function is to *interpret* or classify the open class lexical choices of clauses which make them specific. Without the clauses making them specific within adjoining sentences, these nouns are almost meaningless labels for information. Only the plural noun *the results* is not made specific as clause in the letter. Instead of dismissing this as exophoric reference, we note that the plural noun signals itself being made specific by much more than one clause or sentence. Either this is assumed knowledge of the reader, or it is an indication to the reader as to what kind of information to look for in sentences outside the letter.

Two important terms for discussing how the unspecific noun is made specific are: *specific by identity* (where the item is named or identified by pre- or postmodifiers), and *specific by clause*. Specific by clause means that the noun, in addition to being identified , is specified by clause as well. Thus, in 'The problem of dealing with criminals is that they are largely anti-social rebels', the postmodifier 'of dealing with criminals' identifies the problem, the that-clause which follows provides specifics by clause.

Significantly for the purposes of this letter, one noun, the plural noun *results* which is identified as *the results of ZPG's 1985 Urban Stress Test* is not directly made specific by clause within the letter, though is it connected indirectly to other identified plural unspecific nouns which belong to the same larger report, on which presumably the "top news story" was based: *conditions in our cities*, *problems*, *population-linked pressures*, *population-linked stresses*, and *consequences*. These nouns, though identified by pre- and postmodifiers, are also not made specific by clause in the letter. As plural nouns they signal specification by two or more clauses at the very least in the larger report that the letter assumes a knowledge of. We ought also to note that 'specific by clause', may in individual cases be a linguistic understatement for two or many more sentences.

A defining characteristic of two of the above unspecific nouns is that they must be made specific by *two* clauses or members. In the nouns cited above, they are: *consequences* and *results*. These are nouns of the *Clause Relations* (Vocabulary 3, Winter 1974/1977) In Example 1, the noun *the result* explains this point of two clauses supplying its specifics:

> EXAMPLE 1: In some places there was no rain at all. *The result* was the same — the farmers lost their always precarious crops of maize, and the herdsmen saw their cattle die in thousands. N.S 128

We can show that *the result* is being made specific both by the preceding clause and by the coordinated clauses which follow the dash sign. We can put the preceding clause into a what-question which asks that the noun *the result* be specified in the reply: *What* was *the result* of *there being no rain at all in some places?*" Only the clauses beginning with: 'the farmers lost their always precarious crops of maize etc.' can be the answer. We could also show that the two clauses specify *result* by rewriting the second sentence replacing the complement *the same* by the subordinator 'that'. (I have already explained this principle in Winter 1977:75/76)

A very crude formula for writing a *precis* of the larger report would be as follows: Find the metalanguage nouns which *classify* the open class unspecific nouns of the *subject matter* (e.g. results,, problems and consequences). Using your discretion, take out as much of their *specifics by clause* as you can, and use their significant unspecific nouns to represent the specifics of subject matter, taking care you give sufficient *identification* of the unspecifics of subject matter. Adding other associated unspecific nouns to the above list, we have a rough precis of the contents of the larger report:

Segment 9: "..we had blown the whistle on *conditions in their cities*."

Segment 10: "..concerned citizens want to know *what* they *can do* to hold local officials accountable for tackling *population-related problems that threaten public health and well-being*."

Segment 11: "...ZPG's 1985 Urban Stress Test is the first survey of *how population-linked pressures affect* U.S. cities."

Segment 18: "..Activists need materials to warn community leaders about emerging *population-linked stresses* before they reach *crisis stage*."

Segment 19: "..national government continues to ignore *consequences of uncontrolled population* growth." (Note *growth* as another unspecific)

Segment 20: "..*decisions* ..by local official.. could dramatically affect the *quality of our lives*. (Note Evaluation)

Segment 21: "...elected officials and the American public *need the population-stress data* revealed by our study.

Note how the noun *population* is a key identifier in compound words for four of the unspecific nouns here. From this list, the reader knows what kind of information to look for outside the letter. For a very different way of reducing a larger text to its topic essentials (possibly by non-arbitrary automatic means), see Hoey (in press) for a proposal about the systematic repetition of the sentence.

PART 2: THE STRUCTURE OF THE DISCOURSE

2. The Unit of Written Sentence

In this section, we consider the sentence as our primary unit of analysis and the fact of paragraphing, and how it can affect the meanings of the sentences in their relations with adjoining sentences. We start with the observation that, for the purposes of analysing the sentences in this letter, the orthographic boundaries of capital letter and fullstop coincide conveniently with the grammar of sentence; that is, all the sentences in the 13 paragraphs are independent clause. This accounts for Segment 4 to Segment 23, followed by Segments 28 and 29 as the Post Script. As we shall see, the punctuation and the typography is particularly interesting in this letter as a way of focussing on particular clause relations. Paragraphing is a particularly helpful in showing the intended significant sentence breaks where the text has to be read out aloud.

For example, in the relation between Segment 14 and Segment l5, Segment 14 is a *Evaluation* of need which predicts the statement of *Reason* which follows in Segment l5: *why* do you urgently need our help to use it well?"

> (13) The Urban Stress Test translates complex, technical data into an easy-to-use *action tool* for concerned citizens, elected officials and opinion leaders. (14) But to use it well, we urgently need your *help*.
>
> (15) *Our small staff is being swamped with requests for more information and our modest resources are being stretched to the limit.*

Segment l4 is loosely coordinated as surprising by *But* as the second sentence in a paragraph which describes the ease with which the Urban Stress Test can be used. The use of the coordinator *But* implies a denial of the expected complacency that such a successful test does not need our help. As part of the meaning of this paragraph, the statement of its usefulness and the need for help is seen as semantically belonging closely together. The paragraphing break between Segment 14 and 15 emphasises the meaning of Segment 15 which is presented as sole sentence in a new paragraph marked off from the rest. This focusses upon the two-clause coordination of *Reason*. There is further emphasis on this sentence by underlining. These emphases stress the dual role of Segment 15 in two interpretations. The first is as Reason, the second interpretation placed upon Segment 15 is that of an evaluated Situation which implies the Problem of understaffing and modest resources for disseminating the Test.

Following this last paragraph, we have Segment 16 and 17 in their own paragraph, now back to the normal indentation of the letter. As with Segment 14, we have another Evaluation, this time of Segment 15. It predicts the *Reason* in Segment 17: "*Why* is our support *now* so critical?"

> (16) Your support now is critical. (17) *ZPG's 1985 Urban Stress Test* may be our best opportunity ever to get the population message heard.

The adverb *now* in Segment 16 implies that our support was not critical before the events of Segment 15. As Reason for our support, Segment 17 is also a speculative Evaluation of *ZPG's 1985 Urban Stress Test* as 'may be our *best* opportunity ever to get the population message heard'. In contrast with the similar relation between Segment 14 and 15, the relation between Segment 16 and 17 is presented in their own paragraph, this time focussing upon the meaning of the two members, Evaluation and Reason, as semantically belonging closely together. Note the stressing of the subject *ZPG* etc here by underlining.

Similar considerations apply to the rest of the paragraphing. In advertising, which we will take up below, there is a marked tendency for the advertiser to use paragraphs in this way, especially using one paragraph alone for purpose of emphasising the meaning of a sentence.

3. Question Criteria

In this section, we consider the most obvious of all means of analysis. This is the use of questions because of their power of specifying replies. Question criteria should be regarded as a primitive tool of analysis. The reader might ask: If it is primitive, why use it at all? If we define information as being composed simply of Questions (asking for information) and Answers (giving information) and, further, if we assume that all sentences we see in a text can be answers to specific questions which we the readers might ask of the writer, then it is a useful exercise to examine what questions can be rationalised from the sentences the author wrote. Certainly, our search is on written sentences; certainly there can be criticisms of this as a tool of analysis, on the grounds that, after all, the writer did not use questions and answers here, and certainly we will be bringing more to the text than is actually justified by the choice of words, etc. in the text. But the point of interest is to see how we might go about inventing questions which fit compatibly into the context of the adjoining sentences. If our invented question makes more sense of the particular connection between two sentences or clauses, then this question may be thought of as representing its informational role in the text.

The use of questions as representing meaning was advocated by Anna Granville Hatcher as long ago as 1956, and has since been used by myself, (Winter 1968 and elsewhere), Widdowson (1978), Gray (1977), Edmondson (1981), and others, particularly those who have continued the development of my studies of clause relations, Hoey (1983) and Jordan (1984).

One of the chief weaknesses of inventing questions is that we may sometimes not understand the subject matter of the text, so that inventing questions for it may require considerable effort at understanding what the writer has written in his or her sentence. To this danger, we can add a further one: the difficulty of determining the writer's intention. Sometimes we will have to show what assumptions (preambles) we perceive to account for the sentence we find. These assumptions may at best be good guesses about what the writer intended to communicate.

Nevertheless, when investigating the meaning of items in context, questions should be our first line of defence. Questions at least are familiar instruments of communication to both student and teacher alike, where the various theories of sentence relations are not. The question of a semantic framework between sentences and clauses follows next.

4. The Notion of Clause Relations as Framework

In this section, we have to face the fact that there have been many proponents of sentence relations and ask ourselves where do we have to go next? As readers of this book, you will by now have worked through several kinds of propositional analysis, of which R.S.T (Rhetorical Structure Theory) appears to be one of the easiest approaches for neophyte students to follow. I called my semantic propositions between sentences and clauses 'Clause Relations'(Winter 1968, 1971, 1974, 1977, 1979, 1982 and 1986). Parallel approaches in the late 1960's, the 1970's and 1980's were Beekman & Callow (1974), Robert Longacre (1968) (1974) and (1979), Hoey (1979) and (1983), Jordan (1978) and (1984), Mann and Thompson 1987, and finally, Thompson and Mann 1987. The point here is that all of these approaches were largely intuited analyses of the relations between sentences according to a limited set of predetermineed propositions, of which propositional calculus is an obvious model.

The early criticisms, criticisms which are still being made for all such analyses, centred on the main weakness of our clause relational approaches. This was that we were accused of including far more in our analyses than was said in the texts, our criteria notwithstanding; and we were criticised for using a particular clause relation if only because it was compatible with meaning of the sentence as intuited by the analyst rather than the intended reader. These criticisms are being met by research into all aspects of explicit connection for the clause and sentence. Fries (1982:50-64) in a study of the role of repetition in interpreting a text, concludes: "..while a propositional analysis may be necessary to describe the meanings of a text it is not sufficient, for it does not provide a means of comparing the messages of the text. Such an understanding is, I believe, essential to understanding texts."

It should be self-evident that, as proponents of the idea of a finite set of clause relations, we should consider seriously what items there are in the clause which signal particular clause relational meanings. Obvious connectors which are compatible with clause relational meaning are *conjuncts* (Quirk et al 1972:520), *subordinators* and *coordinators* which are subject to the same singular diffuseness of meaning which covers the two sentences or clauses of a relation just as the idealised proposition (clause relation) does.

Taking *conjuncts* as the most natural items to signal the meanings of particular clause relations, we won't get far with the letter because it has only one, the paired contrastive correlative conjuncts *At first...Now* between Segments 9 and 10. Here they serve to mark a contrast between the situation pertaining at two times. This contrast in turn serves as a Basis for the Evaluation in Segments 7 and 8.

Taking subordinators of the Adverbial kind, there are only three: the *when*-clause of Segment 7 signals a time relation prior to the Situation reported in these segments.

The *before*-clause in Segment 18 is a signal of the undesirable Situation for emerging population-stresses to reach, and the *even though*-clause in

Segment 19 concedes as known the "fact" that the Government "continues to ignore the consequences of uncontrolled population growth" and its main clause denies the conclusion which would otherwise be made: that ZPG can do nothing. All three subordinators are important connections in the letter.

If we rely on the above connections by conjunct and subordinator, we are not going to get too far in analysing the letter, and must look to other features of connection that might help in recognising clause relational cues in the sentence. An insight into such cues might be provided by considering those *lexical items* which can in some way paraphrase the meanings of conjuncts and subordinators. These lexical items are what I have called Vocabulary 3 (Winter 1975/6), as a third way of connecting clauses after the subordinators as Vocabulary 1, and conjuncts as Vocabulary 2.

Vocabulary 3 has the grammar of lexical items, namely that of nouns, verbs and adjectives. For instance, the noun *example* has the definite article *the* and the premodifying adjective *classical* in the sentence:

> EXAMPLE 2: The Wall Street Crash of 1929 was *the classical example* of a loss of investor confidence.

Examples of Vocabulary 3 in the letter are the nouns *results* and the verb *affect* in Segment 11 and the noun *consequences* in Segment 19. These are very important to the message status of the letter, but they are merely part of a larger Metalanguage vocabulary whose cohesive feature is that of connecting the *unspecific* to the *specific*. We will return this kind of connection when we consider *Unspecific* as fundamental connective in Part 3 below. In the meantime we must consider what particular clause relations might be useful for analysing our letter.

In Thompson and Mann: (1987:3), the writers note that: "The collection of particular relations is not taken as fixed, but is open to modification and additions. Although it is an open list, it appears to be very stable for most uses of text. It appears to be culturally specific." However, for the purposes of trying out their model, they must use the set of 15 relations they propose for their analysis, and to that extent it is practically fixed.

There is no point in attempting to justify the range of relations for any discourse or text model in such a short text as the letter here. Let us look at Clause Relations in principle by considering what a clause relation means. For the purpose of the definition, I shall conflate the notion of sentence and clause in clause, so that Clause Relations also means Sentence Relations. It now follows:

> "A Clause Relation is the shared cognitive process whereby we interpret the meaning of a clause or a group of clauses in the light of their adjoining clause or group of clauses. Where the clauses are independent, we can speak of 'sentence relations'." (Winter 1986:91; See also Hoey 1983:19)

As we are speaking of a shared cognitive process for the meaning of clause, it implies that there must be a limit to the number we can share. I see the limit as something like the limit to the number of subordinators or conjuncts which we have in English. (We can group subordinators and conjuncts according to their typical clause relations, Winter 1977:22-3) The point at issue here is that when any two sentences are put together for the purpose of communicating a message and make sense to the decoder, they do so because they are compatible in meaning with our consensus of expected meanings between sentences.

5. Clause Relations for a Fund-Raising Letter

For the purpose of analysing the letter, I am going to ignore discussing the primary detail of the Clause Relations which I have described elsewhere. I am going to introduce the clause relation structures which I find most useful to describe the grouping of sentences from Segment 4 to Segment 10 as I see the whole appeal of the letter centering around this grouping of sentences. We need what I call the the larger clause relation of *Situation* and *Evaluation* in which *Evaluation* can predict *Basis/Reason*, and a Logical Sequence Relation in which *Imperative* can predict *Basis/Reason*. An explanation now follows of *Situation* and *Evaluation*, a basic text structure (also called a *larger clause relation*: a larger clause relation is one whose binary members can consist of further membership of clause relations).

In Winter (1982:190-2) and particularly in Winter (1986:96-102), I claimed that *Situation* and *Evaluation* represented one of *two* basic text structures, the other being *Hypothetical* and *Real* in which Hypothetical (represented by the adjective *hypothetical*) is Hypothetical Situation, and Real (represented by the adjective *real* as in the question: "what is his *real* reason?") is Evaluation of likely reality. (In investigating clause relations, I follow the practice of taking a characteristic lexical item to represent its relation.) We do not need Hypothetical and Real for this letter, and will focus on *Situation* and *Evaluation*. We can represent these two members by their unspecific nouns *situation* and *evaluation*.

If we think of Situation and Evaluation as basic message structure or *carrier*, a message structure which may contain all other clause relations, then it is easier to grasp what is meant by its *two* members. The first member, *Situation*, is what do you *know*, the second member, *Evaluation*, is what do you *think* about what you know, or how you do *interpret* what you know? The second member is important because it can predict a *basis* or *justification* (reason) for your interpretation. I see interpretation as the key element in the message, the subjective side, the reception of which may depend very much on the basis or reason offered as its objective counterpart.

More specifically, we can state the three elements of Situation and Evaluation for the listener who might ask the following questions from us: Having had X identified for us (What are you talking about?), we ask you: "what is the Situation/circumstances/set-up for X?" The question for the next member is: "What do you think about the Situation for X?" How do you see/interpret/view the Situation for X? or What is your Evaluation/assessment/comment on the Situation for X? An answer to this last question raises the question: "How do you *know* (you are correct in your assessment)?" What *makes* you says that? *Why* are you saying that? What *reasons* or *grounds* have you got for saying that?

Adapting all this to the letter, we take the first seven sentences from Segment 4 to Segment 10 which we represent below. As we noted earlier, the paragraphing is interesting. The 3 sentences of Situation are focussed on as one whole, being placed in their own paragraph. The same kind of focus applies to the 2 sentences of the Evaluation, but the clause relation of Matching Contrast (Winter 1974) between the two sentences of the Basis of Evaluation is emphasised by appearing *separately* as their own paragraphs. (Matching Contrast is what I have called Comparative Denial: what is true of X is not true of Y (in respect of Z feature)) As noted earlier, this relation is signalled by the paired correlative conjuncts *At first..Now*.

SITUATION: Segments 4 to 6

(4) At 7:00 a.m. on October 25, our phones started to ring. (5) Calls jammed our switchboard all day. (6) Staffers stayed late into the night, answering questions and talking with reporters from newspapers, radio stations, wire services and TV stations in every part of the country.

EVALUATION (*OF SITUATION*): Segments 7 and 8

(7) When we released the results of ZPG's 1985 Urban Stress Test, we had no idea we'd get such an overwhelming response. (8) Media and public reaction has been nothing short of incredible.

BASIS (*OF EVALUATION*): Segments 9 and 10

(9) *At first*, the deluge of calls came mostly from reporters eager to tell the public about Urban Stress Test results and from outraged public officials who were furious that we had "blown the whistle" on conditions in their cities.

(10) *Now* we are hearing from concerned citizens in all parts of the country who want to know what they can do to hold local officials accountable for tackling population-related problems that threaten public health and well-being.

Addressing the questions to Susan Weber, Executive Director:

"*What* was the *situation* you found at ZPG Headquarters (following the recent release of the results of ZPG's 1985 Urban Stress Test): *How* did the release of the results actually *affect* you all at ZPG?"

= Segments 4 to 6.

"What do you *think* of the *response* (when you released the results of ZPG's 1985 Urban Stress Test)?

= Segments 7 and 8.

"*What, in fact*, was so overwhelming about the *response*, and *what* is it about media and public *reaction* that *makes it* nothing short of incredible?"

= Segments 9 and 10 in turn.

For the moment, this level of detail of discussion of the above grouping of sentences will suffice for illustrating *Situation* and *Evaluation*. We have already discussed the Evaluation Segments 7 and 8 in some detail when we considered the immediate contextual role of the unspecific nouns *response* and *reaction* as belonging to the same metalanguage as the Vocabulary 3 item *results* here.

I see the whole of the letter as built around two Situations for ZPG: the first is the favourable Situation arising out of the release of ZPG's results, the second is the unfavourable Situation in which the ZPG organisation finds itself to exploit the results (Segment 15). At this point the genre of the letter enters into our consideration, a professional fund-raising approach. As a fund-raiser, Susan Weber has to describe the problems and solutions for safeguarding ZPG's existence in a manner which will persuade new readers to provide funds.

The very broad analysis above is a poor reflection of the other information that the letter conveys about the background to the results of ZPG's 1985 Urban Stress Test. We will get some idea of what is meant by information when we discuss candidates for the metalanguage below. In addition to the nouns *results*, *reaction*, and *response*, other unspecific nouns which classify the information of its identificatory specifics of the subject matter of the letter are: action, choices, conditions, consequences, contribution, coverage, criteria, data, decisions, growth, help, (local) level, limit, materials, message, pressures, problems, quality of life, questions, stage, stresses, support and test.

Of these, '(taking) action, consequences, contribution, criterion, decisions, message, problems, questions, stage and test' are metalanguage nouns of the clause. 'Data, criteria, help, (local) level, limit and support can also be regarded as metalanguage if seen as related to the notion of message, not as specifying the clause, but as specifying the meaning of the phrase. 'Information, quality of life, limit, resources and story' are unspecifics whose specifics are understood.

I see Susan Weber combining the task of asking for funds and other assistance with informing the reader of ZPG's *results* as a necessary part of the asking for funds. We have already seen how she uses the *unspecific plural nouns*: results, conditions, problems, pressures, stresses, consequences in the precis outlined on page 4 as describing the significant specifics by two or more clauses of information to be found outside the letter.

6. Linguistic Features of Advertising

In this section we take up the question of how the genre of the letter affects its choice of linguistic resources, and consequently affect how we analyse and understand its meaning and purpose. I see this letter as an advertisement selling the idea of ZPG to potential contributors of cash and other assistance. It is similar to consumer advertising because it has linguistic features we expect of advertising.

We can describe advertising as the language of unmitigated self-praise (favourable self-evaluation) of the product or service which is presented as the *unique solution* to the customer's *problem*. In the letter, this uniqueness is expressed directly by the adjective *first* in 'the nation's *first* survey of how population-linked pressures affect U.S. cities'. A characteristic way of signalling this uniqueness is in the repetition of the unique brandname e.g. ZPG's 1985 Urban Stress Test.

Any criticism (unfavourable evaluation) of the product or service is *not* of the product itself but of rival brands or of the consequences of *not* using or buying the product or service. As self-praise, consider especially the tone of 'seven day's wonder' that accompanies the description of the *Situation* at ZPG's headquarters which is described from Segment 4 to Segment 10, and the sustained favourable Evaluation that accompanies the mention of the results of ZPG's 1985 Urban Stress Test throughout the letter, and the Stress Test itself as below:

EVALUATIONS OF THE RECEPTION OF THE RESULTS:

Note that S.7 is preceded by the furious activity of reporters asking questions, which in itself implies a favourable evaluation of the *results*.

S.7 We had *no idea* we'd get such an *overwhelming* response (to the results)

S.8 Media and public reaction (to the results) has been *nothing short of incredible*

S.9 "*deluge* of calls" and "reporters *eager* to tell the public about Urban Stress Test results"

S.9 "outraged public officials who were *furious* that we had *blown the whistle* etc." Evaluation by public officials implying effective results.

S.28 "*top* news story by hundreds of newspapers and TV stations from coast to coast"

S.29 "this *remarkable* media coverage" (of the results)

EVALUATIONS OF THE TEST ITSELF:

Note how Segment 10 leads with an Evaluation of the significance of what the test measures:

S.10 "population-related *problems* that *threaten* public health and well-being"

S.11 "created after months of *persistent* and *exhaustive* research" and "the nation's *first* survey.."

S.13 "an *easy-to-use* action tool.." Note the advertising rhetoric of making things *easy* for the consumer as in the compound word *easy-to-use* (Leech 1966:59)

S.17 "our *best* opportunity *ever* to get the population message heard"
Perhaps one of the most obvious linguistic features that distinguishes advertising from other genres is the high degree of repetition of the highly unique *brandname* (Leech 1966:21). Consider how often the brandname, *ZPG*'s *1985 Urban Stress Test*, is repeated in one form or another. We find that out of 22 sentences, there are 12 overt repetitions after the covert repetitions of Segments 5 and 6:

Note how the mention of the results of ZPG's 1985 Urban Stress Test is covert within Segments 5 and 6.

Segment 7: the results of ZPG's 1985 Urban Stress Test
Segment 9: Urban Stress Test results
Segment 11: ZPG's 1985 Urban Stress Test
Segment 12: It
Segment 13: The Urban Stress Test
Segment 14: It
Segment 17: ZPG's 1985 Urban Stress Test
Segment 18: ZPG (ambiguous for staffers?)
Segment 21: our study = ZPG Test
Segment 23: The Urban Stress Test
it
Segment 28: the results of ZPG's 1985 Urban Stress Test

In ordinary communication, such as letters to friends, such detailed unique lexical repetitions would be off-putting. In commonsense terms, when we as readers try to follow the meanings of sentences, we go by the sustained repetition of topic. What the strategy of the advertiser does is force us to link the brandname with the topic, and sometimes the brandname dominates the topic as does *ZPG's 1985 Urban Stress Test* here. There is no escape for the reader, and it is this kind of extra repetition of items within the individual noun phrases, together with the high degree of favourable self-evaluation that alerts the reader to its 'selling approach'.

Returning to self-evaluation, we also note that in addition to Evaluation Clause, advertising presents its product or service as *unique* while making the unmarked use of favourable *Evaluatory additions* (How good is it?) at every conceivable syntactic opportunity in any clause relation whatever. This is the difference in selling a car between: "I've got a car to sell you" and "I've got a *truly fantastic* car to sell you!" Compare this with the similar difference for Segment 11 between A and B below:

> A: ZPG's 1985 Urban Stress Test is the survey of how population-linked pressures affect U.S. cities.
>
> B: ZPG's 1985 Urban Stress Test, *created after months of persistent and exhaustive research*, is the *nation's first* survey of how population-linked pressures affect U.S. cities.

We observe the influence of Evaluatory additions within a sentence whose underlying semantics is an answer to the question: "What exactly *is* ZPG's 1985 Urban Stress Test?" This would simply be a question for *identification*. Things of course are not as simple as this. Using the clause relation of Evaluation (What do you think of the car?) has its price in credibility: it predicts Basis/Reason for the Evaluation (What is it about the car which makes you say the car is truly fantastic? What's so fantastic about it?). If persuasion is to succeed, everything depends on (a) who is doing the evaluating, and (b) the quality of Basis/Reasons as information to support the Evaluation. Obviously the Basis/Reason must also be favourable: To a gadget fiend: I've got a truly fantastic car to sell you; it has every gadget known to man." A list of gadgets then follows, providing the specifics for the unspecific 'every gadget known to man'.

We have already noted how the clause relation of Evaluation predicts Basis/Reason. Now we have to explain what is meant by prediction with *Imperative Clause*. A noticeable characteristic which Advertising Imperative Clauses share with the electioneering manifestoes of politics is that its main imperative may end the text e.g "Vote for Mrs Thatcher!" Here the whole of the text which precedes the Imperative provides the Basis/Reason for voting. The letter is also constructed like this. A brief description of the contextual role of Imperative Clause now follows.

7. The Discourse Role of the Imperative Clause

In this section, we are faced with one of the obvious features of a fund-raising letter, how the Imperative Clause is worded when the writer comes down to asking for hard cash. We ought to note that there is a strong resistance by the decoder for the writer to overcome, especially where the decoder has strong feelings about carrying out the imperative. We are, so to speak, linguistically free human beings; we have a very strong tendency to why-question any imperative before we will carry it out. The requirement runs something like this: if an Imperative Clause is *not* preceded by a Reason, then we predict that the next clause(s) will provide the Reason. If, however, the Reason *does* precede the Imperative Clause, then it is linguistically complete, and no longer predicts the Reason-to-come:

EXAMPLE OF IMPERATIVE < REASON:
Speaker A: "Get out of here fast!"
Speaker B: "<*Why* should we get out of here fast?"
Speaker A: "The ceiling's going to fall in on us!"
EXAMPLE OF REASON > IMPERATIVE:
Speaker A: "The ceiling's going to fall in on us!"
Speaker B: "What should we do about it now?>"
Speaker A: "Get out of here fast!"

The important linguistic point about prediction of Basis/Reason by an Imperative Clause, where the Basis/Reason does not precede it, is *not* that the fulfilment of the prediction is obligatory but rather that the target of the imperative knows when it is not being fulfilled. The Imperative "Get out of here fast!" is a very likely single clause sentence which implies compelling reasons for obeying the Imperative. A terrified tone of voice would suffice for a Reason which could come later.

In wording the desired Imperative, the writer has the age-old psychological problem of confronting the reader with a direct or immediate demand for hard cash. It would be like starting an electioneering pamphlet with 'Vote for Margaret Thatcher' with the rest of the pamphlet providing Reasons for doing so. Like voting, giving cash requires a hard decision. She solves the problem by a successive mention of the unspecifics *your help*, *your support*, *your contribution*, to "Please make a *special contribution*" in Segment 22, preceding the final point of actually asking for hard cash in Segment 23.

PART 3: THE UNSPECIFIC AND ITS DEMAND FOR SPECIFIC LEADING TO METALANGUAGE NOUNS

8.1 Introduction

In Part 3, we consider how metalanguage nouns fit into the greater notion of unspecific versus specific, what problems there still are in identifying metalanguage nouns, how the problems are being tackled. To answer these questions, we need to understand how the notion of a metalanguage arose out of research into elements which might signal the meaning of clause relations. In particular, we will concentrate on examining the notion of Vocabulary 3 whose deficiencies of analysis and application raised the question of a larger metalanguage to which Vocabulary 3 belongs. We need to consider how Vocabulary 3 was first described in 1975 and 1977 as *lexical items* which signal the meanings of clause relations, and the subsequent discoveries leading to the claim that there is a larger metalanguage which also signals what unique clauses can mean, and which can be clearly isolated for research purposes by syntactic means.

8.2 The Background to Vocabulary 3

The idea for a clause relational metalanguage arose out of my early work on the suspect features of sentences which I thought might contribute to realising the meaning of a particular clause relation. At this time, I was concerned with describing what conjoined *two or more* clauses or sentences. In my research into systematic repetition as the most fundamental connector of the clause, I had noted that certain so-called lexical items played a role in connecting clauses rather like that of adverbial subordination (*as*, *after*, *because*, *if*, *since*, *when*, *where*, *whereas*, *why* etc and sentence connection by such conjuncts as *accordingly*, *consequently*, *however*, *nevertheless*, *so*, *therefore*, *thus*, *yet* etc.

Pursuing the idea that Vocabulary 3 must be a limited Vocabulary like Vocabulary 1 (subordinators) and Vocabulary 2 (conjuncts), I decided to let the numbers stand for the degree of established knowledge with Vocabulary 1 as the most known and Vocabulary 3 as the least known. Since it is less well established than Vocabulary 1 and 2, I shall give a fuller list of some of its nouns:

achievement, addition, affirmation, antonomy, basis, cause, comparison, concession, consequence, contradiction, correction, denial, difference, distinction, error, exception, explanation, fact, feature, form, general, grounds, hypothesis, instance, justification, kind, manner, match, means, object, opposite, particulars, point, reason, reality, repetition, requirement, resemblance, result, reversal, sameness, similarity, specification, statement, synonomy, truth, uniqueness, way etc.

I decided to state my case for regarding these lexical items as closed-set in meaning by setting out five criteria of closed-set meaning:

Criterion 1: This is the notion of a closed set vocabulary There are no completely new items created over very long periods, but old ones can be supplemented in such informal creations as: "There are no *strings attached*" for "There are no *conditions* or *requirements* to be met".

Criterion 2: They can supplement questions, and so narrow down the reply in terms of a particular clause relation e.g. The noun *purpose* and the verb *serve* in "What *purpose* would his visit serve?" As has become apparent subsequently, this criterion also applies to the larger metalanguage outside clause relation paraphrase. Metalanguage items specify particulars of information to be supplied in phrase, clause or sentence e.g. the noun *procedure* in the question: "What *procedure* should we adopt for the procession?"

Criterion 3: They can paraphrase conjunctions or connection. This is especially noticeable with many subordinators and conjuncts eg. The paraphrasing of the subordinator *because* in *A* by the noun *reason* in *B*:

> *A* The committee dismissed him *because* he was completely unreliable in the crises they faced.
> *B* The committee's *reason* for dismissing him was that he was completely unreliable in the crises they faced.

(Some Vocabulary 3 nouns fail this criterion. Other metalanguage nouns also fail it.)

Criterion 4: They can *anticipate* the clause relation which follows their sentence. The adjective *opposite* in 'opposite views' signals the contrast which is made specific by the next two sentences.

> We have *opposite* views of how to run an office. He keeps his office neat and bare; I inhabit mine.

The notion of *anticipation* was then an acknowledgment of their potential forward signalling properties; that is, their unspecifics could be followed by their clause relational specifics of at least two clauses in the next sentence(s). This makes them *cataphoric* as opposed to *anaphoric*.

(A vocabulary of Metalanguage nouns other than Vocabulary 3 also meets this criterion for the clause(s) or sentence(s) that makes them specific.)

Criterion 5: Their nouns have the *negative property* of failing to fit the grammar of simile framework which accepts open class nouns as "making sense".

In 1977, I had already noted that in addition to rejecting Vocabulary 3 nouns, there were problems with certain abstract nouns which would not fit the simile criterion such as the noun *arrangement* in "*It is like* an arrangement." Since then I have been slowly investigating the notion that Vocabulary 3 nouns belonged to a larger closed set vocabulary of our Metalanguage.

8.3 Updating Vocabulary 3

In this section, we note revisions to the above description in the light of further work on the vocabularies of connection. Since 1977, the significance of Criterion 2 and Criterion 4 has changed. Both Criterion 2 and Criterion 4 are now conflated as being part of the more fundamental linguistic phenomenon of *the inherent unspecific* power of a larger metalanguage which includes Vocabulary 3. In the use of questions of Criterion 2, the unspecificness of the metalanguage item is direct: *What problem* does he face with his classes?

In Criterion 4, the notion of *anticipation* of the coming clause relation is now seen simply as the case where the *unspecific* item precedes its *specific* lexical realisation. The then novel notion of anticipation is now replaced by the notion of seeking the *inherently unspecific item* in the sentence, and of asking whether its open class specifics have preceded it, or followed it, or have not been offered in the text itself. We will return to this decoding approach below.

The key research question now is just where does Vocabulary 3 fit into the larger metalanguage? If Vocabulary 3 covers meanings of how one clause relates to another what role does the remaining metalanguage play in the meaning of the text?

Earlier we noted a criticism of the clause relational approach which assigns a small set of propositions to account for all relations between sentences. This was the criticism that, in our intuition of what was an appropriate relation between sentences, we were accused of including far more in our analyses than was said in the text. In Winter 1974 and 1977, I noted that a defining feature of Vocabulary 3 nouns was that they "*said what the relation between two clauses was*". Since then, I became increasingly aware that Vocabulary 3, important though it was in Clause Relations also made explicit by subordinators and conjuncts, was merely part of a larger whole which I am calling the metalanguage. If Clause Relations is to be a really adequate way of accounting for sentences in texts, then all of the metalanguage items which "say" what an individual clause means has to be brought into it.

9.1 The Present Approach

The present work on these nouns is directly related to an interesting monograph by Gill Francis (1986) on what she calls *Anaphoric Nouns*, and most recently to an equally interesting monograph by Roz Ivanic (1989), who following Vendler 1968, calls them *Container Nouns*. These are the nouns which Halliday and Hasan (1976) call '*general nouns*' and Jordan (1986) calls '*generic nouns*'. Francis introduced a neat clarificatory point about her set of *Anaphoric Nouns*. She observed that their meanings could be regarded as *stereotypes*. In Winter 1977:86 I noted, following Schon (1963), that metalanguage items which include these nouns were '*fixed* or *central metaphors*' and that one of their significant linguistic properties was that they could not fit the *simile framework*. A semantic characteristic of many open-class nouns is that you can convert them into metaphors by placing them in the simile framework e.g. the metaphor of 'sin' as in Example 3:

EXAMPLE 3: The division of Germany *is* rather *like sin*. Everyone is against *it*; everyone thinks *it* is inevitable.

Notice the change of truth for the date of this example since 1966.

9.2 The Notion of Lexical Uniqueness

For the purpose of understanding the significance of the relation between *unspecific* and *specific* in this paper, you will need to understand what the effect of being unspecific is, and especially what relation it bears to the message structure of the letter. In the above example, the notion of *sin* presented as a metaphor, is unspecific, and would be *meaningless* except as potential subject matter if there were *no lexical realisation* to provide its specifics in the next clause or clauses. The two clauses which follow specify *how* the division of Germany is rather like sin, but *without them we have a sentence which does not communicate* because the metaphor sin is meaningless to us *without its specifics by clause*. In the full example above, we have the minimal *completion in a clause relation* because the unspecific 'like sin' has been specified, and in this case, explained as well.

The point is that the first sentence is almost meaningless because it is unspecific. For the unspecific to communicate, it must be made specific (in contexts where it is not known by the decoder) by the next sentence(s) to become *lexically unique*.

To become a *significant message*, it has to become lexically unique through the open-class specifics of its second sentence. In principle, this applies to the metalanguage, they are ways of classifying open class specifics, but do not in themselves constitute message structure. Consider the difficulty of guessing precisely what the nouns 'a tricky *situation*', and 'public *opinion* being *split*' mean in the following sentences:

EXAMPLE 4: Admittedly, the L.S.E authorities had to cope with *a tricky situation*.

EXAMPLE 5: Public *opinion is split*, too, over Article 587:

In Example 5, we have the open-class noun (public) *opinion* whose specifics by clause will be contrastive. Metalanguage Nouns derive their meaning from the choices of open-class specifics which *connect* them within or across sentence boundaries. This observation was made in Winter 1975 and 1977, for a restricted number of nouns, Vocabulary 3.

In Section 1, we noted that there were two *kinds* of *specificness* required to complete the meanings of the unspecific noun; this was *specific by identity*, and *specific by clause*. At the last resort, all specificness means open-class lexical choice. The term we will use for the making specific of the unspecific is *lexical realisation*.

We have already noted that the terms *anaphoric* and *cataphoric* suffice if only to indicate the *direction* of the lexical realisation by specifics for the unspecific. They are merely aspects of the *function* of inherently unspecific items in their connection with the words of adjoining clauses of the text. What we are concerned with here is the unspecific metalanguage noun in its function of being made specific by clause, irrespective of whether the specifics by clause has either preceded or followed it.

We ought also to note that the function of unspecificness applies equally to all open class nouns except that their completion by specifics applies across all clause relational boundaries. It is after all the unspecific open-class nouns which govern the unique subject matter of any text.

9.3 Investigating the Meaning of Noun

Since this article is about unspecific metalanguage nouns, we will need to discuss in more detail what is meant by unspecific, and what kinds of specific realisation they require to complete their contextual meanings. In this paper, we are concerned with two kinds of specific realisation. The first is specifics of *identity*, and the second is *specifics by clause*.

(1) *SPECIFICS OF IDENTITY*

Taking the unspecificness by identity first, any open class noun such as *man*, *cat*, *wife*, etc can be unspecific in a context. In "There's *a man* standing in our garden, the man can be specified as *the* man *next door* (*who* is he?); in "there's a cat climbing up our tree," a cat becomes *the neighour*'s cat (*whose cat* is it?); in "I was talking to somebody's *wife*," that wife can be specified as the wife *of the local magistrate* (*whose wife* is she?); and so on. The function of premodifiers (*neighbour*'s cat) and postmodifiers (the man *next door*) is to provide *immediate specifics of identity*. The point is that open-class nouns do not refer to the meanings of unique clauses.

What is clause-relational about specifics of identity is that is is a naming process; it names the actors, participants to the clause which will distinguish its unique clause from all others.

The requirement of the specifics of identity applies equally to all other kinds of noun. Take the unspecific open class noun *banking*, and modify it as the *problems* of *banking*". The question which this new noun phrase structure raises is: what particular parts of banking constitute the problems?

The answer to this question is controlled by the closed-class item *problems* which specifies not only the identities within *banking* but also determines the nature of *specifics* by *clause*. These specifics by clause will be compatible with the meaning of problem.

(2) *SPECIFICS BY CLAUSE*

What is not generally recognised is that a *relative clause* does *not* provide what I calling specifics by clause. It provides specifics, either of identity or evaluation of the noun head, and so can indirectly identify it. In Example 6 below, the noun *population-related problems* has postmodification with the relative *that*-clause.

> EXAMPLE 6: (10) Now we are hearing from concerned citizens in all parts of the country who want to know what they can do to hold local officials accountable for tackling population-related *problems that threaten public health and well-being*.

The plural noun *problems* is identified by its premodifier as 'population-related problems'. The relative clause *evaluates* the *problems* but does not provide specifics by clause of the meaning of *problem* itself. A strong hint of what its specifics by clause might be is provided by the identification and description of the Test in two segments that immediately follow. The other unrealised unspecific by clause which is carried over is the indirect question 'who want to know *what they can do*'.

This is new territory. We can provisionally distinguish by means of syntactic criteria between unspecifics of the metalanguage and other kinds of unspecifics. The distinguishing feature is in *how the two kinds of unspecific require specifics by clause*. As there is another difference within metalanguage itself, we will simply note what happens with *open-class unspecifics* as 'other kinds'(e.g. *conditions at home* below), before tackling the metalanguage itself.

(2.1) *SPECIFICS BY CLAUSE FOR OPEN-CLASS UNSPECIFICS*

In the Precis supplied on Page 4, there are three already identified open class nouns, *conditions in their cities*, *population-linked pressures*, and *population-linked stresses*. As plural unspecifics, the three plural nouns *conditions*, *pressures,* and *stresses*, can only be lexically realised by at least two or more clauses, but they do not control the form their clauses can take. They cannot be used to refer to the meaning of a clause or a clause relation, but may be made specific by the nouns of their own subject matter. The noun *conditions in their cities* is not the closed class *condition* of Vocabulary 3 (paraphrasable by if-clause, Criterion 3), but is the open class noun *condition* meaning health or well-being as in the EXAMPLE 7 where the unspecific *conditions* of the second sentence is specified by all the sentences that follow it as a list:

> EXAMPLE 7: His marriage was in tatters. *Conditions* at home were terrible. The house was in a shambles. His wife drank. The children screamed all day, and his mother-in-law had moved in to restore order.

This is not simply a case of *Elaboration*, but elaboration as part of the *Basis* for the *Evaluation* as 'terrible'. Unlike the metalanguage nouns, the noun *conditions* does *not refer directly* to *the meanings* of the *unique clauses* which follow or precede them. Notice too how the unspecific idiomatic 'marriage *in tatters*' has its specifics guided by the next unspecific '*conditions* at home'.

(2.2) *SPECIFICS BY CLAUSE FOR THE METALANGUAGE*

As noted earlier, we can divide the metalanguage into two kinds. The first are the directly clause-relational nouns such as the Vocabulary 3 nouns which require their specifics by *two unique clauses*; that is, they *classify* their clause relation *according to the lexical realisation made in both of its clauses* for their Vocabulary 3 noun. The second are the remaining metalanguage nouns which require their specifics by *one* clause or more unique clauses, but do not otherwise restrict the clause relations of the clause which make them specific.

Putting this difference between Vocabulary 3 nouns and their cousins, the nouns of the metalanguage, more simply: Vocabulary 3 specifies the lexical choice of *two clauses of their clause relation*; the metalanguage noun specifies the meaning of *one or more clauses* in *other clause relations*. The significance of this difference will become clearer below.

9.4 Syntactic Criteria for the Noun 'Problem'

Pride of place goes to Vendler 1968 who first used syntactic criteria to classify as 'Container Nouns' the nouns that fitted the slot of subject or complement in clauses of the pattern:

N is Noun Clause
Noun Clause is N

where Noun Clause is 'that-clause', 'to-clause' and 'wh-question clause' or a nominalisation, and N is Container Noun. In Winter 1982:65, I noted that Noun Clause like that-clause is where we "talk about a clause." The 'that-clause' is illustrated by Example 9 and the 'to-clause' by Example 10 below, where we consider the item *problem* as 'Container Noun'. To this syntactic criterion, we add another: noun clause in apposition to noun as illustrated by Example 8. There are other criteria such as Noun head postmodified by prep plus ing-clause e.g. 'various methods *of treating green fly infestation*'. In this construction, the postmodifying clause supplies both the identity and the specifying clause. These are described by Tim Johns as structures of complementation (in preparation). However, for the purpose of illustration, the above two criteria will suffice.

The noun *problem*, and its predicted partner *solution*, are nouns of the metalanguage which are also clause relational; they meet Criterion 2 and 4, but fail Criterion 3 given in Section 8.2. They are intimately connected with the larger clause relations of *Situation* and *Evaluation*. As noted earlier, these larger clause relations are carriers for all the remaining 'standard' clause relations. Their metalanguage property of signalling *the meaning of a clause as such* will now be illustrated by Examples 8, 9 and 10 respectively.

In Example 8 below, the noun *problem* is followed by a that-clause *in apposition* which provides *its specifics by clause* within its own noun phrase structure:

> EXAMPLE 8: The P.W.R is the world-wide "standard" reactor. While this brings advantages on knowhow, it also brings the *problem that* the U.K. may be influenced by the effects of foreign experience, particularly safety standards. In recent years, these have become notably more stringent, especially in the U.S. and West Germany. N.S.885

Contrast this kind of postmodification by relative clause with that described for Example 6 above, where the relative clause is not providing specifics by clause for the meaning of the noun *problem*.

In Example 9 below, the noun phrase *A further problem* is subject of a special clause pattern *S P C*, where *P* is the verb *be*, and *C* is a *that-clause*. This that-clause complement provides the *specifics by clause for its subject*, (a further) *problem*.

> EXAMPLE 9: Although the reserves are vast, this supply will also run out in the not-too-distant future. *A further problem is that* although methane is an excellent fuel, chemically it resists the changes needed to make it into a useful feedstock. N.S. 167

In Example 10 below, we have the noun *The problem* in the same special clause structure as Example 9 but instead of a *that-clause*, we have a *to-infinitive clause*:

> EXAMPLE 10: The threat to warships in the 1980s and beyond lies above all in the accurately guided anti-ship missile launched beyond the range of the ship's weapons. *The problem* is *to defeat the missile*, irrespective of its terminal velocity and trajectory. N.S 119

In all of the above examples, the specification by clause of the noun *problem* is provided by a subordinate clause within its own sentence. Contrast this, with the specification by *sentences* which follow its sentence in Example 11 below:

In Example 11, in the idiomatic verb "*face a..problem*", the premodifying adjective *dual* signals that *two* separate sets of specifics by clause follow. These are confirmed by the correlative conjuncts *First* and *Second* respectively:

> EXAMPLE 11: The (French) defence establishment is faced with *a dual problem. First* it needs to boost its efforts to get wind of military-useful technology at an early stage. *Second*, it is trying to persuade researchers that it is a good thing to work for the military. Apart from any moral objections, researchers are scared that they will be deprived of fame and fortune by military secrecy. N.S.126

10.1 A Statement about Research

The present approach to the metalanguage owes much of its progress and methodology to the work of Timothy F Johns of the Department of English, University of Birmingham, who has developed an efficient program of linguistic retrieval for the study of English texts, using micro-computers. This program produces concordances for any word or phrase which enable us to study the collocations to the left or to the right of the item being studied. Timothy Johns uses his "*Conc*" program to produce teaching material (T.F Johns 1988). His approach to teaching is bold and unorthodox. He gets the computer to produce various items in collocational context selected by himself (for instance, the modal verb *should*) and gets the students (foreign learners) to discover for themselves the various the meanings of *should* from its various contexts. Both teacher and student learns new facts of the language and the knowledge is cumulative.

In advising me how to use my personal computer for linguistic retrieval, Tim Johns has given me some guidance based on his own observations in teaching of the importance of structures of complementation (the *that*-clauses cited for the noun *problem* above) for the kind of noun vocabulary that accompanies them. I must now turn the linguistic significance of the slots for nouns which are connected to such that-clauses.

A large group of metalanguage nouns can be isolated syntactically in databases by searching for, and provisionally listing, the nouns found in the special clause S P C, and in apposition to that-clause. Only nouns of this kind fit this position where they *classify the meaning of a their clause* as such. From a database of roughly 1.3 million words, I have isolated the following nouns against each syntactic position. Roz Ivanic 1989:8 tentatively notes a vocabulary of 40 container nouns. As this work is also in its tentative stage, I will simplify description of the largest vocabulary by only taking every 5th noun. The number found in my database is shown in brackets.

(I) *Nouns in apposition* (57): acknowledgement, announcement, assessment, calculations, complaint, demonstration, fact, finding, idea, knowledge, point, probability, sign, theory, view.

It is interesting that, in a study of subject and complementation in the clause, Huddleston 1971:197 notes a vocabulary of 42 nouns in a science corpus of 135,000 words. Of these, the noun *fact* accounted for 51 out of 148 occurrences. Notice also that the increase from 42 per .135 million to 57 per 1.3 million words is a mere 15 items.

(2a) *S P C clause where C is that-clause (145):* advantage, argument, assumption, belief, cause, clue, consensus, corrollary, dilemma, downside, episode, exception, explanation, fact, feature, gist, idea, impression, irony, lesson, judgment, news, peculiarity, possibility, question, reality, result, role, situation, snag, thesis, tragedy, verdict, view, word, worry.

It should be obvious that some of these nouns have verbal origins e.g. 'argument' as in 'he argued that..'

(2b) *S P C clause where C is a to-infinitive clause (82):* achievement, answer, brief, contribution, decision, effect, hope, intention, method, need, objective, plan, policy, proposal, remedy, response, role, solution, strategy, tactic, task, test, way.

Of the 82 items here, 34 occur only in this frame e.g. aim, approach, brief, contribution, goal, job, purpose, reaction, stage, step, strategy, task, test, way etc. The Complement slot in (2) above can also be filled by the other non-finite clause *ing* as in "My problem is getting to work by bus" but I am ignoring examples of these.

10.2 Implications for the Description of Clause (Sentence) Relations

We have already noted that the linguistic feature which distinguishes between metalanguage nouns, which includes Vocabulary 3, and open class unspecific nouns (e.g. conditions in our cities) is that metalanguage nouns signal the meanings of clauses or sentences, whereas open class unspecifics do not refer to the unique meanings of the clauses where the specification of their nouns can be found. Within the metalanguage, Vocabulary 3 may signal what the meaning of two clauses of their clause relation is; the remaining metalanguage nouns signal what the meaning of a clause is; that is, they both classify *what kind of information their clause(s) present*. In other words, we could regard both kinds of metalanguage noun as universals of meaning for the clause to cut across all subject matter.

There are other candidates for metalanguage nouns which remain to be investigated. These are the nouns that are to be made specific by phrase of some kind. An example is the noun 'level' in 'local level' where the adjective local determines what is to be chosen for the head 'level': 'local officials', 'elected officials and the American public.' This metalanguage would be universals by phrase.

Until Clause Relations, as previously described, and similar schemes take fully into account the role of the metalanguage in classifying information of the clause and phrase, such schemes will never adequately describe the information content of the sentences in the text. The 'notionally complete' set of semantic propositions or clause relations are only part of crucial universals which are still being explored. What we need to find out is how the metalanguage operates as part of clause relational meaning and as an independent system of its own.

After the systematic repetition of the clause and its topic, the relation of unspecific and specific is the most fundamental connection between clauses and sentence. Indeed, we could theorize that the unspecific open-class nouns govern the subject matter which their lexical realisation by specifics produces, but that the metalanguage, whether of Vocabulary 3 or other metalanguage, may otherwise govern whatever lexical realisation is required for the subject matter.

Put differently, the point about the metalanguage combining with the unspecifics of subject matter is that it dominates the choice of specifics of, and hence the universal information content, of any informative text. I hope I have shown that this is true of the examination of the letter which follows next.

PART 4: EXAMINATION OF THE LETTER IN THE FRAMEWORK OF QUESTIONS AND ANSWERS

We are now going to examine the nouns in each sentence and consider their connective relation as *unspecifics* to *their specifics*. From the way the letter is written we have to assume that the reader does not know the details of the release of the results of ZPG's 1985 Urban Stress Test. Thus in Segment 6, he would have no idea of what the reporters were asking the staffers questions about. We are kept guessing until Segment 7.

All questions which are not answered in the letter are marked (RQ) meaning *read about it* outside the letter. These questions are intended to represent unspecific nouns (shown in bold type) whose *specifics by clause* is to be found by the reader outside the letter. A significant number of the questions have *preambles* (Harper 1987). A preamble is the linguistic situation on which a question is based.

Preambles are undoubtedly controversial, but the actual questions which the sentences answer can equally be seen to be those which the writer *chooses to answer for the reader*. This will explain the oddness of detail to some of the questions e.g. Q.11, 12, 15, 16, 21 and 23.

The candidates for the metalanguage are: questions, results, test, response, reaction, blown the whistle, problems, criteria, requests, information, resources, support, message, contribution, (taking) action, consequences, stage, level, decisions, data, study, and story.

TOPIC CHUNK 1: THE RELEASE OF THE RESULTS OF ZPG'S 1985 URBAN STRESS TEST

The questions are indented to distinguish them from their answers, and are numbered from 1 to 23 and shown thus: Q.12. The answers are shown with their Segment numbers. Notes are shown in brackets both with questions and with answers. The proposed sentence (clause) relations are shown as headings over each answer.

SEGMENTS 4 TO 6: SITUATION AT ZPG AFTER RELEASE OF ZPG's RESULTS

"Q1. What was the Situation for you at ZPG (immediately after you released the results of ZPG's 1985 Urban Stress Test? How did the release of these results affect you (Susan Weber and the staffers) at ZPG office at that time?"

SEQUENCE OF EVENTS FOR SITUATION

(4) At 7:00 a.m. on October 25, our phones started to ring.

"Q.2 What happened with the phones after that?"

(5) *Calls* jammed our switchboard all day.

"Q.3 How did your staffers cope with these *calls*, and who were they from and what were they about?"

(6) Staffers stayed late into the night, answering *questions* and *talking* with reporters from newspapers, radio stations, wire services and TV stations in every part of the country.

"Q4. What were you answering *questions* and *talking* with reporters about? (This is answered as part of 7, which is answering a question for Evaluation of Situation)

(Note that the bracketed after-clause does not occur in the letter and so the noun *calls*, the noun *questions*, and the verb *talk* are used unspecifically. The last two, questions *about what*? and talking *about what*? are both specified in the when-clause in 7 by the same noun phrase 'the *results* of ZPG's 1985 Urban Stress Test.' The important point for the letter is that the noun *results*, though identified as 'ZPG's 1985 Urban Stress Test', is unspecific by clause)

SEGMENT 7 TO 8 = *EVALUATION OF SITUATION*

"Q.5 What did you think the *response* would be like, when you released the *results* of ZPG's 1985 Urban Stress Test.?"

(7) When we released the *results* of ZPG's 1985 Urban Stress Test, we had no idea we'd get such an overwhelming *response* (from reporters whom we were talking with etc) (to these results)

"(RQ.1) What are these *results* of ZPG's 1985 Urban Stress Test?

"Q.6 That was the Media you were talking about. What has the *reaction* (to the release of these results) been like from the public as well as the media?"

(8) Media and public *reaction* has been nothing short of incredible.

SEGMENTS 9 TO 10: *BASIS BY SPECIFICS FOR EVALUATION*

"Q.7 What in fact was so overwhelming about the *response*, and what was it about the media and public *reaction* that has been nothing short of incredible? How is their reaction to be seen in the nature of their calls?" (This is a question demanding the *specifics by clause* for *response* and *reaction*)

BASIS. FIRST MEMBER OF CONTRAST

(9) *At first*, the deluge of calls came mostly from reporters eager to tell the public about Urban Stress Test results and from outraged public officials who were furious that we had "*blown the whistle*" on *conditions* in their cities.

(RQ.2) "What *conditions* in their cities?"

(Note the idiomatic "blown the whistle". We could regard all idiomatic phrases as potential metalanguage)

"Q.8 That was only the Media reaction. You have unexpectedly included public officials in with the Media. That was a very strong reaction from them. What about the public who are on the opposite side to public officials. What was their reaction like?

BASIS: SECOND MEMBER OF CONTRAST

(10) *Now* we are hearing from concerned citizens in all parts of the country who want to know *what they can do* to hold local officials accountable for tackling population-related *problems* that threaten public health and well-being.

(RQ.3) "What *population problems* that threaten public health etc?"

TOPIC CHUNK 2: DESCRIPTION OF THE URBAN STRESS TEST

"Q.9 What is it about ZPG's 1985 Urban Stress Test that has created such interest? What has it got to do with population-related problems that threaten public health etc? How can you hold local officials accountable for tackling this? What *is* the ZPG Urban Stress Test? How did it come into existence?

IDENTIFICATION OF TEST

(11) ZPG's 1985 Urban Stress Test, created after months of persistent and exhaustive research, is the nation's first survey of *how* population-linked *pressures affect* U.S cities.

(R.Q4) "What population-linked pressures, and how do they affect U.S. cities?"

"Q.10 Describe the Test. What is it designed to do? How does it measure population-linked pressures that affect U.S. cities? What criteria does it use?

DESCRIPTION OF TEST

(12) It ranks 184 urban areas on 11 different criteria ranging from crowding and birth rates to air quality and toxic wastes.

"Q.11 What does the test do with all this data?"

FUNCTION OF TEST

(13) The Urban Stress Test translates complex, technical *data* into an easy-to-use action tool for concerned citizens, elected officials and opinion leaders.

TOPIC CHUNK 3: HELP IN USING THE TEST

"Q.12 That's great, but *what* do you *need* (in order) to use it well?"

CONCESSIVE EVALUATION OF NEED

(14) But to use it well, we urgently need your *help*.

(This sentence itself is *purpose* = to use it well, and *achievement of purpose* = we urgently need your help)

"Q.13A What kind of help?" (Not answered here, and becomes *your support* in 16, *your contribution* in 18, *a special contribution* in 22 and finally cash in 23)

"Q.13B *Why* do you (at ZPG) urgently need our *help* to use it well?

STATEMENT OF REASON AND STATEMENT OF NEW SITUATION

(15) Our small staff is being swamped with *requests* for more *information* and our modest *resources* are being stretched to the limit. (The relation between the coordinated clauses connected as 'expected' by the coordinator *and* is Matching Compatibility where the second member answers the question: *and what else is true of* ZPG's circumstances?" Note also *requests for information* "about ZPG")

"Q.14 Things look bad at ZPG for your use of the test. You said you needed our help urgently. Just how urgently do you need it?

EVALUATION OF NEW SITUATION CONFIRMING EVALUATION OF SEGMENT 14

(16) Your *support* now is critical.

(Note that this not so much as the restatement of the sentence in Segment 14 as a reformulation of your *help* as your *support*, with its new meaning for *help*. Segment 16 should be seen as *Confirmation* for what is true in Segment 14)

"Q.15 Why is our support for ZPG now so critical?"

REASON FOR EVALUATION AND ALSO EVALUATION

(17) ZPG's 1985 Urban Stress Test may be our best opportunity ever to get *the population message* heard.

TOPIC CHUNK 4: HOW OUR CONTRIBUTION ENABLES ZPG TO GET THE TEST TO THE RIGHT PEOPLE

"Q.16 What *can* you do with our contribution? How *could* our contribution *enable* ZPG to get the population message heard? What do you mean by population message?

POSSIBILITY OF ENABLEMENT FOR ZPG

(18) With your *contribution*, ZPG can arm our growing network of local activists with the *materials* they need to warn community leaders about emerging population-linked *stresses* before they reach the *crisis stage*.

(Note that your *support* has been reformulated as your *contribution*, the meaning now clearly changes to giving money. Note also that *population message* has been specified as *the materials* they need to warn etc.)

"R.Q6 What emerging population-linked stresses and what crisis stage?" (Note that *crisis stage* is an Evaluation of Situation to be avoided)

"Q.17 Can your local activists *really* take any action on your own *when* our national government continues to ignore the consequence of uncontrolled population growth? (The subordination by the circumstantial *when* presents its clause as taken for granted as true. The yes/no-question with the insertion of the adverbial *really* implies the answer *no you can't*)

CONFIRMING POSSIBILITY OF ENABLEMENT FOR ZPG
(19) (Of course we can!) Even though our national government continues to ignore the *consequences* of uncontrolled population *growth*, we can *act* to *take* positive *action* at the *local level*.
(The sentence which follows 'Of course we can' provides Basis for Affirmation as possible. In the letter the main clause is underlined to emphasise it as a positive conclusion to be drawn from negative basis: we can act positively *in spite of* the government's inaction. See Thompson and Mann 1987 for Concessive)

"R.Q7 what *consequences* of uncontrolled population growth?"

"Q.18 How can you take positive action at local level? What kind of positive *action* and what do you mean by *local level*?

THE INSTRUMENT OF ENABLEMENT
(20) Every day *decisions* are being made by *local officials* in our communities that could drastically affect the quality of our lives.
(Note *decisions* is only evaluated but not specified until S.21 where it is reformulated as *choices in planning for people*)

"Q.19 You haven't said what positive action you can take at local level. Instead, you talk about vital decisions made by local officials. What has this got to do with your taking positive action with them?

THE ACHIEVEMENT OF INSTRUMENT
(21) To make sound *choices* in planning for people, both elected officials and the American public need the population-stress *data* revealed by our study.

TOPIC CHUNK 5: MAKING THE CONTRIBUTION SPECIFIC

"Q.20. You have said how our contribution could enable you ultimately to influence the decisions of elected officials by using the Stress Test to guide them in sound choices on which to base their decision-making. We have got the picture now. *What should we do about* the contribution itself? *What kind of contribution* do you want us to make?"

IMPERATIVE: INSTRUMENT RESTATED
(22) Please *make a special contribution* to Zero Population Growth today.
(Notice how compatibly Segment 15 would fit here as a Reason for carrying out the imperative:

(15) Our small staff is being swamped with *requests* for more *information* and our modest *resources* are being stretched to the limit)

"Q.21 What do you mean by a special contribution here? What *will* be done with what we give, does it matter how much we give?

ACCOMPLISHMENT OF INSTRUMENT

(23) Whatever you give — $25, $50, $100 or as much as you can — will be used immediately to put to use the Urban Stress Test in the hands of *those* who need it most.

Note how the verb *need* is strategically repeated throughout the letter from Segment 14 to Segment 23:

S.14 But to usc it wcll, wc *nccd* your hclp

S.19 ..the materials they *need* to warn community leaders about the emerging *population-linked stresses* before they reach the *crisis stage*.

S.21 ...both elected officials and the American public *need* the *population-stress data* revealed by our study.

S.23 ....to put the Urban Stress Test in the hands of those who *need* it most)

TOPIC CHUNK 6: POSTSCRIPT ABOUT TOPICS 1 AND 4

(Segment 28 can be seen as a strengthening of the favourable Situation 1 as part of the reasons for the Imperative Clause and its specifics of Segments 22 and 23. Similarly, the implied Imperative in Segment 29: We hope you'll help us... can be seen to follow as consequence of Segment 28)

"Q.22 Earlier you talked about the great enthusiasm of the various kinds of people who called you about the results of ZPG's 1985 Urban Stress Test. You did not mention the actual news coverage itself. How was it treated as a news story?

(28) P.S. The *results* of ZPG's 1985 Urban Stress Test reported as a top news *story* by hundreds of newspapers and TV and radio stations from coast to coast.

"RQ.8 *What* was the *story*?"

"Q.23 So what other kind of help do you need in addition to funds?

(29) I hope you'll help us monitor this remarkable media coverage by completing the enclosed reply form.

References

Beekman, John, and John Callow
1974 *Translating the Word of God*. Michigan: Zondervan Press

Bolinger, D.
1980 *Language the Loaded Weapon*. London: Longman.

Edmondson, W.
1981 *Spoken Discourse: A Model for Analysis*, London: Longman.

Francis, Gill
1986 *Anaphoric Nouns*. (Discourse Analysis Monograph 11). English Language Research, University of Birmingham.

Fries, P.
1982 "On repetition and interpretation." *Forum Linguisticum* 8/1.

Gray, B.
1977 "From discourse to dialog." *Journal of Pragmatics* 1/3.

Halliday, Michael, and Ruquiya Hasan
1976 *Cohesion in English*. London: Longmans.

Harper, Nicholas
1987 "A Study of replacement and associated phenomena in questions and their answers." PhD Dissertation, Hatfield Polytechnic.

Hoey, Michael
1979 *Signalling in Discourse*. (Discourse Monographs *No. 6*). University of Birmingham: English Language Research.

1983 *On the Surface of Discourse*. London: George Allen & Unwin.

1988 "Discourse Properties of the Criminal Statute." In: Charles Walter (ed), *Computing Power and Language*, 69-88, New York: Quorum, Greenwood Press.

1991 *Patterns of Lexis in Text*. Oxford: Oxford University Press.

Huddleston, R.D.
1971 *The Sentence in Written English*. Cambridge University Press.

Ivanic, Roz
1989 "Nouns in search of a context." *Lancaster Papers in Linguistics* 59.1-23.

Johns, Timothy F.
1988 "Whence and whither concordancing?" In: Bongaert et al. (ed.). *Computer Applications in Language Learning,* Dordrecht: Foris.

(forthcoming) *Microconcordancing: A Manual of Data-Driven Learning*. Oxford University Press.

(forthcoming) "*Should* you be persuaded."

Jordan, Michael

1978 The principal semantics of the nominals 'this' and 'that' in contemporary English writing." Ph.D Dissertation, Hatfield Polytechnic.

1980 "Short texts to explain Problem-Solution — and vice versa." *Instructional Science* 9.221-252, Amsterdam: Elsevier Scientific Publishing Co.

1981 "Structure, meaning and information signals of some very short texts." *Lacus Forum*, 410-417.

1984 *Rhetoric of Everyday English Texts*. London and New York: George Allen & Unwin.

1985 "Some advances in clause-relational theory." In: Benson and W.S. Greaves (eds). *Systemic Functional Approaches to Discourse*. Ablex, 282-301.

Longacre, Robert E.

1970 "Sentence structure as statement calculus." *Language*, 46:4.783-815.

1972 *Hierarchy and Universality of Discourse Constituents in New Guinea Languages*. Washington D.C.: Georgetown University Press.

1979 "The paragraph as a grammatical unit." *Syntax and Semantics*, Vol 12: Discourse and Syntax New York: Academic Press. 115-134.

Mann, William C., and Sandra A. Thompson

1986 "Relational processes in discourse." *Discourse Processes* 9:1.57-90.

1987 "Rhetorical structure theory: Theory of text organisation." In: Livia Polanyi (ed.) *Discourse Structure*. Ablex.

1988 "Rhetorical structure theory: Towards a functional theory of text organisation."

Quirk, R. et al.

1972 *A Contemporary Grammar of English*. London: Longman.

Schon, Donald

1963 *Displacement of Concepts*. London: Tavistock Publications.

Thompson, Sandra, and William C. Mann

1987 "A discourse view of concession in written english." *Language and Topics: Essays in Honour of M.A.K Halliday*, Amsterdam/Philadelephia: John Benjamins.

Vendler, Z.

1968 *Ajectives and Nominalizations*. The Hague: Mouton.

Widdowson, H.

1978 *Teaching Language as Communication*. Oxford: University Press.

Winter Eugene O.

1968 "Anaphoric Sentence Adjuncts" Part 3 of "*Sentence and Clause in Scientific English*." Osti Report 5030, R.D. Huddleston, R.A. Hudson, E.O. Winter, and A. Henrici. University College London.

1970 "Connection in science material: A proposition about the semantics of clause relations." C.I.L.T Reports and Papers 7: "*Science and Technology as a Second Language*," (London Centre for Information on Language Teaching and Research), 41-52.

1974 "Replacement as a fundamental function of repetition: A study of its principal features in the clause relations of contemporary English." Ph.D. Dissertation, University of London.

1975 "A look at the role of certain words in information structure." *Informatics 3*, Proceedings Aslib Co-ordinate Indexing Group conference, April 1975, 85-97.

1977 "A clause-relational approach to English texts." *Instructional Science* 6:1.1-93.

1979 "Replacement as a fundamental function of the sentence in context." *Forum Linguisticum*, 4:2.95-133.

1982 *Towards a Contextual Grammar of English*. London and New York: George Allen & Unwin.

1986 "Clause relations as information structure: Two basic text structures." In: M. Coulthard (ed.) *Talking about Text*. Discourse Analysis Monograph 13, University of Birmingham, 88-108.

(forthcoming) *Meaning and the Metalanguage of English*. London: Hyman and Unwin.

An Integrated Three-Pronged Analysis of a Fund-Raising Letter

Michael P. Jordan
Queen's University at Kingston, Ontario, Canada

This chapter introduces and justifies the need for an integrated analysis by three methods: clause relations, lexical connection, and problem-solution structures. Each method is explained and used as the basis for analyzing the text, and the integrated results are presented on a detailed diagram of connections supplemented by textual discussion, a schedule of lexical connections, a semantic field of connection, and a list of typical clause relations. Reflections on the analysis and the three methods are provided.

1. Introduction

1.1 *General Background and Approach*

The analytical technique outlined and exemplified in this chapter integrates three analytical techniques into a single detailed analysis, shown principally by Figure 1 and supported by Figures 2 and 3 and the detailed explanations provided. The three methods used are: a clause-relational analysis, a lexical/continuity explanation, and a problem-solution approach.

The clause relational aspects of the total analysis, the heart of the work presented here, is a complex amalgam of several approaches to complex text analysis, notably the "clause relations" of Winter (1968, 1971, 1974, 1977, 1982), Hoey (1979, 1983, 1986 (with Winter)), Dea (1977) and myself (1978, 1985c/e, 1988a, 1989a); the "relational propositions" of Beekman

(1970a/b/c), J. Callow (1970a/b), K. Callow (1970), Blight (1970) and Beekman and Callow (1974); the calculus and speech notion systems of Longacre (1972, 1976, 1983); and the "rhetorical structure theory" of Mann and Thompson (1986, 1987, 1989). This central thrust is supplemented by a lexical/continuity analysis based on early work by Christophersen (1939) and Hawkins (1978) and my later developments (1981a, 1982a/b, 1984a, 1985a, 1985b, 1986). To complement these two methods of analysis, the more general problem-solution analysis integrated with them is based on work by Winter (1974), Hoey (1979, 1983a), and myself (1980, 1981b, 1984c, 1989b). More specific explanations of the principles and origins of the three methods are provided later in this chapter.

1.2 *Premises*

The overall premise of the three-pronged analysis used here is that we can determine a meaningful and very detailed analysis of the way the text works as language and communication in terms of three inter-related and overlapping systems:

(a) connections between statements identifiable as being one of a small set of semantic text relations (see Figure 4 for a proposed set), or as any of a large number (possibly infinite) of complex combinations of these relations;
(b) lexical continuity in both thematic and non-thematic positions, including the ways writer/speakers provide detail about the major topics in the text; and
(c) the problems, solutions and evaluations (with basis and assessment) involved in the thoughts, actions, aspirations and decisions discussed in the text.

Whether systems (a) and (c) can or should be regarded as a single system is problematical. Mann and Thompson (1986) identify "solutionhood" — though not "problemhood" — as just one of their relations, and I have discussed (1985f) the closeness of the problem-solution binary pair of relations with that of purpose-means (also known as the "instrument" relation). In both the Zero Population Growth text, and in many others, there are instances in which the problem-solution meanings appear very similar to the other semantic relations (of Basis, Effect, Manner, etc.). In other instances, however, problems (and their solutions and evaluations) appear to be different in nature than the defined closed set of relations. This remains unresolved.

A further premise of the approach used here is that we analyze the text from beginning to end rather than seeking to determine a central theme or proposition — perhaps later in the text — around which the text might rhetorically revolve. This start-to-finish analysis is ideal for lexical continuity, where only the occasional cataphoric reference leads to a slight complication. For the clause-relational aspect of the analysis, there are greater difficulties which are created by pre-subordination, clause dominant adjuncts (especially attitudinals such as *Hopefully*), and inner clause assessments (such as the hypothetical *may be*). Complications also occur when a statement is made and the reader/hearer does not know what it is in connection with until later in the text — the deliberate suspense created in some communications. In all these instances, the connections are shown in Figure 1 as going *backward* in the diagram (instead of the normal forward progression) to recognize nuclearity in a rather basic form. Mann and Thompson use a similar method in their use of arrows in rhetorical structure diagrams, and for them nuclearity is a more important principle for analysis.

1.3 *Organization of this Chapter*

The next part of this chapter (Section 2) explains the need for a system of analysis which goes beyond just the relations between clauses. Lexical continuity and problem-solution aspects are also shown to be essential parts of the system, and this analysis seeks to show the inter-dependence of these three methods in a full analysis of connections within the text.

As, however, the three methods of analysis used here can be viewed, at least initially, as separate systems, each is dealt with separately, in the order: clause relations (Section 3), lexical connections (Section 4), and problem-solution aspects (Section 5). Within each of these three major groups, there is discussion of first the theory, then the application to practical text analysis, and finally the analysis of the Zero Population Growth text as the central theme of this book.

The final part of this chapter (Section 6) provides discussion regarding the effect of integrating the three methods, the advantages of the overall approach adopted here, and some reflections on the analysis and the methods used.

2. The Need for an Integrated Approach

2.1 *Clause Connections*

It is generally understood that clauses and sentences are connected together by definable meanings (such as Solution, Enablement, Assessment, Time, Means, Purpose). This is shown by Beekman and Callow's example (1974:317):

1. (Christ) has now reconciled you (to God)
2. by means of dying physically — MEANS of 1.
3. in order that you will be holy — PURPOSE of 1.

That is, the first clause enters into a relationship of Means with the second (providing the means of reconciliation), and of Purpose with the third (providing the purpose of the reconciliation). Following both Beekman and Callow and also Healey (1965), the term "Means" is used here rather than the more usual "Instrument," as I feel it is a clearer indication of the relation, and is often signaled by the item "means."

2.2 *Clause and Lexical Connections*

We also know that texts exhibit cohesion between their parts by virtue of the interconnections of lexical meanings, as discussed, for example, by Halliday and Hasan (1976):

(1:1) Wash and core the six cooking apples. Put them into a fireproof dish.

Halliday and Hasan point out that the cohesive agency, or texture, is accomplished by the co-referentiality of the substitute item *them* and its referent *six cooking apples*.

But there must also be an element of textual cohesion in this example by virtue of the order of the instructions, and the clear possibility of the interposing question from the reader "What do I do next?". That is, there is an unsignaled relation of Time (Next) between the clauses as well as the lexical connection Halliday and Hasan identify. If this were not so, the example

(1) Wash and core six cooking apples. Preheat the oven to 350° F. (Philip Harben's Cooking Encyclopedia, Odhams. 1955:13)

would have no texture beyond the collocational connection (or regular co-occurrence; see, for example, Crystal and Davy, 1969 :56) between *cooking* and *oven*.

We must also recognize that co-referentiality is merely the means by which we can say something more about something already included in a text — and that information thus provided may also have a clause relational connection between the clause containing the original lexical item! Thus in the text:

(2) The variety of apples known as Bramley's Seedlings is generally regarded as being the most suitable for baking. This apple when baked turns to a light, fluffy, creamy mass. ibid.

we have to recognize the texture between the two sentences as having two components:

(a) the Detail about this type of apple communicated by means of the referent/substitute pair; and
(b) the reason (or Basis) for the view (or Assessment) expressed in the first clause.

Thus the second sentence has a relationship both with the nominal group as grammatical subject of the first sentence, and also with the whole of the first sentence:

The variety of apples known as Bramley's Seedlings

is generally regarded as being the most suitable for cooking.

DETAIL: *This apple* when baked turns to a light,
BASIS: fluffy, creamy mass.

In addition, we can recognize the words *when baked* as providing the Circumstances under which the remainder of the second sentence is true. This relation *within* the second sentence must also be accounted for in the final analysis, but it does not affect the argument being presented at this stage. Such complexities are discussed later in Section 3.7.

2.3 *Complex Mediating Questions*

The analysis for Example 2 shows that the second sentence simultaneously provides answers to two questions about two separate (and definable) parts of the previous text:

> "What can you tell me about Bramley's Seedlings?" and "What is the Basis/reason for the generally accepted view that Bramley's Seedlings are the most suitable for cooking?"

Conflated, these two questions, become the sort of complex question used by Winter (e.g. 1974, 1983) to explain complex clause relations:

> "Can you tell me something about Bramley's Seedlings that justifies the generally regarded view that they are the most suitable for cooking?"

Such an approach is in line with Beekman and Callow's comment that each proposition is related in some way to another proposition or to the theme being developed (1974:283), where "theme" is being used to mean topic of discussion. Clearly the two types of connection are not mutually exclusive. See Jordan 1978 for a detailed discussion of the more complex approach used here compared with the textual analysis provided in Halliday and Hasan 1976.

2.4 *The Problem-Solution Element*

The two systems of clause relations and lexical continuity are quite clearly related in actual language. It is therefore essential to integrate them in some way as part of an explanation of the textual connection. Less easily integrated are the problems and their solution and related evaluations.

In Example 2, however, we can recognize the earlier problem (the need for a suitable cooking apple), the solution (the selection of Bramley's Seedlings), and the evaluation by comparison (*most suitable*). This third element of the overall method of analysis described and used here provides a vital bridge between the more technically linguistic principles of clause relations and lexical continuity, and the more general concepts of rhetoric and document purpose. It also yields a deeper understanding of the meanings in the text, and provides meaningful insight into the aims, problems, desires, actions and thoughts of the writer and those described or alluded to in the text.

2.5 *Overall Analysis of the Text*

An overall general analysis of the ZPG letter is provided here to help to substantiate the need for an integrated approach to its analysis. It also provides the reader with an understanding of the areas of the document which rely more significantly than other parts on each of the three systems of analysis described here.

The purpose of the letter is to convince readers to send money to the ZPG organization to help them to overcome the major perceived problem of overpopulation. (Constant references to the United States indicate that the problem is being restricted to the United States.) Thus essentially we have a major problem, for which Zero Population Growth is the proposed solution, and the organization "Zero Population Growth" is seeking funds (a solution) to alleviate their problem of poor funding in their efforts to achieve their goal.

Thus rhetorically problems and solutions are of great importance in this text, and the writer explains the problems the organization has in meeting the need to provide better publicity for their publication. To convince readers that publication is worth the time and money distributing — as a step toward the ultimate goal of achieving ZPG — the text describes the publication and the effect they feel it will have when presented to various levels of government and the public. This means that, in addition to explaining the problems and possible solutions, the text also uses description extensively.

The main topics of discussion and description are the proposed solution Zero Population Growth (in the USA) and the organization called Zero Population Growth. These, with many other sub-topics (see Figures 1 and 2), are re-entered many times in many ways throughout the text to achieve the lexical connections. While lexical connection is an important aspect of the letter at all points in the text, it is the predominant form of connection through Segments 11-18, which essentially describes the Urban Stress Test and the complex problem-solution grouping of the need to communicate it, the problems of swamped staff, and the needed solution for more money to achieve the distribution. The relative simplicity of the text at this phase can be seen by the simplicity of analysis compared with the earlier and later parts of the text — see Figure 1.

In addition to problem-solution aspects and lexical connections, we find relations within and between clauses throughout the letter. These are particularly complex for Segments 4-10 and 20-23, and together the three forms of connection combine to produce a quite detailed explanation of the cohesion in the text.

3. Clause Relations

3.1 *Basic Theoretical Framework*

The approach adopted here for the analysis of the meanings within and between clauses is based initially on the quasi-diagrammatic form used by Beekman and Callow (1974), as shown in their example given earlier. The diagrammatic form used here, again illustrated earlier, provides a clear and direct way of indicating what the relationships are between without the need for numbering and cross-references. It also enables us to add other elements of lexical connection and problem-solution meanings to the diagram to show how the three systems interrelate in a total holistic analysis of text. (Both methods allow us to indicate that the first *two* clauses of Beekman and Callow's example form the initial part of the Purpose relation — which I feel is a more accurate interpretation of the text they use.)

While many linguists adopt the approach of using single words to denote the relationships between clauses and sentences, Winter (e.g. 1974, 1982) uses quite long sentences to indicate the relation. Winter bases his work on Hatcher's proposal (1956a) and analysis (1956b), in which she appeals to the question-and-answer technique in establishing the semantic connections between sentences. Gray (1977a/b) points out that well-formed texts answer questions raised or implied earlier in the text. Hoey (1983:28-29) discusses the use of a range of questions in terms of "broad" and "narrow" questions for the shorter and longer forms respectively. Earlier (1978) I discuss the implications of mediating questions between clauses in terms of: the total version (containing the full referent); the substitute version using substitute items *this* or *that* or a substitute clause (e.g. *"This is done by...*); and the abbreviated version using single item indicators (e.g. Purpose, Means). And both Edmondson (1981) and Widdowson (1978) have used questions to represent meaning between statements.

We are essentially saying the same thing, and there is clear recognition that the questions can be depicted in any form as long as we realize that the single-item notation (e.g. Agent, Purpose, Cause, Enablement) refers to a definable referent (the first part of the binary clause relation) and that it is incomplete in respect of tense and modality — which of course are included in the full question form. Both tense and modality are essential elements of the total semantic connection between the clauses, but they are not included in the diagram here (Figure 1) in the interest of simplification. No doubt simple codes could be added to each single-item indicator to include this information if the analyst requires it.

3.2 *Origins and Definition*

The origins of the study of clause relations can be traced to Sweet's analysis of the try-succeed binary pair (1891) and to inter-clause connections discussed by Jespersen (1914-49) and Poutsma (1926-29). Beardsley (1950) appears to have been the first to apply these relations to the organization of discourse, and Quirk's (1954) study of the concessive relation in Old English also had discourse implications. He defines the relation as:

> "Perhaps the most satisfactory statement to use as a working guide is that the concessive relation may be said to exist between parts of an utterance when one part is surprising in view of the other." (p.6)

A similar definition is given in Quirk et al 1972:

> "Concessive conjuncts signal the unexpected, surprising nature of what is being said in view of what was said before." (p.874)

Although the actual meaning of the concessive relation has since been questioned (see Jordan 1985e and Thompson and Mann 1986 and 1987, for example), Quirk clearly expresses the concept of relations existing between clauses and sentences. Winter (1974) defines the clause relation in the following manner:

> "A clause relation is how we understand a sentence or a group of sentences in an adjoining context of another sentence or group of sentences." (p.172A)

More recently Hoey and Winter (1986) adopt a very complex definition involving the cognitive process and the product from the points of view of the readers' interpretations and the writer's choices of lexis, grammar and intonation. For the purpose of this analysis (and I find for most purposes), a simple definition will suffice:

> "A clause relation is the meaning between two coherent stretches of text."

where "coherent" means any stretch of text which can be epitomized and/or talked about in some way in the text. This follows Beekman and Callow's (1974) point that relations occur between different levels of the discourse.

Thus a clause relation is a text semantic notion of binary connection between potentially *any* two parts of a text, whether they are clauses or sentences, or paragraphs — or even nominal groups or single words. This is a much broader concept of semantic text relation than has hitherto been envisaged, as it recognizes that there are many such relations within as well as between clauses and sentences (Jordan, 1989a), and that nominal-subjects can have such relationships with their predicates, that adverbs can have such relations with the remainder of the clause, etc. (Jordan 1990). Thus we must take the term "clause relation" as one of convenience only, and not allow the use of the term to obscure the reality of inter-strata connections in actual language.

In essence, the clause relation without tense and modality is indicated as:

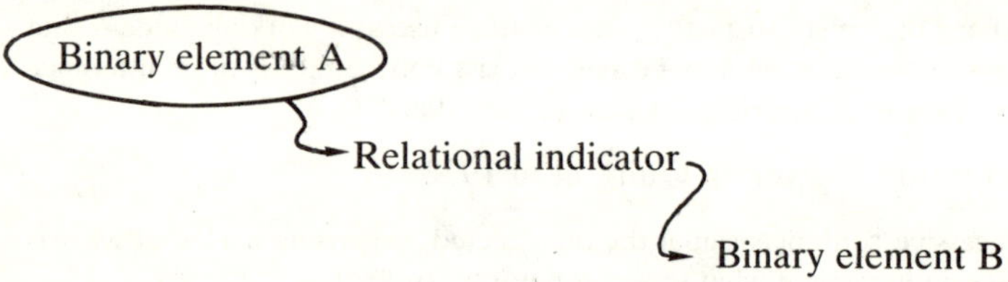

and it is necessary in the analysis to indicate these three elements clearly for each relation.

3.3 *Combinations of Relations*

We must not, of course, expect to find relations in real language coinciding exactly with such a crude model of textual semantics, and we must be prepared to use the different relations in combination to achieve an accurate analysis. In Segment 11 of the ZPG letter, for example, we must recognize *after* as indicating not only a subsequent Time relation with the preceding main clause, but also indicating the Cause of the information in that clause.

In an earlier analysis (1978), I identified three types of combination ("simultaneous," "joint" and "combined" relations) based partly on notions expressed by Greenbaum (1969) and Karlsen (1964) regarding the need to identify more than one relation between stretches of text. It has become apparent from later analyses (including this present one) that it may be naive to seek such a neat classification. There are so many possible types of combination in actual texts that the more sensible approach is to allow the diagram of the relations to indicate the combinations rather than attempting to classify them. However, certain typical clusters of relations (e.g. known information plus new relation in subordinate clause, comparison clusters, and defining detail clusters) are apparent in this text and in others. These are useful clusters for the analyst to consider in understanding a text.

3.4 *Depicting Combinations in Practice*

As mentioned earlier, the term "clause relations" is actually a misnomer, as the system of analysis applies exactly the same whether we are dealing with relations between clauses or between sentences — or indeed between nominal groups, paragraphs, or any combination of these. We are dealing with the semantic notions of meaning which exist between *any* two coherent passages of text. These relations can best be seen by analyzing in some detail the clausal connections within Segment 20. Using van Dijk's point (1973) that statements can be written in equivalent form as separate sentences, we can write this sentence as:

1. Decisions could affect the quality of our lives.
2. They could affect them drastically.
3. These decisions are being made.
4. They are being made by local officials.
5. These officials are in our communities.
6. This is all being done every day.

The relations between these separate sentences can be shown as:

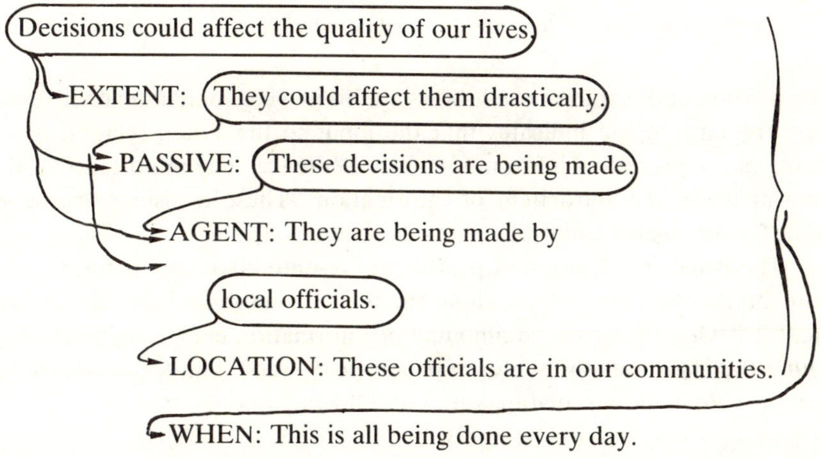

The same meanings and relations are shown in the arrangement of actual text as shown in Figure 1. In using this approach, I am claiming more than van Dijk's (1973) point that one property of a text grammar is that it must:

> "consider the relations between clauses in complex or compound sentences as special cases of the more general textual relations between sentences."

I am claiming that they are the *same* relations, and also that they transcend boundaries within as well as between the clause and the sentence — see Jordan (1988, 1989a, 1990).

The relational indicators in this analysis (Extent, Passive, Agent, Location and When) show the relations which exist between two defined parts of the text. The full question forms of these relational indicators would also include within them the first part of the binary relation:

- To what extent could the decisions affect the quality of our lives?
- What is being done to these decisions?
- Who is making these decisions?
- Where are these officials?
- When is all this being done?

In Figure 2, and in the sketch above, there are occasions when two or more parts constitute the input to the binary relation. As an example, the input to the Agent question has not only the initial statement as input, but also the "answers" to the Extent and Passive questions. That is, the input to the Agent relation is all the preceding information in the sentence, and the full mediating question for the Agent relation is:

> "Who are making decisions that could drastically affect the quality of our lives?"

The method of illustration used shows all this in a convenient manner. Similarly the large brace indicates that the input to the When relation is the whole of the preceding information in the sentence. The importance of the knownness of the third item of information "These decisions are being made." is discussed under the next subsection (3.3).

The principle of different parts being re-entered as inputs to the relation applies many times throughout the text. It is perhaps best seen in Segment 29, where progressive amounts of information cumulate in relations within the clauses as the sentence progresses — and then the whole of the sentence enters into a relation with the following one.

3.5 *Other Complications*

The major difficulty in analyzing text is not simply the recognition of the relations which exist between and within different grammatical and textual units, but in the recognition of the combinations of these relations and in their explanation. Several complex combinations are apparent in the ZPG letter. Some have a single input having a dual relation with (i.e. simultaneously answering two questions about) the second part of the relation. Define/Detail and Assessment/Detail pairs are common here.

Others are even more complex, with the second part of the relation simultaneously answering different questions about (i.e. having different relations with) separate parts of the text. Segment 6 is an example of complex relations. The whole of Segment 6 is an Effect of Segment 5 and provides information in Connection with it and Segment 4; the second part of Segment 5 is also a Cause for the first part of Segment 6. The Summary of Relational Connections (Section 3.7) provides further discussion of the relations in the text and their complexities.

Besides containing many complex combinations, this text also includes three other complications which are discussed here. These are: the assessment and other relations (e.g. of doubt) integrated within the grammar of the clause, or as adjuncts to it; the co-hyponymic comparisons; and the known passive main clauses used as basis for the new information in the following subordinate clause.

The difficulty of integrated relations occurs with *mostly* (S9) and *may be* (S17) which contain relational information bound within the grammar of the clause. The meaning of *mostly* dominates the meaning of the remainder of the clause it forms a part of, indicating that the statement "the deluge of the calls came from reporters" is only partly true, and is true to the extent that most of them came from that source. This is indicated in Figure 1 as a True relation with an input of the major part of the segment; the question is: "Is that true?" and the answer of course is "mostly."

In this text, *mostly* is a sentence adjunct dominating the meaning of the whole clause. With *may be* (and with all modals), however, a grammatical change has to be made to form the neutral definite *is* from the hypothetical *may be*. For this the verb *is* has been included in parentheses to complete the input part of the True question yielding the *may be*.

The second area of difficulty involves comparisons with co-hyponyms. The approach used to analyze these parts of the text is based initially on

Winter's (1974) treatment of comparison as "comparative denial" for which the question mediating between the two statements in comparison is "Is that true for Y?," where Y is a co-hyponym of X, the topic of the first statement. It also leans of Grimes' (1975) discussion of "collateral inversion," in which what is not true is a clear harbinger for what is true. Further discussion and exemplification of the approach used here to explain comparison can be found in Jordan 1982b, 1986, and 1989a.

For the comparisons of Segments 11 and 17, the Assessment relations have inputs of co-hyponyms as well as the topic being discussed as the two elements for comparison. This approach relies on the entry of new topics into the text with the relationship between topics already in the text being made clear in the comparison. In Segment 10 and 11, however, Segment 9 was true *At first*, but was not true *Now*; this is a comparative denial as a function of time with the mediating question being "Is this true now?", and involves collateral inversion as we are told what is true now. Collateral inversion also plays a role in understanding the comparison of Segment 19; for this the question is "Is that true for us too?," the implicit reply (shown in parentheses in Figure 1) is *No.* and the statement of what can be done is given in the main clause as collateral inversion of the subordinate clause. That is, the concessive meaning with the denial of the implicit conclusion that nothing can be done is followed by the statement of what *can* be done.

The third difficulty involves known passive main clauses used as the basis for new information in the following dependent clause. In Segment 29, for example, the information in the main clause *The results of the ZPG's 1985 Urban Stress Test were reported* is already given earlier in the text, and it therefore has no direct informational function. Gopnik (1972) uses the term "included paraphrase" to describe such occurrences, using the example "A table was purchased." as being included within "David purchased a table." The above example is a rather obvious extension of Gopnik's approach.

The role of the passive component is to allow readers to know what the remainder of the sentence is about. In Winter's terms the mediating question between the earlier parts of the text and this sentence is "In what manner and by whom and where were the results of the ZPG's Urban Stress Test reported." This approach poses the practical difficulty that the question includes open-system lexis, which obviously cannot be classified within a closed system of clause relations. To overcome this difficulty, I include the information as a known passive clause (Gopnik's included paraphrase) about an earlier topic and then add the other relations in the dependent clause to show the relations present within the sentence. Jordan 1988a contains further discussion of the need for this approach and its compatibility with the closed system of clause relations used as a premise for this analysis.

3.6 *Meanings and Scope of the Relations*

It is major premise of this chapter that coherent stretches of text are connected to other coherent stretches of text by means of complex combinations of a relatively small set of semantic relations.

Figure 4, based on that found in Jordan (1988a), is a proposed list of these relations together with brief details of their origin. In that diagram, the relations are arranged in semantic groupings, and are shown in pairs where appropriate. Although the meanings of the relations are fairly self evident from the single item labels given them, the questions listed for each relation help to identify the relations and distinguish between them. In practice, however, it is not always easy to determine which relation — or relations — are present, especially when complex combinations are present.

3.7 *Summary of Relational Connections*

This summary provides a brief analysis of the relational connections within and between the segments of the text. It is intended to support the analysis presented in Figure 1, and should be read in conjunction with it. Note that the lexical and problem-solution connections are dealt with in the two subsequent major sections.

The pre-subordinate clause of Segment 4 indicates When the action of the main clause happened. Both parts of Segment 4 enter into a joint Subsequent/Connection relation with both parts of Segment 5, saying that what happened after the action of Segment 4 indicates the Duration of the action. Only Segment 5 enters into the relations with Segment 6, as the starting to ring did not cause staffers to be late. The Effect relation is between all of Segments 5 and 6 and is also in Connection with the phone calls. The reason (or Basis for the decision) for staffers staying late is provided in the second part of Segment 6, in which a joint Source/Location relation and a secondary Location relation are included.

Segments 5 and 6 are re-entered as the non-thematic joint Assessment/ Classification nominal *such an overwhelming response* in the main clause of Segment 7, which provides an Assessment of the survey results and gives time (*When*) and Circumstance relevance in the pre-subordinate part of the segment. The theme of Segment 8 (*Media and public reaction*) is both an associate of the survey results and an imperfect synonym of Segments 5 and 6, allowing these segments to be Assessed as Segment 8.

Segments 5 and 6 are Assessed for the third time, this time as *the deluge of calls*, in Segment 9 to provide further Source details, modified first by the True relation (introducing *mostly*) and then by the Time comparison with Segment 10 signaled by *At first* and then *Now*. Within Segment 9 the reporters are Defined and Detailed, and their Purpose is indicated; also the outraged officials are Defined and Detailed as part of the Emotive Effect-Cause binary pair. Segment 10 contains Location and Detail information about the concerned citizens followed by joint Desire/Purpose information in the relative clause, which also shows an Effect of the survey results.

At Segment 11, the types of relation change from being complex relational/descriptive to being predominantly descriptive with problem-solution elements. Within this mainly descriptive (i.e. relying of lexical connections) section of text — up to Segment 18 — there are a few clause relations, notably the co-hyponymic comparisons as part of the descriptions, the minor Purpose relations, and the Assessment of the ZPG publication. The complication in Segment 11 involves the known passive *created*, which is complemented by the Cause and the Previous efforts, and is followed by the comparative Assessment with other surveys.

The powerful signaling of *But* in Segment 14 mediates between the good assessments of the previous three segments, and the problem created for the organization in trying to met the demand for it. (See Jordan 1985e for discussion of such uses of *But*, *However*, etc.) Segment 12 contains Defining/Detail in the non-finite *-ing* clause, and Segment 13 contains a Purpose for the generic Classification *tool*. Segment 14 contains a Purpose clause with embedded Manner information to support the main clause, and with Extent information added. Segment 15 is essentially co-ordinated Basis for the plea for help in Segment 14, with the first part also containing the Cause of the swamping. The support needed is Assessed in Segment 16, followed by Basis for that Assessment in Segment 17 in the form of a comparison with other opportunities.

The remainder of the main text deals with anticipated effects of the funds being sought, starting with the Enablement relation dominating Segment 18, which contains Purpose and When relations within it. The relation within Segment 19 is shown as a joint comparison/concession relation as it appears to have elements of both types of connection. These are both shown in a form compatible with the remainder of this analysis; the comparison involves the denial of Truth for ZPG and the concession is the denial of the expected Assessment, both being followed by the collateral inversion to indicate what is true.

With the When adjunct *Everyday* dominating, Segment 20 contains included Extent and Passive information followed by an Agent and Locating/Defining information. In Connection with these decisions, and as an Assessment based on it, Segment 21 contains Passive known information complemented by the Agent — all as input to the pre-subordinate Purpose clause.

Segment 22 contains To Whom indirect object information, with the When relation having inputs from both parts. Further information to Detail all of Segment 22 is given in Segment 23 together with an interrupting Example, a known Passive for the complementing When detail, and the post-subordinate Purpose relation.

Segment 29 has a chain of relations (known Passive, Manner, Agent, and finally Location). It is then Assessed as the non-thematic *this remarkable media coverage* in Segment 30, which provides information in Connection with the coverage expressed as the writer's Desire. The Means of the first clause is given in the final subordinate clause.

4. Lexical connection

4.1 *The Topics*

Lexical continuity is achieved in this text through various inclusions of the major concept Zero Population Growth and its many associates. In this context Zero Population Growth has two meanings, leading to two identifiable topics for the letter: the organization "Zero Population Growth"; and the aim (a proposed solution to the perceived problem of overcrowding) of achieving Zero Population Growth. These two related topics are indicated as "org" and "aim" respectively in the following discussion and the illustrations. We know these are the topics of the letter by the large number of lexical connections that are present and their occurrence in thematic positions of the sentences and clauses. The term "topic" is used here in the sense of "discourse topic" as used by Keenan and Schieffelin (1976) and van Dijk (1981). The approach adopted here is not inconsistent with that of Givón (1983), who proposes a hierarchy of continuity for topics of texts.

At a hierarchically higher level than ZPG aim and ZPG org, the topic U.S.A. dominates the meaning of both of these main topics of the document. There are many references to the U.S.A., which tell us that the area of interest is in the United States and not the global picture: *the country* (S6,S10), *the nation's* (S11), *U.S. cities* (S11), *our national government* (S19), *the American public* (S21), and *from coast to coast* (S29). In particular the fact that the ZPG survey determines the effect of overpopulation on U.S. cities (S11) tells us that the concern of ZPG org is with the United States rather than the world. Thus the main topic ZPG aim must be seen as being related to the U.S.A. rather than the wider issue worldwide. That is, ZPG aim = the aim of achieving Zero population Growth in the U.S.A., and ZPG org = the American organization called Zero Population Growth.

Also there is no mention of media publicity from outside the United States, lending support to the contention that this is presented as a national rather than a global issue. In Figures 1 and 2, the superordinate topic U.S.A. is shown as a controling theme of the discussion, and the various reentries of U.S.A. are indicated as lexical connections in Figure 1.

All sub-topics are derivable from the two main topics and the U.S.A. These are shown on Figure 1, and the semantic connections between the topics and the many sub-topics are illustrated in Figure 2 supplemented by a detailed listing of these connections as Figure 3. The use of such diagrams as Figure 2 to illustrate a complex semantic field of connections is discussed and derived in my analysis of complex lexical cohesion (1985a).

4.2 *Basic Continuity*

The topics are re-entered into the text by basic, associated and grammatical means, which are discussed in this and the next three sub-sections.

Basic continuity involves the use of repetition (full and partial), substitution, clausal ellipsis (deletion), acronyms, synonyms, naming and generic nouns (Jordan 1984a). In basic continuity the meaning of the topic (or referent or antecedent) is not altered or added to; the referent is simply included again in the text so that more can be said about it, and it can occur in both thematic and non-thematic (Jordan 1985b) positions. Information can, of course, be added to the new nominal (e.g. the addition of *small* to the associate *Our...staff* in S15), but the base nominal itself does not change the meaning of the referent in basic continuity.

Basic continuity is indicated as several entries for the same referent in Figure 2, and all triggered associates (see next sub-section) contain a form of basic continuity, as indicated in the schedule of lexical connections (Figure 3).

4.3 *Associated Connection — Background*

The key to understanding many of the lexical connections in the ZPG letter lies in recognizing nominal groups which are "associated" in some way with one or more of the topics. These were named "associated nominals" simultaneously and independently by Hawkins (1978) and myself (1978), following work on the English articles in context by Christophersen (1939) rather than the "associations" of Dixon (1971) and Grimes (1975). Their categories of inclusion and components are included in the sense used here, but I use the term purely for lexical connections between nouns and noun groups, and do not include the vaguer notions of connotation and collocation included within their use. Also the emphasis here is on the linguistic recoverability of the referent or "nuclear" concept in the new nominal. I prefer Hawkins's term "trigger" to avoid confusion with Beekman and Callow's (1974) and Mann and Thompson's (1986, 1987, 1989) use of "nuclear."

Christophersen points out that, once a particular book has been established as a topic in a text, it is quite reasonable to write "The author is unknown.", where *The author* is associated is some clear way with the original term. The original term is the "trigger," and we can recognize the existence of untriggered (e.g. *The author*), pre-triggered (e.g. *The book's author* or *its author*), and post-triggered (e.g. *The author of the book*) associates of the trigger (Jordan 1981a). For pre- and post-triggering, we can recognize the use of a form of basic continuity as part of the complex associated nominal.

4.4 *Associated Connection — Application*

In the ZPG letter, if we take ZPG org as topic, we can recognize these three forms of association:

S6	Staffers	untriggered — no mention of the trigger *ZPG*
S11	ZPG's Urban Stress Test	pre-triggered — *ZPG* precedes the association in possessive form
S3	Friend of ZPG	post-triggered — *ZPG* follows the association

Although most of the associations are quite easily recognized as such, others need a little thought. For example, *Susan Weber* (S26) is Identified as an Executive Director (S27) (an untriggered associate of ZPG org), *the overwhelming response* (S7) is a response to the Urban Stress Test, and the *population-related problems* (S10) are associated with ZPG aim as it is the initiating problem which ZPG aim seeks to redress. All associations are included in Figure 2, with indications of the types of associate and their triggers being included in the schedule of connections as Figure 3.

Some associations contains a "Vocabulary 3" word as defined by Winter (1977). These words indicate the presence of a clause relation with the trigger, and are typified by the words used to signify these relations (e.g. *cause*, *basis*, *comparison*, *purpose*). An example in this letter is *the consequences of controlled population growth* (S19), which indicates a cause-effect relationship with unspecified effects. Also *the results of ZPG's 1985 Urban Stress Test* includes the item *results* to indicate a cause-effect relation between the test and the data yielded by it.

4.5 *Multi-Stage Associations*

The existence of two or more stages of association has already been recognized (Jordan 1982a, 1984a, 1985a), and this principle is crucial to the understanding of the lexical connections in this text. If, for example, we take ZPG (org) as a trigger, we can easily recognize *ZPG's 1985 Urban Stress Test* as a first stage of association. We can now take that associated nominal as our new trigger for the second stage, which is *the results of ZPG's 1985 Urban Stress Test*. The first stage is pre-triggered by *ZPG's*, and the second stage is post-triggered by *ZPG's 1985 Urban Stress Test*.

There is no theoretical limit to the number of stages of association possible in a text. In this letter, we can recognize a three-stage associate *Media and public reaction* (to the results of the ZPG's 1985 Urban Stress Test), which is untriggered. There is even a four-stage association as *decisions that could affect the quality of our lives* (USA → US citizens → our lives → the quality of our lives → and the final nominal) with an included cause-effect relation signaled by *affect*.

A further complication discussed elsewhere (Jordan 1985a) and apparent in this text is the occurrence of dual triggering, in which two (or conceivably more) triggers combine within a single associated nominal. Thus in S11, the complex nominal *the nation's...cities* has triggers of the superordinate U.S.A. as well as the Urban Stress Test (an associate of ZPG org). All these complications are included in detail in Figures 2 and 3.

4.6 *Grammatical Topic Connections*

Although most of the references to the topics of discussion in the text are achieved through basic and associated connection, some are achieved through grammatical means within the sentence. Relative clauses, *-ed* clauses, *-ing* clauses, verbless clauses and locative clauses are all present in the text, and are included in all three figures. The useful generalization of defining and non-defining is also apparent in Figure 1 through the identification of defining detail in several of the segments of the text.

4.7 *Indicating Lexical and Relational Connections*

A difficulty is often created in text analysis by the fact that many nominal groups not only re-enter a topic (in basic or associative form), but also provide some information about it. This additional information can take the form of the choice of lexis (e.g. *This ploy* carries meaning as well as re-entering the referent), as predicative adjective (e.g. *Our small staff*), or as many other complications within the grammar of the nominal group.

In Figure 1, relational connections are indicated thus

Basis:

as explained in Section 3, and the lexical connections are indicated with an arrow from the referent to the new nominal which is underlined with a broken line thus

When both relational *and* lexical connections occur in the same nominal, this is indicated using both systems, for example:

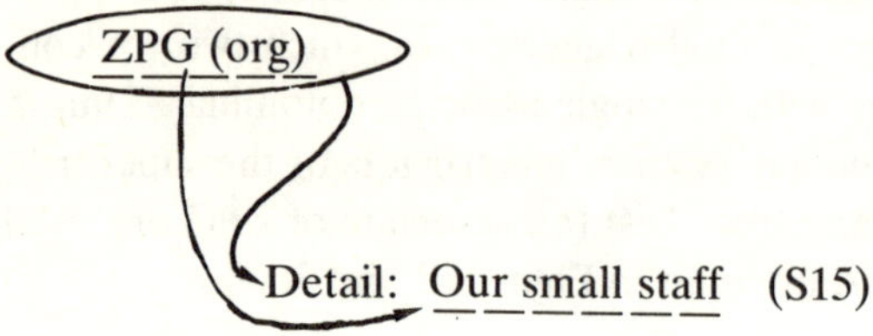

The relations included with such nominals are identified in the schedule (Figure 3).

5. Problem-Solution Analysis

5.1 *Background*

Many texts are centrally concerned with problems, and their solutions, and evaluations of these solutions. This text is no exception, and it is possible to understand the main needs and aims of the writer (and the approaches taken to overcome the associated difficulties) through an analysis in terms of problems, solutions and implementation.

This area of analysis was pioneered by Winter (1976), who discovered that many technical texts followed a pattern of "Situation-Problem-Solution-Evaluation." Working with him, Hoey describes many of the related signals of these categories of information (1979), and explains many aspects of the method of analysis (1983a). Also working with Winter, I expanded the theory using a 12-step process and algorithm to depict the sequence from initiation through fruition (1980), developed the ideas into a working analytical rhetoric of text (1984b), and applied the approach to ESL teaching (1984c) and the teaching of technical writing (1989b). While many other workers have recognized the importance of problem solving as a basis for understanding language and the writing process (and many other aspects of life), the work introduced above seeks to provide a linguistically sound detailed analytical method for understanding many aspects of everyday English texts.

5.2 *Complex Analysis*

Winter and Hoey have concentrated on fairly short texts which exhibit the four part structure of Situation-Problem-Solution-Evaluation, together with many of the complications within these categories of information. In my work in this area of analysis, I have also sought to apply the underlying concepts to texts which do *not* follow this pattern, recognizing how the method helps us to understand texts having many problems, or many solutions, or with parts of the structure omitted, or for very short texts such as "Mind the Gap," "Steep Hill" and "Go Slow" (1981b, 1984b), which indicate Solution-Problem, Problem and Solution respectively. I have also sought to define the difficult concept of "Evaluation" in terms of the binary clause-relational pair Assessment/Basis (1984b, 1988b).

There is no doubt that the ZPG letter does not follow the basic four-part structure, but that does not invalidate the technique as a means of analyzing this text, as we can now apply the principles to a wide array of texts which do not follow this structure. Many texts, and this one is a good example, have many important elements involving problems, solutions and evaluations; but we must not expect to find them in a neat four-part structure for each text.

In fact the great difficulty of analyzing many texts using the problem-solution approach is that the problems, solutions and evaluations occur at different points in the text, and in different orders and at different levels of hierarchy, with solutions having their own problems, etc. The text we are analyzing here is a prime example of such complexities. While the main problem may be alluded to earlier in the text, the first specific mention of the problem comes in Segment 10 as *population-related problems*, and the superordinate situation occurs only in Segment 19 as *uncontrolled population growth* within the problem-related wider associated nominal *the consequences of uncontrolled population growth*. The solution, of course, is Zero Population Growth (aim), and the survey of results and the actions ZPG org intends to tak eto publicize the results of their survey are steps toward achieving that goal. And although there are many evaluations (Assessments) — some with Basis — these are usually assessments of the survey and not of the proposed solution: ZPG aim. (This is not a criticism of the text, as the aim of the letter is to solicit funds to support publicity of the survey results, and is not intended to convince readers of the merits of ZPG aim itself — presumably the survey does that.)

As mentioned earlier in this chapter, it is problematic whether problem-solution structures can or should be considered as clause relations in the same way we consider the other clause relations. As with many other texts here we have examples where "problemhood" and "solutionhood" could be considered in a clause-relational manner. The swamping of staff and the stretching of resources being solved by the hoped-for contributions from readers are clear examples. However the overall aim, its situation, the role of the survey and its results, and their evaluations are all matters that cannot conveniently be handled in this way. These and other problem-solution aspects of the text are analyzed here in the manner described and exemplified with over 100 examples in Jordan 1984a, and following the guidelines for textual analysis provided there in "A Guide to the Analysis of Text" (p.136-139). The major problems and solutions with their evaluations are discussed first, followed by a listing of other minor problem-solution aspects of the text.

5.3 *Major Concepts*

The overall situation is *uncontrolled population growth* (S19) which, in spite of the negative prefix, is not necessarily a problem. Uncontrolled population growth has been with mankind for centuries, but it is only in the last few decades that population problems have arisen in the world.

These problems are mentioned several times in the text. In Segment 19, the use of *ignore the consequences* indicates a problem perceived within the general situation, as *consequences* is here used is its negative (problem-signaling) sense. This meaning is made much clearer by *population-related problems* (S10), followed by *threaten public health and well-being* (S10), *population-linked pressures* (S11), and *emerging population-linked stress* (S18).

The solution to these problems is *Zero Population Growth* aim, and *Zero Population Growth* org has conducted the survey and is distributing this solicitation for funds as part of a campaign to bring this solution about. One possible Means of achieving the solution is for *our national government* (U.S.) to take some action (S18) — we are not told what! — but that appears to have failed as they *continue to ignore* the problem (S18). An alternative Means of overcoming the problem is to *take positive action at the local level* (S19), and that is the thrust of this present campaign. To achieve this aim, the organization has commissioned a survey of the Effects of increased population on *184 urban areas* in *U.S. cities* (S12,S11). ZPG org is now proposing to give wide publicity to the results in the hope that local officials and community leaders will take action to implement the solution. (Again the Means by which this could be accomplished is not discussed.)

The immediate aim, therefore, is to convince public officials and others of the problem and its Extent, and to hold them *accountable for tackling* the problem (S10). The survey results are thus perceived as an *easy-to-use action tool* presumably to help officials implement zero population growth (S13). ZPG org has established a network of local activists, and now wishes to arm them with the survey results (S18); the aim in doing this is to provide them with the basis for warning community leaders of the problems before these problems become too severe (S1). The need for local action to be taken by ZPG org, and the need for the survey results to achieve this is stated in Segments 19 and 21.

The major concepts relating to problem-solution structures can be shown as:

uncontrolled population growth (S19)	SITUATION
population-related problems (S10) population-linked pressures (S11) population-linked stresses (S18)	PROBLEM
Zero Population Growth (aim) (S1) federal action (S19) (not taken)	SOLUTION
local action (S19,20) knowledge of problem through survey results (S5,10,13,17,18,19,21,23)	EVALUATION

5.4 *Minor Concepts*

Apart from the major considerations of problems and their attempted solution and the Means of implementing it, other problem-solution structures are apparent in the text, and these are included in Figure 1. These minor structures are:

(a) The problem of staffers having to stay late answering calls jamming the switchboard (S5,6); this was rather a pleasant "problem" for the ZPG org executive. There was no immediate solution; the staffers just had to put up with it.

(b) The survey results created a problem for the outraged officials, who sought a cathartic solution by complaining about the whistle blowing (S9). This is an example of what I have called a "people problem" (1984c), in which an effort to create or implement a solution by one party causes a problem for another.

(c) The reporters, officials and concerned citizens had a need-to-know problem, which was satisfied by the information provided during their telephone calls (S6,9,10).

(d) In Segment 14, *But* provides the transition introducing the problem for ZPG that financial help is needed. Their attempted solution is this letter to solicit funds to provide that help. Details of the problem are provided in Segment 15.

(e) A further need arises in Segment 29 because of the media coverage. This need, clearly specified in Segment 30 as *help us cover this remarkable media coverage*, has an attempted solution in the form of the Means by which the monitoring can be achieved (S30).

6. Reflections

6.1 *The Analysis*

6.1.1 *Problem-Solution Features*

The problem-solution analysis enables us to comprehend the general purpose of the organization and the letter within the wider context of situation (overpopulation). It also provides a comprehensive account of the major and minor aims, purposes, problems and solutions of those involved in the organization, the survey, and the resulting media attention.

This approach yields more of a rhetorical or "non-technical" analysis in the form of an exegetic description of the text, using specific signals in the text as evidence for the connections claimed. We must not expect different analysts to produce identical analyses of the same text when using this method, as the analysts' individual descriptive styles and analytical abilities will inevitably lead to different responses. However, the substance, as opposed to the form, should be the same for all analyses of the same text using this approach. Any initial variations of the connections reported should be resolvable and ultimately made definitive given a text and any vital background information.

This particular problem-solving approach to text analysis (Jordan 1989a) has been used for the past 7 years by freshman to senior students. It has become clear that any text involving problems and solutions — and very few do not — can be analyzed at the rhetorical level with clear expectations for the analysis, to the extent that an "answer guide" of the expected answer can be prepared. Students respond positively to the approach, and to its use in class discussions, tests and examinations.

A possible misconception of this approach might be that it is severely limited because it only deals with problems and solutions. Clearly Problem-Solution is very close to Purpose-Means (Jordan 1985f), Cause-Effect is commonly involved with problem identification, evaluation is a general term for Basis-Assessment, and relations of Agent, Location, Time, Source, Circumstance, Cognition and others are often associated with the main features of problem and solution — as with the ZPG letter, for example. Also writers use description (and thus lexical connection) when dealing with problems and their solutions. Thus a fully detailed rhetorical account of a text could include all other features of connection the analyst wishes to include. It could even be argued that the more technical accounts of lexical connection and clause relations support the more general framework of analysis by the problem-solution approach. The method is limited only by the analyst's ability to comprehend and describe language structures and their methods of signaling.

6.1.2 *Lexical Connections*

Figures 1, 2 and 3 show the extent by which the theory of lexical connection discussed here can be applied to a complex text. In Figure 1 we see at a glance the superordinate *U.S.A.*, the topics (*ZPG* org and *ZPG* aim), and various sub-topics (e.g. *Friend of ZPG* and *ZPG's Urban Stress Test*) and other subordinate topics, and how they connect with the passages in the text to provide the lexical continuity.

Figure 2 shows how these topics, sub-topics and all nominals associated with them are connected semantically; the nominals are displayed hierarchically as stages of association. Figure 3 provides a detailed account of each connection, the method of connection, the triggering if appropriate, and the stages of association.

Although such lexical connections are always an important feature of complex texts, they usually only provide a partial analysis of a text such as the ZPG letter. Fortunately, however, there are many texts which rely entirely or almost entirely on such connections, and this has been used as the basis for a linguistic definition of the genre of description (Jordan 1984b). Such texts provide excellent preparatory study for students, as they do not also contain the complexities of problem-solution and clause relational connections found in other texts. With little exception the results of analysis using the principles explained here, are quite definitive; any differences can usually be easily resolved through discussion.

Although much work has been done in lexical connections, the concepts of collocation, and perhaps also allusion, could be usefully added. Connections between nouns and verbs (rather than just between nominals and other nominals) could also perhaps be incorporated into the overall method, and we also need to include analysis of implicit connections (e.g. implicit agent, implicit object, implicit locatives). However, even at this stage, the approach used here to indicate lexical connections seems to provide a detailed and defensible analysis of the lexical connections in almost any text.

6.1.3 *Clause Relations*

The clause relational analysis used here is both the most far reaching and the most contentious of the three methods used here. Many of the relations listed in Figure 4 are already well accepted, but some need further definition and classification to allow more definitive analysis. There could well be other relations that need to be identified, or some of those listed could perhaps be subdivided into sub-groups of relations.

The main features of the clause relational analysis used here, however, lie in more than the actual relations between the relations. More important are: (a) the consistent use of these relations within as well as between clauses and sentences, (b) the use of complex combinations to explain the total semantic connections between parts of the text, and (c) the integration of these relations with both lexical connection and problem-solving aspects of textual continuity.

Take, for example, the connections within and between Segment 30 and the remainder of the text. Lexically, we need to account for the pronouns *I* (referring to the writer *Susan Weber*), *you* (referring to the addressee *Friend of ZPG* org) as co-hyponymic first-stage associates of *ZPG* org, and *us* (referring to *ZPG* org), and the endophoric associate *enclosed reply form* (= reply form enclosed *with this letter*). We must also recognize that the preceding sentence is classified and epitomized as *this...media coverage* with the added assessment from the writer of *remarkable* to create the object of *monitor*, thus yielding the perceived need (a problem) to be overcome.

Clause relationally, the writer is providing information in connection with the details in Segment 29, and is expressing a need (*hope*) in the matrix clause with both main and subordinate clauses as inputs. The *by...-ing* Means clause indicates the means by which readers can provide this help, thus overcoming the problem.

If we are to provide a full account of the connections within this sentence and the connections it has within itself and between other parts of the text, we cannot evade any of these items of continuity. We could attempt to find a question which mediates between Segment 30 and the remainder of the text:

> "How would you classify and characterize this media coverage and provide detail in connection with it which involves the reader's requested action in helping the organization to meet the perceived need of monitoring the media coverage and providing the means of achieving this aim, and which expresses the writer's desire in this matter?"

Besides including many open-system lexical items (and thus preventing any reasonable classification of such connecting methods), such a question is far too unwieldy. Also from a theoretical point of view, such a question fails to clearly identify what some of the relations are between, especially for connections within the segment itself.

The overall method of analysis used here shows all these connections, and shows clearly what the connections are between and what type of connections they are. It also shows all this in a graphic presentation, in a short space, and in a manner consistent with other analyses and established principles of language connection.

6.2 *Pitfalls Avoided*

6.2.1 *The Writer's Intention*

The discussion and diagrams offered here form an unashamedly *linguistic* analysis, in which the text actually provided is analyzed without reference to what the writer might or might not have had in mind in preparing the letter. The approach has been to study what is there — not what we might deduce could be in people's minds from the text offered. If we seek to guess the writer's intentions, we become embroiled in literary-style argument, and become forced to introduce extra-textual background and other evidence for intended meaning; we also elevate the writer's intention (or at least our perception of it) to a level at least as important as the actual communication. While such an ethnomethodological approach could yield interesting perceptions of the text and its role as a communication, it would tell us little about the way English text inter-connects to form meaningful statements within an overall document — and that is the aim of this analysis.

Thus the "function-based" analysis of what we perceive the writer *intended* to achieve with each part of the text is not included here. In my view we cannot possibly know — or reliably guess — what was in the writer's mind (even if we asked her) in composing each part of the text, and we must instead analyze what she *did* write. The main lesson we should have learned from the trauma in linguistics over the past 30 odd years is that we should only analyze what is there — not what we envisage might or should be there in people's minds.

6.2.2 *Reader Reaction and Interpretation*

Similarly this analysis steers clear of any analysis regarding the possible reaction of, or interpretation by, the readers to statements in the document based on their earlier understanding or earlier background knowledge. Again we do not know what these are, and can only guess. More importantly, we must expect different readers to have different interpretations and different reactions, so there seems little point in attempting to determine the understanding, interpretation or reaction of readers to the text as a whole or to specific parts of it.

In any event I feel that such an analysis should properly be conducted within the frameworks of communication theory, psychology or perhaps literary analysis rather than linguistics which, as a science, should rely solely on primary data and established principle of interpreting and assessing that data within established frameworks. The work of de Beaugrande (1980) and de Beaugrande and Dressler (1981) are examples of how we can easily forget the importance of grammar and lexis in concentrating on how readers are thought to process discourse.

6.2.3 *Nucleus/Satellite and Hierarchy*

If we accept Longacre's (1968) principle of sentence margins and their relations with the nucleus, and Mann and Thompson's (1986, 1987, 1989) developments of nuclear and satellite elements of a text, we must then distinguish between grammatical nuclei and rhetorical nuclei. In Segment 7, for example, there can be no question that we have a main clause as a grammatical nucleus and a subordinate satellite dominated by the subordinator *When*. But rhetorically, we could certainly argue that the information in the subordinate clause is dominant, as this is vital new information at that stage in the discourse and the stress test and the results are very important subtopics throughout the text. In any event the designation of rhetorical nucleus is arguable, whereas the designation of grammatical nucleus is not.

As another example, the main clause of Segment 29 (*The results ...were reported*) can hardly be regarded as rhetorically nuclear, as we already know that information. The vital new information comes in the grammatically dependent remainder of the sentence. A similar argument applies to Segment 23, and there are many other instances in the letter in which the question of rhetorical nucleus is at least open to question and interpretation.

Nuclearity between sentences and larger sections of discourse can only be rhetorical, and we must accept that lexis as well as clausal statements can be "nuclear" — especially the stress test dominating Segments 11 — 13, and the media coverage forming the basis of discussion for Segments 29 and 30. In fact the "nucleus" for descriptive texts is, by definition (Jordan 1984b), a noun or nominal group rather than a clause or sentence. In description, there is no nuclear statement — only details about the topic of discourse.

Nuclearity is dealt with in this analysis through the clause relational question-and-answer principle. We can see in Figure 1 what is being entered into the new relation, and we can see that some relations are semantically subordinate to others. The notion of parallel relations is also obvious in the analysis, although many such combinations have different inputs.

The early work of Longacre (1968) and Beekman and Callow (1974) regarding nuclearity and parallelity with both nominal and clausal inputs needs to be combined to allow this interesting line of enquiry to develop. Pending completion of that work, no attempt is made here to introduce these concepts into the analysis in any other way than is portrayed by the relations depicted in Figure 1. While it may be possible to determine with some reliability the patterns of nuclearity for a rather coarse rhetorical analysis of the letter, that does not appear possible, with our current understanding of text, for a more detailed analysis of the document.

The concept of lexis being at different levels of hierarchy is dealt with through the semantic field of connections and associations in Figure 2, which clearly shows the hierarchy of the various stages of association. This is supported by the detailed schedule of lexical connections in Figure 3.

Because this analysis treats the text as a self-contained communication in its own right without comparison with other texts of a similar or dissimilar type, this chapter makes no attempt to reach conclusions regarding the way or extent to which the letter conforms to similar communications in the genre. However, it should be clear that similar analyses of other such letters are almost certain to yield interesting results regarding the stylistically significant elements of this form of letter. The work could then be applied more widely by comparing this form of letter with the wider genres.

6.3 *Non-Technical Features*

6.3.1 *Detailed Analysis*

The analysis provides a great deal of detail which would not be readily apparent from a careful reading by a non-linguist. Although non-linguists might be expected to provide a reasonable account of the problems and solutions discussed in the letter, they would not be able to identify the specific signals which indicate the various categories of information. They would also be unlikely to be able to explain in detail what the categories are and how they relate to one another to create a detailed rhetorical account of the problems and solutions related to ZPG (aim and org), the survey, its results, the resulting media coverage, and the problems and solutions connected with that media coverage and the opportunity it presents. The problem-solving approach is thus a valuable first step in taking discerning readers from a general fuzzy analysis, to a much more detailed one based on the linguistic signals present in the text.

The lexical analysis even more clearly takes the general reader into a deeper understanding of the continuity of the text. Few non-linguists could be expected to understand the great degree of complication of the lexical connections apparent here without the benefit of such an analysis. The levels of association, the interaction of the superordinate *U.S.A.* with the main topics *ZPG* (aim and org), the recognition that *ZPG* has two meanings here, and the complications of basic and associative connections with and without triggering would not be recognized by even a careful reading by non-linguists.

The clause relational analysis provides a further order of complexity which the non-linguist could not be expected to extract from the text. The many complications within the clause that create semantic connections both within and between the clauses and sentences, the way larger elements of the text (e.g. Segments 5 and 6) are epitomized, re-entered into the text, and Assessed as part of later discussion, and the real complexity of comparison and concession in the letter are but a few examples of the richness of understanding offered by this analysis.

In total, the integration of these three approaches shows to the non-linguist (and perhaps even to some linguists) an amazing amount of connection and interconnection at the rhetorical, grammatical, lexical and relational levels which would not be apparent on even a very careful reading.

6.3.2 *Relational Affinities*

Although no definitive conclusions should be reached from a detailed analysis of this one short text, some general observations of the overall three-pronged method may be useful. It seems clear that many sentences are semantically structured in a branching manner in which the information cumulates as the inputs for questions for the next stage of the sentence. The clearest examples of this are Segments 23 and 29, but the branching is also apparent in almost all of the sentences of the text. This is certainly not a necessary feature of semantic sentence structure, but it may well be a very common technique.

Many other relational affinities appear to be interesting possibilities for further study:

(a) the Assessment/Detail and Define/Detail pairings, as any information provided about something is also potentially evaluative in nature, and detail often also tends to define;
(b) the importance of Locatives and Time, Manner, and Extent adjuncts (*in our communities*, *at the local level*, *At first*, *Now*, *immediately*, *today*, *well*, *urgently,*), as relations answering Where, When, How, and Extent questions about the remainder of the clause or sentence; and, more generally,
(c) the almost constant need to recognize the existence of many relations

occurring simultaneously, often with different parts of the earlier text being inputs to the clause-relating question.

6.3.3 *Other Interesting Features*

The three Agent relations (indicating agentive passives) and the agentless passive of Segment 23 are noticeable in the five sentences of Segments 19-29. Clearly the passive can be a powerful tool in dramatic forceful writing — despite vociferous claims to the contrary by writing experts who do not study language. The causative passive (and the following implicit causative passive) of Segment 15, and the agentless passive of Segment 11 make this even clearer.

The problems and solutions are often signaled in terms of the Purpose or Means relation (Segments 10, 18, 21, 30), but also in less well-signaled ways. Signaling of "problem" is achieved clausally or lexically (e.g. *stress*, *jammed*, *furious*, *blown the whistle*, *threaten public health and well-being*, *swamped*, *stretched to the limit*, *affect* (assumed adversely) *the quality of our lives (the American public need)*. Solutions are indicated as donations (*Your support*) or as actions (e.g. *talking with reporters*, *tackling population-related problems, arm our growing network*). Assessments are even harder to identify, as they occur within the grammar of the nominal group (e.g. *such an overwhelming response, the nation's first survey*, *our best opportunity*), by the comparisons, and through all identifications of problem (which is a negative evaluation of a thing or situation).

6.4 *Technical Features*

6.4.1 *Uniqueness*

The approach used here is a serious attempt to account *fully* for all the semantic connections in the text, whether they occur as morphology, lexis, nominal groups, clauses, sentences, or larger elements of the discourse. Thus each of the three branches of analysis seeks to go beyond generalities and beyond the application of connecting principles that apply only at sentence or clause level. van Dijk's (1973) notion of the complex sentence being decomposable into separate items of information (applied practically in Strong's (1973) composing book on sentence composing) is taken very seriously here. The logical extension of that principle is that virtually *any* element of the clause in context must be suspect as a potential clause relational, lexical or problem-solution feature of connection in the wider discourse.

This philosophy pervades all three methods of analysis. The problem-solution discussion goes beyond the generalities of the subject to a potentially very detailed analysis in which often morphology (e.g. *ir*, *un*, *icide*, *anti*, *over*, *free*, and the comparatives and superlatives) play important roles in signaling problems, solutions and evaluations. At the other extreme, the same consistent principles can be used to understand the overall structure of many large documents with a macro-structure following the problem-solution pattern and with micro-structures of description (lexical connection) and/or clause relations.

Similarly the lexical analysis seeks to close the gap between the established principles of co-referential connection and the more general concepts of collocation and allusion. The basic elements of lexical connection (repetition, substitution, synonymy, etc.) are included, of course; but the major type of connection seen in this and most other texts also involves various types, stages and combinations of associations with one or more trigger. The system is further enriched by the inclusion of Assessments within the nominal group, by the use of co-hyponyms and explicit or implicit comparators, and by the integration of information about lexical features of the text and the clauses and sentences of which they grammatically and semantically form an essential part.

The third element of the overall analytical approach is a rigorous application of the relations between propositions, whether these are communicated in nominal, clausal or sentential form. Again this element goes beyond the usual application by seeking to recognize, based on Winter's use of questions as the main identifying criterion, how many different parts of the text answer questions about other parts of the text. However, the approach is still compatible with the relations defined by many other linguists who have sought to identify and define a quite small closed set of semantic relations as possible semantic universals of human communication.

6.4.2 *Problems and Extensions*

Analysis of the clause relations in this text has raised several theoretical problems, many of which I had to address as three separate papers as necessary background for this present chapter. The first (1988a) shows that the complex questions containing open-system lexis used by Winter (1974, 1982) are indeed compatible with the desirable need to define a closed system set of semantic "clause relations." The second (1989a) shows how the theory of clause relations can be applied to relations within as well as between clauses, and provides an introductory comparison between the clause relational approach used here and the rhetorical structure theory of Mann and Thompson (1986, 1987, 1989). The third (1990) explains the use and complexities of clause relations within the nominal group.

However, problems still remain, and the method needs further work and extension in at least the following areas:

(a) clarification of the weak Connection relation (Jordan 1974) with its typical signaling of *In this connection*,
(b) a deeper understanding of how the entering and re-entering of lexical items into the text affect clause relations,
(c) clarification of the definitions for the relations and refinement of their categories and sub-categories,
(d) a clearer way of indicating relations going backward in the text or recognition of inverse relations (What happened then?, What happened under those Circumstances?),
(e) possible further integration of problem-solution concepts with the other clause relations, and
(f) a greater understanding of how the conjuncts and adjuncts relate to the relations between parts of text.

We must also accept Longacre's (1972) challenge of identifying the surface signals of all the relations as well as seeking to define them.

6.4.3 *Toward a Text Grammar*

The notion of "text grammar" has been with us for some time, and some determined efforts have been made to provide the basis for such an understanding — notably Pike (1967) and Pike and Pike (1977), van Dijk (1972, 1973), Werlich (1976), Winter (1982) and Longacre (1976, 1983). It is clear from this work that we must be able to account for the semantic connections at *all* levels of discourse, from the whole document, large sections and paragraphs, right into the sentence and clause — and even into the semantics of single items and nominal and verbal groups.

The need is for a system of continuity which can be applied consistently at all these levels of text, and which can show how the smallest part of language in context (even, for example, prefixes as "problem" indicators) is used as means of achieving continuity and cohesion in the text. While the method presented here appears to have many of the necessary features for such a grammar, it does so only by relying on three rather separate principles of language connection and by showing how these systems work together to achieve the overall cohesion in the text.

What other systems must be added or incorporated? Are the notions of theme and rheme essential elements to an eventual understanding of text structure and signaling? Can we more fully integrate Winter's work on repetition and replacement — or his important notion of the predicatability of unspecifics? Can participant involvement be integrated with these other systems, and can we incorporate metaphor as paradigmatic choice within a consistent framework of clausal semantics and connection?

More importantly, perhaps, we must now ask whether it will ever be possible to create a single overall descriptive apparatus to account for the many complex forms of cohesion in natural language — or whether that account must necessarily remain rather piecemeal. Are we forced to accept that textual cohesion is created using several complex overlapping mechanisms, each of which can become dominant in certain restricted forms? If so, we must determine the level of definiteness or scientificness of each mechanism we propose. Where on the scale from the social sciences to the humanities does each technique lie — and how do they interface with principles of rhetoric and ethnographic studies?

These and possibly many other matters remain to be resolved before we can approach a workable text "grammar."

References

Ballard, D.L., R.J. Conrad, and R.E. Longacre
1971 "The deep and surface grammar of interclausal relations." *Foundations of Language*. 7. [Also in R.M. Brend (ed.) *Advances in Tagmemics*. Amsterdam: North Holland, 1974.]

Beardsley, M.C.
1950 *Practical Logic*. New York: Prentice Hall.

Beekman, J.
1970a "Propositions and their relations within a Discourse" *Notes on Translation*. 37.

1970b "A structural display of propositions in Jude." *Notes on Translation. 37.*

1970c "Structural notes on the book of Jude." *Notes on Translation*. 37.

Beekman, J. and J. Callow
1974 *Translating the Word of God*. Grand Rapids, MI: Zondervan.

Blight, R.C.
1970 "An alternate display of Jude." *Notes on Translation* 37.

Brown, G. and G. Yule
1983 *Discourse Analysis*. Cambridge: Cambridge University Press.

Callow, J.C.
1970a "Structural notes on the book of Jude." *Notes on Translation* 37.

1970b "An outline of Jude." *Notes on Translation* 37.

Callow, K.
1970 "More on propositions and their relations within a discourse." *Notes on Translation* 37.

Christophersen, P.
1939 *The Articles: A Study of their Theory and Use in English*. Copenhagen: Muskaard.

Cook, W.A.
1972 "A set of postulates for case grammar analysis." *Language and Linguistics Working Papers*, 4.

Crystal, D. and D. Davy
1969 *Investigating English Style*. London: Longman.

Dea, W.H.
1977 *The Sentence and Beyond: Clause Relations and Analysis of the Language of Literature*. M. Phil Thesis. The Hatfield Polytechnic, Hertfordshire, England.

de Beaugrande, R.A.
1980 *Text, Discourse, and Process: Toward a Multidisciplinary Science of Texts*. (Advances in Discourse Process 4). Norwood, NJ: Ablex.

de Beaugrande, R.A. and W.U. Dressler
1981 *An Introduction to Text Linguistics*. (Longman Linguistic Library 26). London: Longman.

Dixon, R.
1971 "A method of semantic description." In D.D. Steinberg, and L.A. Jakobovits, (eds), *Semantics: An Introductory Reader in Philosophy, Linguistics and Psychology*. Cambridge: The University Press.

Edmondson, W.
1981 *Spoken Discourse: A Model for Analysis*. London: Longman.

Givón, T.
1983 *Topic Continuity in Discourse: A Quantitative Cross-Language Study*. Amsterdam/Philadelphia: John Benjamins.

Gopnik, M.
1972 *Linguistic Structures in Scientific Texts*. (Janua Linguarum Series Minor 129). The Hague: Mouton.

Gray, B.
1977a "From discourse to dialogue." *Journal of Pragmatics* 1/3.

1977b *The Grammatical Foundations of Rhetoric: Discourse Analysis*. (Janua Linguarum Series Minor 51). The Hague: Mouton.

Greenbaum, S.
1969 *Studies in English Adverbial Usage*. London: Longman.

Grimes, J.
1975 *The Thread of Discourse*. The Hague: Mouton.

Hatcher, A.G.
1956a "Syntax and the sentence." *Word*, 12.

1956b "Theme and underlying question." *Word*, 12, monograph 3.

Healey, P.
1965 "Levels, constituent strings and agreement in telefol syntax." Thesis, Australian National University, Canberra.

Halliday, M.A.K. and R. Hasan
1976 *Cohesion in English*. London: Longman.

Hawkins, J.A.
1978 *Definiteness and Indefiniteness: A Study of Reference and Grammaticality Prediction*. London: Croom-Helm.

Hoey, M.P.
1979 *Signalling in Discourse*. (Discourse Analysis Monograph No. 6). University of Birmingham, England.

1983a *On the Surface of Discourse*. London: George Allen and Unwin.

1983b "The place of clause relational analysis in linguistic description." *English Language Research Journal* 4.

Hoey, M.P. and E.O.O. Winter
1986 "Clause relations and the writer's commmunicative task." In B. Couture, (ed.), *Functional Approaches to Writing*. London: Frances Pinter.

Hutchins, W.J.
1977a "On the Problem of "Aboutness" in Document Analysis," *Journal of Informatics*. 1,1.

1977b "On the structure of scientific texts." *UEA Papers in Linguistics*. 5,3.

Jespersen, O.
1914-49 *A Modern English Grammar on Historical Principles*. Heidelberg: Winter, and London: George Allen and Unwin.

Jordan, M.P.
1978 "The principal semantics of the nominals 'this' and 'that' in contemporary English

writing." PhD Thesis, The Hatfield Polytechnic and Birmingham University, England (see *Dissertation Abstracts International*, sec. C, Summer 1978, 38, 533).

1980 "Short texts to explain problem-solution structures — and vice versa." *Instructional Science* 9.

1981a "Some associated nominals in technical writing." *Journal of Technical Writing and Communication* 11/3.

1981b "Structure, meaning and information signals of some very short texts." In W. Gutwinski, and G. Jolly, (eds), *The 8th LACUS Forum*, Columbia SC: Hornbeam Press.

1982a "The thread of continuity in functional writing." *Journal of Business Communication* 19/4.

1982b "Co-associative lexical cohesion in English texts." *Technostyle* 2/2.

1984a *Fundamentals of Technical Description*. Malabar FLA: Krieger.

1984b *Rhetoric of Everyday English Texts*. London: George Allen and Unwin.

1984c "Structure, style and word choice in everyday English texts." *TESL Talk*, 15/1 and 2.

1985a "Complex lexical cohesion in the English clause and sentence." In A. Manning, P. Martin, and K. McCalla, (eds), *The 10th LACUS Forum*. Columbia, SC: Hornbeam Press.

1985b "Non-thematic re-entry." In J.D. Benson, and W.S. Greaves, (eds), *Systemic Perspectives in Discourse*. Vol 1, Norwood, NJ: Ablex.

1985c "Some clause relational associated nominals in technical English." *Technostyle* 4/1.

1985d "Systems of logic in technical writing." *Technostyle* 4/3.

1985e "Some relations of surprise and expectation in English." In J. Hall, (ed.), *The 11th LACUS Forum*. Columbia SC: Hornbeam Press.

1985f "Towards an integrated theory of textual cohesion." *Midland Association for Linguistic Studies*. University of Birmingham, New Series, 10.

1986 "Co-associative lexical cohesion in promotional literature. *Journal of Technical Writing and Communication* 16/1 and 2.

1988a "Some advances in clause relational theory." In J.D. Benson, and W.S. Greaves, (eds), *Systemic Functional Approaches to Discourse*. Norwood NJ: Ablex.

1988b "The language of evaluation." *Technostyle* 6(2).

1989a "Relational propositions within the clause." In S. Embleton, (ed.), *The 15th LACUS Forum*. Lake Bluffs IL: LACUS.

1989b "How to plan and write problem-solving documents." In L. Beene, and P. White, (eds), *Solving Problems in Technical Writing*. Oxford: The University Press.

1990 "Clause relations within the anaphoric nominal group." In M.P. Jordan, (ed.), *The 16th LACUS Forum*. Lake Bluffs IL: LACUS.

Karlsen, R.

1964 *On 'Identifying,' 'Classifying,' and 'Specifying' Clauses in Current English: Zero, Ellipsis and Explicit Form*. Arbok for Universititetet i Bergen, Humanistik Serie, 4, Bergen: Norwegian University Press.

Keenan, E.O. and B. Schieffelin

1976 "Topic as discourse notion." In C.N. Li, (ed.), *Subject and Topic*. New York: Academic Press.

Labov, W.

1972 *Language of the Inner City: Studies in the Black English Vernacular*. Philadelphia PA: University of Pennsylvania Press.

Labov, W. and J. Waletsky

1967 "Narrative analysis: oral versions of personal experience." *Essay on the Verbal and Visual Arts*. Seattle WA: University of Washington Press.

Longacre, R.E.

1968 *Discourse, Paragraph and Sentence Structure in Selected Philippine Languages*. Dallas TX: Summer Institute of Linguistics Publications in Linguistics and Related Fields 21/1 and 2.

1972 *Hierarchy and Universality of Discourse Constituents in New Guinea Languages*, Georgetown: Georgetown University Press.

1976 *An Anatomy of Speech Notions* (Peter de Ridder Publications in Tagmemics). Lisse: Peter de Ridder Press.

1983 *A Grammar of Discourse*. New York: Plenum Press.

Mann, W.C. and S.A. Thompson

1986 "Relational propositions in discourse." *Discourse Processes* 9/1.

1987 "Rhetorical structure theory: towards a functional theory of text organization." *Text*. 8/3.

1989 "Rhetorical structure theory: a theory of text organization." In L. Polanyi, (ed.), *Discourse Structure*. Norwood NJ: Ablex.

Pike, K.L.

1967 *Language in Relation to a Unified Theory of Human Bahavior*. The Hague: Mouton.

Pike, K.L. and E.G. Pike

1977 *Grammatical Analysis*. Dallas TX: Summer Institute of Linguistics Publications in Linguistics and Related Fields 53.

Poutsma, H.

1926-29 *A Grammar of Late Modern English*. 2nd edition, Groningen.

Quirk, R.
1954 *The Concessive Relation in Old English Poetry*. New Haven, Connecticut: Yale University Press.

Quirk, R., S. Greenbaum, G. Leech, and J. Svartvik
1972 *A Grammar of Contemporary English*. London: Longman.

Strong, W.
1973 *Sentence Combining*. New York: Random House.

Sweet, H.
1891 *A New English Grammar*. Oxford: The University Press.

Thompson, S.A. and W.C. Mann
1986 "A discourse view of concession in written English." In S. DeLancey and R. Tomlin, (eds), *Proceedings of the Second Annual Meeting of the Pacific Linguistics Conference*. November.

1987 "A discourse view of concession in written English." *Language and Topics: Essays in Honour of M.A.K. Halliday*. Amsterdam/Philadelphia: John Benjamins.

van Dijk, T.A.
1972 *Some Aspects of Text Grammars: A Study of Theoretical Linguistics and Poetics* (Janua Linguarum, Series Major 63). The Hague: Mouton.

1973 "Models for text grammars." *Linguistics* 105.

1981 Studies in the Pragmatics of Discourse. The Hague: Mouton.

Werlich, E.
1976 *A Text Grammar of English*. Quelle and Meyer.

Widdowson, H.
1978 *Teaching Language as Communication*. Oxford: Oxford University Press.

Winter, E.O.O.
1968 "Some aspects of cohesion." In R.D. Huddleston, R.A. Hudson, E.O.O. Winter, and A. Henrici, (eds), *Sentence and Clause in Scientific English*. University of London OSTI Project.

1971 "Connection in science material: A proposition about the semantics of clause relations." *CILT* [Centre for Information on English language Teaching and Research] *Papers*, December.

1974 "Replacement as a function of repetition." PhD Thesis, University of London (see *Dissertation Abstracts International*, sec. C, Autumn 1977, 38,4).

1976 "Fundamentals of Information Structure." The School of Humanities. The Hatfield Polytechnic, Hatfield, Hertfordshire, England.

1977 "A clause relational approach to English texts: A study of some predictive lexical items in written discourse." *Instructional Science* (special issue) 6.

1979 "Replacement as a fundamental function of the sentence in context." *Forum Linguisticum* 4.

1982 *Towards a Contextual Grammar of English* London: George Allen and Unwin.

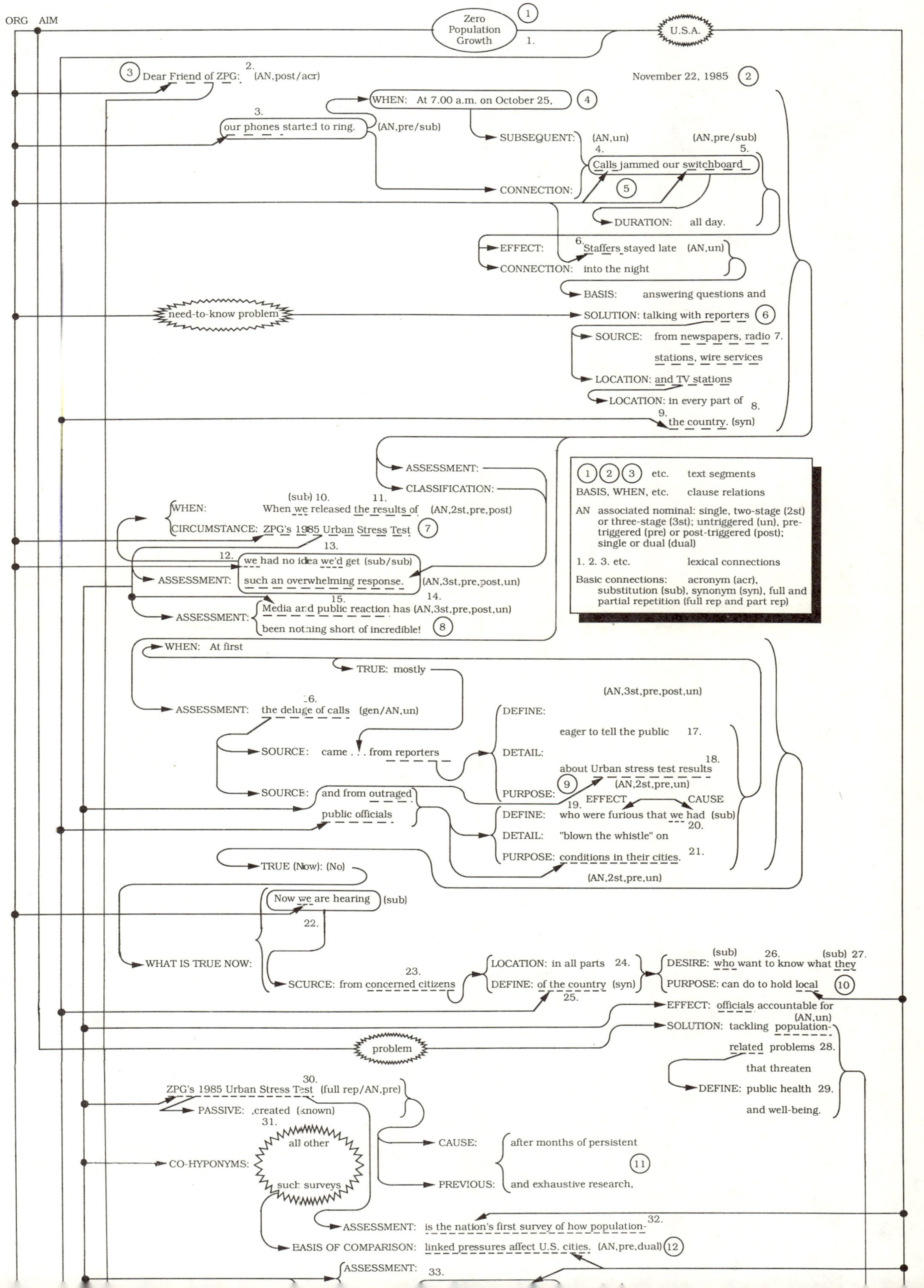
ORG
AIM
Zero Population Growth
1
1.
U.S.A.
3 Dear Friend of ZPG: 2. (AN,post/acr)
November 22, 1985 2
WHEN: At 7.00 a.m. on October 25, 4
3. our phones started to ring. (AN,pre/sub)
SUBSEQUENT: (AN,un) 4. (AN,pre/sub) 5.
Calls jammed our switchboard
CONNECTION: 5
DURATION: all day.
EFFECT: 6. Staffers stayed late (AN,un)
CONNECTION: into the night
BASIS: answering questions and
need-to-know problem
SOLUTION: talking with reporters 6
SOURCE: from newspapers, radio 7.
stations, wire services
LOCATION: and TV stations
LOCATION: in every part of 8.
9. the country. (syn)
ASSESSMENT:
CLASSIFICATION:
WHEN: (sub) 10. When we released 11. the results of (AN,2st,pre,post)
CIRCUMSTANCE: ZPG's 1985 Urban Stress Test 7
13.
12. we had no idea we'd get (sub/sub)
ASSESSMENT: such an overwhelming response. (AN,3st,pre,post,un)
14.
15.
ASSESSMENT: Media and public reaction has (AN,3st,pre,post,un)
been nothing short of incredible! 8
1 2 3 etc. text segments
BASIS, WHEN, etc. clause relations
AN associated nominal: single, two-stage (2st) or three-stage (3st); untriggered (un), pre-triggered (pre) or post-triggered (post); single or dual (dual)
1. 2. 3. etc. lexical connections
Basic connections: acronym (acr), substitution (sub), synonym (syn), full and partial repetition (full rep and part rep)
WHEN: At first
TRUE: mostly
(AN,3st,pre,post,un)
16.
ASSESSMENT: the deluge of calls (gen/AN,un)
DEFINE:
eager to tell the public 17.
SOURCE: came . . . from reporters
DETAIL:
about Urban stress test results 18.
9 (AN,2st,pre,un)
PURPOSE:
SOURCE: and from outraged
public officials
EFFECT CAUSE
19.
DEFINE: who were furious that we had (sub) 20.
DETAIL: "blown the whistle" on
PURPOSE: conditions in their cities. 21.
(AN,2st,pre,un)
TRUE (Now): (No)
Now we are hearing (sub)
22.
WHAT IS TRUE NOW:
23.
SOURCE: from concerned citizens
LOCATION: in all parts 24.
DEFINE: of the country (syn)
25.
(sub) 26. (sub) 27.
DESIRE: who want to know what they
PURPOSE: can do to hold local 10
EFFECT: officials accountable for
(AN,un)
SOLUTION: tackling population-
problem
related problems 28.
that threaten
DEFINE: public health 29.
and well-being.
30.
ZPG's 1985 Urban Stress Test (full rep/AN,pre)
PASSIVE: ,created (known)
31.
all other
CO-HYPONYMS:
such surveys
CAUSE: after months of persistent
11
PREVIOUS: and exhaustive research,
32.
ASSESSMENT: is the nation's first survey of how population-
BASIS OF COMPARISON: linked pressures affect U.S. cities. (AN,pre,dual) 12
ASSESSMENT: 33.

Figure 1

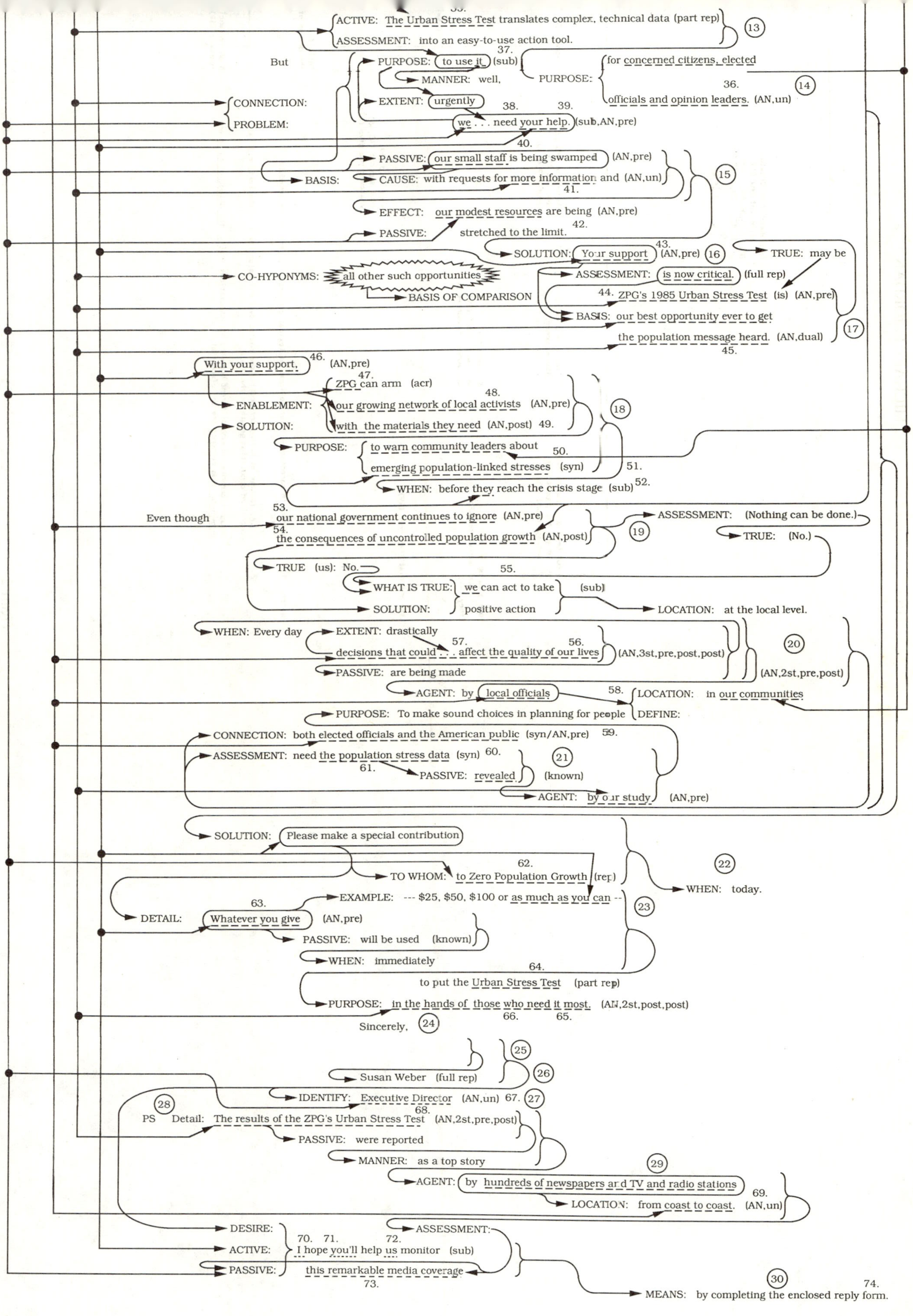

ACTIVE: The Urban Stress Test translates complex, technical data (part rep)
ASSESSMENT: into an easy-to-use action tool.
13
But
37.
PURPOSE: to use it (sub)
MANNER: well,
PURPOSE: for concerned citizens, elected
36.
officials and opinion leaders. (AN,un)
14
CONNECTION:
PROBLEM:
EXTENT: urgently
38. 39.
we . . . need your help. (sub,AN,pre)
40.
PASSIVE: our small staff is being swamped (AN,pre)
BASIS:
CAUSE: with requests for more information and (AN,un)
41.
15
EFFECT: our modest resources are being (AN,pre)
PASSIVE: stretched to the limit.
42.
43.
SOLUTION: Your support (AN,pre)
16
TRUE: may be
CO-HYPONYMS: all other such opportunities
ASSESSMENT: is now critical. (full rep)
BASIS OF COMPARISON
44. ZPG's 1985 Urban Stress Test (is) (AN,pre)
BASIS: our best opportunity ever to get
17
the population message heard. (AN,dual)
45.
With your support,
46. (AN,pre)
47.
ZPG can arm (acr)
48.
ENABLEMENT: our growing network of local activists (AN,pre)
18
SOLUTION:
with the materials they need (AN,post) 49.
PURPOSE: to warn community leaders about
50.
emerging population-linked stresses (syn)
51.
WHEN: before they reach the crisis stage (sub)
52.
53.
Even though
our national government continues to ignore (AN,pre)
54.
the consequences of uncontrolled population growth (AN,post)
ASSESSMENT: (Nothing can be done.)
19
TRUE: (No.)
TRUE (us): No.
55.
WHAT IS TRUE: we can act to take (sub)
SOLUTION: positive action
LOCATION: at the local level.
WHEN: Every day
EXTENT: drastically
57. 56.
decisions that could . . . affect the quality of our lives (AN,3st,pre,post,post)
20
PASSIVE: are being made
(AN,2st,pre,post)
AGENT: by local officials
58.
LOCATION: in our communities
DEFINE:
PURPOSE: To make sound choices in planning for people
CONNECTION: both elected officials and the American public (syn/AN,pre)
59.
ASSESSMENT: need the population stress data (syn)
60.
21
61.
PASSIVE: revealed
(known)
AGENT: by our study
(AN,pre)
SOLUTION: Please make a special contribution
22
62.
TO WHOM: to Zero Population Growth (rep)
WHEN: today.
63.
EXAMPLE: --- $25, $50, $100 or as much as you can --
23
DETAIL:
Whatever you give
(AN,pre)
PASSIVE: will be used (known)
WHEN: immediately
64.
to put the Urban Stress Test (part rep)
PURPOSE: in the hands of those who need it most. (AN,2st,post,post)
66. 65.
Sincerely,
24
25
Susan Weber (full rep)
26
IDENTIFY: Executive Director (AN,un) 67.
27
68.
28
PS
Detail: The results of the ZPG's Urban Stress Test (AN,2st,pre,post)
PASSIVE: were reported
MANNER: as a top story
29
AGENT: by hundreds of newspapers and TV and radio stations
69.
LOCATION: from coast to coast. (AN,un)
DESIRE:
ASSESSMENT:
70. 71. 72.
ACTIVE: I hope you'll help us monitor (sub)
PASSIVE: this remarkable media coverage
73.
30
74.
MEANS: by completing the enclosed reply form.

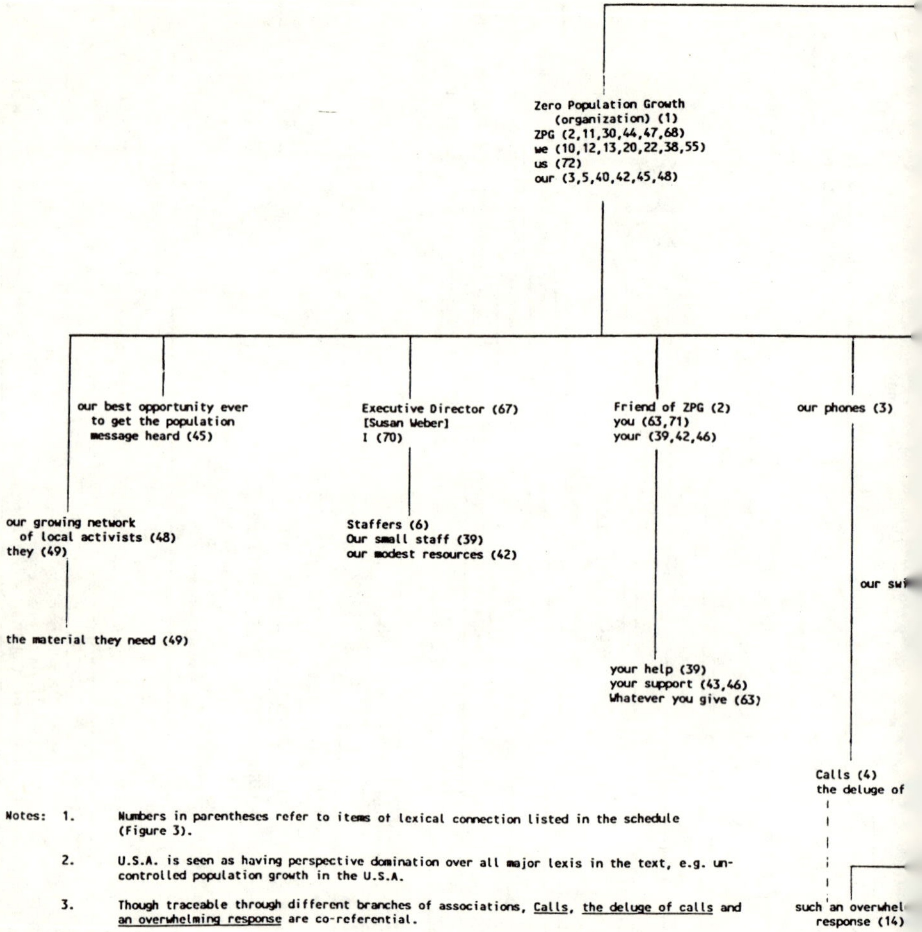

Notes: 1. Numbers in parentheses refer to items of lexical connection listed in the schedule (Figure 3).

2. U.S.A. is seen as having perspective domination over all major lexis in the text, e.g. uncontrolled population growth in the U.S.A.

3. Though traceable through different branches of associations, Calls, the deluge of calls and an overwhelming response are co-referential.

Figure 2

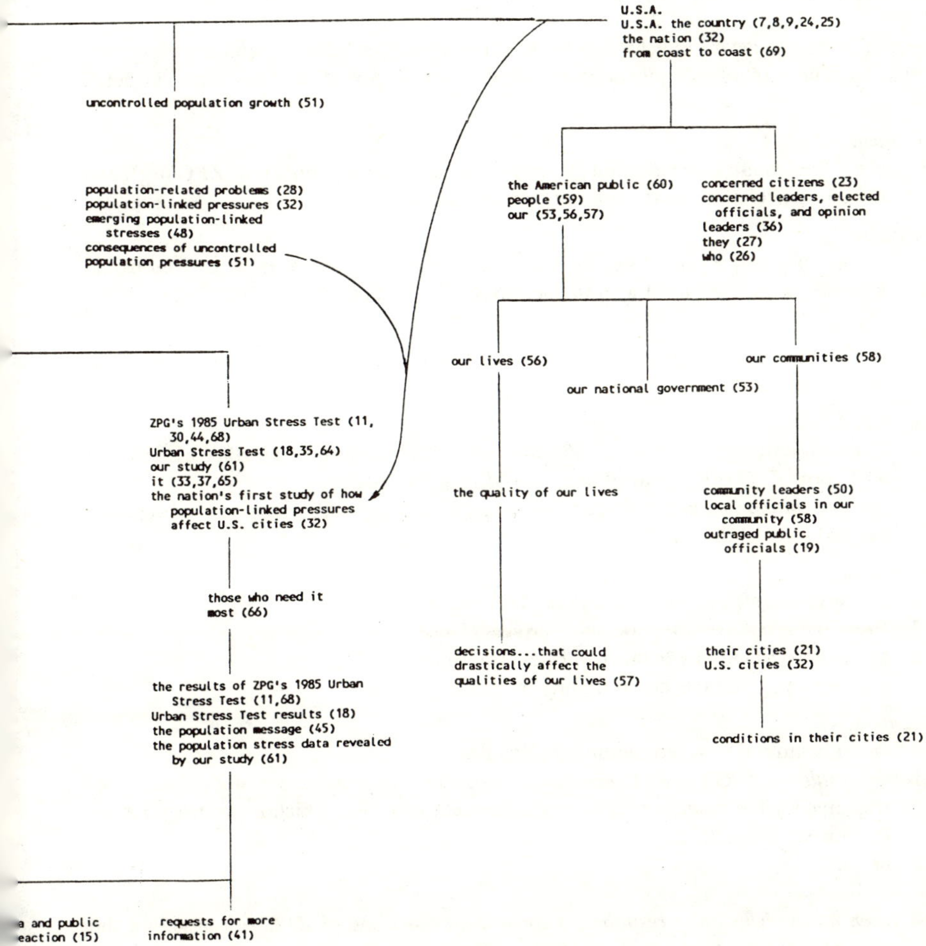
U.S.A.
U.S.A. the country (7,8,9,24,25)
the nation (32)
from coast to coast (69)
uncontrolled population growth (51)
population-related problems (28)
population-linked pressures (32)
emerging population-linked stresses (48)
consequences of uncontrolled population pressures (51)
the American public (60)
people (59)
our (53,56,57)
concerned citizens (23)
concerned leaders, elected officials, and opinion leaders (36)
they (27)
who (26)
our lives (56)
our national government (53)
our communities (58)
ZPG's 1985 Urban Stress Test (11, 30,44,68)
Urban Stress Test (18,35,64)
our study (61)
it (33,37,65)
the nation's first study of how population-linked pressures affect U.S. cities (32)
the quality of our lives
community leaders (50)
local officials in our community (58)
outraged public officials (19)
those who need it most (66)
decisions...that could drastically affect the qualities of our lives (57)
their cities (21)
U.S. cities (32)
the results of ZPG's 1985 Urban Stress Test (11,68)
Urban Stress Test results (18)
the population message (45)
the population stress data revealed by our study (61)
conditions in their cities (21)
a and public
eaction (15)
requests for more information (41)

Schedule of Lexical Connections *(Figure 3)*

Lexical connections are indicated as broken underlining in Figure 1, and are numbered thus: 16. The semantic connections are displayed as Figure 2, and described in detail here.

Segment 1

1. *Zero Population Growth*: seen as two meanings — the organization (*ZPG* org), and the aim (*ZPG* aim), both with implicit perspective *U.S.A*.

Segment 3

2. *Friend of ZPG*: a post-triggered associate of *ZPG* org (*advocate* not *friend* would collocate with *ZPG* aim) with the acronym *ZPG* as basic continuity.

Segment 4

3. *our phones*: a pre-triggered associate of *ZPG* org with possessive substitution *our* as basic continuity.

Segment 5

4. *Calls*: an untriggered associate of *our phones* and therefore a two-stage associate of *ZPG* org: *ZPG* org → our phones → *Calls* (on our phones).
5. *our switchboard*: a pre-triggered associate of *ZPG* org with possessive substitution *our* as basic continuity.

Segment 6

6. *Staffers*: an untriggered associate of *ZPG* org.
7. *from...country*: Defining locative verbless clause.
8. *in...country*: Defining locative verbless clause.
9. *the country*: generic basic continuity of *U.S.A*.

Segment 7

10. *we*: substitution basic continuity of *ZPG* org.
11. *the results of ZPG's 1985 Urban Stress Test*: a two-stage associate of *ZPG* org post-triggered by the associate *ZPG's 1985 Urban Stress Test*, which is pre-triggered by the posssessive *ZPG's*.
12. as 10.
13. as 10.
14. *such an overwhelming response*: a three-stage associate of *ZPG* org based on the untriggered two-stage associate of 11.; it is also basic continuity of the response as indicated in Figure 1, while at the same time both Classifying the calls as a *response* and Assessing them as *overwhelming*.

Segment 8

15. *Media and public reaction*: a three-stage associate of *ZPG* org based on the untriggered two-stage associate of 11.; it is also an overlapping co-hyponym of 14.
16. *the deluge of calls*: basic continuity including Assessment of the response indicated in Figure 1 with repetition of *calls*, and Assessment of *deluge* indicating large quantity.
17. *eager...results*: Defining Detailing verbless clause.
18. *Urban Stress Test Results*: synonym/partial repetition of the two-stage associate 14. with pre-triggering of *Results* by the untriggered *Urban Stress Test*.

19. *who...problems*: Defining basic continuity of *outraged public officials* by relative pronoun (*who*) substitution.
20. *we*: as 10.
21. *conditions in their cities*: a two-stage associate pre-triggered by possessive substitution *their* and then post-triggered by the first stage *in their cities*.

Segment 10

22. *we*: as 10.
23. *concerned citizens*: an untriggered associate of *U.S.A.* and a partitive of *the American public*.
24. *in...country*: Defining Locative verbless clause.
25. *the country*: repetition of the earlier *the country* as basic generic continuity of *U.S.A.*
26. *who...problems*: Defining basic continuity of *concerned citizens* by relative pronoun (*who*) substitution.
27. *they*: substitution basic continuity of *concerned citizens*.
28. *population-related problems*: a superordinate (*pre*-associate) of *ZPG* aim, as the problems are the initial stimulus for the aim and activities of the organization as attempted solutions to the problems.
29. *that...well-being*: Defining basic continuity of *population-related problems* by relative pronoun (*that*) substitution.

Segment 11

30. *ZPG's 1985 Urban Stress Test*: full repetition of the post triggering of 11. as a one-stage associate of *ZPG* pre-triggered by the possessive *ZPG's*.
31. *created*: non-defining *-ed* clause about the stress test.
32. *the nation's first survey of how population-linked pressures affect U.S. cities*: this complex nominal group contains an embedded associate *U.S. cities* pre-triggered by the partial acronym *U.S.* and the synonym *population-linked pressures* for the earlier *population-related problems*; these are embedded within the larger nominal group dominated by the associate *the nation's first survey*, which is pre-triggered by the possessive form of the *nation* (for *country*) and contains the superlative assessment compared with other surveys. (See Figure 2.)

Segment 12

33. *It*: substitution as basic continuity for the stress test.
34. *ranging...wastes*: Defining *-ing* clause about the *11 different criteria*.

Segment 13

35. *The Urban Stress Test*: partial repetition of 30.
36. *concerned leaders, elected officials and opinion leaders*: a complex untriggered associate of *U.S.A.* containing non-co-referential repetition of *concerned citizens* and *officials*.

Segment 14

37. *it*: as 33.
38. *we*: as 10.
39. *your help*: a pre-triggered associate of the earlier *Friend of ZPG* (Segment 2) and therefore a two-stage associate of *ZPG* org.

Segment 15

40. *Our small staff*: a pre-triggered associate of *ZPG* org with possessive substitution *Our* as basic continuity; possibly a synonym or near synonym for the earlier untriggered *Staffers* of Segment 6; contains the Assessment *small* within the nominal.
41. *requests for more information*: an untriggered associate of the stress test results in 11. and 18.
42. *our modest resources*: a pre-triggered associate of *ZPG* org with possessive basic continuity *our*; semantically parallel to, and possibly inclusive of, the *Our small staff* of 40.; contains the Assessment *modest* within the nominal.

Segment 16

43. *Your support*: an associate of *Friend of ZPG* pre-triggered by the possessive *Your*; it is therefore a two-stage associate of *ZPG* org; synonym of 39.

Segment 17

44. *ZPG's 1985 Urban Stress Test*: full repetition of 11. as a pre-triggered associate of *ZPG* org.
45. *our best opportunity ever to get the population message heard*: synonym (*population message*) for the stress test results embedded within the larger pre-triggered associated nominal, with possessive substitution of *ZPG* org being accomplished by *our*.

Segment 18

46. *your support*: a synonym or overlapping co-hyponym of 39. and 43. as an associate of *ZPG* pre-triggered by *your*.
47. *ZPG*: acronym as basic continuity for *ZPG* org.
48. *our growing network of local activists*: an associate of *ZPG* org pre-triggered by the possessive basic continuity *our* and with the added Assessment *growing*.
49. *the materials they need*: an associate of 48. post-triggered by the nul-signaled relative clause containing the basic substitution *they* for 48.
50. *community leaders*: a pre-triggered associate of *community*.
51. *emerging population-linked stresses*: full repetition from 32. with the added Detailing by *emerging*.
52. *they*: substitution as basic continuity for 51.

Segment 19

53. *our national government*: an associate of *U.S.A.* with possessive pre-triggering by the substitution *our* as basic continuity.
54. *the consequences of uncontrolled population growth*: a post-triggered associate of *uncontrolled population growth*, which is the superordinate situation within which the *population-linked problems* are perceived; this whole nominal is therefore a synonym or overlapping co-hyponym of 28. and 51.
55. *we*: as 10.

Segment 20

56. *the quality of our lives*: a three-stage associate of *U.S.A.* (U.S.A. → the American public → our lives → the quality of our lives).
57. *decisions that could affect the quality of our lives*: a four-stage associate of *U.S.A.* with the three stage nominal 56. in the post-triggering defining relative clause.

58. *local officials in our communities*: a remote co-hyponym of 56. diverging at the second root: (U.S.A. → the American public → our communities → local officials in our communities).

Segment 21

59. *people*: an untriggered associate of *U.S.A.*
60. *both elected officials and the American public*: co-ordinated one-stage associates of *U.S.A.*; the first is untriggered, and the second is pre-triggered by the synonym *American*.
61. *the population-stress data revealed by our study*: synonym for 11. containing a defining *-ed* clause (*revealed*) and the pre-triggered associate (*our study*) as a synonym for the *ZPG's 1985 Urban Stress Test*; the premodification by *population-stress* also indicates that this nominal is a pre-triggered associate of the superordinate *population stress problems*.

Segment 22

62. *Zero Population Growth*: full repetition, probably deliberately ambiguous as to *ZPG* org or *ZPG* aim.

Segment 23

63. *Whatever you give*: a complex associate of *Friend of ZPG* in Segment 2, which is included as the basic continuity substitution *you* within the nominal as necessary complementation for *Whatever*; the implicit indirect object is *ZPG* org.
64. *the Urban Stress Test*: partial repetition of 30. } (The *results* of the text ... *they*
65. *it*: basic substitution continuity of 64. } would have been more correct.)
66. *those who need it most*: one-stage associate of 64. post-triggered by the basic substitution *it* in the obligatory complementation for the generic *those*.

Segment 27

67. *Executive Director*: an untriggered associate of *ZPG* org and a verbless clause in true apposition with Segments 25 and 26.

Segment 29

68. *The results of ZPG's 1985 Urban Stress Test*: full repetition of 11.
69. *from coast to coast*: verbless clause as synonym for (mainland) *U.S.A.*

Segment 30

70. *I*: substitution as basic continuity for Segments 25 and 26.
71. *you*: substitution basic continuity for 2.
72. *us*: substitution basic continuity for *ZPG* org.
73. *this remarkable media coverage*: basic continuity of Segment 29 by the substitute nominal, with the addition of Assessment by *remarkable*.
74. *the enclosed reply form*: one-stage associate of the endophoric *this letter*, which provides partial pre-triggering for the association (enclosed with this letter).

A PROPOSED SYSTEM OF CLAUSE RELATIONS IN ENGLISH (Fig 4)

This is based on an earlier version in Jordan 1988a. See the list at the end for details of the references.

1. *BASIC RELATIONS*

1.1 *Detail Relations* (Ho 83, J84a, K,)

IDENTIFICATION	What is it? (genus)
CLASSIFICATION	What is it? (type)
SPECIFICATION	What is it? (after harbinger)
APPEARANCE	What does it look like?
CHARACTERISTICS	What are its features?
FUNCTION	What does it do?
MATERIAL	What is it made of?
PARTS	What does it consist of?

Many other relations are possible under this category to include any detail about something being described — see Ho83 and J84a. Function-based relations (J84a) takes function as the first relation and adds information regarding the Extent, Means, Manner, Circumstances of the function(s) of a topic; these other relations are listed later.

1.2 *General Relations*

ACTIVE	What did X do?
PASSIVE	What was done to X?
AGENT	Who did that?
SOURCE	What is the source of that information?

1.3 *Logical Relations* (J85c based mainly on B/C, L72 and W77

ASSESSMENT	What does X think of that? What is concluded from that? What has been decided?
BASIS	What is/are the basis/grounds evidence/reasons/justification for that?

The Assessment/Basis binary pair (also known as "Evaluation") deals with conscious thought, reasoning and decision-making (J84b,88a); Assessment often occurs on its own.

CAUSE	What was the cause of that?
EFFECT	What was the result of that?
EMOTIVE EFFECT	What emotional effect did that have on X (a person)?

This binary pair deals with action and reaction, stimulus and unthinking response, and changes brought about by something or an action. Reasoned response is Assessment/Basis. Mann and Thompson (1989) use the terms "volitional" and "non-volitional" to distinguish these pairs of relations.

PURPOSE	What is the purpose/ambition/aim/goal/intent of that or of that person, thing or group?
MEANS (B/CH)	By what means (how) was that done?

Purpose often appears without means, but rarely if ever vice versa. This pair deals with considered, planned intention and the way that is carried out. A four-part structure of

"Situation-Purpose-Means-Result" is often apparent as a document macro-structure or as a grouped micro-structure within a text.

PROBLEM	What is undesirable/unhealthy /harmful/lacking/restrictive inadequate/poor/incomplete/ faulty/unfair etc. about that? (J84b, Index B)
SOLUTION	What will or does overcome the problem? (W74, Hu77a/b, Ho79/83, M/T86)

Problem often occurs without solution, but rarely if ever vice versa. Problem is an adverse Assessment of a thing or situation. A four-part structure of "Situation-Problem-Solution-Evaluation" is often apparent as a document macro-structure (W76, Ho83) or as a grouped micro-structure within the text. Many complex combinations are possible (J80,81b,84b/c,89b).

If we accept that a Purpose is often to overcome a Problem, then the Means of achieving that Purpose is the Solution to the Problem (J85f). Thus these two binary pairs and their complications have a very close affinity. Closely related to these are the recognized pattern for plays and novels (Setting and Exposition-Complication-Resolution-Denouement), and other recognized patterns for narratives: Abstraction-Orientation-Complication-Action-Evaluation-Result or Resolution (La/We, La); and Aperture-Setting-Inciting-Conflict-Climax-Denouement-Suspense-Closure (L).

1.4 *Modal Relations* (C,J78) (with combined Agent relations*)

POSSIBILITY	Can that be done?
CAPABILITY*	Can X do that?
CORRECTNESS	Should that be done?
PROPRIETY*	Should X do that?
NECESSITY	Must that be done?
NEED*	Must X do that?
COMPLETION	Has that been done?
ACHIEVEMENT*	Has X done that?
FUTURE	Will that be done?
INTENTION*	Will X do that?
MANDATE	What mandate is there for that?
AUTHORITY	What authority is there for that?
DETERMINATION*	Is X determined to do that?
PERMISSION*	May X do that?
OBLIGATION*	Is X obliged to do that?
WILLINGNESS*	Is X willing to do that?
DESIRE*	Does X want to do that?

1.5 *Time Relations* (L)

TIME	When did that happen?
BEFORE	What happened previously?

AFTER	What happened after that?
SIMULTANEOUS	What happened at the same time?
INVERTED TIME	What happened then?

These relations are frequently combined with Active and Passive relations to create combined questions such as "What did X do after that?" and "What happened to X at the same time?"

1.6 *Other Substantive Relations*

ACCOMPANIMENT	What accompanied that?
CIRCUMSTANCE (M/T)	Under what circumstances did that happen?
INVERTED CIRCUMSTANCE	What happened under those circumstances?
CONNECTION (J78)	Can you tell me something in connection with that?
ENABLEMENT (M/T)	What enabled that to happen?
EXAMPLE	What is an example of that? (often also a Basis relation)
EXTENT	To what extent is that so?
LOCATION	Where did that happen?
INVERTED LOCATION	What happened there?
MANNER	In what manner was that done?
TRUE	Is that true?

The True relation is the basis for conditionals (If it is true...), hypotheticals (It may be true...), comparisons of topic, time, location and circumstance, and all matching relations.

1.7 *Text Manipulation* (L72, W74, Ho83, M/T)

ELABORATION	Will you elaborate on that?
SUMMARY	Will you summarize that?
REPETITION	Will you repeat that (in the same words)?
PARAPHRASE	Will you repeat that (in other words)?
FORECAST	Will you indicate what is to come?
TRANSITION	Will you indicate how the text is changing?

Note that what Longacre, and Winter and Hoey call "General-Particular" and Mann and Thompson call "Elaboration" relations are included here as:

Generalization-example/specific	Example
Preview-detail	Elaboration
Set-member, whole-part and process-step	Parts
Abstract-instance	Example

2. *MATCHING RELATIONS*

2.1 *Matching Detail*

Based on Winter's (1974) comparative affirmation and denial, these relations include the True relation about a co-hyponym Y of the original X.

TOPIC	Is that also true for Y?
TIME	Is that also true for time Y?
LOCATION	Is that also true for place Y?
CIRCUMSTANCES	Is that also true under circumstances Y?

2.2 *Matching Relations*

There are matching counterparts for most if not all of the basic relations, with the general question "Is that also true of Y."; these are based on Winter's (1974) affirmation and denial. Examples are:

AGENT	Did that person also do Y?
CAUSE	Is that also the cause of Y?
CAPABILITY	Can Y do that too?
TIME	Did Y happen then too?

3. *SPECIAL STRUCTURES AND MEANINGS*

Collateral Inversion (G) What is not True followed by what is; this is called Denial-Correction in Winter 1974.

Concession (Q,W74) The "surprise" involves the implicit denial (True) of the expected conclusion (an Assessment) based on the first part of the statement, followed by a statement of what *is* true (Collateral Inversion). But see Thompson and Mann 1986, 1987. Concession can occur in the more complex "Thesis-Concession-Rebuttal" structure (P,We,J78).

Compatibility/Contrast Viewed as compatibility (e.g. *and*) or non-compatibility (e.g. *but*) of Assessments of a topic or statement.

Comparison More specific here as Matching Detail based on the True relation. Mann and Thompson's (1986) treatment of "thesis-antithesis" is included here more specifically as Matching Truth, Truth + Basis, and Collateral Inversion.

Conditionals Viewed as additional semantics of the True relation mapped over other relations. Beekman and Callow's (1974) Condition-Consequence relation is Cause-Effect with Conditional Cause.

Document structures See discussion under Problem-Solution and Purpose-Means. Document macro-structures can be purely descriptive (containing only Detail relations) or be based on the logical pairs of relations. Other relations and groups of relations occur as micro-structures in the document.

Hypothetical-Real (One of Winter's (1974) wider clause relations) A statement modified by the True relation (hypothetical), followed by another True relation of denial, followed by Collateral Inversion, or by Assessment (reason) for Denial and Basis for that Assessment. Many combinations are possible.

Transition Couplets (J85e) Pairs of information types typically signaled by *but*, *however*, etc.: known/new (W82), problem/mitigation, situation/problem, good Assessment/bad Assessment, new or return to topic, concession, contrast, etc.

KEY TO REFERENCES

B/C	Beekman and Callow
C	Cook
G	Grimes
H	Healey
Ho	Hoey
H	Hutchins
J	Jordan
K	Karlsen
L	Longacre
La	Labov
M/T	Mann and Thompson
P	Poutsma
Q	Quirk
W	Winter
We	Werlich

How I Understand a Text — via the Structure of the Happenings and the Telling of Them

Evelyn G. Pike
Summer Institute of Linguistics
and
The University of Texas at Arlington

0. Introduction

One of the primary goals of the Pikean variety of tagmemics is to describe how a person, how I, can understand what a speaker or writer is trying to communicate. This implies understanding something of the speaker's or writer's emic system. An *emic* system consists of the contrastive, relevant units; the *etic* system, in contrast, is what an outsider must use to begin to discover what is relevant to the insider. It includes understanding something of the tolerance for variation in each emic unit.

Tagmemics is a holistic model of language as communication; the entrance point is social interaction. Prime attention is given to the norms of the language — those patterns of structure which exhibit the most contrastive features, hence are the least ambiguous. As these norms are roughed out, the overall symmetry of the language begins to unfold. These then form the skeleton by which those patterns which exhibit less contrastive features of one given pattern and take on increasingly more contrastive features of a second pattern can be more readily understood. This then, in turn spirals back in increased understanding and some redefining of the norms themselves. Pattern recognition is impossible without description; description is impossible without theory; theory is impossible without some prior description and pattern recognition. A holistic approach requires the integration of the three.

Language is considered to exhibit three semi-autonomous but interrelated structural patterns: phonology (phonemes, syllables, stress groups, pause groups, etc.); grammar (morphemes, words, phrases, clauses, sentences, paragraph on up through conversations); and reference (relations, identities, events, sequences of partially simultaneous and intersecting, purposeful events, through to the whole macro event or description). Referential structure has to do with what the speech or writing is talking or writing about, that is, with what is in the conceptual framework of the speaker/writer. Each of these three hierarchies exhibits part-whole relations; smaller units make up larger units — pattern within pattern. Individuals bring their own personal inventory of linguistic structure to bear in trying to understand and communicate with others. The more similar the emic structures (phonology, grammar, and reference) are, between the persons involved, the more immediate and complete is the understanding.

Tagmemics provides multiple perspectives for viewing data: The perspectives of particle (static), wave (dynamic), and field (relational), allow the analyst to change from one to another as data and interest shift. It also requires starting from a philosophical commitment to reality as known to us in terms of cultural or personal categorization of referential materials. For, along with Immanuel Kant (Manthey-Zorn 1966), tagmemics says that no "thing-in-itself" can be known as an objective thing without an observer.

In tagmemics the form and meaning of every unit are tied together; no form is identifiable without meaning and vice versa. This applies to units in each of the hierarchies.

Tagmemics asks four questions of an item under attention: **What** is it (*class*)? **Where** is it in relation to the immediately larger structure and what is its relative prominence — a cline from most nuclear to most marginal in that structure (*slot*)? **Why** does it occur and what is its function in that structure (*role*)? **How** does it govern another unit or how is it governed by another unit in any part of the total context; is its occurrence obligatory in all contexts or only in some contexts (*cohesion*)? For the referential slot, in addition to the features mentioned above, it also includes the place in space and time of the tagmeme. Referential role captures the human desire to know why things are as they are; what is the purpose or reason involved in any event or state or series of them, hence is introduced by (*in order*) *To* or *Because*. The question of why seems to be especially important to cultures where research and western law are highly regarded and somewhat differently or less so in some face-to-face cultures. The answers to the four questions are the contrastive features of a TAGMEME. Tagmemic labels are designed to be contrastive — if two items have the same label, they are judged to be emically the same; conversely, if they have different labels they are judged to be emically different. It should be noted that the relation which exist between the features of each tagmeme and between tagmemes are not always overt, but are deduced by decoders relative to their real-world knowledge and interests. As noted by Widowson (1988:187), "It is a common place in pragmatics that the interpretation of any discourse, written or spoken, will require the inference of relations between expressions which have not been explicitly spelled out. Confronted with two adjacent expressions, the language user will invoke the cooperative principle in Gricean fashion, assume the second expression is relevant to the first, engage interpretative procedures or practical reasoning and work out the most plausible connection or implicature."

Classes are of two kinds: (1) the lowest (minimal) structures of each hierarchy and (2) constructions (syntagmemes). Members of minimal classes are listed in the lexicon. As for constructions, each is a sequence of tagmemes which also manifests a single tagmeme at a higher level. Each tagmeme of a given construction is an immediate constitutent of that construction; constructions frequently consist of more than two immediate constituents. Any given tagmeme may be manifested by one of several different classes (a paradigmatic set of alternatives). Each of the four features described above is referred to as a *cell*, hence the term *four-cell tagmeme*. A tagmemic formula represents a construction with the sequence of its immediate constituents presented by a sequence of four-cell tagmemes; this is the definition of a construction class. The list of formulas together with a list in the lexicon of the manifesting classes is the core of the tagmemic mechanism for analysis and description. We illustrate with a grammatical formula for full transitive clause roots — examples from the Zero Population Growth (ZPG) letter (full, meaning that all three immediate constitutents are obligatory): S5 *calls jammed our switchboard*, S14 *we urgently need your help*, and S19 *our national government continues to ignore the consequences of uncontrolled population growth*. (Numbered segments refer to location in Zero Population Growth (ZPG) letter. The equals sign is to be read "is made up of".)

Full Transitive Clause Root =
CLASS: Noun Phrase or Pronoun (*calls, we, our national government*)

SLOT: Subject (nuclear)
ROLE: Actor (emic actor — central meaning is "that which does the verbing", not equatable with referential differences in members of the class such as animate versus inanimate)
COHESION: Governs number in the predicate; requires Active Phrase in the predicate; is obligatory in occurrence.

CLASS: Verb Phrase (*jammed, urgently need, continues*)
SLOT: Predicate (nuclear)
ROLE: Statement
COHESION: Requires actor and undergoer in the clause root; is governed by subject constraints for the predicate; is obligatory in occurrence.

CLASS: Noun Phrase or Infinitive Clause (our switchboard, your help, to ignore . . . growth)
ROLE: Undergoer (emic undergoer — central meaning is "that which is verbed"
COHESION: Infinitive Clause or Participial Clause is required with *continue*; is obligatory in occurrence

The classes in each of the tagmemes in each of the three hierarchies form the *greater lexicon*. Most units are simultaneously members of some class in each of the three hierarchies. A simple example would be a dictionary entry, in which the spelling represents the phonological class; the grammatical class is specified, and the stated meaning represents the referential class. An example of a high-level lexicon entry would be a limerick; it is a member of a special phonological class, grammatical class, and referential class, all of which would be indicated in the greater lexicon. Examples of classes included in the greater lexicon, but relevant to only one or two hierarchies include: (1) a class of consonant phonemes like *p*, *t*, *k* as in *pat*, *tat*, *cat* (phonological role of phonological contrastive relevance), but its members are not members of either a grammatical class or a referential class; and (2) the morpheme *but*, which is a member of a grammatical class having a grammatical role of contrast and also a member of the phonological class which includes the phonetic variant [CVC] occurring in several different phonological slot-roles. (cf. Pike and Pike 1983:95). However, *but* has no separate referential meaning and hence is not a member of a referential class. The greater lexicon is the interface between the three hierarchies with the formulas of each of the hierarchies indicating the appropriate place(s) each class may occur.

This is a very brief summary of the theory and mechanism that tagmemics provides. It has proved to be a framework for analysis that allows a quicker entrance into the general structure of a hitherto unwritten language than that provided by a number of other theories. It can address a large body of data, including cultural factors, in an organized system of patterns within patterns reflecting the emic system of the speaker. Analysis is not to be equated with presentation of that analysis; the analysis must be more extensive than the presentation. The answers to the preceding four questions may be annoyingly redundant, particularly in cases of one-member classes, and especially if they occur in one and only one slot in the data. The answers may also be redundant with those relating to higher or lower-level structures. Some parts of the analysis deal with topics that are so extensive that only a lengthy monograph could begin to do them justice. Thus investigators, for presentation, must sort out from their analysis those parts which are relevant to their current interest.

This holistic theory treats vast amounts of data. For a short discussion of a text only a small part of much relevant structure can be presented in any detail. Such detail becomes tedious, so we suggest that the reader attend to the detail to the extent of understanding the goals of the model, then skim the remainder. The data are presented in several ways: in prose style, in lists, in tree diagrams of sections of the data, in tagmemic formulas; all this is for easier understanding.

The referential structure will be presented first, because it is probably one of the more distinctive features of the model. It concerns cultural characteristics necessary to the understanding of people's speech. Note the difference between referential role and grammatical role. The former concerns function in society, whereas the latter concerns the function in the telling.

(For a more extensive treatment of tagmemic theory see Pike 1982. For a tagmemic textbook see Pike and Pike 1982. For a detailed tagmemic description of the grammar and reference of a short narrative, the phonology of a four-stanza poem, and the use of the tetrahedron to explain the relations within the four-cell tagmeme see Pike and Pike 1983).

1. The Referential Structure — What is Being Talked about

The referential structure is by far the largest of the three hierarchies. It is coextensive with the world as perceived or imagined and as it is talked about or could be talked about. The etic referential system is related to all the known cultures of the world just as a phonetic system involves a conflation of the phonemic systems of known languages. The use of texts, formal or informal, oral or written, and direct observation, is the entrance into the relevant features of the culture of any language group. To begin to understand, it is useful to take a text and *list* what happened first, second, etc. Then for each of these small events, each being member of a referential *class*, the other three features of the tagmeme need to be identified: (1) its *slot* features: place in time and space, and prominence; (2) its *role* features: for what purpose or reason would the encoder and participants understand the event to happen; (3) its *cohesion* features: constraints dependent on beliefs, success/failure, communication systems, weather, personal character traits, history, physics, etc. We include only the more obvious of these features. Although every previous experience or happening has some effect on a person's later actions, we include only the more obvious of these features. A list of the events in the ZPG letter together with their slot, role, and cohesion features will be given in section 1.1.

The event level of the referential hierarchy is roughly equivalent to clause level in the grammatical hierarchy; both structures are relatively independent in contrast to lower levels, as is the stress group in the phonological hierarchy. The *macro structure* of the referential hierarchy is made up of **vectors**. Each vector is a purposeful sequence of related happenings from the point of view of a member of the cast. Another way of putting it is that a vector is a sequence of happenings with a common effect, such as the pressures spoken of in the ZPG letter. A cast member may be either a single individual or a group of people working as one, such as the ZPG organization. Vectors are made up of *complexes of events* or a string of events or, only very occasionally, even of just one **event**. Vectors of more than one event are sequences of happenings which are more closely related to each other than they are to events in other vectors and fill a single higher-level slot-role. In turn, complexes are made up of other complexes or events. There are both action and state kinds of events. Events are made up of *identities*. We speak of entity kinds of identities such as people, artifacts, geographical locations. Also there are motion, state, and affective kinds of identities. *Relations* make up the lowest level of the referential hierarchy. We suggest that this level is comparable to the stem-affix relationship in grammar. For instance, the meaning of *on* cannot be known apart from a place relation of two entities to each other — one is *on* the other. Another such relation would be *beside* or *under*. (On the other hand, *if . . . then*, has only grammatical meaning. It is not a relation of the referential hierarchy.) Another kind of referential relation is illustrated by *beautiful* or *small* or *hard*. In order to know what these attributes mean, someone has to judge an identity to have such an attribute. Relations cannot be known apart from something else. In this sense they are "bound," much like affixes.

Underlying every text is the relation, actual or potential, of the encoder to the decoder. That relation is the *I-Thou-Here-Now Axis* in which *I* is the encoder, *thou* is the decoder, both in the same place and time. For communication to take place all four elements are required. The significance of *here* and *now* for speaking and hearing is modified somewhat for writing/filming and reading/viewing. Encoders produce the language product, and it is necessarily limited by their personal phonological inventory, their own grammatical inventory, and their own referential inventory. It is at this level that most of the governing cohesion originates. Many linguists differentiate cohesion and coherence, two standards of textuality as presented by Beaugrande and Dressler (1981:3-4). Tagmemics also differentiates the two, but with different labels: grammatical cohesion and referential cohesion respectively. The encoding of the referential structure is closely related to two additional standards of textuality to be found in Beaugrande and Dressler (1981:7): intentionality and acceptability. Encoders choose the topic appropriate to their interests and to those of their chosen audience (decoder). The audience can choose whether to continue the decoding process or not; hence the success of the communication is dependent on both parties.

How close the decoder's understanding is to the encoder's intent differs from person to person. As a decoder of the ZPG letter, I can state only what I understand the message to be. In order to understand some messages the study of many other texts is often required — that is what education is all about: The phonological, grammatical and, especially the referential structure of an individual is continually being revised and enlarged.

1.1 *Events*

Now we consider events. How many minimal events need to be included in a useful list? I would reply by asking an analogous question as to how detailed must a phonetic transcription be. My answer is that it needs to be sufficiently detailed to allow me to use it to understand speakers and to sound enough like them in order to be understood by them. Likewise I need enough detail in my list of events to allow me to understand the ZPG letter and to be able to respond to it appropriately. To state the fact that the staff is breathing is superfluous for this text.

The notion of script is important here (Schank and Abelson 1977). A larger event may be made up of smaller, predictable events which are expected by members of a cultural group. Hence the closer the referential structure of the decoder to that of the encoder, the fewer will be the details needing to be addressed overtly. In this regard, when I was working with a text in India, being ignorant of many of such scripts, I had to address much more detail, in order to understand, than would a local person; in the process, my referential structure was greatly enlarged! I had to get additional texts to be able to understand the original one. This is done continually in conversation as when we ask if the speaker meant this or that, etc.

Each referential event (RE) in our list for the ZPG letter is labeled by a number (RE1, RE2, etc.) showing essentially the relative order in which it began or is expected or hoped to begin, i.e., RE1, RE2, etc. In the letter most of the relative timing is not too crucial; therefore is not as detailed as some other texts would require. Each event is stated in the now time of its happening. Usually an active paraphrase is used rather than a stative one, since, in general, actions tend to be more prominent than states. At least research is frequently concerned with how or why states have come into being and such inquiry permeates our culture. Paraphrases (what the speaker/writer would agree to be a restatement of what was meant) are used extensively to understand both grammatical meanings (largely grammatical role) as well as referential meanings. Such paraphrases are in reality additional texts. The information that I have included in slot, role, and cohesion is derived from the letter itself or is what I, as decoder, guess the people involved would agree to. If it is not, then to that extent I have misunderstood the message. A list of events is actually a bookkeeping device (much as a tentative phonetic chart is) to sort out relevant structures. The list here, then, is reordered in subsequent sections to show the immediate constituent relations of the events.

In the following list of referential events in the ZPG letter, notice that the event labeled as class is only a member of a class. Displays 2 and 3 present classes of events with two examples of the class *Creative Event*, but only one of *Desired Affective Event* (wanting to produce an effect). Much work remains to be done to identify classes and their membership, at this level as well as all other levels. The particular instance, rather than the generalities that class implies, is largely what is presented here. Many people have worked extensively in this area, and even though they don't make overt the kind of contrast between reference and grammar that tagmemics does their work is very relevant to tagmemics. Note particularly that Longacre (1983:174) has at least forty-eight different classes listed in his scheme of case frames for verbs. Semantic inventories in Grimes (1986) are especially relevant to referential classes and an interlocking network of lexical systems. The lexical decomposition of Dowty (1979), also adopted by Foley and Van Valin (1984), would be another fruitful entry to the understanding of this very intricate area of study.

It is to be noted that any one event may be referred to at various places in the text, early or late, and not necessarily in the order of the actual chronology of that event in relation to other events. For each event we give the number of the segment(s) which refer to or imply that event. Also note that Referential Events 1-6 form the first of six immediate constituents of the total text (cf. sec.1.3). Referential Event 8 (RE8), which speaks of the organizing of ZPG, is an example of an event that subsumes a whole set of events in a script that, in turn, sets up a whole organization including its office. RE29 subsumes a letter-writing script.

The actual referent of the 1985 Urban Stress Test (UST) is not clear from the letter. In S11 it is described as being created after being researched. It would seem then to be a list of questions or topics to be used as a tool for making a survey, but not the survey itself. But the last part of S11 states that it *is* the survey. In S12 it ranks 184 areas; in S17 it is an opportunity. In these last two instances, it would seem that the report of the survey is referred to rather than the test itself. Sorting out the events in this part of the letter brought out these ambiguities.

Each event is a member of a referential class. The slot feature of relative prominence of the referential tagmeme has not been included in the following list, because it is in relation to other tagmemes of a construction (rather than in a list) that prominence is relevant. Notice also that the role derives from the immediate purpose (personal) or reason (either personal or nonpersonal) stated or implied in the letter, whereas the cohesion derives from the larger cultural framework constraining the occurrence of a particular member of the class manifesting the tagmeme. This is analogous to the grammatical cohesion agreement of a particular time morpheme in the verb with the time in the clause or paragraph or larger context. As yet there is no etic list of the features for each cell of a referential tagmeme comparable to the one for grammar in Pike and Pike (1982:397-409). However, analysts from closely related backgrounds, after some discussion, usually approach a consensus of relevant statements for each cell. If no consensus is reached, then, to that extent, each analyst understands the text differently.

Note that future events RE33-RE39.2 are inferred from the letter. For these the decoder relies on his knowledge of normal public response to such letters and to understand the alternatives: RE39.1 and RE39.2. (The cohesion abbreviation C/w is to be read "coherent with.")

The list of Referential Events

RE1 **CLASS**: Population-linked pressures affect USA cities. S10, 11, 18
SLOT: From decades before and after 10/25/85; in USA.
ROLE: Because of population density.
COHESION: Coherent with (C/w) style of living, lack of urban services, physical, psychological human needs, and with ZPG beliefs.

RE2 **CLASS**: Overpopulation threatens public health and well-being. S10
SLOT: Same as for RE1.
ROLE: Because of insufficient space and services.
COHESION: Same as for RE1.

RE3 CLASS: People become crowded in urban areas to varying degrees. S12
SLOT: Same as for RE1.
ROLE: Because of unlimited birth rate which differs from area to area (by far the most nuclear cause indicated by this text as seen in S19 relative to the country's "uncontrolled population growth" as well as the title of the organization as seen in the letterhead and throughout the text); other reasons for population concentrations such as population movement from rural to urban areas (deduced from S12 which seems to contrast "crowding" with "birth rates").
COHESION: Same as for RE1.

RE4 **CLASS**: Births occur in differing numbers from urban area to area. S12
SLOT: Same as for RE1.
ROLE: Because more children are born in some areas than in others.
COHESION: C/w natural processes, and with ZPG beliefs.

RE5 **CLASS**: Pollution of air occurs at differing levels from urban area to area. S12

SLOT: Same as for RE1.

ROLE: Because of differing amounts and degrees of air pollution sources.

COHESION: C/w geographic features such as space, air currents, etc., and with ZPG beliefs.

RE6 CLASS: Toxic waste occurs at differing levels from urban area to area. S12

SLOT: Same as for RE1.

ROLE: Because of differing density of various toxic waste sources.

COHESION: C/w waste disposal systems and with ZPG beliefs.

RE7 **CLASS**: National government ignores consequences of uncontrolled population growth. S19

SLOT: Time before and after 11/22/85; in USA.

ROLE: To not increase the government's involvement in concerns which are personal (more recently labeled "invasion of the bedroom"), local, and state.

COHESION: C/w majority of citizens' concepts of the appropriateness of the national government's responsibilities; C/w many other features, and with ZPG beliefs.

RE8 **CLASS**: People organize ZPG including choice of organization name, election of officers, and setting up of office. S1, also the first page top, bottom, and upper left margin of ZPG letter

SLOT: Some time, probably several years, before 10/25/85; in an unknown location.

ROLE: To have a more concerted effort via zero population growth to eliminate population-linked pressures affecting U.S. cities.

COHESION: C/w social concerns of many people in the USA.

RE9 **CLASS**: ZPG invites individuals to be sponsors of ZPG. The first page lower left margin of ZPG letter

SLOT: Soon after organization; probably in the office.

ROLE: To validate the reliability of people in ZPG and importance of their goals.

COHESION: C/w the need of the public to have evidence of the legitimacy of ZPG.

RE10 **CLASS**: ZPG very carefully and diligently prepares research topics and methods: their Urban Stress Test (UST). S11

SLOT: Largely before actual fieldwork but probably extending into the actual fieldwork itself; probably in the office, but probably in field areas as well.
ROLE: To have an optimally useful investigation.
COHESION: C/w recognized research procedures.

RE11 **CLASS**: ZPG persistently and exhaustively researches conditions in 184 urban areas. S11, 12
SLOT: Many "months" before 10/25/85; in various parts of USA.
ROLE: To rank many urban areas according to 11 different criteria of population-linked pressures.
COHESION: C/w ZPG goals.

RE12 **CLASS**: ZPG prepares the report indicating the results of UST. S12-14, 17, 21, 23
SLOT: Probably is begun somewhat before all the fieldwork is finished and extends to just before the release of the results to the media; from the office.
ROLE: To organize and summarize what the fieldwork indicates.
COHESION: Same as for RE10.

RE13 **CLASS**: ZPG releases UST results. S7
SLOT: Immediately before 10/25/85; from the office to unknown publisher(s)/person(s).
ROLE: To let public know how population-linked pressures affect US urban areas.
COHESION: C/w effective methods of implementing change in USA.

RE14 **CLASS**: Reporter(s) read(s) UST results and report(s) to media. S7, 30, etc.
SLOT: Immediately before 10/25/85; in USA.
ROLE: To have interesting items for readers/viewers/listeners.
COHESION: C/w current media practices.

RE15 **CLASS**: Many hundreds of newspapers, TV stations, and radio stations report UST as a top news story. S29
SLOT: Immediately before 10/25/85 and during subsequent days; in USA. S4, 29, 30
ROLE: To have interesting items for their readers/viewers/listeners.
COHESION: Same as for RE14.

RE16 **CLASS**: Elected officials and American public receive population-stress data. S21, 18
SLOT: Immediately before 10/25/65 and into the future; in USA.

ROLE: Because ZPG wants them to have it, and because it is available.
COHESION: C/w the notion people have of an appropriate way to begin to address a problem.

RE17 **CLASS**: UST stimulates great interest. S8
SLOT: On release of the report; in USA.
ROLE: Because of public concern for welfare of people.
COHESION: C/w individual and group concerns in USA.

RE18 **CLASS**: ZPG phones ring.
SLOT: 7 a.m., October 25, 1985; in ZPG office.
ROLE: Because of public interest.
COHESION: C/w methods of communication.

RE19 **CLASS**: Reporters from newspapers, radio stations, wire services, and TV stations call ZPG. S6
SLOT: 10/25/85; from their offices/other in USA.
ROLE: To get more information to pass on to the public. (This is in addition to the role of RE14.) S9
COHESION: C/w media practices.

RE20 **CLASS**: Outraged and furious public officials call ZPG. S9
SLOT: Same as for RE19.
ROLE: To object to the report and its implications and/or to object to ZPG activities.
COHESION: C/w their view of their public responsibilities.

RE21 **CLASS**: Staffers answer questions over telephone. S6, 10
SLOT: 10/25/85 and probably on following days; in ZPG office.
ROLE: Because people have called in asking questions.
COHESION: C/w ZPG's desired relations with the public.

RE22 **CLASS**: Staffers give information over telephone. S6, 10
SLOT: Same as for RE21.
ROLE: To get widest possible distribution of ZPG information.
COHESION: C/w ZPG's goals.

RE23 **CLASS**: Public response surprises ZPG staff. S7, 8
SLOT: 10/25/85 and after; wherever they are.
ROLE: Because of so much public response.
COHESION: C/w their normal expectancy of public response to work of a small, little-known group.

RE24 **CLASS**: ZPG staff works far beyond standard levels. S5, 6, 7, 8
SLOT: 10/25/85 and after; in office, and possibly elsewhere.
ROLE: Because public wants more information.
COHESION: Same as for RE20.

RE25 **CLASS**: Concerned citizens call ZPG. S10
SLOT: After 10/25/85 and toward 11/23/85: from various places in USA.
ROLE: To get more information in order to hold local officials accountable for population-related problems.
COHESION: C/w citizen-felt responsibility toward elected officials and local conditions.

RE26 **CLASS**: ZPG's modest resources are being stretched to their limit. S15
SLOT: After 10/25/85; wherever ZPG works.
ROLE: Because of increased demands on staff and materials.
COHESION: C/w budgetary reality.

RE27 **CLASS**: More people join network of local activists. S18
SLOT: Before 11/22/85 and hopefully after; in USA.
ROLE: Because of ZPG's work.
COHESION: C/w increased public interest when definite information is made available.

RE28 **CLASS**: Local activists warn community leaders about population-linked stresses. S18
SLOT: When potential supporters contribute; in USA.
ROLE: To get help to address population-linked problems.
COHESION: C/w ZPG goals and with accepted ways of initiating change.

RE29 **CLASS**: Susan Weber writes ZPG letter to "friends" (potential supporters) asking for their help, support, and contributions. S26
SLOT: 11/22/85; in ZPG office.
ROLE: To get more money and other kinds of help for ZPG.
COHESION: C/w citizens' felt responsibility to improve environment and Weber's responsibilities as Executive Director of ZPG.

RE30 **CLASS**: Weber suggests that friends give $25/$50/$100/ as much as they can. S23
SLOT: 11/22/85; in letter from the office.
ROLE: To get gifts of more than a dollar or two from each.
COHESION: C/w effective cost realities.

RE31 **CLASS**: Susan Weber expresses her hope that ZPG friends will help monitor top news stories. S30
SLOT: Same as for RE30.
ROLE: To gain more information and possibly to get a response from people who would not give money.
COHESION: C/w accepted means of getting help.

RE32 **CLASS**: ZPG's friends must augment ZPG's resources. S16, 14
SLOT: 11/22/85; from all parts of USA to ZPG office.
ROLE: Because there is no other source of income and income is needed immediately.
COHESION: C/w customary methods of supporting nonprofit organizations.

RE33 **CLASS**: Friends receive ZPG letter.
SLOT: After 11/22/85; in home/office.
ROLE: Because of ZPG effort and US postal service.
COHESION: C/w communication systems.

RE34 **CLASS**: Some ZPG friends give money. S16, 18, 22, 23
SLOT: After receiving ZPG letter/other ZPG information; from home/office.
ROLE: To help and encourage ZPG.
COHESION: C/w understood needs of ZPG.

RE35 **CLASS**: Some ZPG friends complete the form.
SLOT: After receiving ZPG letter; in home/office.
ROLE: Same as for RE34.

RE36 **CLASS**: Fewer ZPG friends than those in RE35 return the form.
SLOT: Same as for RE35.
ROLE: Same as for RE34, and because of normal inertia or lack of interest.
COHESION: Same as for RE34.

RE37 **CLASS**: ZPG uses money and other help given by friends. S23, 30
SLOT: After 11/22/85 when money, forms, and any other help arrives; in office/other.
ROLE: To put the UST results and/or other materials in hands of those who need it most. S23
COHESION: C/w ZPG goals and promises.

RE38 **CLASS**: Some people take positive ZPG action in local community (at local level). S18, 19, 22, 23
SLOT: After 11/22/85, but more in future; in USA.
ROLE: To lessen population-linked problems.
COHESION: Same as for RE27.

RE39 ALTERNATIVE 1 **CLASS**: Population-linked stresses do not reach crisis stage. S18
SLOT: Unknown time after 11/22/85; in USA.
ROLE: Because enough has been done to diminish population-lined problems.

COHESION: C/w success in initiating change in a large population.

RE39 ALTERNATIVE 2 **CLASS**: Population-linked stresses reach crisis stage. S18

SLOT: Unknown time after 11/22/85; in USA.

ROLE: Because not enough has been done to diminish population-linked problems.

COHESION: C/w with failure in initiating change in a large population.

1.2 *Macro Structure*

The whole letter speaks of the macro event, an example of the class Plea for Assistance, and begins to show the immediate constituent relations of the events in the preceding list. We represent it first with a tagmemic formula and follow with a tree diagram which presents the same information, but in addition includes some lower-level constructions within each vector. Plea for Assistance is made up of six immediate constituents — groups of happenings, each with different effects and/or purposes and points of view. The prominence of each immediate constituent in relation to the others of the construction is a cline indicated from high prominence to least prominence as follows: Nucleus+, Nucleus, Nucleus−, Margin+, Margin, and Margin−. The contrastive vectors are: Pressure Vector, ZPG Vector, Media Vector, Friends Vector, Public Vector, and Official Vector. (Again the equals sign in a tagmemic formula is to be read "is made up of.")

ZPG Plea for Assistance =

CLASS: Pressure Vector RE1-6

SLOT: Nucleus−; decades before and after 10/25/85; in USA.

ROLE: Because of population density.

COHESION: Coherent with (C/w) beliefs of ZPG.

CLASS: ZPG Vector RE8-12, 17-24, 29-32, 37, 16, 27-28, 38-39

SLOT: Nucleus+; before and after 10/25/85; in USA.

ROLE: To prevent population-linked stresses reaching crisis stage.

COHESION: C/w success/failure of ZPG goals dependent on RE39 Alternate 1 or 2.

CLASS: Media Vector RE14-15, 17, 19, 23

SLOT: Margin; immediately before 11/22/85; in USA.

ROLE: Partial means of solution.

COHESION: C/w information dispersement.

Figure 1: Referential Structure: Vectors down to events

CLASS: Friends Vector RE33-36
SLOT: Nucleus; after 11/22/85 into future; in USA.
ROLE: Partial means of solution.
COHESION: C/w current ways of assisting groups.
CLASS: Public Vector RE16, 20-22, 27, 38
SLOT: Margin; before and after 11/22/85.
ROLE: Means of change (Positive public opinion is essential for most substantial changes in USA.).
COHESION: C/w felt responsibility.
CLASS: OFFICIAL VECTOR RE7, 16, 20
SLOT: Margin; same as for RC5.
ROLE: Official function.
COHESION: C/w job description.

1.3 *Event Structure*

Time and space permit only sketchy presentations of lower-level referential structure. In section 1.2 a skeleton presentation of structure down to events was given. Now are presented examples of the composition of the event level. Figure 2 presents the class Creative Event (two examples RE10 and 12,) but only RE10 is developed down to relation constituents.

Examples of Creative Event:
RE10 ZPG very carefully & diligently prepares research topics & methods.
RE12 ZPG prepares the report indicating the results of UST.

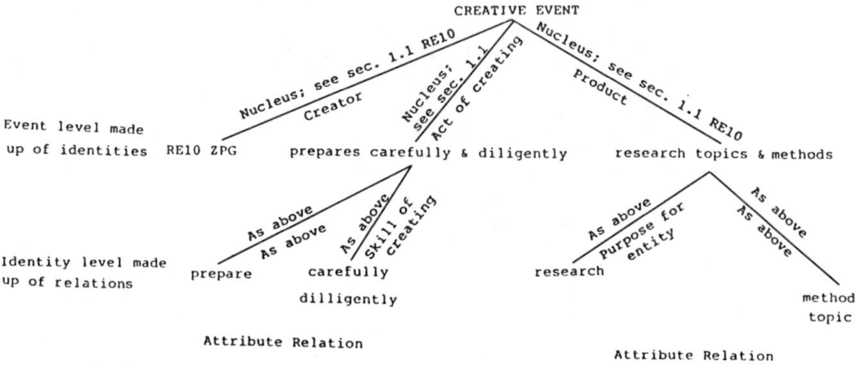

Figure 2: Referential Structure: Creative event down to relations.

Creative Event has three immediate constituents: *ZPG* with the role of **creator**, *prepares carefully and diligently* with the role of **act of creating**, and *research topics and methods* with the role **product**. Each of the last two constituents are identities within which are attribute relations. **Skill of creation** is the role of both *carefully* and *diligently* as attributives to *prepare*. **Purpose for entity** is the role of *research* as attributive to *method* and *topic*.

Example of Desired Affective Action Event:

RE38 Some people take positive ZPG action at local level.

Paraphrase: Some people do ZPG suggested acts toward elected officials/community leaders.

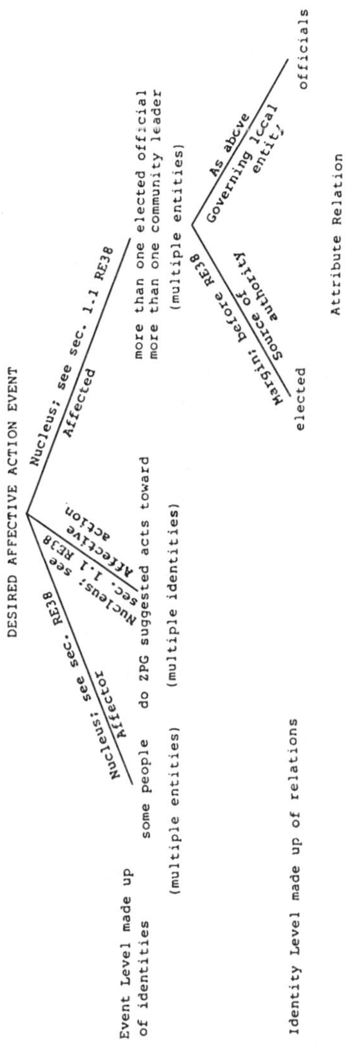

Figure 3: Referential Structure: Desired affective action event down to relations.

1.4 *Identities and Relations*

Figure 3 presents example RE38 of the class Desired Affective Action Event.

1.4.1 *Identities*

The class ZPG is the nuclear entity (one kind of identity) and cast member in the text. Its basic role is **initiator of action**, but some of its other roles include **experiencer** as well as **patient**. It is made up of a group of people as seen in the members of its paraphrase set: S6 *staffers*, S4 *our*, S7 *we*, and S30 *us*. The paraphrase *Zero Population Growth*, in S22 and in the logo, as well as the abbreviation ZPG in S7, etc., probably give more emphasis to the organization as a whole than do the first four paraphrases. The full use of the name in S22 may be given to suggest that contributors should use the full name to make out checks. The initials are less formal than the full form and are probably used to take up less space in the letter. Note that S19 *we* and S19, 20 *our*, include not only ZPG, but the friends as well — the inclusive use of first person plural. The meaning of *our* in S17 is not clear as to whether or not friends are included *in our best opportunity*.

Susan Weber is another entity and is included in the paraphrase set with *Executive Director*, in S27 and in the printed stationary, and the pronoun S30 *I*. The latter is less formal and promotes a more personal relation with the friends than do the other paraphrases.

Initiating entities: *friend*, *reporter*, *official*, *citizen*, *Susan Weber*. Instruments: *phones*, *switchboard*, *newspaper*, *radio station*, *test*. Time identities: S17 (*best opportunity*) *ever*; S20 *every day* (*decisions*); S22 *today*; S23 *immediately*; S16 *now*. Quantities such as S12 *184* (*areas*) are not attributes, but indicate the number of entities involved; also, plural indicates that more than one entity is involved. Grammatically a quantity is subordinate to a noun and the plural suffix to a noun root or stem, but they are not subordinate referentially.

Among action and state identities are the following: Affective Action: S5 *jam* (*Calls jammed our switchboard*); S11 *affect* (*pressures affect U.S. cities.*). Search Action: S11 *research* (*exhaustive research*). Requiring Something State: S14 *need* (*we urgently need your help*), and S23 *those who need it most*. Much is yet to be done in this area.

1.4.2 *Relations*

We list just a few relations: Attribute relation: S21 *sound* (*choices*); S9 *outraged* (*public officials who were*) *furious*; S23 "needy" *those who need*; S20 *drastically* (*affect*) in which an action is understood to be done intensely and with a negative effect. It is assumed that differences in meaning within each of the above relations are not in the relationship, but rather in the nature (referential subclasses) of the identity and characteristics involved. Ownership relation: S4 *our* (*telephones*); S7 *ZPG's* (*1985 Urban Stress Test*), supposing that ZPG owns the copyright, but there is an additional relationship of Target-source. Allegiance relation: S3 *friend of ZPG* (relation of friend to ZPG). Partitive relation: S6, 10 (*part(s)*) *of the country*; S30, 7 *I vs. we*. Comparison relation: S11 *first survey* (of two or more); S17 *best opportunity* (of three or more); S23 *those who need it most* (of three or more). Target-source relation: S7, 29 *results of ZPG's 1985 Urban Stress Test* in which *of* introduces the source which is *ZPG's 1985 Urban Stress Test*, and *results* is the target. The embedded *ZPG's . . . Test.* was listed as exhibiting an ownership relation, but I understand the ownership relation to be less basic than the target-source relation; ZPG is the source and UST is the target; thus ZPG's UST exhibits at least two relations.

This is a very thin sketch of our referential framework. Considerable work remains to be done and the work of many other scholars has much to contribute in this area.

2. The Grammatical Structure — the Telling

2.1 *General Characteristics*

Grammar differs from reference in various ways. A very basic difference is that of sequence. The referential sequence of happenings (chronological sequence) is a fixed sequence. ZPG released the results of the test before their phones started to ring; that sequence is irreversible, but grammatically they tell about the ringing of the phones (S4) before they tell about releasing the results of the test (S7). Susan Weber could have used the chronological order for the telling order, had she wanted, but she could not have changed the happening order. Grammatical order is not fixed; referential order is. Even in languages as some on the island of New Guinea in which very little deviation from the chronological order is allowed within certain structures, there is some deviation such as within quotations. Moreover, referentially, many things happen at the same time. No doubt various members of the ZPG staff were working simultaneously at different tasks, but to tell about that simultaneously is impossible since words are spoken in sequence. Even simultaneous events have to be reported in sequence: *Bill, John, and Joe sang*.

Another difference between grammar and reference is the kinds of classes, slots, roles and cohesion in each. Consider the second clause of S19, *we can act to take positive action at the local level*. That information is accounted for referentially as Referential Event 38 with the role of **lessening population-linked problems**, but grammatically it is an Independent Clause with the role of **contrast** (in relation to the preceding dependent clause *Even though our national government* . . . which has the role of **point-of-reference**).

For the grammatical hierarchy in English, the following levels are posited: conversation, exchange, monolog, paragraph, sentence, sentence stem, clause, clause root, phrase, word, stem morpheme cluster, with morpheme classes as minimal classes. Minimal classes in each of the hierarchies do not constitute a level, but only fill slots in some level. Conversation and exchange have the common meaning of "social interaction"; monolog and paragraph have the common meaning of "theme development"; sentence, clause, and clause root have the common meaning of "proposition"; phrase and word have the common meaning of "term"; morpheme cluster (stem) and morpheme have the common meaning of "lexical packaging."

As mentioned earlier, the I-Thou-Here-Now Axis underlying every stream of speech is the source of major governing constraint features. The grammatical structures used by encoders are confined to their personal inventories of structures and of their esthetic competence. They choose, among other things, the genre, the addressee, (hence the level of politeness that is required), and the basic grammatical cohesive time line of the text. Longacre (1983, 1988) makes extensive use of tense and aspect in discussing various kinds of information in a text which relates to cohesion as presented here, as do Halliday and Hasan (1976:186ff). For the ZPG letter the use of *we* for the writer and *you* (singular, as indicated by the salutation *Dear Friend* . . . S2) for the reader was the cohesion feature chosen by the writer. She also chose to use the cohesion feature of basic discourse time as future for desired action on the basis of the present and past time of other actions.

On the other hand, the other parties of the axis, the hearers/readers, use their own inventory of grammatical structures to understand those of the speakers and frequently that structure is enlarged by what is heard/read.

2.2 *Business Letter*

The ZPG letter is a member of the grammatical class Business Letter (Bus Let) but the nucleus of the letter, having the role of **primary request**, is filled/manifested by the grammatical class Request Discourse, which is a subtype of hortatory discourse. This hortatory classification follows the genre criteria of Longacre (1983): (1) It exhibits agent orientation — how the friends should act. (2) It does not exhibit contingent temporal succession such as a narrative exhibits. (The text does speak of a succession of events, but not contingent succession; the requested act of friends is not determined on any of their previous acts.) (3) It exhibits the feature of projection (future acts) by which a hortatory discourse contrasts with a eulogy, within Longacre's behavioral classification.

This text is a request type of discourse rather than the more general hortatory one, because, although a command form is used in the nucleus of the text, it is mitigated by the use of the politeness marker *please* in S22. The notion of degrees of deference is important (cf. MacArthur 1979, Doty 1984, Hurlbut 1984). These distinctions are accounted for in grammatical role. Doty (1964), for example, posits five degrees of mitigated commands for a Tiruray text of the Philippines. For the ZPG letter there are only three such degrees: S22 **request** (there are no direct commands), S30 **mitigated request**, and S14, 16, 18 **implicit request**. Compare these with the role of **request thesis** for S22 *Please make . . . contribution*; the role of **mitigated request thesis** for S30 *I hope . . .*; **implicit request thesis** for S14 *we . . . need , S16 Your support now is critical*, and S18 *With your contribution . . . .*

The grammatical analysis of the letterhead is omitted except to say that *ZERO POPULATION GROWTH* in the logo is a noun phrase and is the title of the organization of which Susan Weber is a member. (For more discussion of the letterhead see sec. 3.) The letter proper has five immediate constituents:

(1) S2 Date Phrase filling the margin of Business Letter with the role of time; coherent with (C/w) setting the now time of the writing as the point of reference for previous vs. future actions.

(2) S3 Salutation Noun Phrase filling the margin of Bus Let with the role of direct address; C/w being identified as second person singular; obligatory in occurrence.
(3) S4-23 Request Discourse filling the nucleus of Bus Let with the role of primary request; C/w formal deference to addressee; is obligatory in occurrence. (cf. Displays 4A, 4B, 4C).
(4) S24-27 Sign-off Formula filling a margin of Bus Let with the role of sign-off; C/w use of *we* for the total ZPG organization; is obligatory in occurrence.
(5) S28-30 Dependent Request Paragraph (Para) filling a margin of Bus Let with the role of secondary request; C/w Weber's personalizing the message in the use of *I*; is optional in occurrence.

2.3 *Request Discourse*

The grammatical structure of the Request Discourse is presented here in the form of an outline rather than by formulas. Every construction carries the function of the role of its including structure. Thus even though a role is labeled only **thesis**, it is the thesis of its including structure, as, for example, in the following outline, in 212.2 S20-21 Reason Para, whose nucleus with the role of **thesis** is filled by Independent Sentence (Ind Sent). That particular thesis is an **amplification thesis** by virtue of the fact that it is dominated by the role of amplification in its including structure. Also note that by following the nucleus of each construction down the hierarchy, the nuclear thesis of the whole discourse is found: S22 the Request Sentence (see Displays 4A, 4B, 4C). Likewise, by following the nucleus of each construction of the first margin of the discourse, the nuclear problem is found in 1222.1 S14 with the role of **implicit request**, which is dominated by **problem thesis** role. Cohesion features of lower levels are omitted if they have been accounted for in including structures. (The numbers in the outline of Request Discourse S4-23 that follows are also the ones used in the displays.)

1 S4-15 Induction Paragraph (Induc Para) filling the margin (of Req Disc) (probably more marginal in relation to the second immediate constituent) with the role of **problem/reason for request**; C/w governing cohesion features of the I-Thou-Here-Now Axis and Business Letter), C/w topics of the nucleus of Request Discourse.

1.1 S4-10 Attestation Para filling the margin (of Induc Para) with the role of **evidence**

11.1 S4-8 Induction Para filling the nucleus (of Attest Para) with the role of **thesis**.

111.1 S4-6 Amplification Para filling the margin (of Induct Para) with the role of **evidence**.

1111.1 S4 Independent Sentence (Ind Sent) filling the margin (of Ampli Para) with the role of **setting**.

1111.2 S5 (Ind Sent) Ind Clause (Note: S5 is simultaneously an independent sentence and a clause because there are no sentence margins, thus the immediate constituents of S5 are clause immediate constituents. In such instances of a lower level structure being also a higher level structure; the higher level structure will be in parentheses accompanying the class exhibiting immediate constituents.) Ind Clause fills the nucleus (of Ampli Para) with the role of **thesis**.

1111.3 S6 (Ind Sent) Clause Coordinate Complex filling the margin (of Ampli Para) with the role of **amplification**.

111.2 S7-8 Simple Para filling the nucleus (of Induc Para) with the rolc of **thesis** (of Induc Para).

1112.1 S7 Ind Sent filling the margin (of Simp Para) with the role of **setting**.

1112.2 S8 (Ind Sent) Equative Clause Root filling the nucleus (of Simp Para) with the role of **thesis**.

11.2 S9-10 Sequence Para filling the margin (of Attest Para) with the role of **evidence**.

112.1 S9 Sequence Sent filling the nucleus (of Seq Para) with the role of **sequence thesis 1**.

112.2 S10 Sequence Sent filling the nucleus (of Seq Para) with the role of **sequence thesis 2**.

1.2 S11-15 Simple Para filling the nucleus (of Induc Para) with the role of **problem thesis**.

12.1 S11-12 Identification Para filling the margin (of Simp Para) with the role of **introduction**.

121.1 S11 (Ind Sent) Equative Clause Root filling the nucleus (of Ident Para) with the role of **item**.

121.2 S12 (Ind Sent) Ind Clause filling the nucleus (of Ident Para) with the role of **function**.

12.2 S13-15 Point of Reference-Contrast Para filling the nucleus (of Simp Para) with the role of **problem thesis**.

122.1 S13 (Ind Sent) Ind Clause filling the margin (of Pt of Ref Para) with the role of **point of reference**.

122.2 S14-15 Reason Para filling the nucleus (of Pt of Ref Para) with the role of **contrast**.

1222.1 S14 Contrast Sent filling the nucleus (of Reas Para) with the role of **implicit request**.

1222.2 S15 (Ind Sent) Clause Coordinate Complex filling the margin (of Reas Para) with the role of **reason**.

2 S16-23 Reason Para filling the nucleus (of Req Disc) with the role of **requested solution**; C/w embedding structure, C/w governing topics of margin of Request Disc.

2.1 S16-23 Reason Para filling the margin (of Reas Para) with the role of **reason**.

21.1 S16-18 Reason Para filling the nucleus (of Reas Para) with the role of **Thesis**.

211.1 S16 Ind Sent filling the nucleus (of Reas Para) with the role of **implicit request**.

211.2 S17 (Ind Sent) Ind Clause filling the margin (of Reas Para) with the role of **reason 1**.

211.3 S18 Ind Sent filling the margin (of Reas Para) with the role of **reason 2**.

21.2 S19-21 Amplification Para filling the margin (of Reas Para) with the role of **reason**.

212.1 S19 (Ind Sent) Point of Reference Sentence Stem filling the nucleus (of Ampli Para) with the role of **thesis**.

212.2 S20-21 Reason Para filling the margin (of Ampli Para) with the role of **amplification**.

2122.1 S20 (Ind Sent) Independent Clause filling the margin (of Reas Para) with the role of **reason**.

2122.2 S21 Ind Sent filling the nucleus (of Reas Para) with the role of **thesis**.

2.2 S22-23 Amplification Para filling the nucleus (of Ampli Para) with the role of **request thesis**.

22.1 S22 Request Sent filling the nucleus (of Ampli Para) with the role of **request thesis**.

22.2 S23 (Ind Sent) Ind Clause filling the margin (of Ampli Para) with the role of **amplification**.

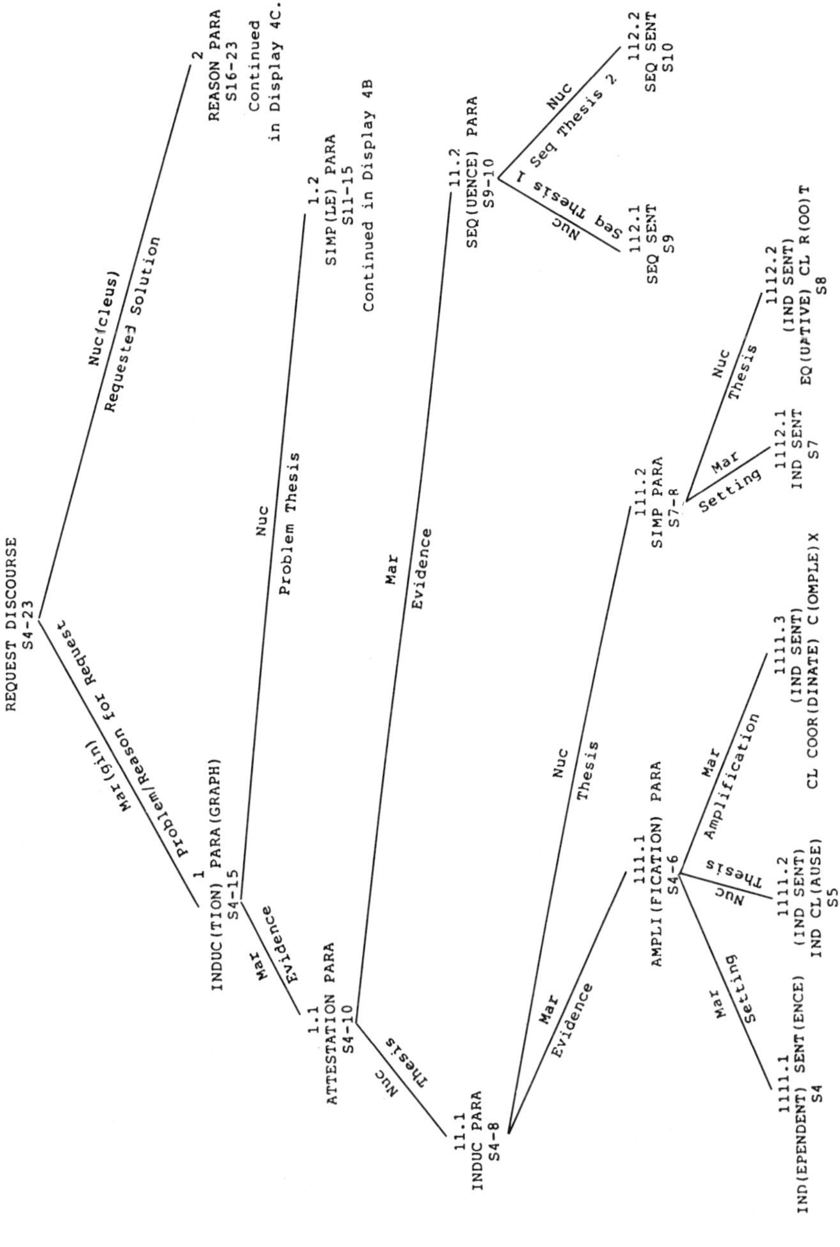

Figure 4a: Grammatical Structure: Upper levels down to sentence.

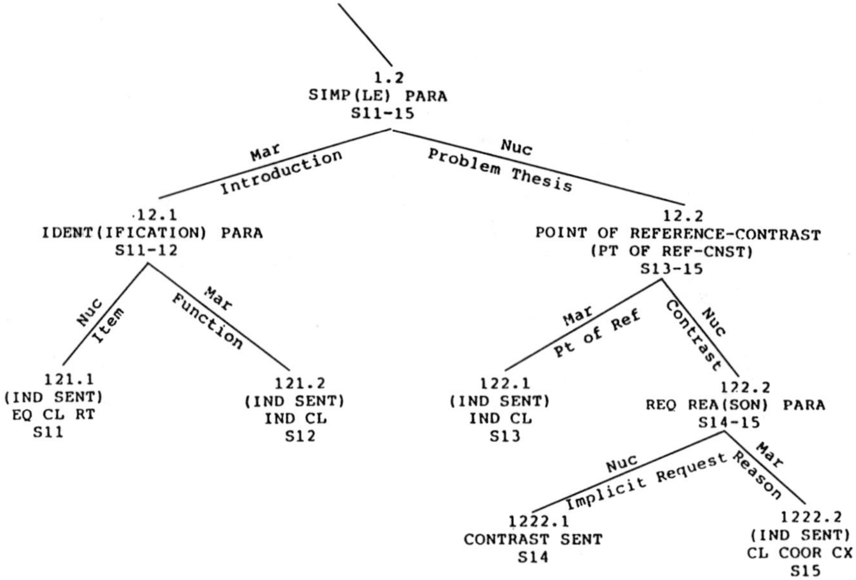

Figure 4b: Grammatical Structure: Continuaiton of display 4a.

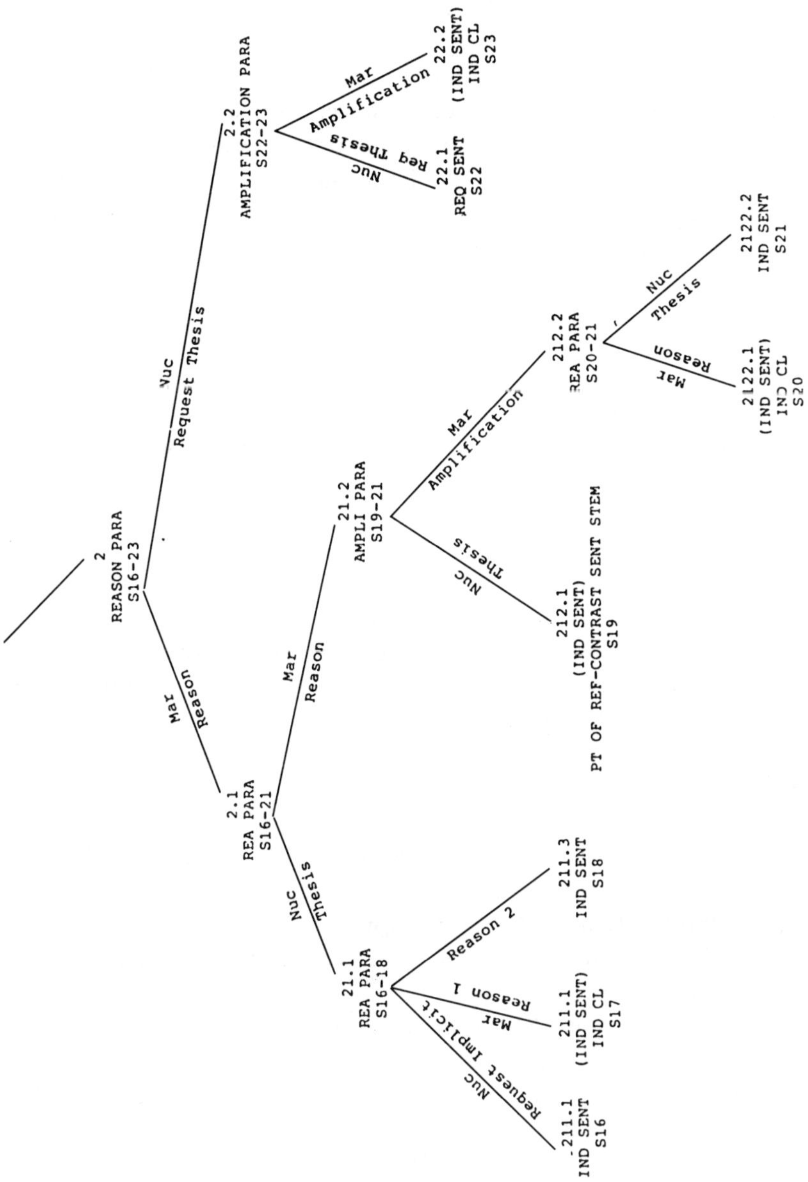

Figure 4c: Grammatical Structure: Further continuation of display 4a.

2.4 *Lower Levels of Grammatical Structure*

The structure of the Business Letter has been presented in the form of an outline, but for a sample of some of the lower-level structures the form of tagmemic formulas will be used, giving one or two examples of each structure. Each of the following section, 2.4.1 through 2.4.7, presents a different formula. Each of the immediate constitutent tagmemes that make up the formula begin with CLASS, followed by the class name and example(s), together with its slot, role, and cohesion.

2.4.1 *Point of Reference-Contrast Sentence Stem* =
CLASS: Point of Reference Clause S19 *Even though our . . . growth*; SLOT: Margin; ROLE: Pt of Ref; COHESION: Obligatory.
CLASS: Ind Clause S19 *we can act . . . level*; SLOT: Nucleus; ROLE: Contrast; COHESION: Obligatory.

2.4.2 *Pt of Ref Clause* =
CLASS: Pt of Ref Marking Phrase S19 *Even though*; SLOT: Margin (closed class); ROLE: Pt of Ref; COHESION: Obligatory.
CLASS: Full Transitive Clause Root (optionally expandable to Ind Clause) S19 *our national government . . . growth*; SLOT: Nucleus; ROLE: Pt of Ref; COHESION: Obligatory.

2.4.3 *Ind Clause* =
CLASS: Intransitive Clause Root S19 *we can act*, or Full Transitive Clause Root S19 *our national government . . . growth*; S5 *Calls jammed our switchboard*; SLOT: Nucleus; ROLE: Proposition; COHESION: Governed by theme constraints of the context; obligatory.
CLASS: Infinitive Clause S19 *to take . . . action*; SLOT: Margin; ROLE: Purpose; COHESION: Optional.
CLASS: Location Phrase S19 *at the local level*; SLOT: Margin; ROLE: Location; COHESION: Optional.
CLASS: Time Phrase S5 *all day*; SLOT: Time; COHESION: Governed by time of the Axis mentioned above; optional.

2.4.4 *Full Transitive Clause Root* =
CLASS: Noun Phrase (for development of NP see Fries 1970) S5 *calls*; S19 *our national government*, SLOT: Subject; ROLE: Actor (emic grammatical

actor, not equatable with referential differences in members of the class); COHESION: Governs number in the predicate (same for all subject slots); requires Active Verb Phrase in the Predicate (same for all subjects with the role of actor); obligatory.
CLASS: Verb Phrase (for development see Pike and Pike 1983) S19 *continues*, S5 *jammed*; SLOT: Predicate; ROLE: Statement; COHESION: Requires Actor and Undergoer in the clause root; obligatory.
CLASS: NP or Infinitive Clause S5 *our switchboard*, S19 *to ignore . . . growth*; SLOT: Adjunct; ROLE: Undergoer; COHESION: Inf Clause/Participial Clause is required with *continue*; obligatory.

2.4.5 *Intransitive Clause Root* =
CLASS: Pronoun S19 *we*; SLOT: Actor; ROLE: Statement; COHESION: Obligatory.
CLASS: VP S19 *can act*; SLOT: Predicate; ROLE: Statement; COHESION: Requires an actor, but no undergoer or scope in the clause root; obligatory.

2.4.6 *Passive Transitive Clause Root* =
CLASS: NP or *Whatever* Clause S20 *decisions*, S23 *whatever you give . . . you can*; SLOT: Subject; ROLE: Undergoer; COHESION: Requires a passive verb phrase in the predicate (as do all subjects with a role of either undergoer or scope); obligatory.
CLASS: Passive VP S20 *are being made*, S23 *will be used*; SLOT: Predicate; ROLE: Statement; COHESION: Requires an undergoer and tolerates an actor in the clause root; obligatory.
CLASS: *By* Phrase S20 *by local officials* (ambiguous as to whether *in our communities* is in the NP or if it is a clause modifier); SLOT: Adjunct; ROLE: Actor; COHESION: Optional.

2.4.7 *Item Noun Stem* =
CLASS: Transitive Verb Root S19 *govern*; SLOT: Nucleus; ROLE: Item; COHESION: Obligatory.
CLASS: Nominalizer Suffix S19 *-ment*; SLOT: Margin; ROLE: Itemization; COHESION: Obligatory.

2.5 *Some Morpheme Classes and Some of their Members*

The following data are from Sections 2.4.1 through 2.4.7.
Transitive Verb Root: *ignore*, *continue* (*continue* is a process and requires infinitive/participial clause as undergoer, cf. Quirk, Greenbaum, Leech, and Svartvik 1972), *make*, *govern* (can be nominalized).
Intransitive Verb Root: *act*
Modal Verb Root: *can*
Item Noun Root: *official*, animate, feminine/masculine; *dollar*, inanimate; *consequence*, inanimate
Time Noun Root: *day*
Subject Pronoun: *we*, *you*
Possessive Pronoun: *our*
Tense Suffix: {*-Z*} third person singular
Nominalizing Suffix: *-ment*

3. Phonological Analog: Letter Lay-out

The phonology of spoken communication may be compared to the layout of printed matter. Layout is very important to communication. As a teacher, I know that an efficient layout of an exam can shorten the time a student requires to take that exam. Since this is a very rudimentary sketch of a phonological analog, see Pike and Pike (1983), chapter 2 for the actual recorded phonology of a poem.

The layout of the ZPG letter exhibits analogies to the three phonological systems: segmental, suprasegmental (pitch, stress, length), and subsegmental (voice quality, rate, etc.). First, we consider analogies to phonological segments. The largest of these, in the letter, are the two pages. Within these two contrastive pages are orthographic paragraphs. The first of these is on the first page: Segment 1 (S1), the logo.

Others are the two paragraphs in the left margin: Officers and Sponsors. The segments indicated by the black squares in the address at the bottom of the page might be treated as three others. These paragraphs printed on the stationary are contrastive with each other and with those in the letter proper.

The date, S2, is another layout orthographic paragraph, as is the salutation, S3. These paragraphs are contrastive with each other as well as with those which are indicated by indentation of the first line and separated by double spacing. S15 is another contrastive paragraph, indented both on the left and right, hence with shorter lines, probably to give it extra prominence. Orthographic paragraphs tend to be coextensive with some grammatical and some referential units (see secs. 1 and 2).

Paragraphs are in turn made up of lines. Their length varies according to available space and length of words at the end of the line. Lines are much less frequently coextensive with a grammatical or referential unit than are orthographic paragraphs.

Lines are made up of words separated by spaces. Some words are made up of forms separated by hyphens, while these and other words are made up of letters. The signature of the author contrasts with her identification; the former is in script (legal) and the latter is typed (legible).

Next we consider suprasegmental analogs. These are largely the punctuation. Note the contrast between periods (not ones indicating abbreviations), commas, and dashes; the exclamation mark probably would indicate an intersection of suprasegmental (high falling pitch) with subsegmental (intensity and duration) features.

Additional subsegmental analogs are: underlining (not the underlining indicating a title), size of type, a full form versus its initials, and possibly numerals rather than the spelling out of numbers. These features are in general used to increase prominence in contrast to their context. In this text numerals are more prominent than their spelled-out form would be because the basic system is with letters — the infrequently used numerals stand out. However, it might be simply a matter of following a particular style manual, or both. The full form of Zero Population Growth in S22 is used, I would guess, not only for contrastive prominence as mentioned , but also to indicate the way checks should be made out. As for size of type, the larger it is, the greater is the prominence.

4. Conclusion

Tagmemic theory offers a systematic, coherent way of addressing vast amounts of relevant data in sets of patterns within patterns, all of which are needed to understand even this short ZPG letter. Some of the presuppositions and aims of tagmemics include:

1. To use replicable etic tools to identify emic/relevant/contrastive structures in a language.

2. To attend particularly to the patterns of norms of the language in order to understand the relation of off-norm patterns to the larger system developing any one area according to need, interest, and time.

3. To identify the part-whole relations in the three hierarchies of phonology, grammar, and reference.

4. To recognize that each unit is a form-meaning composite; one is not discoverable or relevant without the other.

5. To use the four questions basic to the tagmeme to identify coherent system in large bodies of data.

6. To understand that no scientific or artistic statement can be made without explicit or implicit observer involvement; this implies an inevitable indeterminacy in all scientific observation, description, and theory. The best one can hope for is substantial inter-observer agreement, growing over time.

References

Beaugrande, Robert de and Wolfgang Dressler
1981 *Introduction to Text Linguistics*. New York: Longman.

Doty, Steve
1984 "Mitigation in a Tiruray sermon." *Studies in Philippine Linguistics*. 5/1,66-79.

Dowty, David
1979 *Word Meaning and Montague Grammar*. Dordrecht: Reidel.

Foley, William A. and Robert D. Van Valin, Jr
1984 *Functional Syntax and Universal Grammar*. New York: Cambridge University Press.

Grimes, Joseph E.
1986 *Semantic Inventories on Small Computers*. Dallas: Summer Institute of Linguistics.

Halliday, M.A.K. and Ruqaiya Hasan
1976 *Cohesion in English*. London: Longman.

Hurlbut, Hope M.
1984 "Do as I say: a study of selected features of hortatory discourse in Eastern Kadazan." *Studies in Philippine Linguistics* 5/1,118-160.

Kant, Immanuel
[1938] 1966 *The Fundamental Principles of the Metaphysic of Ethics*. Otto Manthey-Zorn. New York: Appleton-Century-Crofts.

Longacre, Robert E.
1983 *The Grammar of Discourse*. New York: Plenum Press.

1987 "The semantics of the storyline in East and West Africa." *ournal of Semantics* 5,51-64.

McArthur, Harry S.
1979 "The role of aspect in distinguishing Aguacatec discourse types." In Linda Jones, (ed.), *Discourse Studies in Mesoamerican Languages. Vol 1: Discussion*. (= Summer Institute of Linguistics Publications in Linguistics 58.) Dallas: Summer Institute of Linguistics and University of Texas at Arlington.

Pike, Kenneth L.
1982 *Linguistic Concepts*. Lincoln, NE: University of Nebraska Press.

Pike, Kenneth L. and Evelyn G. Pike
1982 *Grammatical Analysis*. Summer Institute of Linguistics (= Publications in linguistics 53.) 2nd ed. Dallas: Summer Institute of Linguistics.

1983 *Text and Tagmeme*. Norwood, New Jersey: Ablex.

Quirk, Randolph, Sidney Greenbaum, Geoffrey Leech, and Jan Svartvik
1972 *A Grammar of Contemporary English*. New York: Seminar Press.

Schank, Roger C. and Robert P. Abelson
1977 *Scripts, Plans, Goals and Understanding*. Hillsdale, New Jersey: Lawrence Erlbaum Associates.

Widdowson, N.G.
1988 "Poetry and pedagogy." In Deborah Tannen, (ed.), *Linguistics in Context: Connecting Observation and Understanding*. Norwood, New Jersey: Ablex, 183-197.

II. LEXICO-GRAMMATICAL APPROACHES TO THE TEXT

The five papers in Section II have in common that they all approach the ZPG letter in terms of the relationship between lexicon and/or grammar, on the one hand, and the text, on the other. All five papers subscribe, some more tacitly than others, to a continuum between lexicon and grammar, and each of them deals with some aspect of this continuum in his or her paper.

Each of the first two papers in this section, those by Chafe and Prince, builds on its author's previous work in considering the text from the perspective of how lexical and grammatical choices are used. The other three, those by Halliday, Martin, and Benson and Greaves, approach the text from the point of view of systemic functional grammar.

Chafe's paper considers the ZPG letter in terms of general differences between writing and speaking, focussing on the way in which speakers and writers use grammatical means to manage the rate at which information is imparted to an audience. Chafe considers the lexical and grammatical properties of what he terms an 'idea' in spoken and written language. Chafe shows that, while speakers tend to restrict themselves to one 'new' idea at a time (i.e., per intonation unit), the ZPG text illustrates the grammatical devices that writers use to increase the density of new ideas per unit.

Prince considers the semantic and grammatical choices behind the grammatical category of 'subject', exploring the ways in which subjects and non-subjects differ from one another along the dimensions of definiteness and information status. Differentiating between what she terms 'Discourse-status' and 'Hearer-status', she shows that subjects are more likely than non-subjects to be definite and to represent both 'Discourse-old' and 'Hearer-old' entities.

Halliday uses systemic functional grammar to examine several prominent lexico-grammatical features of the ZPG text. Halliday shows how selections made within certain categories such as 'theme', 'transitivity', and 'nominalization' affect the flavor of the text and the effect it has on the reader, and, more generally, how lexico-grammatical choices create meaning at the textual level.

Martin focusses on the interpersonal function of a text, that function whereby a writer uses the text as an expression not only of attitudes and evaluations but also of his or her relationship with the reader. Martin shows that interpersonal meaning is realized in clause structure prosodically, that is, as a semantic motif running through the clause. He shows in particular how lexico-grammatical systems convey the expression of attitude and evaluation in the ZPG text.

Benson and Greaves' paper is concerned with the patterns of lexical collocations, and what these can tell us about certain aspects of the meaning of the text, the way it puts this meaning across to its intended readers, and its setting within the framework of institutional organizations. Benson and Greaves apply to the ZPG text a computational package called CLOC, which identifies recurring lexico-grammatical collocational patterns. By comparing the ZPG letter with certain other texts, Benson and Greaves are able to show how these collocations reveal the topic of the ZPG letter, its method of appealing to the reader, and the influence of the medium of communication.

Following our desire to help the student, some issues raised by these papers are highlighted below. Because these papers are more diverse, we cannot ask questions that span the whole collection. Instead, we contrast particular papers.

Consider how Chafe's findings might fit into the systemic framework. Does his use of the term "information flow" indicate that he is dealing with ideational functions? Does the speaker's use of assumptions about what is new to the hearer put this into the systemic interpersonal category? Or does the connection to intonational prominence put it into the textual category?

Comparing Prince with Chafe, how does "information-status" compare with the various statuses that Chafe discusses? Are they working with the same concepts? How are these related to the "given" and "new" varieties of "information focus" in Halliday's paper?

Consider the three systemic papers. Benson and Greaves' mechanically derived classes and co-ocurrence patterns could be compared with the classes and co-ocurrence patterns in Halliday's Figure 3. To what extent do they agree? What are the unique contributions from each author's methods?

Martin's paper suggests that interpersonal structure can be realized in a prosodic (distributed) fashion, as well as the more familiar constituent-based fashion. How would such choices of prosodic or constituent realization affect what is discovered by Benson and Greaves' CLOC program? Would anything be overlooked or counted twice?

Finally, for all of the papers in this section (or even the entire volume), we notice that nearly every author identifies Segment 22, "Please make a special contribution to Zero Population Growth today," as having a special, crucial status for the text as a whole. What is this special status? What attributes of this Segment or its role do several authors agree on? Compare the methods used for identifying this sentence as crucial. Which methods are simply readers' intuitions and which can be stated more precisely?

Which papers seem most insightful overall? How does insightfulness relate to the methods that were used?

The Flow of Ideas in a Sample of Written Language*

Wallace Chafe
University of California, Santa Barbara

I am going to use the ZPG letter to explore some ways in which writing differs from speaking. Specifically, I will be exploring the extent to which writers may be relieved of certain constraints which, for speakers, are imposed by the necessity of producing language in real time. Underlying this discussion will be the notion that speakers create language on-line, more or less in synchrony with their (and their listeners') thought processes. As a result the flow of spoken language tends to proceed at approximately the same pace as the flow of thought (cf. Chafe 1979). Writers, on the other hand, produce language at a necessarily slower pace, from which they derive both advantages and disadvantages. On the one hand, the absence of time pressure may tempt writers into creating a kind of language that is badly misaligned with any natural flow of thought, whether within their own minds or within the minds of their readers. On the other hand, the extra time and the editing ability enjoyed by writers offer them the opportunity to produce a kind of language that can flow with grace and elegance. The most effective writers may be those who are intuitively sensitive to the natural constraints of thought and language flow. This article begins with a glance at some of these constraints as they are manifested in speaking, to focus then on how and to what extent they may be relevant to writing as exhibited in this particular writing sample.

In the process I will be exploring several techniques that may prove helpful in analyzing written language in these terms. I emphasize the word

*I am grateful to William Mann, Marianne Mithun, and Sandra Thompson for their helpful comments on earlier drafts of this paper.

explore, since neither the findings nor the techniques discussed here can be regarded as firmly established. Everything that follows is intended in the spirit of testing ways of clarifying aspects of language (and thought) that need to be better understood.

1. Spoken Language Preliminaries

Since my focus here will be on a written, not a spoken text, I cannot dwell long on properties of thought and language flow in spoken language. I am going to proceed under the surely unwarranted assumption that the properties in question have been satisfactorily demonstrated for speech, and will concentrate on showing their relevance to writing. As a partial justification for this stance, I can point out that this article forms a sequel to an earlier article on spoken language, at the end of which I mentioned that an extension to written language would be in order (Chafe 1987).

There are two constraints that appear to be difficult for speakers to overcome in casual, unplanned conversation. I will refer to them as the *one-new-idea-at-a-time* constraint and the *light-subject* constraint. The one-new-idea-at-a-time constraint assumes that a basic unit of spoken language is the *intonation unit*, which functions as the verbal expression of a single focus of consciousness (Chafe 1980). Specifically, it limits an intonation unit to no more than one *idea* that has the status of *new* information, although such a unit may at the same time express additional ideas that have the status of either *given* or *accessible* information. The light-subject constraint has to do with grammatical *subjects*. Specifically, it restricts a grammatical subject to information that is *not* new, limiting it to information that is either given, as is usually the case, or at least accessible.

Obviously there are two questions that need to be answered at this point. First, what is meant in these formulations by the term *idea*? Second, what does it mean for an idea to be *given*, *accessible*, or *new*? In providing some brief answers to these questions I will use for illustrative purposes the following excerpt from a recorded conversation:

(1) ... The ^^tape ^recorder when it
(2) ... when it ^shows ^^red,
(3) ^^that's when it really ^picks ^^up ^^well huh?

The three dots indicate pauses, the carets indicate accents (two carets primary accent and one caret secondary accent), the comma shows a clause-final intonation, and the question mark a yes-no question intonation. The division into three lines reflects a segmentation into intonation units, each such unit ending in a recognizable phrase-, clause-, or sentence-final pitch contour, and usually showing other manifestations of prosodic integrity that set it apart from adjacent intonation units (Chafe 1987 and elsewhere). (Lest there be any misunderstanding, I will be using the words *prosody* and *prosodic* to cover intonation, accents, pauses, timing, and the like.)

I will suppose that an idea (pending further elucidation of that term) is *active* in a speaker's consciousness at the moment it is verbalized. An active idea is one on which the speaker is at that moment focusing attention. An idea that has changed from the inactive to the active state in the speaker's consciousness, and that the speaker intends, by verbalizing it, to change from inactive to active in the listener's consciousness, may be said to constitute *new* information. Take for example the idea of the tape recorder expressed in (1) above. Sometime before uttering (1), perhaps during the pause indicated by the three dots, this idea must have become active for the speaker. By uttering (1) he must have intended to activate the same idea in the listener's consciousness.

A new idea is verbalized with a syntactic constituent (a word or sequence of words) containing a primary accent. That is, one of the words in the verbalization of a new idea will contain a syllable with heightened pitch and amplitude and often lengthening. In (1), for example, there is a new idea that is verbalized with the words *the ^^tape ^recorder*, a noun phrase expressing the idea of a physical object. In (2) another new idea is verbalized with the words *it ^shows ^^red*, a clause expressing the idea of an event. In (3) there is a new idea that is verbalized with the words *it really ^picks ^^up ^^well*, another clause and another event.

Although a new idea is typically verbalized by a sequence of words containing only one primary accent, the reader may have noticed that the last example contains two such words, *up* and *well*. If ideas are ultimately defined in terms of referentiality — as mental representations of objects, states, or events — there are certain limited and specifiable conditions under which their linguistic expressions may exhibit multiple primary accents. Later we will see what some of those conditions are, and why it is useful to allow for such cases. For now we can notice that one such case may involve the modification of a lexical item like *pick up* by a degree adverb like *well*, both being accented.

Once activated, an idea may remain for a time in the active state. While it is in that state it may be said to constitute *given* information. Whereas new ideas are verbalized with a sequence of words containing a primary accent, given ones are typically verbalized in more attenuated ways, in English usually with an unaccented pronoun. In (2) and (3) above the idea of the tape recorder is verbalized with the pronoun *it*.

Sooner or later, every active idea loses its active status. The capacity of focal consciousness is very limited, and as new ideas are added old ones must leave. When an idea ceases to be fully active it does not immediately return to the inactive state, but becomes for a time *semi-active*. More research is needed on the nature and effects of semi-activation, but roughly speaking this is a state that functions as a holding area for ideas that may later be reactivated as they reenter the discourse. It is also a state within which separately activated ideas are conceptually integrated into a larger picture. Semi-activation presumably has a great deal to do with preserving coherence within a discourse.

What is of special interest here is the possibility that the reactivation of a semi-active idea, if and when it occurs, may exact a smaller cognitive cost than does the activation of an idea that was previously inactive. An idea that has been reactivated from the semi-active state may be called *accessible*. The lesser cost of an accessible idea is evidenced in the fact that, whereas an intonation unit may express only one new idea, it may express in addition one or more accessible ideas.

Once reactivated, an accessible idea will be subject to the same fate as any other activated idea, sooner or later becoming semi-active again, and eventually inactive. Ideas thus have what we can call an *activation history* within a discourse. For example, an idea might begin as inactive, then be activated as a new idea, remain for a time as a given idea, then for a time be semi-active, perhaps then be reactivated, this time as an accessible idea, remain in the given state again for a time before again becoming semi-active, and then finally be reduced to the inactive status. Such a sequence typifies the kind of activation history an idea might have within a particular discourse.

Just what is it that has such a history? What is the locus of activation? What is it that may be at one time inactive, later active, later semi-active, and so on? Put differently, what is it that is treated by language as new, given, or accessible information? The locus of activation is not some segment of language, but rather a cognitive unit that may be verbalized by a segment of language. It is the kind of unit I have loosely been calling an *idea*.

Approached through language, an idea is the sort of cognitive unit which, when its status is new or accessible, may receive expression in a sequence of words containing an accent, or which, when its status is given, may be expressed by an unaccented pronoun. Approached cognitively, an idea may be the mental representation of a person or object (*the tape recorder*), of a state (*it shows red*), or of an event (*it really picks up well*). It is fundamentally, then, the mental representations of objects, states, and events that I am calling ideas.

It is possible for intonation units to express more than one idea in this sense. Intonations units, of course, may include linkages to other intonation units, as exemplified by the *when* in (2) above. They may also include interactive signals like the *huh?* in (3). They may include contrastively accented items, like the word *^^that's* in (3). But most significant for us here will be the fact that an intonation unit may express a cluster of ideas, all of which are active at the time. None of the intonation units in (1) through (3) above contains more than a single idea, but we can look at the following example from Chafe (1987), in which the speaker referred to an undergraduate class he once had,

... where ^^everybody ¦ ^^loved ¦ the ^^instructor,
acc new acc

This intonation unit contains, in addition to the word *where* that links it to the preceding context, three words or word sequences that verbalize three separate ideas. I have shown the boundaries between them with the symbol "¦". The important finding in such cases is that, so far as spoken language is concerned, only one of the ideas within a single intonation unit will be new. In this example there are reasons for regarding the ideas expressed by *everybody* and *the instructor* as accessible, and only that expressed by *loved* as new. I have indicated the activation status of each idea with the notation *acc* or *new* below its verbal representation.

Intonation units, then, besides containing linkages and various other textual and interactive devices, often verbalize clusters of ideas. When they do, so far as spoken language is concerned, only one of the ideas may be new. The remaining, accessible idea(s) serve to provide a context for the one new idea. This is the one-new-idea-at-a-time constraint.

It can be seen that the example above adheres to this constraint:

(1) ... The ^^tape ^recorder when it
(2) ... when it ^shows ^^red,
(3) ^^that's when it really ^picks ^^up ^^well huh?

The speaker may have tried to violate it in (1), but got no further than the words *when it*, being forced by the one-new-idea-at-a-time constraint to truncate the intonation unit at this point. He then paused, and was able in (2) to produce an intonation unit in which the idea introduced in (1) had acquired the status of given information, which it maintained through (3).

The same example also illustrates the second constraint that will occupy us here. The light-subject constraint allows a grammatical subject to be given or accessible information, but not new. In (1) the speaker began by verbalizing *the tape recorder* as a disembodied topic, separated from and unintegrated into any following grammatical structure. Since it was new information at this point, he could not immediately use it as a subject. But with the idea of the tape recorder activated he was free to use it as a given subject in (2), and again in (3).

If the constraints which this example illustrates are generally applicable, it would be impossible for a casual conversationalist, operating in the same context, to produce a single intonation unit like the following:

When the tape recorder shows red is when it really picks up well.

The reasons are two: this would be an intonation unit containing three separate new ideas, and it would contain a subject that expresses new information. I believe it is not intuitively obvious that such an intonation unit would be ruled out of unplanned spoken language, but in fact the two constraints it violates do appear to apply to most unplanned spontaneous speech. It may be useful to characterize such a concocted intonation unit, not as ungrammatical, but as *unsayable*. We will see that writers can and do violate these constraints; that something analogous to this example would not be *unwritable*.

2. Written Language

As a prelude to examining written language in these terms, we need to consider how several factors that are relatively well defined in speech are reflected in writing. In particular, we need to ask whether written language has anything analogous to accents and intonation units. What exactly would it mean to refer to prosodic criteria in writing, if writing is a visual medium and prosody is a property of sound, not sight? In Chafe (1988) I observed that many writers and readers experience a kind of auditory imagery that includes intonation contours, accents, and pauses. Imagery of this kind can be interpreted as a manifestation of a covert prosody of written language, one of whose principal qualities is the presence of segments akin to accents and intonation units.

In part the boundaries of mentally imaged intonation units are signaled by an author's punctuation. The primary function of punctuation seems always, in fact, to have been to guide the reader toward a prosodic interpretation resembling the author's own auditory imagery. There are several factors, however, that keep us from equating punctuation units with intonation units. For one thing, there is some punctuation that is determined by nonprosodic factors, whether grammatical or simply arbitrary. For another thing, authors differ greatly in the extent to which they exploit punctuation to reflect their prosodic intentions. There are, furthermore, changing fashions in this regard: English authors during the nineteenth century made considerably greater use of punctuation for this purpose than have more recent writers, and different punctuating conventions remain associated with different contemporary genres. The upshot is that we cannot use punctuation as the sole guide to the prosody associated with a piece of writing, even though it can be a useful guide up to a point, and a better guide with some kinds of writing than with others.

One way of obtaining additional information on the prosody of written language is to have it read aloud. Oral reading forces written language to take on a prosody that is in some respects closer to that of spoken language. I have found, for example, that the intonation units of oral reading consistently show a mean length of about five or six words, regardless of how the passage was punctuated (Chafe 1988). This is the typical mean length of spoken intonation units. It evidently reflects a strong constraint on oral language production, regardless of whether the language was spoken to begin with, or whether it was originally intended to be read silently. By forcing writing to become, to a limited extent, speech, we force it to be governed by some of the same production constraints that govern real speech.

Any particular instance of reading aloud is almost certain to contain idiosyncrasies. Any particular reader will introduce some prosodic breaks in peculiar places that are of no interest beyond that particular reading. However, such idiosyncrasies are smoothed out across a variety of readings, especially readings by different people, and one discovers that different oral readers have much in common. I will describe here some findings that are based on tape recordings of nine different people reading aloud the ZPG letter.

These readings were transcribed with particular attention to intonation, marked with (1) periods and commas for falling and non-falling final contours of intonation units; (2) carets for accents, primary and secondary; and (3) sequences of dots for pauses, distinguished as very brief (two dots) or normal (three). From these nine oral readings a composite version was constructed in the following way. If at least seven of the nine readers introduced an intonation unit boundary, an accent, or a pause, that feature was accepted in the composite version. When these seven, eight, or nine readers differed as to whether there was a falling or non-falling intonation, a primary or secondary accent, or a brief or normal pause, preference was given to the majority. For example, if five oral readers used a falling pitch and two a non-falling one, the composite version accepted the falling pitch. The following illustrates the nature of this composite read-aloud version. The punctuation marks that were present in the original letter are also included, followed by an asterisk. The punctuation marks at the very ends of lines reflect the prosody of the oral readings. In other words, (1) ended with a falling pitch, (2) with a non-falling, and so on.

(1) ^^Dear ^^Friend of ^^ZPG:*.
(2) ... At ^^7:00 ^^a.m. .. on ^^October ^^25,*,
(3) ... our ^^phones started to ^^ring.*.
(4) ... ^^Calls ^^jammed our ^^switchboard ^^all ^^day.*.
(5) ... ^^Staffers ^^ stayed ^^late into the ^^night,*,
(6) .. ^^answering ^^questions,
(7) and ^^talking with ^^reporters from ^^newspapers,*,
(8) .. ^^radio ^stations,*,
(9) .. ^^wire ^services,
(10) and ^^TV ^stations,
(11) .. in ^^every ^part of the ^^country.*.

Since there was very high agreement among the oral readers on this way of interpreting the text, and since it was far from completely determined by the punctuation of the written original, this version presumably brings the text closer to the way it might be produced if it were spoken language. Of course, it is not spoken language. For one thing, many of the particular intonation contours used by the oral readers would not be mistaken for those of a natural conversationalist. The oral readers sounded like oral readers. In addition, no one familiar with transcripts of real spoken language would mistake this version for such a transcript, even though its intonation units have a mean length of 5.4 words, a length quite typical of speaking. Our concern below will be with ways in which the *wording* of the letter fails to conform to spoken language constraints, even when certain aspects of its prosody have been forced to do so.

We can note in passing that the mean length of the *punctuation units* (sequences of words between punctuation marks) in the letter itself was 10.4 words, or about twice as long as the intonation units produced in the oral readings. I take that to mean that the letter-writer used punctuation about half as often as she might have if she had followed a completely spokenlike punctuation style. I hasten to add that such a style would be inappropriate in a letter of this kind, and that this writer's usage fits well with the current preference for an *open* style of punctuating. I found punctuation units of about this length in a front-page news report, as well as in a software advertisement appearing in a popular magazine.

3. Identifying Separate Ideas

How can these intonation units, based on the oral readings, be further segmented into units that express separate ideas? As a first step we can insert provisional boundaries so that there is one and only one word with a primary accent within each such segment. Unaccented words and words with secondary accent can be distributed so that constituent relations are preserved. I will exemplify this procedure with intonation unit (46) and a few of the units following it. (The numbering of these intonation units comes from a segmentation of the entire text that will be presented below.) Sometimes this procedure requires a recognition that one idea has been inserted within another, as in (46), where I have shown that *small* was inserted within *our staff* by enclosing it in square brackets:

(46) ... Our [^^small] ^^staff,
(47) is being ^^swamped with ^^requests,

(48) .. for ^^more ^^ information,
(49) ... and our ^^modest ¦ ^^resources ¦ are being ^^stretched to the ^^limit.*.

Although this provisional segmentation into ideas can be accomplished in a fairly mechanically way, it is not entirely satisfactory as a segmentation into expressions of separate ideas. One problem is the uncertainty associated with distinguishing secondary from primary accent. If, for example, *modest* had been transcribed as having secondary accent for the majority of the oral readers, then the boundary between it and *resources* in (49) would not have been inserted. This difficulty may be to some extent alleviated by the following considerations.

Whereas there may be a tendency for each content word to be given a primary accent, several content words often combine to form a single lexicalized unit, and thus to express a single idea. I will distinguish the following three types of lexicalized word sequences (cf. Pawley 1985):

(a) idioms
(b) lexicalized phrases
(c) lexicalized frames

The clearest cases are idioms, where the meaning of the lexicalized sequence is unpredictable from the meanings of the individual words. An example from the ZPG letter is *blow the whistle*, whose special status the writer signaled by enclosing it in quotation marks. Clearly only one idea is involved here, not the two that the accents on *blow* and *whistle* might suggest.

How do we recognize an idiom, or for that matter any lexicalized word sequence? We could hope that such knowledge is available introspectively to those who know the English language. Knowing what it means to *blow the whistle* on something is as much a part of knowing the contemporary English language as knowing the meaning of *furious*. But not all cases are so clear, and people do vary in their ability to make verbal judgments. In looking for ways to confirm such judgments when they may be in question, I have experimented with a modified use of the cloze procedure (Taylor 1953), a measure of redundancy in which people are asked to fill in blanks that have been inserted, say, for every fifth word in a text. What I did in this case was to insert blanks for every fifth word that was given a primary accent in the composite read-aloud version. The procedure is costly of subjects. Since the blanks were distributed through the text in five different ways, in order to obtain even a modest four responses for each blank it was necessary to distribute the forms to twenty subjects.

Given the context *who were furious that we had "[ ] the whistle" on conditions in their cities*, all four cloze subjects guessed *blown* correctly. Such unanimous predictability helps to confirm the intuition that *blow the whistle* is indeed a lexicalized sequence. The predictability need not extend in both directions. Of the four who were shown the version *who were furious that we had "blown the [ ]" on conditions in their cities*, two guessed *cover*, having a different idiom in mind.

In addition to idioms, there are lexicalized word sequences in which the constituent elements have retained their usual meanings, so that the meaning of the sequence is largely predictable from the meanings of its parts. I am calling such sequences *lexicalized phrases*. Though semantically transparent, they have become frozen through frequent use. An example is *stretch to the limit*, which we met in (49) above. Of course the word *stretched* is used here metaphorically, but we are concerned, not with the metaphoric use of individual words, but with the lexicalization of the entire sequence. Given the context *our modest resources are being stretched to the [ ]*, three of the four cloze subjects guessed *limit*. I take this again as evidence that the phrase *stretch to the limit* is lexicalized, since one of its accented words is predictable, given the other.

There are some phrases that are lexicalized in a particular context, though they would not be in isolation. A good example from the letter is *ZPG's 1985 Urban Stress Test*, whose parts were largely unpredictable in its first occurrence, but became predictable when it was repeated. It may be noted that this phrase was underlined each time it appeared in the letter, as a signal of its lexicalized status.

The largest number of lexicalized phrases in the ZPG letter were found to be either adjective-noun sequences like *public reaction* or *toxic wastes*, verb-object sequences like *answer questions* or *ignore the consequences*, or noun-noun compounds. Later I will devote more discussion to the adjective-noun and verb-object types. The following is a list of instances of the noun-noun type. Again, the numbers refer to intonation units in the version of the complete text that will be given below. I hope that the lexicalized nature of these sequences, supported by the cloze test, will be apparent to the reader:

radio stations (8, 84)
wire services (9)

TV stations (10, 84)
Stress Test (12)
Urban Stress Test (37, 76)
Urban Stress Test results (20)
ZPG's 1985 Urban Stress Test (28)
U.S. cities (32)
birth rates (35)
air quality (36)
action tool (40)
opinion leaders (43)
community leaders (43)
population growth (60)
population-stress (68)
Zero Population Growth (70)
news story (82)
media coverage (85)
reply form (86)

Other lexicalized phrases in the letter belong to miscellaneous grammatical constructions. For example:

late into the night (5)
nothing short of (adjective)! (16)
hold accountable (25)
easy-to-use (40)
the quality of our lives (64)
those who need it most (76)
from coast to coast (84)

Besides idioms and lexicalized phrases, there is a third type of lexicalized word sequence in which the content words are subject to replacement by synonyms, thus allowing for a set of phrases that are not verbatim repetitions. *Lexicalized frames* of this sort are captured well by the cloze test. An example is *swamped with requests* in (47). No one guessed the word *swamped*, and only one person guessed *requests*. However, the alternatives to *swamped* were *flooded*, *besieged*, *bombarded*, and *overwhelmed*, all of which make similar semantic contributions. The alternatives to *requests* were *demands*, *inquiries*, and *calls*. What has been lexicalized here is evidently not the particular word sequence *swamped with requests*, but a consistent semantic frame that can be verbalized in a variety of relatively synonymous ways.

A few examples of other lexicalized frames in the ZPG letter, with alternatives supplied through the cloze procedure, include:

need (require) your help (support) (45)
modest (meager, few) resources (funds) (49)
crisis (critical) stage (level, point) (59)
sound (intelligent) choices (decisions, judgments) (65)
top (major) news story (item) (82)

Having identified instances of these various types of lexicalized sequences, we can consolidate certain of the provisional ideas within the earlier example as follows, where segmentation has been made only between separate ideas:

(46) ... Our [^^small] ^^staff,
(47) is being ^^swamped with ^^requests,
(48) .. for ^^more ^^ information,
(49) ... and our ^^modest ^^resources ¦ are being ^^stretched to the ^^limit.*.

Two of these intonation units (47 and 48) can now be seen to express only one idea each, while (46) and (49) express two. (46) contains the ideas expressed as *our staff* and *small*. (49) contains the ideas expressed as *our modest resources* and *are being stretched to the limit*.

Beyond lexicalized word sequences, there are other cases of words with primary accent that may not signal separate ideas. In the cases to be discussed now I have found that, if they were to be interpreted as expressions of separate ideas, they would constitute annoying minor exceptions to generalizations that otherwise hold up well. Since there are plausible independent reasons for not regarding these items as expressions of separate ideas, the unitary interpretations seem justified.

One such case is that of numerals. The enumeration of a referent appears not to be conceived of independently of that referent, but to combine with it to form a single composite idea. For example, imagine someone saying in an appropriate context *She had ^^three ^^oranges*. The idea expressed by the phrase *three oranges* evidently does not involve the separate conceptualization of threeness and orangeness, but rather the idea of both simultaneously. This conceptual act may be different from that involved in, say, *She had some ^^unripe ^^oranges*, where there is a greater separability of the idea of unripeness from the idea of orangeness. This difference may help to explain why *She had some ^oranges that were ^^three* is peculiar in a way that *She had some ˆoranges that were ˆ ˆunripe* is not. On this basis we can treat the following as expressions of single ideas:

184 urban areas (33)
11 different criteria (34)

The same interpretation can be given to several cases of a vaguer kind of enumeration:

the deluge of calls (18)
months of ... research (29)
hundreds of newspapers (83)

In a similar category are several phrases with quantifiers that can also be interpreted as expressions of unitary ideas:

all day (4)
every part of the country (11)
all parts of the country (24)
every day (63)

Other cases of words that may receive primary accent without expressing separate ideas are words that convey the degree or intensity of something; for example *urgently*, *drastically*, and *ever* in the following (cf. Chafe 1987:35):

we urgently need your help (45)
may be our best opportunity ever (52)
that could drastically affect the quality of our lives (64)

Finally, there are constructions that have a *presentative* function. They express the existence, arrival, or perception of some new referent, and in so doing they need not be regarded as having an idea status separate from that of the new referent itself. Often these presentatives are weakly accented, good evidence that they do not express separate ideas. An example is *came from* in:

came mostly from reporters (19)

I will extend the same interpretation to cases like *hearing from*, in spite of the fact that it was given primary accent by most of our oral readers in:

Now we are hearing from concerned citizens in all parts of the ' country (24)

4. Distinguishing Accessible and New Information

The next step is to distinguish those ideas that express accessible information from those that express new. The results of the cloze test can be of help here also, but only in concert with other considerations. Above all, the cloze results need to be interpreted with reference to particular contexts; looking at one intonation unit in isolation fails to provide sufficient evidence for an adequate analysis.

Before discussing specific cases of accessible and new information, in order to have all the necessary contexts before us I will present first the entire text, segmented into intonation units (the numbered lines) and expressions of ideas (separated by "¦"). Below the expression of each idea I will show my decision as to whether it expresses accessible (acc) or new information. For accessible ideas I have attempted to show the sources of their accessibility, either with a number referring to the intonation unit in which the idea was previously activated, or to some other source. For example, the *Dear* in (1), which perhaps should not be considered the expression of an idea at all, is accessible on the basis of the well-known epistolary salutation. The idea expressed by *ZPG* in the same intonation unit is accessible from the letterhead. Only the idea expressed by *Friend* is new, as reflected in the fact that the cloze subjects guessed such irrelevant words here as *Sirs*, *President*, *Patron*, or *Jim*. Following a presentation of the entire text in these terms, I will discuss some of the more interesting decisions regarding accessibility as opposed to newness.

(1) ^^Dear ¦ ^^Friend ¦ of ^^ZPG:*.
acc(formula) new acc(letterhead)

(2) ... At ^^7:00 ¦ ^^a.m. ¦ .. on ^^October ¦ ^^25,*,
new new new new

(3) ... our ^^phones started to ^^ring.*.
new

(4) ... ^^Calls ¦ ^^jammed our ^^switchboard ¦ ^^all ^^day.*.
acc(3) acc(3) new

(5) ... ^^Staffers ¦ ^^stayed ^^late into the ^^night,*,
new new

(6) .. ^^answering ^^questions,
new

```
(7)  and ^^talking with ^^reporters ¦ from ^^newspapers,*,
         new                          new

(8)  .. ^^radio ^^stations,*,
        new

(9)  .. ^^wire ^^services,
        new

(10) and ^^TV ^^stations,
         new

(11) .. in ^^every ^^part of the ^^country.*.
      new

(12) ... When we ^^released the ^^results ¦ of ^^ZPG's ¦ ^^1985 ¦
              new                            acc(1)        new
     ^^Urban ¦ ^^ Stress ^Test,*,
      new        new

(13) ... we had ^^no ^^idea,
      new

(14) we'd ^get such an ^^overwhelming ^^response.*.
     new

(15) ... ^^Media    ¦ and ^^public ^^reaction,
        acc(7-10)         new

(16) has been ^^nothing ^^ short of ^^incredible!*.
     new

(17) ... At ^^first,*,

(18) .. the ^^deluge of ^^calls,
      acc(4)

(19) .. came ^^mostly from ^^reporters,
      acc(7)

(20) .. ^^eager to ^^tell the ^^public ¦ about ^^Urban ^^Stress ^^Test
        new                             acc(12)
     ^^results.

(21) ... and from [^^outraged] ^^public ^^officials,
                   new        new

(22) .. who were ^^furious,
      acc(21)
```

(23) .. that we had "^^blown the ^^whistle" ¦ on ^^conditions ¦ in
new new new
^^their ^^cities.*.

(24) ... ^^Now we are ^hearing from ^^concerned ^^citizens ¦ in
new acc (11)
^^all ^^parts of the ^^country,

(25) .. who ^^want to ^^know what they can ^^do ¦ to ^hold
new new
[local ^officials] ^^accountable,
new

(26) ... for ^^tackling [^^population-^related] ^^problems,
new acc(letterhead)

(27) .. that ^^threaten ¦ ^public ^^ health ¦ and ^^well-being.*.
new new new

(28) ... ^^ZPG's ^^1985 ^^Urban ^^Stress ^Test,*,
acc(20)

(29) ... ^^created ¦ after ^^months of [^^persistent and]
new new new
^^exhaustive ^^research,*,

(30) ... is the ^^nation's ¦ ^^first ¦ ^^survey,
acc(24) new new

(31) of how [^^population-^^linked] ^^pressures,
acc(26) acc(26)

(32) .. ^^affect ¦ ^^U.S. ^^cities.*.
acc(how)acc(23)

(33) ... It ^^ranks ¦ ^^184 ^^urban ^^areas,
new new

(34) .. on ^^11 ^^different ^^criteria,
new

(35) .. ^^ranging ¦ from ^^crowding ¦ and ^^birth ^rates,
acc(33) new new

(36) .. to ^^air ^^quality ¦ and ^^toxic ^^wastes.*.
new new

(37) ... The ^^Urban ^^Stress ^Test,
acc(28)

(38) ^^translates ¦ ^^complex,*,
new new

(39) .. [^^technical] ^^ data,
new

(40) .. into an [^^easy-to-use] ^^action ^tool,
new new

(41) for ^^concerned ^^citizens,*.
acc(24)

(42) ... ^^elected ^^ officials,
new

(43) .. and ^^opinion ^leaders.*.
new

(44) ... But to ^^use it ^^well,*,
new

(45) we ^^urgently ^^need your ^^help.*.
new

(46) ... Our [^^small] ^^staff,
acc(5) new

(47) is being ^^swamped with ^ ^requests,
new

(48) .. for ^^more ^^information,
new

(49) ... and our ^^modest ^^resources ¦ are being ^^stretched to the
new new
^^limit.*.

(50) ... Your ^^support ^^now ¦ is ^^critical.*.
acc(45) acc(45)

(51) ... ^^ZPG's ^^1985 ^^Urban ^^Stress ^Test,
acc(37)

(52) .. may be our ^^best ^^opportunity ^^ever,
new

(53) .. to get [the ^^population ^^message] ^^heard.*.
new acc(20)

(54) ... With ^^your ^^contribution,*,
acc(50)

(55) ^^ZPG ¦ can ^^arm ¦ our [^^growing] ^^network ¦ of
acc(51) new new new new
[^^local] ^^activists,
new

(56) .. with the ^^materials they ^^need,
new

(57) .. to ^^warn ¦ ^^community ^^leaders,
new acc(43)

(58) .. about [^^emerging ¦ ^^population-^linked] ^^stresses,
acc(31) new acc(31)

(59) ... ^^before they ^reach the ^crisis ^^stage.*.
new

(60) ... ^^Even though our ^^national ^^government ¦ ^^continues ¦
new new
to ^^ignore the ^^ consequences ¦ of [^^uncontrolled]
new acc(35) new
^^population ^growth,*,

(61) ... we can ^^act,
new

(62) .. to take [^^positive] ^^action ¦ at the ^^local
new new acc(25)
^^level.*.

(63) ... ^^Every ^^day ¦ ^^decisions are being ^^made ¦ by ^^local
new new acc(25)
^^officials ¦ in our ^^communities,
acc(57)

(64) .. that could ^^drastically ^^affect the ^^quality of our ^^lives.*.
new

(65) ... To make ^^sound ^^choices ¦ in ^planning for ^^people,*,
acc(63) new

(66) ... both ^^elected ^^officials,
acc(63)

(67) .. and the ^^American ^^public,
acc(41)

(68) .. ^^need the [^^population-^^stress] ^^data,
new acc(58)

(69) .. ^^revealed by our ^^study.*.
acc(51)

(70) ... ^^Please ¦ ^make a [^^special] ^^contribution ¦
acc(formula) acc(54) new
to ^^Zero ^^Population ^^Growth ¦ ^^today.*.
acc(55) new

(71) ... ^^Whatever you ^^give--*,
new

(72) ... ^^$25,*,
new

(73) ... ^^$50,*,
new

(74) ... ^^$100,
new

(75) ... or as ^^much as you ^^can--*,
new

(76) will be used ^^immediately ¦ to put [the ^^Urban ^^Stress
new new acc(69)
^^Test] in the ^^hands of ¦ ^^those who ^need it ^ ^most.*.
new

(77) ... ^^Sincerely,*,
acc(formula)

(78) ... ^^Susan ^^Weber*,
new

(79) ... ^^Executive ^^Director*.
new

(80) ... ^^P.^^S.*.
new

(81) ... The ^^results of ^^ZPG'S .. ^^1985 ^^Urban ^^Stress ^Test,
acc(20)

(82) .. were ^^reported ¦ as a ^^top ^^news ^^story,
acc(19) acc(16)

(83) by ^^hundreds of ^^ newspapers,
acc(7)

(84) and ^^TV ¦ and ^^radio ^stations ¦ from ^^coast to ^^coast.*.
acc(10) acc(8) acc(24)

(85) ... I ^^hope you'll ^^ help us ^^monitor ¦ this [^^remarkable]
new acc(82) new
^^media ^^coverage,

(86) .. by ^^completing ¦ the ^^enclosed ^^reply ^form.*.
new new

On what basis, then, were the ideas in this text characterized as accessible or new? It may be helpful to make at least a rough distinction between ideas that are accessible from *context* and those that are accessible from *inference*, though the distinction is surely a continuous and not a discrete one. In general it is the ideas that are accessible from context that are the easier to establish, since one need only look back at the preceding text to see whether the idea in question was previously verbalized. For example, after the idea expressed as *ZPG's 1985 Urban Stress Test* had been introduced in (12), it was accessible in (20), (28), (37), (51), and (81). Beyond that, since (12) introduced *the results* of ZPG's 1985 Urban Stress Test, subsequent references to *results* (of the test) were also accessible, as in (20) and (81).

Nearly as easy to establish is the accessibility of *the deluge of calls* in (17), established initially by the *calls* (which *jammed our switchboard*) in (4), but reinforced by mention of *an overwhelming response* in (14), as well as by the fact that *media and public reaction* was described as *incredible* in (15) and (16). Three of the four cloze subjects guessed *calls* in (17), the fourth guessing *responses*. A similar example is the accessibility of *with your contribution* in (54). Intonation unit (45) mentioned *your help*, and (50) mentioned *your support*. That this help and support would take the form of a contribution is inferrable, especially in the context of such a letter. In (54) we are dealing with an accessible meaning rather than a specific lexical item: none of the cloze subjects guessed *contribution*, but two guessed *help* and the others *support* and *donations*.

Inference is clearly involved in the accessibility of *calls* in (4). Intonation unit (3) introduced the idea of phones ringing, from which it is a small step to the inference that calls were coming in. Two of the cloze subjects guessed *calls* in (4), and one *callers*. A bigger inferential step may be involved in the accessibility of *reporters* in (7), but it was guessed correctly by all the cloze subjects, presumably because they saw the following word *newspapers*. *Population-related* in (26) is an idea accessible to any informed addressee of this letter, or to anyone who had noticed the letterhead. Various possibilities, however, were open to the cloze subjects here. While one guessed *population-related*, two thought of *stress-related*, and one *health-related*. In (29), given the context *ZPG's 1985 Urban Stress Test, created after months of persistent and exhaustive [ ]*, two of the cloze subjects guessed *research*, the others guessing *investigation* and *labor*. Evidently the idea that is captured by the intersection of these words was accessible here. I hope that these examples have illustrated how the identification of accessibility can be accomplished through contextual analysis aided by the cloze results.

5. Findings

What is to be made of all this? My principal aim has been to establish whether, and how, writing allows a relaxation of the constraints that govern the distribution of new information in spoken language. The one-new-idea-at-a-time constraint limits spoken intonation units to no more than one new idea. Certainly that constraint does not apply in the letter. Of its 86 intonation units established through oral reading, 24 of them, or 28%, contain more than one new idea.

Given the circumstances of writing, it is not surprising that this should be so. The one-new-idea-at-a-time constraint arises from the dynamics of idea activation in real time, by which the mind activates a single piece of new content at roughly one- or two-second intervals, the time occupied by the production of successive intonation units. Producing language in real time, a speaker is unable to activate more new items during such an interval. A writer, in contrast, is able to create a roughly analogous piece of language during a much longer, potentially unrestricted time interval, having thus ample time to activate several ideas that are new.

Halliday (1987) has suggested that written language, compared with spoken, has a higher *lexical density*, as measured by the proportion of words that are content words as opposed to function words. This letter bears out his suggestion: content words constitute 60% of all the words in it. I have found a typical proportion for conversational language to be more in the neighborhood of 40%. Such a finding can, however, be enriched through the discovery that written language may also contain a higher density of new information, in the sense just described. It is not the content words per se that carry an increased cognitive load, but their combination into lexicalized word sequences expressing unitary ideas, and the density of idea clusters in terms of new information.

Beyond this general observation, however, it should be of particular interest to linguists to discover the specific grammatical devices writers use in order to increase the density of new ideas. It appears that writers are able to extend certain grammatical constructions which, in speech, are generally restricted to one new idea, to instances that express more than one. This is an important characteristic of written language: its potential for increasing the new-idea density of constructions that speakers can use only within the limitations of one-new-idea-at-a-time. How that happens can be illustrated first with the construction that consists of an attributive adjective followed by a noun.

Whereas *predicate* adjectives have been found to occur with approximately equal frequency in both spoken and written language, *attributive* adjectives occur with considerably greater frequency in the more planned kinds of written language (Chafe and Danielewicz 1987:100-101). On examining the specific ways in which attributive adjectives are used in speaking, we find that they seldom lead to the inclusion of two new ideas within a single intonation unit. Speakers are limited to several other usages.

Many attributive adjectives in both speech and writing belong to idioms (like *red herring*) or lexicalized phrases (like *public health*) in which the adjective and noun together express a single idea. Typically in such cases the adjective receives secondary accent and the noun primary. I cite here a list of examples from the ZPG letter, but such examples can equally well be found in speech. Where the cloze subjects came up with alternative formulations I have included them in parentheses:

public reaction (response) (15)
concerned citizens (24, 41)

local officials (25, 63)
public health (27)
exhaustive research (29)
urban areas (33)
toxic wastes (36)
complex data (38)
elected officials (42, 66)
modest (meager) resources (funds) (49)
best opportunity (chance) (ever) (52)
population-linked stresses (58, cf. 31)
national (federal) government (60)
local level (62)
sound (intelligent) choices (decisions, judgments) (65)
the American public (people) (67)
Executive Director (79)
enclosed reply form (86)

There are other adjective-noun sequences in which the noun expresses accessible rather than new information, such examples also being in accord with the one-new-idea-at-a-time constraint. The following examples from the letter belong to a type that could also occur in spoken language:

our [small] staff (46)
acc new

a [special] contribution (70)
acc new

this [remarkable] media coverage (85)
acc new

But writing, unlike speech, allows the extension of this pattern to cases in which both the adjective and the noun express ideas that are new. The following are some examples from the letter:

outraged ¦ public officials (21)
new new

an [easy-to-use] action tool (40)
new new

our [growing] network
new new

Speakers would not normally have produced sequences like these. The writer of the ZPG letter had the leisure to activate separately the idea expressed by the adjective and that expressed by the noun, and she had no trouble in combining them within the adjective-noun construction, a construction familiar enough in speech, but one that speakers are prevented by the one-new-idea-at-a-time constraint from using in this way.

Another construction that writers may use to express two new ideas, though speakers do not, is the combination of a transitive verb with its object. Certainly lexicalized verb-object constructions would not be out of place in speech. The following are examples of this type from the letter:

jam (bombard, deluge, invade) the switchboard (4)
answer questions (6)
release the results (findings) (12)
have no idea (13)
get (receive) a response (14)
tell (inform) the public (20)
"blow the whistle" (23)
tackle problems (26)
need (require) your help (support) (45)
reach the crisis stage (59)
ignore the consequences (60)
take action (62)
make decisions (choices) (63)
affect the quality (of our lives) (64)
make (sound) choices (65)
need the data (68)
make (send) a contribution (70)
complete the reply form (questionnaire) (86)

The verb-object construction also appears in both speech and writing under circumstances in which one of the ideas is accessible. Examples like the following, then, would not be ruled out of spoken language by the one-new-idea-at-a-time constraint:

warn ¦ community leaders (57)
new acc

monitor ¦ this ... media coverage (85)
new acc

It is the cases in which both the verb and the object express separate new ideas that present something uniquely writtenlike. The letter provides the following examples:

it ranks ¦ 184 urban areas (33)
new new

translates complex, technical data (38-39)
new new new

Here again we see a grammatical pattern that is by no means rare in speech extended in writing to denser concentrations of new information.

A third commonly used construction is that in which two noun phrases or other grammatical entities are conjoined with *and*. While lexicaled sequences of this sort are frequent in speech (*bacon and eggs*, *pins and needles*), sequences with two new items are not. The ZPG letter offers:

crowding ¦ and birth rates (35)
new new

air quality ¦ and toxic wastes (36)
new new

Having looked at the adjective-noun, verb-object, and conjoining constructions from this point of view, when we turn to the subject-predicate construction we might be tempted to regard it as just another example of the same kind: a construction in which both constituents, in this case the subject and the predicate, are rarely both new in speaking, but can be so treated in writing. Because of the special discourse functions of grammatical subjects, however, we find some narrower constraints at work here.

So far as lexicalization is concerned, aside from formulaic discourse markers like *you know* and *I mean* and proverbs like (*The early bird catches the worm*), idioms and lexicalized phrases that consist of a subject followed by a transitive predicate are rare. Furthermore, in contrast to the cases we have been considering, one of the constituents, the subject, has a strong tendency to be given information. When it is not given, when one constituent is new and the other accessible, in speech it is nearly always the subject that is accessible and the predicate that is new. In short, the relation between subject and predicate is a highly asymmetric one with respect to the distribution of new information.

The following example from the letter, where the subject *we* expresses a given referent, accords with the most common pattern of speech:

we urgently need your help (45)

An example with an accessible subject, also not uniquely written like, is the following:

the Urban Stress Test ¦ translates ... data (37-39)
acc new

The kind of new-subject instance that is unique to writing appears in the following examples:

staffers ¦ stayed late into the night (5)
new new

our modest resources ¦ are being stretched to the limit (49)
new new

our national government ¦ continues ¦ to ignore the consequences (60)
new new new

The proportions of given, accessible, and new subjects are typically very different in speaking and writing. The overwhelming majority of subjects in casual spoken language are given, with perhaps 15% or so being accessible, and virtually none being new. The ZPG letter, in contrast, shows only 43% of its subjects expressing given information, nearly as many (37%) expressing accessible information, and fully 20% expressing new information. The subject-predicate construction, then, provides us with a special example of another grammatical pattern that is constrained in speaking, but that can be extended to a wider range of possibilities in writing (Cf. Chafe 1991).

6. Summary

What I have tried to show, using the ZPG letter as evidence, is that writing provides the opportunity to violate two constraints that are imposed on language by the economy of information flow. One is the constraint that allows only one new idea within each idea cluster (as expressed by an intonation unit). The other is the constraint against grammatical subjects that express new ideas. In the course of exploring violations of these constraints in the ZPG letter, we looked for a consensus on its prosody in oral reading. With such a prosody established, we found ways to segment the idea clusters expressed by intonation units into separate ideas, a pursuit that led us to examine instances of lexicalization. We then looked for ways of distinguishing accessible ideas from new ones. In the end we saw how particular grammatical constructions have come to be used by writers to combine separate new ideas, thus exceeding the bounds of spoken language.

This discussion has been an initial exploration of a territory that needs much more attention. I can only hope that it will suggest that further exploration will be worthwhile, while providing some ideas and methods that may prove useful on subsequent forays into the same area. It is an area that will have to be better understood if we are going to know more about how thought and language interact in real time.

References

Chafe, Wallace

1979 "The flow of thought and the flow of language." In T. Givón, (ed.), *Discourse and Syntax*. New York: Academic Press.

1980 "The deployment of consciousness in the production of a narrative." In Wallace Chafe, (ed.), *The Pear Stories: Cognitive, Cultural, and Linguistics Aspects of Narrative Production*. Norwood, NJ: Ablex.

1987 "Cognitive constraints on information flow." In Russell Tomlin, (ed.), *Coherence and Grounding in Discourse*. Amsterdam: John Benjamins.

1988 "Punctuation and the prosody of written language." *Written Communication* 5.395-426.

1991. "Grammatical subjects in speaking and writing." *Text* 11.45-72.

Chafe, Wallace and Jane Danielewicz

1987 "Properties of spoken and written language." In Rosalind Horowitz and S. Jay Samuels, (eds), *Comprehending Oral and Written Language*. New York: Academic Press.

Halliday, M.A.K.

1987 "Spoken and written modes of meaning." In Rosalind Horowitz and S. Jay Samuels, (eds), *Comprehending Oral and Written Language*. New York: Academic Press.

Pawley, Andrew

1985 "Lexicalization." *Georgetown University Round Table on Languages and Linguistics 1985*. Washington: Georgetown University Press.

Taylor, Wilson L.

1953 "Cloze procedure: a new tool for measuring readability." *Journalism Quarterly* 30.414-438.

The ZPG Letter: Subjects, Definiteness, and Information-status*

Ellen F. Prince
University of Pennsylvania

0. Introduction

Although terms like 'discourse analysis' and 'text analysis' have been around for over 35 years (e.g. Harris 1952a,b), there is still no one generally accepted theory of discourse on the basis of which one might provide *the* analysis of a text. For one thing, one may take two different tacks: the 'humanistic' tack, according to which one seeks to discover what is special about or unique to a particular text, what sets it apart from all other texts of its class or genre, and the 'scientific' tack, according to which one seeks to discover what general principles of texthood are discernible from a single token of text.

In what follows, I shall take the latter approach. That is, I shall assume that a particular naturally-occurring text, the Zero Population Growth fund-raising letter chosen for analysis by the editors of this volume, is an unexceptional member of its class of texts and therefore is representative of that genre. Although, as it turns out, I shall present some evidence that suggests that parts of this text are not as natural as they might have been, I shall present no evidence that the text is in fact different from any other in

*I should like to thank Susan Pintzuk and Shana Poplack for their invaluable help. Thanks are also due Deborah Dahl, Bob Frank, Jeanette Gundel, Larry Horn, Aravind Joshi, and Yael Ziv for their very helpful discussions and research (which is of course not to suggest that any of them agree with anything in this paper). Finally, *bolshoy spas'ibo* to Tom Samuelian and Sasha Bobilev. This research was supported in part by NSF IRI84-10413-A02 (A.K. Joshi, Principal Investigator).

its genre, since such a demonstration would require an additional corpus of analogous texts.

Second, a text may be analyzed with respect to any number of variables: syntactic patterns, syntactic complexity, register, rhetorical devices, presuppositions and narratee,[1] and so on, and a complete analysis of any text would deal with all possible variables. Clearly, that is beyond the scope of this paper as well as the competence and interests of its author. Rather, I shall look at just one feature: how subjects differ from nonsubjects in the text. More specifically, I shall investigate the differences between subjects and nonsubjects with respect to one formal phenomenon, definiteness, and one discourse phenomenon, the information-status of the entities that the subjects and nonsubjects represent.

1. Overview of the ZPG Letter

Before proceeding with a discussion of the analysis, however, let us first consider briefly the general content and syntactic form of the ZPG letter.

1.1 *Content of the ZPG Letter*

The letter, addressed to 'Dear Friend of ZPG' and signed by its executive director, is primarily an appeal for money. The particular pretext for this instance of fund-raising is that (A) a study of urban population-related problems carried out and published by the organization has elicited an enormous number of requests for information, (B) it is very important for the cause that these requests be answered, and (C) the organization cannot meet these demands without more money, presumably for extra postage, printing, staff, phone lines, and so forth. A secondary goal of the letter is a request to the addressee to fill out an enclosed questionnaire about what they have heard about the above-mentioned study and where.

1.2 *Syntactic Form of the ZPG Letter*

First, there are 56 clauses, distributed as follows:

(1) Clauses in ZPG letter:

	Finite Segment #	Nonfinite Segment #	Total
Main:	23: 4,5,6,7,8,9,10, 11,12,13,14, 15(2x),16,17,18, 18,19,20,21,22, 22,23,29,30	[D.N.A.]	23
Subord.:	16: 7(2x),9(2x), 10(3x),11, 18(2x),19,20, 23(3x),30	17: 6(2x),9,10(2x), 11,12,14,17,18, 19,21(3x),23, 30(2x)	33
Total:	39	17	56

These clauses display a fair amount of syntactic variation. Five finite clauses are passive (Segments 15 (2x), 20, 23, 29), and there is one parenthetical (Segment 23). In addition, there is a good deal of embedding of finite clauses — three complement clauses (Segments 7, 9, 30), six relative clauses (Segments 9, 10 (2x), 18, 20, 23), two free relatives (Segments 11, 23), one indirect question (Segment 10), three adverbial clauses (Segments 7, 18, 19), and one comparative subdeletion (Segment 23).[2] Finally, there is some noncanonical word order: three preposed adverbial phrases (Segments 4, 9, 10), four preposed infinitivals (Segments 14, 18, 20, 21), and two preposed finite adverbial clauses (Segments 7, 19), and there is one extraposed relative clause (Segment 20).

Interestingly, however, there is no clause in which arguments of the verb — (surface) subject or object NPs — occur out of their canonical position.[3] That is, there is no Topicalization, no Inversion, no Dative-Shift or Particle-Shift, and no Heavy NP-Shift. In addition, there are no There-sentences. Thus, this text lends itself well to a study of the discourse-related properties of canonical subjects and objects, in particular to those that tend to distinguish (canonical) subjects from other verb-arguments.

2. Two Properties of Subjects: Definite and 'Old'

As is well known, NPs representing discourse entities, or 'referring expressions' in the broadest sense, do not occur in different syntactic positions randomly. Among other things, it has often been claimed or argued that whether an NP is a subject or not is related to its definiteness and to the information-status of the discourse entity it represents: subjects tend to be definite and tend to represent old information.[4] Note that these are simply statistical tendencies. See, for example, the comparison of subjects and topics in Li and Thompson 1976, where it is argued that the tendency of subjects to be definite and 'old' corresponds to a categorical requirement for topics.

Of course, what is at issue here are 'canonical' subjects, subjects which occur in unmarked/canonical position. In English, this means preverbal subjects, as in (2), in contrast to noncanonical subjects, as in (3):

(2) a. *Lee* bought a book.
b. *The book* was written by a Russian.
c. Tomorrow *she*'ll buy another book.

(3) a. There was *a book* on the shelf.
b. On the table was lying *a pamphlet.*
c. Nothing else did *I* see.

That is, the sentences of (2), whether active (2a,c) or passive (2b), whether subject-initial (2a,b) or not (2c), have their subject in the canonical preverbal position. In contrast, the sentences of (3) have their subjects in some noncanonical postverbal position.[5]

As mentioned above, the particular claims we shall consider about the relationship between definiteness and information-status, on the one hand, and subjecthood, on the other, are basically that canonical subjects tend to be *definite* (e.g. Li and Thompson 1976, Givon 1976, Keenan 1976, inter alia) and to represent *old information* (e.g. Linde 1973, Chafe 1976, Keenan 1976, Silva-Corvalán 1983, Lambrecht 1986, inter alia). In what follows, we shall analyze the ZPG letter with respect to these two claims. In particular, we shall consider the following questions. First, given that information can be 'old' in a variety of ways, which definition of 'old' information is relevant to subjecthood? And, second, can we tease apart the importance of 'old' information from that of definiteness? That is, are these two independent variables each having an effect on subjecthood, or does one in fact follow from the other? However, before dealing with the details of the analysis, a discussion of these two phenomena is in order.

2.1 *Definiteness*

Although the notion of definiteness/indefiniteness seems to be relatively straightforward, it in fact has been subject to a good deal of confusion. In particular, it is taken to be a formal property of NPs but, often at the same time, it is also taken to be a conceptual property of entities in a discourse model.

Formal definiteness pertains to the marking of the NP as definite or indefinite in those languages like English which have such a marking. Marking of definite NPs in English may be done by the definite article (*the*), demonstrative articles (*this*, *that*, and so forth), possessive adjectives (e.g. *my house*, *her work*), personal pronouns (e.g. *I*, *they*), and (unmodified) proper nouns (e.g. *Sandy*, *Bill Mann*, *Italy*). In addition, certain quantifiers (e.g. *all*, *every*) have been argued to be definite. Marking of indefinite NPs in English may be done by the indefinite articles (*a*, the zero article) and by other quantifiers, including the numerals (e.g. *some*, *any*, *one*, *six*). Thus, whether a given NP is formally definite or indefinite is decidable, entirely and exclusively, on the basis of the form of that NP.

At the same time, it is frequently claimed that only indefinite NPs may occur in, say, There-sentences (e.g., most recently, Safir 1985:91). This predicts the difference in grammaticality/felicity found in the two versions of (4b) (the symbol # indicates that the sentence is infelicitous):

(4) a. A/The man was in the room.
b. There was a/#the man in the room.

However, as noted in Rando and Napoli 1978, Ziv 1981, and elsewhere, it is simply not true that only indefinites may occur in There-sentences, as shown in 5:

(5) a. There were the same people at both conferences.
b. There was the usual crowd at the beach.
c. There was the stupidest article on the reading list.

Likewise, if the claim that only indefinites occur in There-sentences is to account for all the facts — that is, that all and only indefinites occur in There-sentences — then a problem arises with plural generics, which are formally indefinite but which cannot occur in There-sentences. That is, the same formally indefinite NP can have a generic understanding, as in (6), or a nongeneric understanding, as in (7); only the nongeneric understanding is available in There-sentences, as in (8):

(6) a. I love *bagels*.
b. *Unicorns* are quite popular in some philosophy circles.

(7) a. I bought *bagels*.
b. I dreamt that *unicorns* were grazing in front of College Hall.

(8) a. There are *bagels* with cinnamon nowadays.
b. There are *unicorns* in front of College Hall.[6]

At this point, one often hears that certain indefinites are 'really' definite (e.g. Safir 1985) and that certain definites are 'really' indefinite (e.g. Prince 1981a), but then one is construing the terms as relating to information-status and no longer as decidable on the basis of linguistic form. Obviously, one is perfectly free to use the terms 'definite/indefinite' for information-statuses, but then one must keep in mind that is what one is doing and not use definiteness for analyses based on form (e.g. Safir 1985 and elsewhere; compare Milsark 1974). Of course, for crosslinguistic or historical purposes, it might make sense to talk about 'formal definiteness' vs. 'informational definiteness' so as to be able to compare different formal systems for marking the same informational classes. In what follows, however, I shall take 'definiteness' to be a formal category and use other terms for the informational. That is, with respect to the issue at hand, I shall construe the claim that subjects tend to be definite as a claim that subjects are more likely than nonsubjects to be formally definite, and it is this claim that I shall test with respect to the ZPG letter.[6]

2.2 *Information-Status*

As is well known (Allerton 1978, Prince 1981b, Horn 1986, inter alia), the terms 'old/given' and 'new' information have meant a variety of things over the years. However, I think we can differentiate three notions of 'old/new' information.

2.2.1 *Old/New: Focus-Presupposition Constructions*

First, let us distinguish one sense of old/new information so that we may proceed to ignore it, since it is not particularly relevant to the ZPG letter. This is the sense of old/new typically exemplified by sentences like (9):

(9) a. It's *John* I like.
b. What he ate was *a/the banana*.

That is, such 'focus-presupposition' constructions (Chomsky 1971) structure the proposition that they convey into two parts, an open proposition, as in 10a, and an instantiation of the variable in that open proposition, as in 10b:

(10) a. I like X.
b. X = John.

As is often noted (Chomsky 1971, Prince 1978, Horn 1981, Wilson and Sperber 1979, Delahunty 1982, Gundel 1985, inter alia), the open proposition is generally taken to be 'old' information, already in the discourse-model or at least known or inferrable, while the focus is taken to be the 'new' information.

In terms of linguistic form, focus-presupposition constructions are marked by stress or by syntactic form (in conjunction with stress): it-clefts, wh-clefts, Topicalization, Focus-Movement, and so forth (Prince 1986).

However, there are virtually no focus-presupposition constructions in the ZPG letter. (Clear exceptions are the free relatives in Segments 11 and 23.) Of far greater relevance to the present study are the two other notions of old/new information, and it is to them that we shall now turn.

2.2.2 *Old/New: in the Hearer's Head*

Information, by which is here generally meant 'entities'/referents, may be old/new with respect to (the speaker's beliefs about) the hearer's beliefs. Thus, for example, when I utter (11) to a colleague, I presume that this colleague already has a mental entity with the attribute of having the name *Sandy Thompson* and will believe that this is the entity I am speaking of:

(11) I'm waiting for it to be noon so I can call *Sandy Thompson*.

That is, in this situation, the NP *Sandy Thompson* represents information that I, the speaker, take to be old — with respect to my hearer's head (Christophersen 1939, Chafe 1976, 1987). Conversely, if I were to want to convey the same general information to my neighbor (who I believe does not know Sandy Thompson), I might say something like (12):

(12) I'm waiting for it to be noon so I can call *someone in California*.

That is, I believe my neighbor does not already know of Sandy Thompson, I believe that this particular entity is new — with respect to my hearer's head. The type of 'old' information exemplified in (11), i.e. old (only) with respect to the hearer's beliefs, has been called a variety of things in the literature: 'in the permanent registry' (Kuno 1972), 'Culturally copresent'

(Clark and Marshall 1981), 'Unused' (Prince 1981b), among other things. With such an understanding of 'old' information, 'new' information would then be an entity assumed not to be already known to the hearer, or what I have previously (Prince 1981b) called 'Brand-new'. Perhaps more easily remembered terms — though no more euphonious — would be Hearer-old and Hearer-new.

With respect to linguistic form, Hearer-old entities are typically definite, as is the proper name *Sandy Thompson* in (11); Hearer-new entities are typically indefinite, as is *someone in California* in (12). Likewise, the indefinite in (13a) tells the reader that the kid that threw up is Hearer-new — some unknown-to-hearer kid, while the definite in (13b) tells the reader that the sick kid is Hearer-old — some known-to-hearer kid, say, the speaker's:

(13) a. In the park yesterday, *a kid* threw up on me.
b. In the park yesterday, *the kid* threw up on me.

While this correlation of definite NPs with Hearer-old entities and of indefinite NPs with Hearer-new entities is typical, it is by no means perfect. For one thing, both indefinite and definite NPs may represent Inferrable entities, to be discussed below.

Second, some definite NPs represent Hearer-new entities; this is in fact the case in (5) above, where definites 'behave like' indefinites, i.e. occur felicitously in There-sentences. In point of fact, There-sentences do not require indefinite NPs at all; rather, they require Hearer-new NPs. Thus, for example, *the same people* in the There-sentence in (5a), while formally definite, evokes an entity that is Hearer-new: the hearer learns that some set of people were at one of the conferences and that some set of people were at the other conference and that the two sets were the same. This set of people, however, is presented as not already known to the hearer. Compare (14a) with (14b) (= 5a):

(14) a. The same people were at both conferences.
b. There were the same people at both conferences.

Note that (14a) is ambiguous: the set of people at both conferences may be some set not already identified to the hearer (Hearer-new), or it may mean that some previously identified set of people (Hearer-old) was also at both conferences. Thus (15a) may entail (15c) but (15b) does not entail (15c):

(15) a. Nine hundred people attended the Institute and the same people were at both conferences.

b. Nine hundred people attended the Institute and there were the same people at both conferences.
c. The set of nine hundred people attended both conferences.

Third, some indefinite NPs represent Hearer-old entities. This is the case, for example, with generics, mentioned above. That is, if a speaker thinks the hearer knows the meaning of some noun, a minimal condition on its normal felicitous use, and if that noun denotes an entity-type, then the speaker must assume that the hearer already knows that there is a class of such entity-types; therefore, generics are Hearer-old. As for the unavailability of generic understandings in There-sentences, as illustrated in (8) above, note that this follows automatically from the discourse constraint on There-sentences that their logical subject be Hearer-new.[8]

In sum then, Hearer-status is typically but not categorically marked by definiteness, with Hearer-old entities typically being represented by definite NPs and Hearer-new by indefinite.

2.2.3 *Old/New: in the Discourse-Model*

Instead of assessing the age of an entity from the point of view of the hearer's head, we may assess it from the point of view of the discourse-model being constructed during discourse processing. Thus, an entity may be old/new with respect to the discourse model, or 'Discourse-old'/'Discourse-new'.

That is, an NP may refer to an entity that has already been evoked in the prior discourse-stretch, or it may evoke an entity which has not previously occurred in the prior discourse-stretch. For example, if (11) and (12) above were each discourse-initial (or, more likely, if they were preceded by simply 'Hi, what are you doing?'), both *Sandy Thompson* and *someone in California* would evoke *new* entities in the discourse-model, or 'Discourse-new' entities, regardless of the fact that the former was Hearer-old and the latter Hearer-new. Thus, Discourse-newness tells us nothing about an entity's Hearer-status. Of course, an entity's status as Hearer-new would tell us something about its Discourse-status: it would necessarily be Discourse-new, since hearers are expected to remember what they have been told.

With respect to linguistic form, consider (16b), as a response to (16a) (= 11):

(16) a. I'm waiting for it to be noon so I can call *Sandy Thompson*.
b. Why are you trying to get in touch with *Sandy Thompson*?

The italicized NP in (16b) represents an entity that has already been evoked in the discourse and is therefore Discourse-old. Note that the Discourse-new *Sandy Thompson* in (16a) is formally indistinguishable from the Discourse-old occurrence of the same NP in (16b). In fact, it is interesting that, in English at least, there is virtually no marking of an NP with respect to the Discourse-status of the entity it represents. Of course, if an NP is indefinite and is thereby understood as evoking something Hearer-new, we can infer Discourse-new. However, if it is not so marked, then, with one exception, we cannot tell from its form whether it has occurred before in the discourse.

The one possible exception to the generalization that Discourse-status is not marked (except insofar as it follows from Hearer-status, which typically *is* marked) is that of pronouns. Pronouns indicate that the entities they represent are salient, i.e. appropriately in the hearer's consciousness (Chafe 1976, Clark and Marshall 1981, inter alia), at that point in the construction of the discourse model. Therefore, they are presumably already in the discourse model. Therefore, they are Discourse-old.[9] However, at any point in (discourse) time, only a subset, usually proper, of the entities already evoked are salient and hence are representable by a pronoun. Furthermore, the use of a pronoun, especially when the prior mention is in a different sentence, is often optional. Thus, while the use of a pronoun probably entails that the entity it represents is Discourse-old, an entity's status as Discourse-old does not entail that it will be represented by a pronoun.

In sum, while the category of definiteness gives us an approximate marking of Hearer-status (Hearer-old or Hearer-new), there is no analogous marking of NPs according to their Discourse-status (Discourse-old or Discourse-new), although we may get certain clues as to Discourse-status from an NP being marked as Hearer-new or, optionally, as salient Discourse-old.

2.2.4 *Inferrables*

Unfortunately for these relatively neat binary distinctions, there is a third possible status for an entity in the discourse-model: Inferrable. That is, when a speaker evokes some entity in the discourse, it is often the case that s/he assumes that the hearer can infer the (discourse-)existence of certain other entities, based on the speaker's beliefs about the hearer's beliefs and reasoning ability. Consider, for example, (17):

(17) a. He passed by the door of the Bastille and *the door* was painted purple.
b. He passed by the Bastille and *the door* was painted purple.

In (17a), the hearer is assumed to have an entity for the door under discussion before hearing the italicized NP; hence it is Discourse-old. In contrast, in (17b), the hearer is not assumed to already have any mental representation of the door in question, hence it is not Discourse-old. However, this door is treated *as though* it were already known to the hearer. Indeed, the hearer of (17b) knows a great deal about this door — s/he knows which door it is: the door of the Bastille. Hence it is not quite Discourse-new.

Of course, not just any entity can be introduced this way. Minimally, the speaker must have a warrant for believing (A)that the hearer already has the belief that the entity in question is plausibly related to some other 'trigger' entity (*the Bastille*, in 17b), where the trigger entity is itself not (or, minimally, would not be), at the relevant point in time, Hearer-new, and (B)that the hearer is therefore able to infer the existence of the entity in question. Thus I am calling such entities 'Inferrables'. In the case of (17b), at the point of hearing *the door*, the hearer is assumed to have already a mental representation of the building under discussion and also to believe something like 'A building (generally/plausibly) has associated with it a particular door, namely the main door used for entering and leaving.' Compare (18):

(18) #I passed by the Bastille and *the trunk* was painted purple.

In the absence of special prior knowledge (e.g. the Bastille had a trunk nailed on its facade, or the Bastille was in fact a car, in which case it typically had a trunk associated with it, or the Bastille *was* a trunk, in which case *the trunk* would be coreferential with *the Bastille* and Discourse-old rather than Inferrable), (18) is infelicitous, since *the Bastille* is not a trigger for any inferences crucially involving trunks and there is, therefore, no warrant for assuming that the hearer can plausibly infer the existence of this trunk.[10]

Inferrables are thus like Hearer-old entities in that they rely on certain assumptions about what the hearer does know, e.g. that buildings typically have doors in (17b), and they are like Discourse-old entities in that they rely on there being already in the discourse-model some entity to trigger the inference, e.g. *the Bastille* in (17b). At the same time, Inferrables are like Hearer-new (and, therefore, Discourse-new) entities in that the hearer is not expected to already have in his/her head the entity in question. The question then arises whether Inferrables should be collapsed with one or the other category, preserving binariness, or whether they form a separate third category, or whether information statuses are merely points on a continuum, with Inferrables in the middle.

The evidence for collapsing Inferrables with one of the other categories is not straightforward. For one thing, linguistic form will not help to decide, since Hearer-old and Discourse-old entities are generally represented by the same types of NPs. Furthermore, Clark and Haviland 1977 present experimental evidence for the distinctness of Inferrables, based on the length of time hearers take to process them. Finally, Mazzie and Sankoff 1988 show that, in Tok Pisin, an English-based pidgin currently undergoing creolization, there is an ongoing grammaticization of the marking of a certain class of Inferrables but no such grammaticization of the marking of other information statuses.[11]

The last approach, a continuum analysis, is rather troubling on cognitive grounds, as pointed out in Chafe 1976, Contreras 1976, inter alia: what could it mean that there is a continuum between what we have in our head and what we do not? To my knowledge, the only argument for a continuum is presented in Silva-Corvalán 1983. Unfortunately, Silva-Corvalán fails to distinguish Discourse-status from Hearer-status, her chief evidence for a continuum being that (in my terms) a Discourse-new/Hearer-old entity is 'older' than a Discourse-new/Hearer-new entity and 'newer' than a Discourse-old(/Hearer-old) entity.[12]

At the same time, what I am lumping together under the single rubric 'Inferrable' may itself be subdivided, possibly as a continuum, according to the type and ease of inferencing that is required. This is an important area for psycholinguistic research and one that I shall not pursue here.

In what follows, then, I shall simply leave Inferrables as a third category, and we shall see how they are in fact treated in the text analyzed.

As for the linguistic form of NPs representing Inferrables, the situation is fairly complex. If we reconsider (17b), we note that Inferrables may be represented by definite NPs. However, consider (19):

(19) a. I picked up that book I bought and *a cockroach* fell out.
b. I picked up that book I bought and *a page* fell out.

In (19a), the indefinite NP *a cockroach* represents a Hearer-new entity: a cockroach whose existence the hearer is assumed not to already know of. In

(19b), on the other hand, the most usual understanding is that this is not simply any old page but *a page from the book just mentioned*. Thus, for example, the hearer of (19b) can infer that the book became defective, since it is now missing a page; it cannot however be said to be missing a cockroach. Thus, *a page* in (19b) is an Inferrable: the speaker expects that the hearer believes that books typically have associated with them a set of pages and that s/he will infer that this page is one of the set of pages associated with the book in question. Unlike the Inferrable in (17b), however, it is indefinite. The reason for this seems to be that the prior belief involves a set (of pages, in 19b) rather than a single entity (a door, in 17b). As we might expect, if the whole set is evoked, the NP is definite:

(20) a. #I picked up that book I bought and *the cockroaches* fell out.
b. I picked up that book I bought and *the pages* fell out.

(See Hawkins 1978 for the relation of sets to definiteness.)

In sum, Inferrable entities are technically Hearer-new (and, therefore, Discourse-new) but, unlike Hearer-new entities, their existence is assumed to be inferrable by the hearer on the basis of some trigger entity, itself Discourse-old, in combination with some belief the hearer is assumed to have which says that entities like the trigger have associated with them entities like the Inferrable.

2.2.5 *Containing Inferrables*

Finally, in Prince 1981b, I distinguished a fifth category, which I called Containing Inferrables. These are exemplified in (21):

(21) a. *The door of the Bastille* was painted purple.
b. *The pages of that book I bought* fell out.

Once again, we find NPs which are formed in such a way that we 'feel' we are supposed to know about the entity they represent, but in fact we may very well not. These NPs are similar to Inferrables in that they require inferencing on the basis of certain background knowledge we have; the difference is that the entity which triggers the inference is not, as in the case of the Inferrables, necessarily in the prior discourse, but is rather *within the NP itself*. Thus (21a) and (21b) can be quite felicitous where the Bastille and the book in question, though known to the hearer, have not yet been mentioned in the discourse, as well as where the hearer has no prior knowledge of the relevant door or pages.[13] All that is minimally required is that the speaker already know about the Bastille and the book and that the speaker believe that a building like the Bastille typically has a door and that a book typically has pages. Compare with (22):

(22) a. #*The trunk on the Bastille* was painted purple.
b. #*The cockroach in that book I bought* fell out.

It goes without saying that the propositional content in (22) can of course be conveyed; however, in the absence of special beliefs, it would be much more felicitously conveyed along the lines of (23):

(23) a. The Bastille had a trunk nailed to it. The trunk was painted purple.
b. That book I bought had a cockroach in it. The cockroach fell out.

That is, there are constraints on felicitous Containing Inferrables, just as on Inferrables: the inferences required of the hearer must be based on beliefs the hearer can reasonably be expected to have.

As for linguistic form, the most salient feature of Containing Inferrables is their syntactic complexity. They necessarily have some NP contained in them, often within a subordinate clause. Interestingly, it is generally the case that what is a Containing Inferrable for one hearer (or, more likely, reader) can felicitously serve as a Hearer-old, Discourse-new entity for another. For example, imagine that a hearer were told the first sentence of (23a) (*The Bastille had a trunk nailed to it*) in one discourse and (22a) (*The trunk on the Bastille was painted purple*) in a subsequent discourse. The italicized NP in (22a) would still be felicitous, but it would be understood as representing a Hearer-old, Discourse-new entity rather than a Containing Inferrable. Or, more commonly, imagine that half of an audience heard the first sentence of (23a) on one occasion and the other half did not. In a subsequent discourse, the speaker could utter (22a) felicitously to the whole audience: the half that had previously heard the first sentence of (23a) would understand the underlined NP in (22a) as representing a Hearer-old, Discourse-new entity, while the other half would understand it as a Containing Inferrable. As I mentioned in Prince 1981b, this makes Containing Inferrables very suitable for multi-receiver discourse, in particular formal written prose, where the sender either is not sure of the receivers' knowledge/beliefs, or where s/he believes that there are relevant differences among the receivers.

2.2.6 *Information-Status: A Summary*

First, discourse entities may be considered old or new with respect to the hearer, or Hearer-old/Hearer-new. Second, they may be considered old or new with respect to the discourse, or Discourse-old/Discourse-new.

Furthermore, Discourse-status and Hearer-status are partially independent of each other. In particular, Discourse-new tells us nothing of Hearer-status, as shown in (11) and (12) above, and Hearer-old tells us nothing of Discourse-status, as can be seen in (16).

In contrast, the status of Discourse-old is not independent of Hearer-status: if an entity has had a prior evocation in a discourse-model, then it follows that it is now Hearer-old, as well as Discourse-old: hearers are assumed to remember the entities we have told them about, at least for the duration of the discourse. Likewise, if something is Hearer-new, then it must be Discourse-new, for, if it were not, then the hearer would already know about it. Thus, we have the following possibilities, exemplified in (24) and (25) (each consisting of two contiguous discourse segments) and named in (26):

(24) a. I'm waiting for it to be noon so I can call *someone in California*.
b. I figure *she*'ll be up by 9, her time.

(25) a. I'm waiting for it to be noon so I can call *Sandy Thompson*.
b. I figure *Sandy/she*'ll be up by 9, her time.

(26) Hearer- and Discourse-status of a discourse entity:

	Discourse-new	Discourse-old
Hearer-new:	Brand-new: 24a: someone...	[D.N.A.]
Hearer-old:	Unused: 25a: Sandy Thompson	Evoked: 24b: she 25b: Sandy, she

Third, discourse entities may be of a third category, Inferrable, where they are technically Hearer-new and Discourse-new but depend upon beliefs assumed to be Hearer-old, and where these beliefs crucially involve some trigger entity, which is itself Discourse-old, and where they themselves are being treated as though they were Hearer-old and possibly also Discourse-old.

Finally, discourse entities may be Containing Inferrables, similar to Inferrables but containing the trigger entity within their description.

Thus we have a fairly complex interaction of the speaker's beliefs about what the hearer knows, potentially knows, and does not yet know, and this interaction is crucially involved in the production and comprehension of each referring expression in discourse.

3. Goal and Methodology

The goal of the analysis was to determine the following:

(27) a. Are subjects significantly more likely than nonsubjects to be definite?
b. Are subjects significantly more likely than nonsubjects to be Hearer-old entities?
c. Are subjects significantly more likely than nonsubjects to be Discourse-old entities?
d. If the answer to any two of the above is affirmative, are they independent tendencies, or is one a reflex of the other?

The methodology used was quantitative analysis. To that end, a data file was created consisting of each NP in the ZPG letter as a separate token. Each was coded for information-status as discussed above and formal definiteness, as well as for the dependent variable, grammatical role (subject/nonsubject). In addition, a number of other variables were coded for, e.g. NP-type (full NP, pronoun, etc.), clause-type (main, relative clause, indirect question, etc.), syntactic and informational complexity of the NP (i.e. whether it contained a clause and/or other NPs), and so on. The data file was then run on VARBRUL.[14] Certain classes of tokens were ignored: NPs which I could not code (e.g. *the whistle*, Segment 9), subjects represented by a trace (e.g. the subject of *need*, Segment 23), NPs which were not part of clauses (e.g. *Dear Friend of ZPG*, Segment 3), and subjects of nonfinite verbs (e.g. *reporters*, Segment 9).[14] The coding for syntactic information was straightforward. However, a few words are in order on the coding for definiteness and information status.

3.1 *Coding for Definiteness*

Definiteness was construed, as mentioned above, as a formal category. Thus, NPs with definite or demonstrative articles, NPs with universal quantifiers, proper names, and personal pronouns were coded as definite. (NPs like *October 25* were considered to be proper names.) NPs with indefinite articles, including the zero article, and NPs with non-universal quantifiers were coded as indefinite. NPs whose definiteness I could not comfortably code, e.g. *how population-linked pressures affect U.S. cities*, Segment 11, were left uncoded.

3.2 *Coding for Information-Status*

Coding for information-status is never an easy matter, and no doubt other analysts might have a somewhat different coding. For what it is worth, I recoded a number of difficult tokens and the changes had no significant effect on the VARBRUL results. That said, the NPs were coded for information-status as follows:

NPs evoking entities which had already been mentioned in the letter were coded as Discourse-old (= Evoked), exemplified in (28), where the pronoun *they* is understood as referring to the local activists already introduced:

(28) Discourse-old (and, ergo, Hearer-old) = Evoked: '...arm our growing network of local activists with the materials *they* need...' (Segment 18)

NPs evoking entities which had no prior mention in the letter and which I, as a representative intended addressee (who in fact receives large numbers of fund-raising letters from ZPG), had never heard of (and could not infer the existence of) were coded as Hearer-new (= Brand-new), as in (29), where the intended reader is presumably not supposed to have already a mental entity for this complex, technical data:

(29) Hearer-new (and, ergo, Discourse-new) = Brand-new:
'The Urban Stress Test translates *complex, technical data* into...
(Segment 13)

NPs evoking entities which had no prior mention in the discourse but which I already knew of were coded as Discourse-new, Hearer-old (=

Unused), as in (30), where the italicized NP certainly represents an entity I already knew existed:

(30) Discourse-new, Hearer-old = Unused:
'...from reporters eager to tell *the public* about...' (Segment 9)

NPs evoking entities which were not previously mentioned and which I as the reader had no prior knowledge of, but whose existence I could infer on the basis of some entity that was previously evoked and some belief I have about such entities were coded as Inferrable, as illustrated in (31):

(31) Inferrable:
'*Staffers* stayed late into the night.' (Segment 6)

That is, while I did not already have a mental entity for any personnel in that particular ZPG office, this NP did not induce me to create a new arbitrary set of staffers but rather to infer that these were the individuals that staff the ZPG office, since I believe that an organization like ZPG typically has an office, which typically has staffers.

Finally, I took advantage of the situation that one man's Containing Inferrable is another man's Unused, and collapsed the two categories, on the rationalization that, if it is true that speakers (usually, writers) use Containing Inferrables partly because they can be understood also as Unused entities, then the two categories should not differ with respect to the grammatical role of the NP that represents them. For example, consider the italicized NP in (32):

(32) 'When we released *the results of ZPG's 1985 Urban Stress Test...*' (Segment 7)

Clearly, ZPG expects that some readers already know of the entity this NP represents; cf. Segment 30. I, however, did not know of it; for me, and no doubt for many other readers, it was a Containing Inferrable. Clearly, ZPG had to allow for both types of readers. Therefore, it should not be the case that the writer of the letter would treat them differently with respect to subjecthood, the phenomenon being studied here.

4. Analysis

Let us now turn to the quantitative analysis of the NPs in the ZPG letter to see the effect of information-status and definiteness on subjecthood.

4.1 *The Effect of Information-Status on Subjecthood*

In order to check the claim that subjects tend to be 'old' information and, if that claim is correct, to see what is meant by 'old', I ran VARBRUL on the token file, the dependent variable being whether the NP is a subject or a nonsubject. The independent variables were Hearer-status, i.e. whether the entity represented by the NP is Hearer-old or Hearer-new, and Discourse-status, i.e. whether the entity represented by the variable is Discourse-old or Discourse-new. The runs were made twice, once excluding Inferrables, once including them as a third factor in each factor group. In total, 106 NPs were counted in the analysis, of which 31 occur as subjects.

The results show the following: first, taken separately, each information variable — Hearer-status and Discourse-status — is significant; second, both Hearer-old and Discourse-old entities are more likely to be subjects than Hearer-new and Discourse-new, respectively; and, third, the inclusion or exclusion of Inferrables has no significant effect on these patterns. The numbers, percentages, and VARBRUL probabilities of NPs in each category occurring as subjects are presented in (33):[15]

(33) NPs in each category occurring as subjects:

	Hearer-status			Discourse-status		
	Subj/NP	%	Prob.	Subj/NP	%	Prob.
Old:	26/72	= 36%	0.60	24/39	= 62%	0.85
New:	1/16	= 6%	0.15	3/49	= 6%	0.19
Inferrable:	5/18	= 28%	0.50	5/18	= 28%	0.57
Total:	32/106	= 30%		32/106	= 30%	
Significance:	$p < .035$			$p < .001$		

While subjects tend to be old with respect to both Hearer-status and Discourse-status, the figures in (33) lead us to suspect that Discourse-status has a stronger effect. Indeed, when we run the two information-statuses together, the results are clear: given both statuses, the variance is accounted for by Discourse-status, with the effect of Hearer-status completely losing statistical significance. The VARBRUL probabilities and significance figures for this run are presented in (34):[17]

(34) Probs. of NPs as subjects, Hearer-status vs. Discourse-status:

	Hearer-status	Discourse-status
Old:	0.50	0.85
New:	0.51	0.19
Inferrable:	0.50	0.58
Significance:	[Not signif.]	$p < .001$

Thus we may begin to answer the questions we have set out to investigate: the claim that subjects tend to represent 'old' information is borne out by the data in the ZPG letter. However, it is borne out just in case we understand 'old' information to mean 'old in the discourse', or Discourse-old. If we take it to mean 'old for the hearer', or Hearer-old, then the evidence presented here clearly contradicts it. That is, the fact that the hearer is assumed to know of some entity which has not already been mentioned in no way favors that entity for being represented by a subject NP, whereas the fact that some entity has already been introduced into the discourse, whether or not it was known to the hearer before the discourse, does indeed favor that entity for being represented by a subject NP, at least in the ZPG letter.

Finding that Discourse-old entities are favored for subject position, we must now ask whether this is a unitary set or whether it contains subsets which behave differently with respect to occurrence in subject position. One important feature by which to subdivide the set of Discourse-old entities is that of 'activation', as Chafe 1987 has called it. That is, do all Discourse-old entities have an equal chance of occurring in subject position, or do those that are activated at their moment of occurrence have a greater chance than those that are not activated? Given the findings presented by Chafe over the past 15 years, one would certainly expect activation to be a significant factor. I shall try to shed light on the issue, even if not definitively, using the category 'pronoun'.

Clearly, not all activated NPs at any point in discourse-time are represented by pronouns (cf., for example, 16b above). Therefore, a partition of the NPs in a discourse into pronominal and nonpronominal will not necessarily map isomorphically onto a partition of the corresponding entities into activated and nonactivated. However, it must be the case that pronouns *generally* represent NPs taken by the speaker to be activated: how else could the hearer be expected to interpret them? Thus, a partition of NPs into pronominal and nonpronominal should, at the worst, be equivalent to a partition of the corresponding entities into activated and activated-plus-nonactivated. If a statistically significant difference were found, then one might have good reason to infer that activation is significant. In fact, a VARBRUL run of the data with the factor 'Discourse-old' broken up into 'Pronominal' and 'Nonpronominal' shows that pronominal status, and therefore quite possibly activation, does indeed make subjecthood more likely. The figures are presented in (35):[18]

(35) NPs in each category, including Pronominal, as subjects:

	Subj/NP	%	Prob.
Discourse-old Pronominal:	13/16 =	81%	0.94
Discourse-old Nonpronominal:	11/23 =	48%	0.76
Discourse-new:	3/49 =	6%	0.18
Inferrable:	5/18 =	28%	0.57

Significance: $p < .001$

Significance of partitioning Discourse-old into Pronominal and Nonpronominal: $p < .05$

We may now consider the question of whether Inferrables should be collapsed with one of the other categories. In fact, they are not collapsible with Discourse-new, whether or not Discourse-old is subdivided into Pronominal and Nonpronominal.[19] Similarly, they are not collapsible with Discourse-old, when Discourse-old is not subdivided according to pronominal form.[20] Furthermore, Inferrables are certainly not collapsible with Discourse-old Pronominals.[21] However, Inferrables are indeed collapsible with Discourse-old Nonpronominals; the probabilities are presented in (36):[22]

(36) NPs in each category, including Pronominal, as subjects; Inferrables and Discourse-old Nonpronominal collapsed:

	Subj/NP	%	Prob.
Discourse-old Pronominal:	13/16 =	81%	0.94
Discourse-old Nonpronominal + Inferrable:	16/41 =	39%	0.68
Discourse-new:	3/49 =	6%	0.18

Significance: $p < .001$

Significance of collapsing Inferrables and Discourse-old Nonpronominals: not significant

Of course, the figures here are small and the probabilities should be given weight accordingly. Furthermore, the partitioning of Discourse-old on the basis of pronominal form is merely an attempt to investigate salience indirectly. Therefore, we cannot draw definite conclusions about either the role of salience in subjecthood or about the collapsibility of Inferrable entities with Discourse-old Nonpronominals. However, the relevance to subjecthood of Discourse-status — and the irrelevance of Hearer-status — does seem clear, at least in the ZPG letter being analyzed: entities which have previously occurred in the discourse are more likely than those which have not formerly occurred to be represented by NPs in subject position.

4.2 *The Effect of Definiteness on Subjecthood*

We shall now turn to the analysis of the data with respect to the claim that subjects tend to be definite. The figures for definiteness of subjects vs. nonsubjects are shown in (37):[23]

(37) Definiteness of subjects vs. nonsubjects:

	Subj/NP	%	Probability
Definite:	28/73	38%	0.63
Indefinite:	3/31	10%	0.23

Significance: $p < .003$

However, when Discourse-status, with or without Hearer-status, is also taken into account, the favoring of subjects for definiteness is no longer statistically significant, whereas Discourse-status remains significant at greater than the 0.001 level, as shown in (38):[24]

(38) Discourse-status and definiteness of subjects vs. nonsubjects:

Discourse-status:	New = 0.19 Inf. = 0.58	Old Nonpro. = 0.74 Old Pro. = 0.93	$p < 0.001$
Definiteness:	Def. = 0.54	Indefinite = 0.39	n.s.

Thus, of the three factor groups studied — Discourse-status, Hearer-status, and Definiteness, one was found by the VARBRUL program to account all by itself for the subject-nonsubject distribution: Discourse-status. Furthermore, within the Discourse-status factor group, a three-way partition of the factors into Discourse-old Pronominal, Discourse-old Non-pronominal + Inferrable, and Discourse-new, as shown in (36), was found to be the best fit.

5. Discussion

We may now propose answers to the questions raised in (27) above. In the ZPG letter we have analyzed, subjects are more likely than nonsubjects to be definite and to represent both Hearer-old and Discourse-old entities. However, when we run the corpus through the VARBRUL multivariate analysis program, we see that these tendencies are not independent. In particular, the apparent tendency for subjects to be Hearer-old is simply a reflex of a real tendency for them to be Discourse-old; when both are taken into account, Discourse-status accounts for all the variance and Hearer-status loses statistical significance. In addition, the apparent tendency for subjects to be definite is likewise seen to be simply a reflex of their tendency to be Discourse-old; analyzed together with Discourse-status, the effect of definiteness loses statistical significance.

Of course, given the lack of significance of Hearer-status on subjecthood, the lack of significance of definiteness is not surprising, if definiteness is, as it appears to be, a grammaticization of Hearer-status. On the other hand, the lack of significance of Hearer-status, i.e. the fact that an entity's being (assumed to be) known to the hearer does not increase its likelihood of being a subject, may indeed be surprising. What makes it more plausible, however, is the fact that, among Discourse-old entities, those represented by pronouns are more likely to be subjects than those represented by full NPs: if this means that salience is relevant to subjecthood, then it follows that Discourse-old entities, presumably more salient than Hearer-old/Discourse-new (Unused) entities, are more likely than they to be subjects.

These findings, if they are generalizable to other texts, have a possible bearing on a recent controversy about the informational properties of topics. Although we have not here investigated topichood per se, the subjects in the ZPG letter would presumably count as topics following a number of analyses, among them Reinhart 1981, Gundel 1985, and Horn 1986. Reinhart 1981 presents arguments against the widespread view that topics must represent 'old' information; following her analysis, all the subjects in the ZPG letter could be topics. If topichood is in fact a relevant notion for English and if canonical subjects are default topics, the analysis presented here would support her position: although the topics in the ZPG letter are statistically more likely to be 'old', they are not categorically restricted to that status.

In contrast, Gundel 1985 and Horn 1986 argue, along very different lines, for a distinction by what we are calling Hearer-status. First, Gundel 1985 argues that topics follow the 'Topic-Familiarity Principle', i.e. that topics are Hearer-old.[25] If she is correct, and even if this is a strong tendency rather than the fairly categorical principle she presents, we should find Hearer-status to be the significant variable. In fact, as we have seen, it is not.

Finally, Horn 1986, tying (canonical) subjecthood together with topichood, proposes that (canonical) subjects/topics be either 'salient' or 'presuppositional'. From his discussion, I believe that his salient/nonsalient parameter is equivalent to Discourse-status and that his presuppositional/nonpresuppositional parameter is equivalent to Hearer-status, as defined here. If this is correct, we should find that subjects in the ZPG letter are more likely to be Hearer-old/Discourse-new (= Unused) than Hearer-new/Discourse-new (= Brand-new). As we have seen, there may be such a difference, but it is not statistically significant.

Thus, if canonical subjects are default topics, the pattern seen in the ZPG letter indicates that topics may be old or new, but that they are more likely to be already evoked in the discourse than not.

6. Afterthoughts: The Form of Inferrables

Although the results presented here seem (to me) totally intuitive and plausible, I must speak briefly of a certain strangeness in the ZPG letter. While there is nothing incoherent or infelicitous in it, one feature of it strikes me as not being as natural as possible: the form of certain Inferrables.

As mentioned above, NPs representing Inferrables are typically sometimes definite, sometimes indefinite. Generally, they are definite when they refer to some entity E that is related to some other trigger entity T by some belief along the lines of 'A T typically has an E associated with it.' And, generally, they are indefinite when the belief is something like 'A T typically has Es associated with it' and when the Inferrable refers to a proper subset of the set of Es. Thus the Inferrable in (19b) is represented by an indefinite (a page), while the Inferrables in (17b) and (20b) are represented by definites (*the door* and *the pages*, respectively).

Now consider the following Inferrables from the ZPG letter:

(39) a. '[...our phones started to ring.] *Calls* jammed our switchboard all day.' (Segment 5)
b. '*Staffers* stayed late into the night.' (Segment 6)

When originally coding the NPs, I considered *calls* in (39a) to be Hearer-new; further consideration made me realize that these calls are really not new to me: they were the calls that resulted from the phones' ringing. Furthermore, they are presumably all the relevant calls: certainly the author has no reason to implicate that there were also calls that day and night that did not jam the ZPG switchboard. Thus it seemed to me that, while the text is coherent as it stands, *the calls* would have been somewhat more natural than *calls* in this context.

The situation with *staffers* in (39b) is analogous: true enough, maybe some staffers went home and only a proper subset of staffers stayed late into the night, but what would be the point of implicating this? Again, the indefinite does not produce incoherence, but it does seem puzzling.

To test my intuition that definites would be more natural here, I had the letter translated into Russian by a Russian-dominant Russian-English bilingual. I did not tell him my reason for wanting it translated. I then had his translation translated into English by another Russian-English bilingual, this one dominant in English, again with no explanation and of course without showing him the original letter. My purpose was to take the 'content' of the letter through a language with no articles on the assumption that whatever articles occurred in the English translation of the Russian would be at least one other person's objective choice for the most natural. The Russian translation of (39a,b) is presented in (40):

(40) a. '[...nashi t'el'efony natshal'i zvon'it'.]
our telephones began ring
zvonki n'e daval'i pokoya nashemu kommutatoru tsel'iy
rings not gave rest our switchboard whole
d'en'.'
day

b. '*sotrudn'iki* rabotal'i po pozdn'ey notshi...'
employees worked through late night

As expected, the Russian translations of the NPs in question have no marking of definiteness. However, note, that they are in initial (canonical) position. Now consider the English translation of (40a,b):

(41) a. '[...our phones started to ring.] *The ringing* gave our operators no peace all day.'
b. '*Our coworkers* worked till late in the night...'

Note that both NPs are definite. True, in each case, a different noun is used, and I do not know if this should make a difference. However, I am now fairly confident that these indefinites in the original letter are more marked than definites would have been.

As I said at the outset, the sort of analysis done here cannot tell us what, if anything, is special about this text. The bulk of it has attempted to investigate some frequently made claims about subjecthood, and the results of that investigation are plausible indeed. The question raised in this final section about the naturalness of the indefiniteness of two NPs can only be that: a question. Without an exhaustive study of a large number of comparable texts, we cannot even say that this 'unnaturalness' is atypical. Furthermore, even if it were found to be atypical, we still could not determine the reason, we still could not conclude with confidence that the author was, say, a native speaker of some language other than English, or simply idiosyncratic, or a computer text-generation system. Whatever the answer, though, it does seem that he/she/it puts the intuitively right kind of entities in subject position, even if sometimes in not the most predictable form.

Notes

1. The narratee is the abstract individual to whom the narrator is narrating and for whom all entities/beliefs/etc. marked as 'shared knowledge' are in fact shared. See Prince 1980.
2. There are also several syntactically noteworthy nonfinite clauses, e.g. reduced relatives, both active and passive, detached participials, purpose infinitivals, and so forth.
3. I am assuming that the extracted constituents in the headed and free relatives and in the indirect questions have been moved *out* of their original clause. Thus they do not count as occurring noncanonically *within* that clause.
4. Subjects are also frequently said to be agentive, animate, referential, presuppositional, and topical. We shall not deal directly with these claims, though the entire study will be

relevant to the referentiality claim and the analysis we shall present will possibly have a bearing on the presuppositionality and topicality claims, as will be suggested below.

5. Of course, if *there* in (3a) is taken to be the subject, then (3a) has its subject in canonical position.

6. Note that French, for example, would mark generic NPs like (6) as definite and nongeneric NPs like (7) as indefinite:

   (i) a. J'adore *les* beyguels.
   b. J'ai acheté *des* beyguels.

   Not surprisingly, only the indefinite occurs in the French correlate of (8):

   (ii) Il y a *des*/#*les* beyguels à la cannelle de nos jours.

7. No doubt some (or all) of the claims made have really been about informational definiteness; we are of course examining that too, but under the rubric of information-status.

8. In addition, as shown in Dahl 1987, indefinites may refer to Hearer-old entities in certain cases involving attributes.

9. Nevertheless, there are apparent counterexamples to this. First, first and second person pronouns may occur with no prior occurrence of a coreferential nonpronominal NP. However, speakers and hearers are generally taken to be 'situationally' evoked in the discourse model, along with other salient objects in the discourse situation. Second, consider i:

   (i) [A to B, where B is just returning home and where A has been home all day waiting for the plumber.]
   He never showed up.

   Utterances like i may be (and in fact generally are) analyzed as being a noninitial segment of some extended discourse, and, in that extended discourse, the entity represented by the pronoun has in fact been evoked.

10. I have just received a letter which has a message as part of the Post Office cancellation mark. The message is: *Include your apt. # for better service.* I leave it as an exercise for the reader to guess in which city this letter was mailed.

11. This appears to be a reflex of the situation in the substrate Austronesian languages, which is itself still another piece of evidence of the distinctness of Inferrables.

12. Silva-Corvalán's other evidence for a continuum appears to be that, in Prince 1981b, I distinguished more than two information-statuses. However, no arguments are presented for why nonbinariness should entail a continuum, a fairly unusual inference.

13. See Lakoff 1974 for arguments that NPs like *that book I bought* represent entities that are, in our terms, Hearer-old, Discourse-new.

14. VARBRUL is a program written by D. Sankoff to perform binomial logit analysis on linguistic data. The present study used the following VARBRUL software, written by S. Pintzuk: READTOK 1.1, MAKECELL 2.2V, IVARB 2.1, and CROSSTAB 2.1, run on the VAX Cluster, Computer and Information Science Department, Moore School, University of Pennsylvania.

15. Of course, *reporters eager to tell the public about Urban Stress Test results* was counted, as an object of a preposition.

16. For the Hearer-status variable, counting Inferrables, log likelihood = -62.171; ignoring Inferrables, log likelihood = -51.546. Corrected mean for both = 0.28. For the Dis-

course-status variable, counting Inferrables, log likelihood = -48.609; ignoring Inferrables, log likelihood = -37.984. Corrected mean = 0.23, 0.23, respectively.

17. Counting Inferrables, log likelihood = -48.608; ignoring Inferrables, log likelihood = -37.984. Corrected mean for both = 0.23.

18. Log likelihood = -46.266. Corrected mean = 0.23.

19. Discourse-old not subdivided, log likelihood = -51.192; Discourse-old subdivided, log likelihood = -48.849; corrected mean for both = 0.26. In both cases, collapsing of Inferrables with Discourse-new is significant at the .05 level.

20. Log likelihood = -51.489. Corrected mean = 0.23.

21. Log likelihood = -51.417. Corrected mean = 0.23.

22. Log likelihood = -47.133. Corrected mean = 0.23.

23. Log likelihood = -60.729. Corrected mean = 0.27.

24. Log likelihood = -45.866. Corrected mean = 0.22. The levels of significance remain the same if Inferrables are collapsed with Discourse-old Nonpronominals: log likelihood = -46.384; corrected mean = 0.22. Furthermore, as would be expected, VARBRUL analysis of Discourse-status, Hearer-status, and Definiteness simultaneously shows both Hearer-status and Definiteness to lack statistical significance, no matter how the factors in the Discourse-status factor group are partitioned: Discourse-new, Inferrable, Discourse-old, log likelihood = -47.825, corrected mean = 0.22; Discourse-new, Inferrable, Discourse-old Nonpronominal, Discourse-old Pronominal, log likelihood = -45.693, corrected mean = 0.23; Discourse-new, Inferrable + Discourse-old Nonpronominal, Discourse-old Pronominal, log likelihood = -45.689, corrected mean = 0.23.

25. Gundel 1985 adds that the Topic-Familiarity Principle may be suspended under certain conditions, e.g. in 'special uses of language', conditions which do not seem to obtain in the ZPG letter.

References

Allerton, D.J.
1978 "The notion of 'givenness' and its relations to presupposition and to theme." *Lingua* 44,133-68.

Chafe, W.
1976 "Givenness, contrastiveness, definiteness, subjects, topics, and point of view." In C. Li, (ed.), *Subject and Topic*. NY: Academic Press, 25-55.

Chafe, W.
1987 "Cognitive constraints on information flow. In R. Tomlin, (ed.), *Coherence and Grounding in Discourse*. Amsterdam/Philadelphia: John Benjamins.

Chomsky, N.
1971 "Deep structure, surface structure, and semantic interpretation." In D. Steinberg, and L. Jakobovits, (eds.), *Semantics: An Interdisciplinary Reader in Philosophy, Linguistics, and Philosophy*. NY: Cambridge Univ. Press, 183-216.

Christophersen, P.
1939 *The Articles: A Study of their Theory and use in English*. Copenhagen: Munksgaard.

Clark, H. and S. Haviland
1977 "Comprehension and the given-new contract." In R. Freedle, (ed.), *Discourse Production and Comprehension*. Hillsdale, NJ: Erlbaum, 1-40.

Clark, H. and C. Marshall
1981 "Definite reference and mutual knowledge." In A.K. Joshi, B.L. Webber, and I.A. Sag, (eds), *Elements of Discourse Understanding*. Cambridge: Cambridge Univ. Press.

Contreras, H.
1976 *A Theory of Word Order with Special Reference to Spanish*. Amsterdam: North-Holland.

Dahl, D.
1987 "Determiners, entities, and contexts." In Y. Wilkes, (ed.), *Proceedings of TINLAP-3. Theoretical issues in natural language processing*. 133-36.

Delahunty, G.P.
1982 *Topics in the Syntax and Semantics of English Cleft Sentences*. IULC.

Givón, T.
1976 "Topic, pronoun, and grammatical agreement." In C. Li, (ed.), *Subject and Topic*. NY: Academic Press, 149-58.

Gundel, J.
1985 "'Shared knowledge' and topicality." *Journal of Pragmatics* 9.1.83-107.

Harris, Z.S.
1952a "Discourse analysis." *Language* 28,1-30.

1952b "Discourse analysis: a sample text." *Language* 28,474-494.

Hawkins, J.A.
1978 *Definiteness and Indefiniteness*. Atlantic Highlands, NJ: Humanities Press.

Horn, L.
1981 "Exhaustiveness and the semantics of clefts." In V. Burke, and J. Pustejovsky, (eds), *Papers from 11th Annual Meeting of the North Eastern Linguistic Society*. Amherst: University of Massachussetts Department of Linguistics, 125-142.

1986 "Presupposition, theme, and variations." In A. Farley, et al., (eds), *Papers from the Parasession on Pragmatics and Grammatical Theory at the 22nd Regional Meeting*. CLS, 168-92.

Keenan, E.L.
1976 "Toward a universal definition of SUBJECT." In C. Li, (ed.), *Subject and Topic*. NY: Academic Press, 303-33.

Kuno, S.
1972 "Functional sentence perspective: a case study from Japanese and English." *Linguistic Inquiry*. 3.269-320.

Lakoff, R.
1974 "Remarks on this and that." In M. Lagaly, et al., (eds), *Papers from the 10th Regional Meeting*. CLS, 345-56.

Lambrecht, K.
1986 "Pragmatically motivated syntax: presentational cleft constructions in spoken French." In A. Farley, et al., (eds), *Papers from the Parasession on Pragmatics and Grammatical Theory at the 22nd Regional Meeting*. CLS, 115-26.

Li, C.N. and S. Thompson
1976 "Subject and topic: a new typology of language." In C.N. Li, (ed.), *Subject and Topic*. NY: Academic Press, 457-89.

Linde, C.
1973 "Information structures in discourse." In R. Fasold, (ed.), *Variation in the Form and Use of Language*. Washington, D.C.: Georgetown Univ. Press, 205-15.

Milsark, G.
1974 *Existential Sentences in English*. MIT PhD dissertation.

Prince, E.F.
1978 "A comparison of Wh-clefts and It-clefts in discourse." *Language* 54,883-906.

1981a "On the inferencing of indefinite-*this* NPs." In A.K. Joshi, B.L. Webber, and I.A. Sag, (eds), *Elements of Discourse Understanding*. Cambridge: Cambridge Univ. Press, 231-50.

1981b "Toward a taxonomy of given/new information." In P. Cole, (ed.), *Radical Pragmatics*. NY: Academic Press, 223-55.

1986 "On the syntactic marking of presupposed open propositions." In A. Farley, et al., (eds), *Papers from the Parasession on Pragmatics and Grammatical Theory at the 22nd Regional Meeting*. CLS, 208-22.

Prince, G.
1980 "Aspects of a grammar of narrative." *Poetics Today* 1/3,549-563.

Rando, E. and D.J. Napoli
1978 "Definites in There-sentences." *Language* 54,300-313.

Reinhart, T.
1981 "Pragmatics and linguistics: an analysis of sentence topics." *Philosophica* 27,53-94.

Safir, K.
1985 *Syntactic Chains*. Cambridge: Cambridge Univ. Press.

Sankoff, G. and C. Mazzie
1988 "On the development of determiners in Tok Pisin: is grammaticalization inevita-

ble?" Presented at the 12th Annual Penn Linguistics Colloquium, University of Pennsylvania.

Silva-Corvalán, C.
1983 "On the interaction of word order and intonation: some OV constructions in Spanish." In F. Klein, (ed.), *Discourse Perspectives on Syntax*. NY: Academic Press, 117-40.

Wilson, D. and D. Sperber
1979 "Ordered entailments: an alternative to presuppositional theories." In C.K. Oh, and D. Dinneen, (eds), *Syntax and Semantics. XI: Presupposition*. NY: Academic Press. 299-323.

Ziv, Y.
1981 "On some discourse uses of existentials in English, or, getting more mileage out of existentials." Presented at the LSA Annual Meeting, NY.

Some Lexicogrammatical Features of the Zero Population Growth Text

M.A.K. Halliday

0. Introductory

This paper presents a partial interpretation of the ZPG text using systemic grammar. It consists of seven sections: 1, Theme; 2, Information structure; 3, Mood and modality; 4, Transitivity; 5, Clause complexes; 6, Lexical cohesion; 7, Nominalization and grammatical metaphor. For the grammar and its application to discourse analysis see Halliday 1985a, 1985b.

I have used the suggested numbering of the portions of the text, in thirty segments. Of these 30, Segments 1-3 and 24-28 (a total of 8), while they have distinct functions in the structure and format of a letter, have almost none of the features of a clause; they are 'clausettes' in the terminology of the Nigel grammar (Matthiessen 1985: 102-103).

(1-3)	Title Date Address;
(24-28)	Valediction Signature Signatory Status Coda-signal

Four of them (24-27) could be regarded as forming a clausette-complex, of structure $x\beta \quad \alpha 1 \quad \alpha{=}21 \quad \alpha 2{=}2$.[1] Apart from occasional references to §3, I have ignored these segments in the present treatment.

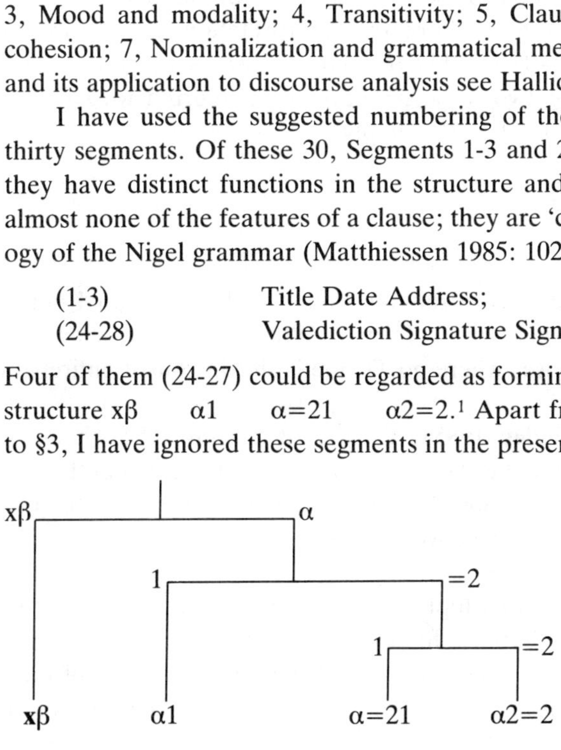

This leaves 22 segments of the discourse. Of these, 13 consist of a single clause ('clause simplex'); the remainder are clause complexes, 4 with two and 5 with three clauses, as follows:

1 clause:	§§ 4 5 8 9 10 12 13 16 17 18 20 22 29	= 13
2 clauses:	§§ 11 14 15 23	(2x4) = 8
3 clauses:	§§ 6 7 19 21 30	(3x5) = 15
		Total 36

giving a total of 36 clauses in all. Note that these are ranking clauses; embedded clauses, which are rank-shifted to become constituents of nominal groups (there are 19 of these), do not participate in the clause-complex structure of the text. Where there is more than one ranking clause within a segment these will be indicated with capital letters A, B, C in the order in which they occur. In § 11, clause B is enclosed inside clause A; in § 14, for simplicity, the initial *but* is assigned to the clause *but to use it well*, which therefore becomes clause A. The analysis of the clause complexes is presented in Section 5; embedded clauses are also listed in that Section.

As always in text grammar, alternative interpretations are possible at numerous points. Ideally, all should be offered and discussed; but this takes too long. Instead, one or two instances have been referred to, so as to suggest the kinds of consideration that apply.

1. Theme

Table 1 shows the Theme of each ranking clause, including textual, interpersonal and topical (experiential) Theme. Whatever is not shown as Theme is the Rheme; clauses where no Theme is shown consist entirely of Rheme.

For Theme see Halliday 1985a, Chapter 3 passim. The Theme is realized by initial position in the clause; it includes the first element that has a function in transitivity (the 'topical' Theme), together with any other elements that precede it; for example *well* + *then* + *surely* + *that* in *well then surely that's the end of the affair*.

As will be noted, almost all topical Themes are unmarked; that is, the Theme is conflated with Subject in declarative and with Predicator in imperative.[2] Hence the three that are marked stand out, and two of them have a significant function in the construction of the text. One of these is

Table 1: Themes of ranking clauses

clause no.	Theme: textual	inter-personal	topical	marked / unmarked
4			at 7 a.m. on October 25	marked
5			calls	unmarked
6A			staffers	unmarked
B			--	
C			--	
7A	when		we	unmarked
B			we	unmarked
C			we	unmarked
8			media and public reaction	unmarked
9	at first		the deluge of calls	unmarked
10	now		we	unmarked
11A			ZPG's 1985 Urban Stress Test	unmarked
B			--	
12			it	unmarked
13			the Urban Stress Test	unmarked
14A	but		--	
B			we	unmarked
15A			our small staff	unmarked
B	and		our modest resources	unmarked
16			your support now	unmarked
17			ZPG's 1985 Urban Stress Test	unmarked
18			with your contribution	marked
19A	even though		our national government	unmarked
B			we	unmarked
C			--	
20			every day	marked
21A			--	
B			--	
C			both elected officials & the American public	unmarked
22		please	make	unmarked
23A			whatever you give — $25 or as much as you can	unmarked
B			--	
29			the results of ZPG'a 1985 Urban Stress Test	unmarked
30A			I	unmarked
B			you	unmarked
C			--	

the Theme of the text-initiating clause (§ 4), *at 7 a.m. on October 25*, which sets the text plan — deceptively, as it turns out — to narrative, by looking like an Orientation; the other is *with your contribution* (§ 18), which finally disposes of the earlier one and reveals the nature of the text as a begging letter. The third of the marked Themes, *every day* (§ 20), introduces a subroutine of 'constantly', perhaps contrasting with the initial time-frame *at 7 a.m. on October 25* but also setting the scene for the intensified imperative Theme *please make* ('so do something') in § 22. So the marked Themes tell their own rather explicit story: 'here's what happened one day — now about your contribution — here's what happens every day — so please!'

Let us now consider the Themes of all ranking clauses, unmarked as well as marked. After the initial time-frame we find eight clauses (§ 5-10) having as Theme *calls, staffers/we, media/calls, we* — alternating between them and us, outsiders and insiders; these are followed by three clauses having the *Urban Stress Test* as Theme (§ 11-13). In other words, having first constructed the theme of 'our relations with the media and the public', the writer then goes on to thematize 'what we did (that brought this about)'. The Theme now returns to 'us' (§ 14-15); but now it is 'poor us' (*our small staff, our modest resources*), so that when it shifts over to 'you' (*your support now*, and the marked *with your contribution*, in § 16-18) it is clear in what role 'you' are being expected to take part.

There is then a brief digression, where the Theme shifts to *our national government* and then (after the marked *every day*) to *both elected officials and the American public*; this serves as the context for again returning to 'you' as Theme, in *please make* (which has the only interpersonal Theme in the text), followed by the long embedded clause thematizing 'your money' (§ 19-23). Interpersed with the 'you' Themes, the Urban Stress Test appears: in § 17 immediately before *with your contribution*, and now in § 29 just before the final segment. In § 30, for the only time in the letter, the writer uses *I*; and the thematic move from 'I' to 'you' in *I hope you'll help* gives the required personal flavour to the carefully contrived little postscript.

The thematic movement of the text clearly bears out Fries' interpretation of clause Theme in terms of the rhetorical concept of 'method of development' (Fries 1981). We could diagram this movement as in Figure 1.

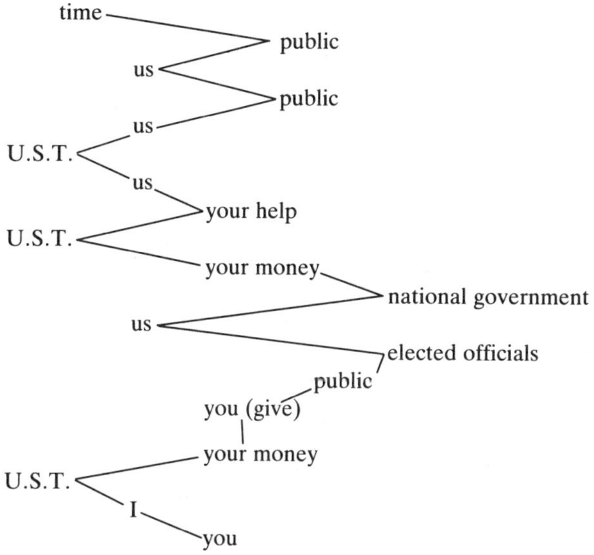

Figure 1: Thematic progression

2. Information Structure (Given and New; Information Focus)

I read the text aloud, to make explicit its 'implication of utterance' (Firth (1968: 30-31). Below is the transcription, in systemic notation. (See Halliday 1967. Note that the italic type identifies the information focus, which is the culmination of the New element — the part that is presented as 'for the listener's attention'.)

3 //1 dear / friend of / Z P / *G* //

4 //3 . at / seven a / *m* on Oc //3 tober twenty / *fifth* our //1 *phones* / started to / ring //

5 //1 calls / jammed our / switchboard / all / *day* //

6 //1 staffers stayed / late into the / *night* //3 answering / *questions* and //3 talking with re/*porters* from //3 *newspapers* //3 *radio* stations //3 *wire* services and T//1 *V* stations in //1 every / part of the / *country* //

7 //4 when we re/leased the re/sults of / ZPG's / nineteen eighty five /

Urban / *Stress* / Test we had //1 no i/*dea* we'd get //1 such an over/whelming re/*sponse* //

8 //3 media and / public re/*action* has been //1 nothing / short of in/*credible* //

9 //4 . at / *first* the //4 deluge of / calls came / *mostly* from re//1 porters / eager to / tell the / public about / Urban / Stress Test re/*sults*//4 . and from / outraged / public of/*ficials* who were //1 furious that we had / blown the / *whistle* on con//1 ditions in / their / *cities* //

10 //4 *now* we're / hearing from con//4 cerned / *citizens* in //3 all / parts of the / *country* who /want to know //3 what they can / *do* to hold //1 local of/ficials ac/*countable* for / tackling //3 population re/lated / *problems* that //1 threaten / public / health and / *wellbeing* //

11 //4 Z P / G's / nineteen eighty / five / Urban / *Stress* Test //4 . cre/ated after / months of per/sistent and ex/haustive re/*search* //3 . is the / nation's / first / *survey* of how //1 population / linked / pressures af/fect / U.S. / *cities* //

12 //3 . it ranks a / hundred and / eighty-four / urban / *areas* on e //3 leven / different cri/*teria* ranging from //3 crowding and / *birth* rates to //1 air quality and / toxic / *wastes* //

13 //4 . the / Urban / *Stress* Test / translates //4 complex / technical / *data* into an //1 easy to / use / *action* / tool for con//3 cerned / *citizens* e //3 lected of/*ficials* and o//1 *pinion* / leaders //

14 //4 . but to / use it / *well* we //1 urgently / need your / *help* //

15 //13 . our / small / staff is being / *swamped* with re/quests for / more infor/*mation* and our //4 modest re/*sources* are being //1 stretched to the / *limit* //

16 //1 your sup/port / now is / *critical* //

17 //4 Z P / G's / nineteen eighty / five / Urban / *Stress* Test may be our / //4 best oppor/tunity / *ever* to //1 get the popu/lation message / *heard* //

18 //3 . with / your contri/*bution* //3 Z P / G can / arm our / growing / network of / local / *activists* with the ma //3 terials they / *need* to //3 warn com/munity / *leaders* about e //3 merging popu/lation linked / *stresses* be //1 fore they / reach / *crisis* / stage //

19 //4 even though our / *national* / government con/tinues to ig/nore the / consequences of / uncontrolled / popu/lation / growth //4 *we* can / act to take //1 positive / action at the / *local* / level //

20 //3 every / *day* //3 . de/cisions are being / *made* by //3 local of/*ficials* in //3 our com/*munities* that could //1 drastically af/fect the / quality of our / *lives* //

21 //4 . to make / sound / choices in / planning for / *people* //3 . both e/ lected of/*ficials* and the A//3 merican / *public* //1 need the popu/lation stresses / data re/vealed by our / *study* //

22 // 3 please make a /special contri/*bution* to /1 zero popu/lation growth to/*day*//

23 //3 . what/ever you / *give* //3 twentyfive dollars / fifty dollars a / hundred dollars or as / much as you / *can* //1 . will be / used im/*mediately* to //1 put the / Urban / Stress Test in the / hands of / those who / need it / *most* //

29 //4 . the re/sults of / Z P G's / nineteen eighty-five / Urban / *Stress* Test were re //1 ported as a / top / *news* story by //1 hundreds of /newspapers and / TV and / *radio* stations from //1 coast to / *coast* //

30 //4 . I / hope you'll / help us / *monitor* this re/markable / media / coverage by com//1 pleting the en/closed re/*ply* form //

The text was difficult to read aloud, and this turned out to be because of its mixed characteristics: presented as a personal letter, and hence in parts like spoken discourse (e.g. § 7), but in fact deliberately composed and so often reaching a very high lexical density (e.g. § 13, with sixteen lexical words in one clause). The more spoken parts read fluently with the tone group mapping generally on to the clause, whereas the clauses in the more 'written' sections were mostly broken up into tone group sequences, with tones 3 3 3 ... 1, such as are typical of loud reading (for example in news bulletins).

Since obviously many other readings are possible I do not propose to make too much of this analysis. But it bears importantly on the previous section, because while (following Fries) the Theme carries the method of development of the text, the New tends to correspond to the rhetorical 'main point'. Fries, who is here treating only written texts, discusses the issue entirely in thematic terms and identifies the main point with the

Rheme; and this is justifiable given that, especially in writing, the information focus typically falls within the Rheme. But the operative category is probably that of the New, so that we could summarize Fries' findings as follows:

> Theme (typically falling within Given) represents 'method of development'
>
> New (typically falling within Rheme) represents 'main point'

The transcription shows what in one possible reading are the prominent motifs within the New.

In this reading, most ranking clauses required more than one tone group; this is predictable, since the text as a whole is clearly more like writing than like speech. Where this effect was simply due to high lexical density the pattern was the one mentioned above: a sequence of tone 3 (low rising) followed by a final tone 1 (falling). Since tone 3, among its other functions, is also the listing tone in speech this pattern also occurred where the clause incorporated a list (e.g. § 6). In other contexts, where a segment consisted of more than one tone group the pre-final tone was usually tone 4 (falling-rising); this is the characteristic tone where the Theme carries a separate tone group (as it often does, especially when a marked Theme), and also where there is a rising dependency in the clause complex (that is, β followed by α; these two are actually the same phenomenon, since where the β-clause does come first it is thereby marked as thematic in the clause complex).

So if we want to establish what it is that emerges as the overall information structure of this text, the motifs that make up the 'main point' as it unfolds, we can examine two sets of instances: (a) the unmarked tonics, (i.e. those which are clause-final — here mainly also final in the segment) which select tone 1; and (b) the tone 4 tonics, which are either marked (not clause-final) or on clauses that are not final in the segment. Those of type (a) will directly reveal the main point; while those of type (b) will express highlighted Themes, sometimes involving a feature of contrast (e.g. national vs. local in § 19), against which the main point is explicitly foregrounded. We can ignore tonics on tone 3. (Tone 13, which occurs rarely here, can be treated as a variant of tone 1.)

The story told by the tone 1 tonics is that the text begins by taking the 'wow!' of publicity as its main point (§ 4-9). Note that the relevant unit is the whole element of clause structure on which the tonic falls; hence, in § 7,

Table 2: Subject, Finite and the selection of mood

clause no.	Subject	Finite	primary tense /modality	mood
4	our phones	started	past	declarative
5	calls	jammed	past	declarative
6A	staffers	stayed	past	declarative
B	--			(non-finite)
C	--			(non-finite)
7A	we	released	past	declarative
B	we	had	past	declarative
C	we	would	future sequent	declarative
8	media and public reaction	has	present [past in]	declarative
9	the deluge of calls	came	past	declarative
10	we	are	present	declarative
11A	ZPG's 1985 Urban Stress Test	is	present	declarative
B	--			(non-finite)
12	it	ranks	present	declarative
13	the Urban Stress Test	translates	present	declarative
14A	--			(non-finite)
B	we	need	present	declarative
15A	our small staff	is	present	declarative
B	our modest resources	are	present	declarative
16	your support now	is	present	declarative
17	ZPG's 1985 Urban Stress Test	may	probability/low	declarative
18	ZPG	can	ability/low	declarative
19A	our national government	continues	present	declarative
B	we	can	ability/low	declarative
C	--			(non-finite)
20	decisions	are	present	declarative
21A	--			(non-finite)
B	--			(non-finite)
C	both elected officials and the American public	need	present	declarative
22	--			imperative
23A	whatever you give — $25, $50, $100, or as much as you can	will	future	declarative
B	--			(non-finite)
29	the results of ZPG's 1985 Urban Stress Test	were	past	declarative
30A	I	hope	present	declarative
B	you	will	future	declarative
C	--			(non-finite)

such an overwhelming response, and in § 8, *nothing short of incredible*. It then moves on to public health and the cities (§ 9-12), and from there to the sense of crisis and appeal for help (§ 14-18). The next five segments re-enact the two previous points with slightly different emphases: the quality of life on a more local level (§ 19-21), and the urgency of the appeal (§ 22-23; note tonics on *today, immediately, most*). Finally the postscript returns to publicity (§ 29) and then requests a reply (§30).

The tone 4 tonics, on the other hand, mainly highlight motifs that we have already identified as Themes: us, our data, our meagre resources, and our Urban Stress Test. Interestingly, the other Themes — you, and the general public — turned out not to be highlighted in this way. But, as already stressed, too much should not be derived from one reading; especially a reading by someone who is an outsider to this sub-culture.

3. Mood and Modality

Table 2 gives the mood of each ranking clause in the text, and the modality if any; and enters the items functioning as Subject and as Finite (verbal operator). All ranking clauses are included, since all may have Subjects; but non-finite clauses do not select for mood, and finite dependent clauses are declarative by default (except for types of projection, which do not occur in this text).

Of the 23 clauses that select for mood (36 ranking clauses, minus four dependent finites and nine non-finites), all but one are declarative. Of the first six of these (§ 4-9), five have past as primary tense (*started, jammed, stayed, had, came*; cf. their dependents *released* and the sequent form *would* in *we'd*); the sixth has primary tense present but secondary past (*has been*, past in present). This reflects the narrative beginning of the text. The tense then shifts to present and remains so up to §21 (*need*).

Then comes the one clause that is not declarative but imperative (§ 22: *please make* ...); this brings about a sudden change in the relationship of writer to reader, the writer shifting to the goods-&-services mode of 'I'm asking you to do something'. On the way to this, however, there has been one modalization (§ 17, *may be*); this — the only expression of probability in the text — has added a feature of tentativeness to the argument that your support now is critical (this may be our best opportunity, but it is important not to be too definite about that because we may want to ask for your support again later on).

After the imperative clause the mood becomes declarative again; and the primary tense switches to future, then past, then future (§ 23, 29, 30): the first to tell you what we are going to do with your money, the second to return to the narrative left unfinished at the beginning, and the last to express another request, this time in the form of a declarative projection by a mental process (affect) verb, *I hope you will ...* . This mildly metaphorical representation is preferred to a direct imperative for the final segment of the letter.

There are two modulated clauses, both of the 'ability' type expressed by *can* (§ 18, *ZPG can arm*; § 19, *we can act*); the Subject in both is 'ZPG'.

We saw in Section 1 that in almost all of the declarative clauses the Subject is also the Theme. Where the two are not conflated (in § 4, 18, 20), the Subjects are *our phones, ZPG* and *decisions*; no pattern there, of course, but it is interesting that the only time *ZPG* appears as a participant (in the transitivity structure of the clause) it is Subject but not Theme. Otherwise, *ZPG* appears only as possessive Deictic, modifying *Urban Stress Test* (elsewhere it is replaced by *we*). So the movement of Subject in the text is similar to the movement of Theme; if anything, because of the instances where the two are dissociated the periodicity between 'us' and 'others' appears slightly more clearly with the Subject. We might recognize phases (as in Gregory 1985: 194-8) as set out in Figure 2:

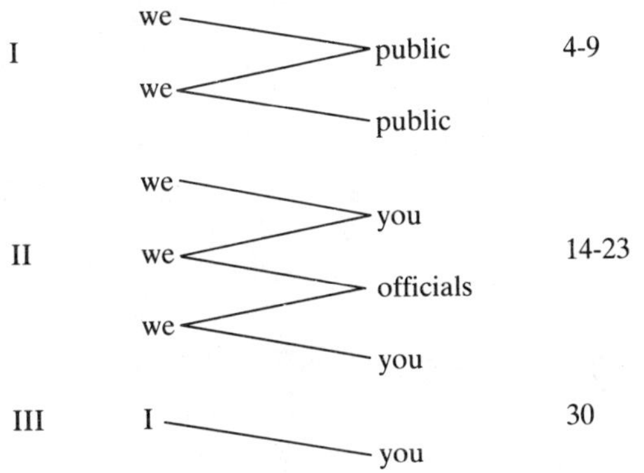

Figure 2: Phases based on Subject selection

— with the Urban Stress Test ('our' test) appearing from time to time as before. But the significance of Subject is rather different from that of Theme; the Subject is the element in which is vested 'modal responsibility'

Table 3: Process types and transitivity functions

clause no.	process type	Process	Medium	other participants and circumstances
4	mat/mid	ring	phones	Time: at 7 a.m. on October 25
5	mat/effec	jam	switchboard	Ag: calls Dur: all day
6A	mat/mid	stay	staffers	Dur: late into the night
B	verbal	answer	staffers	Range: question
C	verbal	talk	staffers	Accomp: with reporters
7A	mat/effec	release	results	Ag: we
B	rel: poss/attr	have	we	Atte: no idea
C	rel: poss/attr	get	we	Atte: response
8	rel: int/attr	be	media & public reaction	Atte: incredible
9	mat/mid	come	deluge of calls	Place: from reporters and public officials
9.1	verbal	tell	(reporters)	
9.2	rel: int/attr	be	(officials)	Atte: furious
9.3	mat/mid	blow	we	Range: whistle Matter: on … their cities
10	verbal	hear	we	Place: from concerned citizens
10.1	mental: cog	know	(concerned citizens)	
10.2	mat/mid	do	(concerned citizens)	Range: what
10.3	mat/effec	hold	local officials	Ag: citizens Atte: accountable
10.4	mat/effec	tackle	problems	
10.5	mat/effec	threaten	public health & well-being	Ag: problems
11A	rel: int/id	be	the nation's first survey	Ag: ZPG's Urban Stress Test
11A.1	mat/effec	affect	cities	Ag: pressures
B	mat/effec	create	(ZPG's Urban Stress Test)	Time: after months of research
12	mat/effec	rank	184 urban areas	(Ag: ZPG's U.S.T.) Manner: on 11 criteria
12.1	rel: circ/attr	range	criteria	Atte: from crowding … to … toxic wastes
13	mat/effec	translate	data	Ag: U.S.T. Atte: into an action tool Cause: for concerned citizens and … leaders

14A	.. ..	use	it	Manner: well
B	rel: poss/attr	need	we	Atte: your help
15A	mat/effec	swamp	staff	Manner/Ag: requests for information
B	mat/effec	stretch	resources	Dist: to the limit
16	rel: int/attr	be	support	Atte: critical
17	rel: int/id	be	the best opportunity	Ag: ZPG's Urban Stress Test
17.1	verbal	hear		Range: population message (Ag: we)
18	mat/effec	arm	activists	Ag: ZPG Manner: materials
18.1	rel: poss/attr	need	they	Atte: materials
18.2	verbal	warn		Rec: leaders Matter: about stresses
18.3	mat/mid	reach	stresses	Place: crisis stage
19A	mental: perc	ignore	national government	Phen: consequences
B	mat/mid	act	we	
C	mat/mid	take		Range: action Place: at local level
20	mat/mid	make	officials	Range: decisions Time: every day
20.1	mat/effec	affect	lives	(Ag: decisions) Manner: drastically
21A	mat/mid	make		Range: choices
B	mat/mid	plan		Cause: for people
C	rel: poss/attr	need	officals and public	Atte: data
21C.1	mat/effec	reveal	(data)	Ag: our study
22	mat/mid	make	(you)	Range: contribution Place: to ZPG Time: today
23A	mat/effec	use	whatever you give	
23A.1	mat/effec	give	whatever	Ag: you
B	mat/effec	put	Urban Stress Test	Place: in hands of those who need it most
B.1	rel: poss/attr	need	(those)	(Atte: U.S.T.) Manner: most
29	verbal	report	newspapers, TV and radio	Range: results of test Role: as top news
30A	mental: aff	hope	I	
B	mat/effec	monitor	media coverage	Ag: we Instig: you
C	mat/effec	complete	reply form	(ag: you)

— on which the validity of the writer's argument is made to rest, in each clause. This appears clearly when we add a response:

Staffers stayed late into the night. — Did they?
Media and public reaction has been incredible. — Has it?
We urgently need your help. — Do you?

It is even clearer in the imperative, where 'modal responsibility' means responsibility for providing the goods-&-services in question:

Please make a special contribution. — Must I?

Note finally that all ranking clauses have positive polarity. The message is a positive one; the only negatives are either ensconced in the lexicon (*ignore, uncontrolled*) or else used in nominal groups to heighten the positive effect (*we had no idea we'd get such an overwhelming response; reaction has been nothing short of incredible*).

4. Transitivity

Table 3 presents the analysis of transitivity, showing the process type and the items occupying the various transitivity functions: the process itself, and any participants and circumstances. These are shown for all clauses, including those that are embedded, since embedded clauses select freely in the transitivity systems. Embedded clauses are numbered .1, .2, .3 &c. following the clause in (a nominal group within) which they are embedded.

There are thus 55 clauses: the 36 ranking clauses already identified, plus 19 that are embedded. The distribution of process types is given in Table 4.

The clear preponderance of material processes (33 out of 55, constant across all clause statuses) would suggest that the text is largely concerned with actions and events; and so at one level it is. However, with the doubtful exception of *hold local officials accountable*, all these material processes, whether middle or effective, represent actions which are either abstract or, if concrete, then of a very general kind. We could categorize these as in Table 5.

These portray a realm where the action is abstract, bland and formulaic. Where there is agency, the Actor/Agent is typically some abstract object or process: calls or requests, a test or a study, pressures, decisions

Table 4. Distribution of process types

	material		mental	verbal	relational		
	effective	middle			identi-fying	attribu-tive	Total
α-clauses	7	6	1	2	2	5	23
β-clauses	6	3	1	2		1	13
[[-clauses	8	3	1	3		4	19
	21	12	3	7	2	10	
Total	33		10		12		55

Notes

1. The three clauses with *make* + Range (*make decisions, make choices, make contributions*) are all interpreted as material: (i) *make contributions,* even if 'unpacked' as *contribute (money)*, would still be material; (ii) *make decisions, make choices* could not be unpacked here as *decide, choose* because they could not project: the attached clauses are clearly expansions (${}^{\times}\beta$ *in planning for people;* =[[*that could drastically affect the quality of our lives*), whereas if the congruent forms were mental they would be able to project — as they could if the nominal groups in question were singular, e.g. *make the (sound) decision/ choice not to pursue the matter further.*

2. The four clauses with *need (we need your help, the materials they need, the public need the data, put the test in the hands of those who need it*) are all interpreted as relational: attributive/possessive, 'must have'. Of these, the first could also be interpreted as mental + projection, congruently *we need you to help us*; but given that *help* is followed by a cohesive lexical chain *support — contribution — contribution — give — $25 $50 or $100,* it seems more appropriate to interpret this too as a possessive.

3. The clause *to hold local officials accountable* ... might by itself be taken as mental, agnate to *hold that local officials are accountable* ('consider that ...'); but this is precluded here by the preceding clause *what they can do*. In this context the interpretation must be as material process, with *accountable* ... as resultative Attribute.

and problems. The only actions performed by human Agents are giving money, tackling problems, releasing results or completing forms (there is also arming activists — with data). Where there is no agency, and the Actor is just the Medium for the action or event, human Actors preponderate; and their actions are vague generalities, like planning, taking action, or making decisions and contributions.

Of the remaining 22 clauses, most (17) are either verbal or attributive. Thus one motif is that of verbal action, with 7 instances of *answer, tell, hear, talk, report* or *warn*. The 10 attributive include the four with *need* (see notes to Table 4), three with *be* (furious, critical, incredible) and three

Table 5: Material processes

	Abstract 'make/be busy'	'do research'	'create/affect/do'	General 'give/use'
effective (Medium/Goal; + Actor/Agent)	calls jam switchboard	we monitor media coverage	test is created	you give (money)
	staff is swamped with requests	we release results	pressures affect cities	we arm activists with data
	resources are stretched	stress data are revealed by study	decisions affect lives	(money) puts test in hands of
	you complete form	test ranks urban areas	problems threaten health	you can (give money)
	officials tackle problems	test translates data		(money) is used
middle (Medium/Actor)	phones ring	we 'blow the whistle'	we act	you make contributions
	staffers stay		we take action	
	calls come		decisions are made	
	stresses reach crisis stage		officials make choices	
			officials plan	
			they do what	

Table 6: Tactic pairs, by taxis and interdependency

	expansion			projection	
	elaborating =	extending +	enhancing x	idea ‘	locution “
hypotactic	1		9	2	
paratactic		2			

others (have an idea, get a response, and *criteria ranging from ... to ...*). Thus the motifs brought out by the transitivity patterns are those of abstract or generalized actions, verbal events, and attributes; the attributes being mainly prerequisites to such actions and events, or their consequences.

All the four most frequent clause types — material effective, material middle, verbal, and relational attributive — are distributed evenly throughout the text; there is no clear pattern of movement from one kind of process to another. This is perhaps partly why I felt that the text lacked direction in its chosen field; it seemed not to be ‘going anywhere’, not even round in a circle.

5. Clause Complexes

As noted in the introduction (Section 0 above), eight of the thirty segments (§ 1-3 and 24-28) consist of clausettes; we shall leave these out of consideration here, and consider the remaining 22 segments. These contain 36 ranking clauses; 13 standing alone (as clause ‘simplex’), 8 in 2-clause complexes and 15 in 3-clause complexes.

There are thus 14 tactic pairs — since a complex of two clauses has just one such pair, while a complex of three clauses has two. Table 6 shows the distribution by taxis and interdependency (logical-semantic relation). The favoured type is hypotactic enhancement; within these, four are clauses of Cause: Purpose, all non-finite with *to: to use it well, to take positive action, to make sound choices, to put the Urban Stress Test in the hands of those who need it most*. Three others are also non-finite: one Manner, *by completing the enclosed reply form*, one Matter, *in planning for people*, and one which could be interpreted as Time: Simultaneity (‘meanwhile’, *answering questions ...*) or alternatively as not enhancing but extending (‘and’). The other two are finite: one Time and one Concession.

Table 7: Ranking clauses: simplexes and complexes

clause no.	symbol	boundaries (first & last word, with conjunction(s) if any; (seg.) = clause takes up whole of segment)
4		(seg.)
5		(seg.)
6A	α	staffers ... night
B	$^{x}\beta_{1}$	answering questions
C	$\beta{+}2$	and talking ... country
7A	$^{x}\beta$	and we ... test
B	$\alpha\alpha$	we ... idea
C	α‘β	we'd ... response
8		(seg.)
9		(seg.)
10		(seg.)
11A	α	ZPG's ... «...» ... cities
B	«=β»	created ... research
12		(seg.)
13		(seg.)
14A	$^{x}\beta$	but to use ... well
B	α	we ... help
15A	1	our ... information
B	$^{+}2$	and our ... limit
16		(seg.)
17		(seg.)
18		(seg.)
19A	$^{x}\beta$	even though our ... growth
B	$\alpha\alpha$	we ... act
C	$\alpha^{x}\beta$	to take ... level
20		(seg.)
21A	$^{x}\beta\alpha$	to make ... choices
B	$\beta^{x}\beta$	in planning ... people
C	α	both ... study
22		(seg.)
23A	α	whatever ... immediately
B	$^{x}\beta$	to put ... most
29		(seg.)
30A	α	I hope
B	‘$\beta\alpha$	you'll ... coverage
C	$\beta^{x}\beta$	by completing ... form

Table 8: Embedded clauses and clause complexes

clause no.	symbol	boundaries (first & last word, with relative or conjunction if any)
9.1	= [[ ]]	eager ... results
9.2	= [[	who were furious
9.3	‘‖]]	that we ... cities
10.1	= [[	who want ... know
10.2	‘‖	what ... do
10.3	ˣ‖	to hold ... accountable
10.4	ˣ‖	for tackling ... problems
10.5	= [[ ]]]]]]]]	that threaten ... well-being
11A.1	‘[[ ]]	how population-linked ... cities
12.1	=[[ ]]	ranging ... wastes
17.1	ˣ[[ ]]	to get ... heard
19.1	=[[	they need
18.2	ˣ‖	to warn ... stresses
18.3	ˣ‖]]	before they ... stage
20.1	=[[ ]]	that could ... lives
21C.1	=[[ ]]	revealed ... study
22A.1	=[[ ]]	whatever you ... can
22A.2	ˣ[[ ]]	as you can
22B.1	=[[ ]]	who need ... most

Three of the four purpose clauses are associated with *need: to use it well we need your help, to make sound choices ... elected officials ... need the population-stress data, [your money] will be used immediately to put the Urban Stress Test in the hands of those who need it most.* This motif also turns up in one of the three embedded clause complexes (see below):

the materials [[they need ˣ‖ to warn community leaders ...]]

This co-occurrence of need (required possession) with purpose lends some sense of urgency to the discourse; and this is perhaps reinforced by the other two purpose clauses, which co-occur with *can do, can act*. Again, one of these sequences is in an embedded clause complex:

citizens ... [[who want to know ‘‖ what they can do ˣ‖ to hold local officials accountable ...]]

while the other is the quaintly worded *we can act to take positive action ...* . But although purpose is clearly the single most favoured form of interdependency (six out of the seventeen tactic pairs), it is never highlighted: all six instances have the simple non-finite form with *to*, instead of a finite clause (e.g. *if we are to* ...), or an explicit conjunction (e.g. *in order to* ...).

Table 7 identifies each of the ranking clauses in the text, showing the tactic status and logical-semantic relationship (interdependency) of those entering into clause complexes. Table 8 identifies the clauses and clause complexes which are embedded in nominal constructions throughout the text.

6. Lexical Cohesion

The main lexical bonding in the text, as is to be expected, is provided by reference to ZPG itself and to the Urban Stress Test. Either *ZPG* or one of its reference items *we, our* occurs in almost all segments in the substance of the letter (16 out of 22, and also in the Address); the *U.S.T.*, or *it*, is mentioned 8 times.

The remaining lexical items cluster mainly into seven sets, which we could label 'action, research, publicity, concerns, stress factors, people, and places'. The items entering into these sets are all nominals (nouns or other constituents of nominal groups), and the chains are purely lexical, not lexico-referential: the only reference item is *such* in § 7.

Taken together, the items in these nine sets (the seven above, plus ZPG and the Urban Stress Test) account for 65% of all occurrences of lexical words in the text (162 out of 250). The remaining 35% include all the verbs and adverbs; high frequency and general lexical items like *idea, limit, trends, day, night;* and items such as *overwhelming, eager, furious, drastic, outraged, remarkable, special, incredible* where the linking motif is interpersonal rather than experiential.

Figure 3 shows the pattern of occurrence of items from the major sets in each of the 22 segments. Either ZPG or the U.S.T. (or both) occurs in all but three (§ 8, 16, 20 — the *our* in § 20 is not referring to ZPG); these connections are not shown. All other co-occurrences are shown by lines labelled with the serial numbers of the segments in question; thus, items from both 'action' and 'research' motifs will be found in § 13, 18, 21. It will be seen that six out of the seven motifs are strongly bonded: apart from 'publicity — concerns', all possible cluster pairs are represented in at least one segment, and the mean number of occurrences of each such pair is three

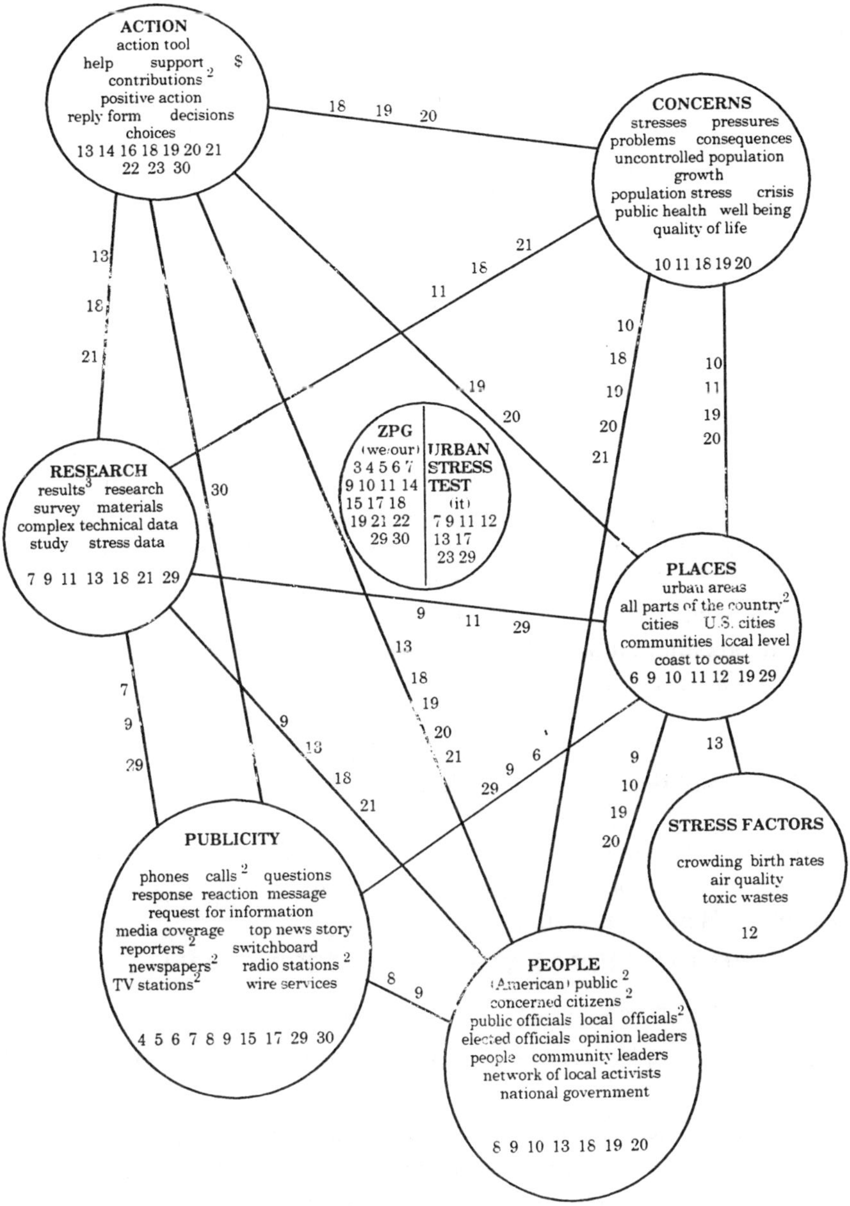

Figure 3: Lexical sets (nominals only) and their co-occurrence patterns

(that is, given six clusters, there are fifteen possible cluster pairs, and the number of pair occurrences in the text, by segment, is 45).

This strongly centripetal bonding, with each motif co-occurring with all the others and with ZPG and the Urban Stress Test, tends to keep the text in one place. There is a slight drift away from 'publicity' in the first part towards 'action' in the second, with a brief return to 'publicity' at the end — the two being then conjoined for the first time in the prosaic appeal to *help us monitor this remarkable media coverage by completing the enclosed reply form*. But there is little other movement. The motifs of research, concerns, places and people occur throughout the text, and there are no less than five segments in which three out of these four occur together (§ 9, 10, 11, 18, 19; *ZPG* also figures in all five).

The exception is the stress factors. These are mentioned only once, in § 12; and they co-occur here only with the motif of place (*184 urban areas*), and with the Urban Stress Test, referred to here as *it* (the only time it is not spelt out in full). ZPG does not occur in this segment. This insulation of the stress factors from the rest of the discourse keeps technical matters firmly at a distance; the effect is somewhat paternalistic, with some such message as 'keep the funds rolling, but don't bother your heads with the difficult stuff — we'll look after all that'. (Compare *translates complex technical data into an easy-to-use action tool*.)

7. Nominalization and Grammatical Metaphor

As one way of exploring the grammatical metaphor I reworded the text in a more congruent form, using the strategy of 'how would I say this to a 12-year-old?'. Here is the result:

KEEPING THE POPULATION NO BIGGER THAN IT IS NOW

4 At 7 a.m. on October 25, our phones started to ring.

5 So many people were telephoning us that the switchboard was jammed all day.

6 Our staff stayed (working) late into the night, answering questions and talking with reporters from newspapers, radio stations, wire services and TV stations in every part of the country.

7 When we told everyone what we had found out by our Urban Stress

Test in 1985 (which shows how people get tired and upset if they live in cities) we'd no idea we'd have so many people taking notice.

8 It was incredible how (much ?) the TV, radio and newspapers, and also ordinary people, talked about it.

9 At first the ones who kept telephoning us were mainly reporters, who were eager to tell people about the results of the stress test, and public officials, who were furious because we had 'blown the whistle on' what it's like to live in their cities.

10 But now we're hearing from ordinary citizens from all parts of the country who are worried and want to know what they can do to get local officials to accept that it's their job to tackle problems coming from overpopulation, if this is (these are?) making people unhappy.

11 When we were creating this Urban Stress Test we had to research persistently and very thoroughly for months; it's the first time anyone in the country has surveyed how much difference it makes having so many people around if you live in U.S. cities.

12 We put 184 urban areas in order according to 11 different properties which we measured, including how crowded they are, how many children are being born, how good or bad the air is, and how much poisonous waste there is around.

13 What we found out with this test is complicated and technical; but we've made the test (the results?) easy to understand so that citizens who are concerned about these things, and elected officials, and people whose opinions count, can use it (them?) to get things done.

14 But to use it well we urgently need you to help us.

15 We have only a small staff, and they've been swamped by being asked so many questions. We haven't enough resources to deal with any more.

16 You have to support us now so that we can survive.

17 The Urban Stress Test may be our best opportunity ever to get people to listen to what we are saying about population.

18 We can use the money you contribute for sending out to the more and more people who are working for us in different places all the information (?) they need in order to warn important members of the com-

munity that people are already beginning to suffer (?) because of overpopulation, before this becomes a crisis.

19 Even though our national government still ignores what happens if the population goes on growing without being controlled, we can try to do something about it in our own neighbourhoods.

20 Every day local officials in our communities are deciding things which will make a difference to the way we live.

21 So that they can choose properly when they plan for people (plan for the population?), both elected officials and the American public need to know what we found out when we studied stresses coming from overpopulation.

22 Please contribute extra money (?) to ZPG today.

23 Whatever you give — $25, $50, $100 or as much as you can — will be used immediately to tell the results to the people who most need to know them (give the test to the people who most need to use it?).

29 The results of the test were reported as a top news story by hundreds of newspapers and TV and radio stations from coast to coast.

30 I hope you'll help us to keep a record of all this remarkable number of reports, by filling in the form I'm enclosing for you to reply on.

When the text is approached from this angle three features seem to stand out: cliches, ambiguities, and grammatical metaphors. As a final step, we will discuss each of these in turn.

(1) Cliches. The cliches seem to cluster around four motifs:
- (i) 'we are under pressure', e.g. *calls jammed our switchboard, the deluge of calls, swamped with requests, resources stretched to the limit*;
- (ii) 'we amaze people', e.g. *met with an overwhelming response, reaction nothing short of incredible, remarkable media coverage;*
- (iii) 'crisis threatens', e.g. *threaten public health and well-being, your support is critical, reach crisis stage, affect the quality of our lives*;
- (iv) 'arm and act', e.g. *arm our growing network of local activists, act to take positive action at the local level*.

It looks as though all these cliches serve a function: that of easing the somewhat awkward disjunction (which appears in the theme and information structures; cf. Sections 1 and 2 above) between two apparently contradictory messages: 'look what we've done — we're great!' and 'we're puny and weak — so help us!' The use of wordings which are so hackneyed that they have lost much of their experiential meaning may help to paper over this contradiction.

(2) Ambiguities. Ambiguity and grammatical metaphor are closely interconnected: grammatical metaphors tend to leave many semantic relationships implicit and by the same token to neutralize certain distinctions. Ambiguities arose in this text particularly in relation to three issues: the nature of the problem, the status of the test, and the kind of assistance requested:

(i) (§ 10, 18) *population-related problems that threaten public health and well-being; emerging population-linked stresses ... reach crisis stage*: is it the size of the population that is becoming threatening and critical, or other factors that arise from this?

(ii) (§ 13, 23) *translates complex data into an easy-to-use action tool; to put the Urban Stress Test in the hands of those who need it most*: is it the test itself, or the results of the test, that are to be made available?

(iii) (§ 22) *make a special contribution to ZPG today:* are we being asked to do something to further the aims of zero population growth, or to give money to a particular organization?

There are other, less salient ambiguities; for example in § 8 and elsewhere referring to the media response (is it the quantity of the reactions that is remarkable, or their nature and quality — many people responded, or people responded favourably?), and in § 21 *in planning for people* (does this mean planning on behalf of the public, or planning what to do as regards the growth of population?).

The word *population* in fact occurs seven times; and every occurrence is framed in one particular kind of grammatical metaphor: where nouns representing processes or attributes function as Head of the nominal group and are preceded by premodifying elements whose semantic relationship to the Head noun is unclear. The examples are:

zero population growth
population-related problems
population-linked pressures

the population message
emerging population-linked stresses
uncontrolled population growth
population-stress data

It will be seen that the word *population* never occurs as Head; it is either a Modifier or else a part of a compound Modifier, and if the latter then followed either by another noun (*population-stress*) or by a verb in V^n form (*population-linked, population-related*). Thus quite apart from the vagueness of the last two, where the sense is 'having some (unspecified) connection with (the) population', each one of these instances is problematic. Population-stress data might be data about the stress caused by the population, or undergone by the population; the population message might be a message about how matters are, or about how they should be, and either concerning or addressed to the population; and even population growth, which presumably must mean people becoming more in number rather than becoming taller and fatter, is introduced in the contradictory context of zero. Nowhere is the concept of 'too many people', overpopulation, made explicit.

It could fairly be said that those to whom the letter is addressed will 'get the message' in all these instances and reject interpretations that are inappropriate; and that it is of no consequence if they are misinterpreted or not understood by others. But, apart from the fact that this seems rather shortsighted — surely the message is one that is intended to be spread? — there is a deeper problem with these rather oblique forms of discourse: that they become so bland as to lose all impact. If the grammar creates a universe of pseudo-objects, like easy-to-use action tools, population-related problems, emerging population-linked stresses approaching crisis stage and positive action at the local level, then all of reality is held at a safe distance; and when these objects are further disneyfied by the use of pseudo-intimacies like dear friend of ZPG, our phones started to ring, our small staff is being swamped, with your contribution, and I hope you'll help us, the underlying message is that life can go on being just one long Happy Hour.

(3) Grammatical metaphors. As is clear from the rewording at the beginning of this Section, the text displays a considerable range of grammatical metaphor: not extremely dense, but varied (cf. Jones *et al.*, 1989: 268-9, 302-4). It would take a separate paper to categorize and describe it in

detail; instead, I shall look at some of its consequences by examining one segment (§ 18).

The following is an informal account of the major decisions that have to be made in interpreting this segment. Not all of these would necessarily be accounted for as grammatical metaphors; some involve lexical metaphor (i.e. metaphor in the usual sense of the term), while others are neutralizations by the grammar of semantic distinctions that are typically not, in fact, made explicit (e.g. *of, -ist* below). Each instance is discussed, and a decision taken among the possible interpretations; the number of possibilities is given in square brackets, usually [2]. A less ambiguous rewording is suggested.

(i) With your contributions, ZPG can arm our network ...

(a) Who are *your* and *our*? 'You' is obviously the recipient of the letter. Assuming that 'we' are the writers, is this *our* anaphoric to ZPG or not? [2] (It is, although the structure is unusual; it would be more usual to write *We at ZPG can arm our ... .*)

(b) *With your contributions:* does this with mean 'giving', as in *with your guns we can arm our militia*, or does it mean 'using'? [2] (It means 'by using your contributions'.)

(c) Your contributions: is 'you' here a possessor, as in *your property*, or is it a participant in some transitivity relation, like *your role* 'the part you play'? (The second; 'you' is Actor in a process of giving, i.e. 'giver'). In that case, has the action been performed or not — that is, is the giving in the past or in the future? [3 options altogether] (The action is in the hoped-for future.)

Rewording: By using the money we hope you are going to give us, we at ZPG can arm our network ...

(ii) ... arm our growing network of local activists with the materials they need ...

(d) *Arm our network with materials*: does this mean 'give our network supplies of weapons' or 'give our network materials which can be used as (if they were) weapons'? [2] (The second.)

(e) What are *materials*: goods-&-services, or information? [2] (Information.)

(f) Who or what are *activists*: people who support activism (cf. *communists*), or people who believe in activity (cf. *relativists*), or people who are active (cf. *sensualists*)? [3] (We ignore 'people who act'! — presumably, people who are active.)

(g) *Our activists*: is 'we' possessor, or in some transitivity function (cf. (c) above)? [2] (The latter: 'on our behalf', 'in our cause'.)
(h) Are *local activists* those in different localities, as in *local representatives*; those in our locality, as in *local doctors*; or those operating within a small area, as in *local government?* [3] (Probably the first.)
(j) In *network of activists*, what is *of*: ownership, as in *house of her parents*; constituency, as in *house of three storeys*; description, as in *house of ill repute*; material, as in *house of cards*; container, as in *house of antiquities*; or collective, as in *house of representatives?* [6] (Presumably the last of these.)
(k) Is the *growing network* expanding in size, like the network surrounding a ball that is being inflated; or is it increasing in numbers? [2] (The latter.)

Rewording: ... we can supply those who are active on our behalf in different localities, now that they are organized into a network and are growing in number, materials that can be used as weapons ...

(iii) ... materials they need to warn community leaders about emerging population-linked stresses ...

(l) What is *to* in *they need to warn*: 'materials they need to warn community leaders about (i.e. that community leaders must be warned about)', or 'materials that they need in order that they can warn community leaders'? [2] (The second.)
(m) Are *community leaders* 'people who lead the community', 'people who hold leading positions in the community' or 'leaders who live in the community'? [3] (Perhaps the second, rather than the first of these.)
(n) What are *emerging population-linked stresses* (cf. the discussion of *population* above)? Are they 'stresses linked to emerging population' or 'emerging stresses linked to population' (i.e. which is emerging, the population or the stresses)? [2] Is *linked to* 'causing', 'caused by' or 'co-occurring with'? [3] Is *emerging* 'coming out', 'beginning to show' or 'increasing'? [3] (Combining the appropriate selection each time we get 'stresses which are caused by population, and which are beginning to show'.)
(o) Is *population* the kind of people, or the number of people? If it is the number, are there too many, or too few? [3 altogether] (Too many.)

Rewording: ... materials that they need to use in order to warn those who hold leading positions in the community about stresses caused by there being too many people, stresses which are now beginning to show ...

(iv) ... before they reach crisis stage.

(q) Who is *they*: the activists, the community leaders, or the stresses? [3] (We can choose 'stresses', because it is the nearest, and because of the collocational relation between *stress* and *crisis*.)

(r) Is *crisis stage* the stage which is a crisis, or the stage where crises occur? [2] (Uncertain.)

(s) If stresses *reach crisis stage*, is this a time, a place, or a degree of intensity? [3] (Probably a degree of intensity; in combination with (r) above, perhaps 'a degree of intensity where crises occur', rather than 'a degree of intensity which is a crisis'.)

Rewording: ... before the stresses become so intense that crises will occur.

It would be possible partially to 'repack' this wording in a way which eliminates some at least of these alternatives; for example:

> Any money that you contribute to ZPG can pay the cost of sending out information to supporters in different localities, so that armed with this information they can warn leading members of the community about the increased stresses brought on by overpopulation before these stresses start to cause a crisis.

Any interpretation of a text involves decisions. Most of these do not engage our attention; we reject improbable alternatives without ever noticing them. In this particular segment we should probably not envisage that *reach ... stage* might refer to a play performed at a theatre, or that *growing network* could be a network for growing plants on, although neither of these is totally impossible. Here I have tried to include only alternatives which seemed reasonably plausible. Note that this is not a composition exercise for purposes of 'improving' the text; there are far too many variables in discourse construction for any operation — even that of reducing ambiguity — to guarantee improvement. (The rewording of the text at the beginning of this Section was different again; it was an intuitive venture at making the text more accessible — something that is connected with 'less ambiguous' but by no means identical with it.)

The present exercise in unpacking and repacking one segment does suggest, however, that this text is somewhat problematic: not so much in the number of possible interpretations as in the number of plausible interpretations offered by its lexicogrammar. If we treated all of those enumerated above as independent of each other we should have a little over 4×10^7 acceptable readings. This is probably more than would be typical of a sentence of comparable length in most kinds of discourse. But it may be typical of this particular register, which we could perhaps characterize as the discourse of the 'soft touch'.

8. Summary

In this paper I have adopted a grammatical perspective on discourse, interpreting the text simultaneously as object and as instance. By bringing a text under attention we assign to it value as an object; this is the activity which turns a text into 'literature' (not thereby implying 'good' literature, of course). By bringing it under grammatical attention we display its properties as an instance; this shows how it means, since every feature it displays is located in the context of its alternatives. These agnate forms, representing what might have been meant but was not, constitute an infinity of shadow texts against which the one in focus achieves its reality.

Among the grammatical systems instantiated in any text we can identify some where the choices made are likely to assume significance: very general categories of theme, transitivity and so on, and also syndromes of features like grammatical metaphor. Selections made within these systems will give the text its distinctive flavour and determine how we evaluate it relative to its socio-semiotic context. We could have examined other features, or explored these ones further — indefinitely further — in delicacy; in stylistic studies we may be treating of choices that are very delicate indeed. But we also have to make choices of our own, especially that between depth and breadth; and in the absence of obvious foregrounding of any one grammatical system it seemed preferable to aim for breadth.

I have not offered more than brief evaluative comments, although no doubt the wording of my own discourse construes an attitude towards its object. What I have tried to do rather is to show the grammar at work creating meaning in the form of written text. We tend to think of grammar as simply taking its orders from above; our own discourse has to make it strange, to show it deautomatized in the text under review. The patterns we bring out create meaning both at their own level and at each 'higher' level that they realize — with which they are related by metaredundancy, in the terms of Lemke's explanatory model (Lemke 1984). I have concentrated on the meaning of the grammar at its own level, trusting to other contributors in the volume to explore the various realms of meaning that lie beyond.

Notes

1. For analysis and notation see Halliday 1985a: 193-202. The following symbols are used:

interdependency:	logical-semantic relations:	
parataxis 1 2 3 ...	= elaborating	expansion
hypotaxis α β γ	+ extending	
	x enhancing	
	' idea	projection
	" locution	

2. For Subject see Halliday 1985a, Chapter 4 passim. The Subject is realized as that element which, together with the Finite verbal operator, constitutes the mood-marking element of the clause; hence, in a declarative clause, the element that is recapitulated in the tag, e.g. *there* in *there's no danger of that, is there?* The unmarked pattern in a declarative clause is that in which the Subject is also thematic.

References

Benson, James D. & William S. Greaves (eds)
1985 *Systemic Perspectives on Discourse, Vol. 1: selected theoretical papers from the 9th International Systemic Workshop*. (Advances in Discourse Processes 15). Norwood, N.J.: Ablex.

Firth, J.R.
1968 "The languages of linguistics". In F.R. Palmer (ed.), *Selected Papers of J.R. Firth 1952-1959*. London: Longman, 27-34.

Fries, Peter H.
1981 "On the status of Theme in English: Arguments from discourse". *Forum Linguisticum* 6 1:1-38. Also in Janós S. Petöfi & Emel Sözer (eds), *Micro and Macro Connexity of Texts*. (Papers in Textlinguistics 45). Hamburg: Helmut Buske Verlag, 1983:116-152.

Gregory, Michael
1985 "Towards 'communication' linguistics: a framework". In Benson & Greaves (eds), 1985:119-134.

Halliday, M.A.K.
1967 *Intonation and Grammar in British English*. (Janua Linguarum Series Practica 48). The Hague: Mouton.

1985a *An Introduction to Functional Grammar*. London, Baltimore & Melbourne: Edward Arnold.

1985b "Dimensions of discourse analysis: Grammar". In Teun A. van Dijk (ed.), *Handbook of Discourse Analysis*, Vol. 2. London: Academic Press, 29-56.

Jones, Janet, Sandra Gollin, Helen Drury, and Dorothy Economou
1989 "Systemic-functional linguistics and its application to the TESOL curriculum." In Ruqaiya Hasan & J.R. Martin (eds), *Language Development: Learning Language, Learning Culture* (Advances in Discourse Processes 27). Norwood, N.J.: Ablex, 257-328.

Matthiessen, Christian M.I.M.
1985 "The systemic framework in text generation: Nigel". In Benson & Greaves (eds) 1985:96-118.

Macro-Proposals: Meaning by Degree

J.R. Martin
University of Sydney

1. How is a Text Like a Clause?

Halliday 1982 suggests that the relationship between text and clause is not arbitrary (as between say clause and syllable), but natural. Realisation between text and clause is, in other words, **symbolic**. It follows that both text and clause are rich sources of metaphor for interpreting each other.

Given our present understanding of discourse and grammar, one is naturally predisposed to using grammar as a source of metaphors for discourse (rather than using discourse, which is less well understood, as a resource for interpreting grammar). And in his paper Halliday points out a number of ways in which a text resembles a clause:

1. A text has structure
2. A text has coherence
3. A text has function
4. A text has development
5. A text has character

Reviewing point 1, Halliday speculates "whether the text may display the same kind of multiple structuring that is found in the clause, ideational, interpersonal and textual, having, potentially at least, an ideational structure relating to its field and an interpersonal structure relating to its tenor..." (Halliday 1982:225), referring to his 1979 analysis of the different types of structure associated with different metafunctional components in the grammar. Matthiessen 1988:157 summarises these as follows, splitting the ideational into its two sub-components, the experiential and logical:

METAFUNCTION	TYPE OF STRUCTURE	PIKE'S TERMS
interpersonal	prosody	field
textual	pulse (culminative)	wave
experiential	constituency	particle
logical	interdependency	–

In this paper the idea that texts have a prosodically realised interpersonal structure alongside an experiential structure realised through constituency will be explored. It will be suggested that texts including and agnate to the ZPG text under discussion do indeed need to be analysed along at least these two dimensions.

2. Experiential Meaning (Constituency Structure)

The analogy between clause and text structure that has been best explored, as least within the systemic tradition, is that a text has constituent structure (Mitchell 1957/1975; Sinclair and Coulthard 1975; Hasan 1977, 1979, 1984; Martin 1984a, 1985a, 1985b; Ventola 1987). Mitchell for example proposes the following structure for market and shop transactions:

Salutation	Enquiry as to Object of sale	Investigation of Object of Sale	Bargaining	Conclusion

Analysis along these lines suggests that texts realising market and shop transactions can be divided into five stages, which typically occur in the sequence outlined above (Mitchell, a fully trained prosodic phonologist of the London School, does in fact allow for non-verbal realisation, optional elements and comments that "*Stage* is an abstract category and the numbering of stages does not necessarily imply sequence in time." 1957:43)

The analysis further suggests that underlying these text structures is a system of text types, relating buying and selling genres in terms of their structural similarities. Mitchell for example considers the similarities and differences between market and shop transactions and auctions, proposing the following related structure for the agnate auction genre:

Opening	Investigation of Object of Sale	Bidding	Conclusion

Experientially derived constituent structures have not been the sole focus of systemic work on genre. The strengths and weaknesses of relating system and process along these lines have been explored by Martin 1985a and Ventola 1987 who argue that a text needs to be seen in dynamic as well as synoptic terms — that is to say, texts have an ongoing interdependency structure analagous to recursive structures deriving from the logical metafunction. And Martin (1986:38-40) analyses culminative Theme-Rheme structures at several levels in the structure of bureaucratic writing. But to date very little has been accomplished on global text structure from either an interpersonal or prosodic perspective.

Adopting this experiential perspective on the ZPG text, one might propose a constituent structure along the following lines (see segmented text in Introduction):

Involvement	Product	Appeal
1-10	11-13	14-30

The function of these stages could be glossed as follows:

INVOLVEMENT – get reader's attention
PRODUCT – describe product offered
APPEAL – solicit contribution, giving reasons

And the text type could be provisionally related to other types of advertisement in something like the following network:

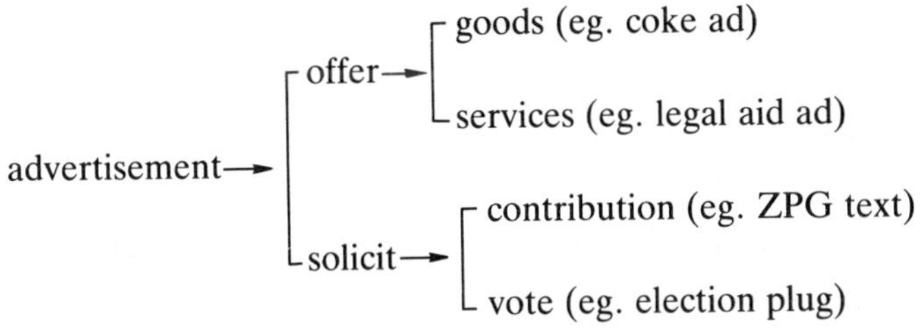

The system/process research paradigm for genre implicated in this section is still in its infancy. And there is still a tremendous amount to be learned about the ways in which genres can be conceived experientially, in constituent terms, as staged goal-oriented social processes. But the paradigm, however successful, is not designed to give a complete account of text structure. For the remainder of this paper, the complementary interpersonal dimension will be in focus.

3. Interpersonal Meaning

Halliday (1971:106) describes the interpersonal function as follows: "Here, the speaker is using language as a means of his own intrusion into the speech event: the expression of his comments, his attitudes and evaluations, and also of the relationship that he sets up between himself and the listener — in particular, the communication role he adopts, of informing, questioning, greeting, persuading and the like." Note that this description covers both personal meaning, the speaker's attitude to the meaning he is making, and **inter**personal meaning, the speaker's relation to his listener.

What is being suggested here is that there is a functional commonality between **acting on** the world, especially other speakers, through Commands, Offers, Questions, Statements and other speech functions, and **reacting to** the world, especially what other speakers have said, through commentary deriving from the systems reviewed in 4 below.

Certainly the grammar of English affords numerous examples of this interdependence. Modal verbs for example are found in indicative but not imperative clauses:

[indicative] *You could come./Could you come*?
[imperative] **Could come.*

Modal adjuncts (Halliday 1985a:50) like *frankly*, *honestly*, *seriously*, *tentatively* are similarly restricted to the indicative, and are further sensitive to the opposition of declarative and interrogative. In declaratives they code the speaker's opinion, but in interrogatives they invite the listener's:

[declarative] *Frankly, I don't like him.*
[interrogative] *Frankly, do you like him?*

And exclamatives grammaticalise high intensity attitude at clause rank:

How well he plays!
What an idiot he is!

Beyond this, as Halliday (1985a:86) notes, the indicative/imperative opposition symbolises the semantic opposition of propositions (exchange of information) with proposals (exchange of goods and services). He goes on to interpret modality (embracing probability and usuality as discussed below) as a scale grading propositions from yes to no and modulation (embracing obligation and inclination as discussed above) as a scale grading proposals from do to don't, as reviewed in section 4 below.

From a discourse perspective, this allows us to interpret Questions as demands for modality and Statements as opportunities to modalise:

Is she coming?
– *Yes/certainly/probably/possibly/no.*

Does she attend?
– *Yes/always/usually/sometimes/no.*

As far as modulation is concerned, Offers express inclination (inviting obligation) whereas Commands assert obligations (inviting inclination):

I'd be happy to take you.
– *Okay, thanks.*

You really should take me.
– *I'd be delighted to.*

The relationship of attitude to mood is perhaps less transparent, but modulation and attitude might be related as follows. The desire to act on the world with a proposal (Offer or Command) is in some sense dependent on dissatisfaction with the ways things are and a desire to make them better — both from the speaker's point of view. Making a proposal thus implies a negative evaluation of the way things are and a positive evaluation of the way they could be. Or to put this another way — attitude is realis; it evaluates what is as good or bad. Modulation is irrealis — it comments that what is shouldn't be (thereby implicitly evaluating it as bad) and what isn't should be (thereby implicitly evaluating it as good). This interaction of modulation and affect is clearly symbolised in the opposition between reaction (realis) and desire (irrealis) in mental processes of affection (Halliday 1985a:106-112). Note the following:

REACTION	DESIRE
I hate going there.	*I'd hate her to go there.*
You love eating clams.	*You'd love her to eat clams.*
I like seeing her.	*I'd like him to see her.*
You adore oysters.	*You'd adore her to eat oysters.*
You despise exams.	*You'd despise him to pass exams.*

Reaction clauses process phenomena — things and acts (i.e. *going there*, *eating clams*, *seeing her*, *oysters*, and *exams*). Desire clauses may also process phenomena, but can project metaphenomena as well — e.g. the ideas *her to go there*, *her to eat clams*, *him to see her*, *her to eat oysters* and *him to pass exams*. As Halliday (1985:336) suggests, this means that desire clauses often function as metaphorical expressions of modulation, as illustrated in the following proportionalities:

I'd permit him to go:he may go::
I'd like him to go:he should go::
I'd love him to go:he must go

Locating semantic and grammatical systems in metafunctional components is less than straight-forward (see Martin 1984b for discussion). However, in light of the kind of interdependency noted in the preceding discussion, for the purposes of this paper both mood (acting on the world) and judgement (reacting to the world) will be taken as critical interpersonal dimensions and explored in the ZPG text accordingly.

4. Prosodic Realisation

Halliday's point about the realisation of interpersonal meaning in clause structure is that it is, potentially at least, non-discrete. In *My firm conviction is obviously that certainly it must be a Range, mustn't it?* for example, a modality of certainty is coded as a semantic motif running right through the clause: *firm conviction, obviously, certainly, must, must*. Prosodic realisation in general poses problems for constituency based grammars, and so it is important to understand exactly what it is that makes them awkward.

Matthiessen in press lists the following systems as problematic in current generative formulations of systemic grammar:

mood number and person (agreement)
moodtag
polarity
reflexivization
key

With the first four systems the problem is that the choice of a particular grammatical feature affects more than one constituent in clause structure. With polarity for example, the choice of negative may be realised across several elements. Matthiessen presents the following examples (negative realisations in bold face):

I ain't never *had* ***no*** *trouble with* ***none*** *of 'em.*
I haven't ever *had* ***any*** *trouble with* ***any*** *of them.*

Key is realised by tone. Here we might say that instead of the realisation of a feature being **distributed** across a number of constituents, the realisation is spread evenly through a constituent — in the case of key, the tone group. This **continuous** realisation is more typical of Firth's use of the term prosody in phonology, although discontinous realisations were certainly recognised — e.g., vowel harmony (see papers in Palmer 1970).

Finally there is the **accumulated** realisation illustrated in the first example given above, where the meaning of certainty is amplified by being selected several times. It is not just the realisation of a particular feature that is prosodic here; the meaning itself has been chosen over and over again and thereby spreads itself across the constituent structure.

Prosodic realisations of interpersonal meaning are also found at group rank, in the context of accumulating attitude. Consider positive and negative attitude in the following nominal groups:

my sweet darling little baby pussy cat
you horrible screaming nasty wakeful cry-baby you

The difference in meaning among accumulating realisations of modality, attitude and other interpersonal systems is a matter of degree. The more a speaker wishes to amplify his position, the more realisations will be used. The grammar piles up meanings across a structure, much as phonology operates gradiently with continuous realisations, adjusting pitch, rhythm, intensity, voice quality and so on to suit a speaker's mood. Poynton 1985:80 refers to the realisation principle under consideration here as **amplification**, which is associated with the *affect* component of tenor in her register theory.

The grammatical systems most strongly associated with amplification appear to be those used by speakers to make judgements of various kinds — systems whose options are graded, with high, median and low values. Modality for example allows for degrees of certainty: possible-probable-certain. In choosing among options such as these, speakers take up positions representing their personal assessment of degree. And they may choose to reinforce their assessment by stamping it several times onto their message as in the prosodic realisations considered above.

This association of gradable systems and prosodic realisation of this kind raises the question of which grammatical systems allow for meaning by degree. These will be addressed in section 5 below. Then later, in section 7, the effect of accumlating meanings of these kinds across discourse units will be considered in an effort to interpret attitude, comment and evaluation in the ZPG text.

5. Gradable Systems

Sapir (1944/1949:123) points out that "Every quantifiable, whether existent (say *house*) or occurrent (say *run*) or quality of existent (say *red*) or quality of occurrent (say *gracefully*), is intrinsically gradable... house A is higher but house B is roomier, while existent C is so much smaller than either A or B that it is "less of a house" than they are and may be put in the class "toy" or at best "shack"." Similarly occurrents like *running* differ with respect to "speed, excitement of runner, length of time, and degree of resemblance to walking." Further "Different examples of "red" similarly exhibit "mores" and "lesses" with respect to intensity, size of surface or volume characterised as red, and degree of conformity to some accepted standard of redness. And "gracefully" is quite unthinkable except as implying a whole gamut of activities which may be arranged in a graded series on the score of gracefulness."

Sapir's comments underline the pervasiveness of meaning by degree in text; they were taken by him as point of departure for a discussion of grammatical comparison. In this paper his remarks will be developed in a different direction in order to focus on the grammaticalisation of grading and its relation to interpersonal meaning.

The first point that needs to be taken up is the difference between graded and gradable items. To take Sapir's example of *house* and *shack*, it is important to recognise that both items enter into two distinct sets of oppositions. On the one hand they enter into oppositions concerned with the classification of experience and are opposed to *flat, apartment, office, school, church, theatre, hotel* etc. On the other they enter into oppositions concerned with the evaluation of experience, and are opposed to *hut, hovel, palace, castle, mansion, pad, shanty*, etc. It is this second set which is inherently graded.

This can be tested in several ways, the general point being that it is not possible to grade nouns like *house* without expressing an attitude towards them, whereas nouns like *shack* are already graded. Consider the following:

It was a mansion:It was quite a mansion::
It was a hovel:What a hovel it was!

It was a church:It was quite a church::
It was a school:What a school it was!

In the first set, the second member of each opposition intensifies the first; but in the second set the opposition is between classification and evaluation. As we grade the ungraded terms, our attitude towards them is invoked.

Some types of intensification draw a clear line between inherently graded and ungraded items. Note the ungrammaticality of the second member of the following pairs:

*It was an absolute mansion:*It was an absolute school::*
*It was such a palace:*It was such a theatre::*
*It was a bit of a hovel:*It was a bit of a church*

The distinction between graded and gradable items raises the question of grammatical resources for grading. A selection from these was illustrated above: *quite a*, *what a*, and *absolute*. Each has the effect of adjusting the evaluation of a graded item or adding an evaluation to an gradable one.

Grading systems arrange comment, evaluation and attitude by degree, generally along a scale with high, median and low values (with various possibilities for fine tuning among these). *Quite* (median) contrasts with *absolute* (high) and *a bit of a* (low) along one of these scales, which is used for evaluating nouns:

an absolute idiot
quite an idiot
a bit of an idiot

Grading systems respond in general to degree questions, usually containing the word *how*. They contrast with systems of measurement which give absolute as opposed to relative values. The examples below contrasts grading with measurement in this way.

How long was he here? — Ages:Three hours::
How many were there? — A few:Three::
How significant is it? — Very:.0001::
How much did he drink? — All of it:24 stubbies

Clearly a full treatment of grammatical resources related to grading is beyond the scope of this paper. Some of the more central of these, especially those most relevant to interpersonal meaning in the ZPG text, will be briefly reviewed here.

The presentation will be organised around clause, nominal group and verbal group systems. A brief comment on lexis will follow. In all cases only representative realisations are specified and only systems with clearly coded degrees of high, median and low will be considered. In the realisations degree will be organised vertically, with the high value at the top.

Following each of these scales an example will be given (enclosed in square brackets) showing the way in which a particular value can be amplified across a clause or group structure in order to bring out the relationship between grading systems of this kind and accumulated prosodic realisation.

5.1 *Clause Systems*

The first five of these systems are taken from Halliday (1985a:334-341) (see also Halliday 1970/1976). These are:

a. probability
   (**How sure** are you?)

This system is realised through corresponding modal verbs and adverbs. It codes speakers' assessment of certainty interpreted as degrees of yes or no:

(it is)
certainly it must be
probably it will be
possibly it may be
(it isn't)

[**I think possibly** it **might** be a Range, **mightn't** it?]

b. usuality
   (**How often** does it happen?)

This system is similarly coded through corresponding modal verbs and adverbs. It grades speakers judgements of usuality in terms of degrees of yes and no:

(it is)
it always must be
it usually will be
it sometimes may be
(it isn't)

[Will he be in this semester?
– He **sometimes may** be **popping in once in awhile**.]

c. obligation
(**How necessary** is it?)

This system codes degrees of obligation to act. It is realised through modal verbs and 'passive participles'.

(do)
you are required to/you must do
you are supposed to/you will do
you are allowed to/you may do
(don't)

[The notice **insists** that it is a **requirement** that all employees **must** return to duty at 1pm.]

d. inclination
(**How keen** are you?)

This system deals with degrees of willingness to act. It is realised through modal verbs and corresponding participles and adjectives.

(do)
I'm determined to/I must do
I'm keen to/I will do
I'm willing to/I may do
(don't)

[**I'm willing** to make **my inclination** that I **may** do it clear.]

e. subjectivity (Halliday's *orientation*)
(**How objective** is that?)

This system allows each of the preceding four systems to be graded in terms of how subjectively probability, usuality, obligation and inclination are expressed. For example, taking modality as an exemplar:

(She knows)
I expect she knows
She'll know
She probably knows
It's likely that she knows/She's likely to know
(Her knowledge)

[**Certainly** he is **surely** coming **definitely** at 6.]

The explicitly subjective (*I expect*) and explicitly objective (*It's likely*) forms in fact treat the assessment itself as a clause, potentially debatable apart from the proposition it's assessing. That this is a marked, though possible, option can be seen in the tag: *I expect she knows, doesn't she?*, not *I expect she knows, don't I?*

The following network sums up these five systems:

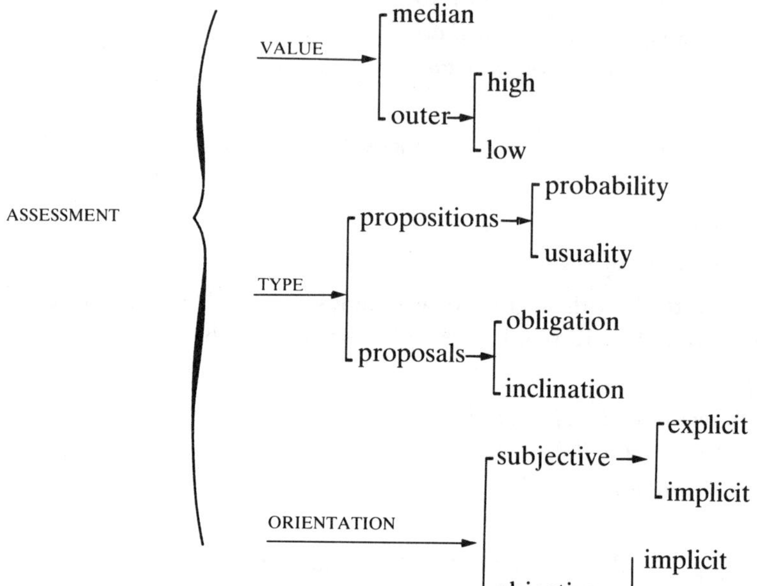

f. commitment

(**How thoroughly** did he do it?)

This system codes the degree of commitment with which some action is undertaken. It is realised through manner adverbs (see Quirk et al.'s 1972 8.18 ff discussion of what they call emphasizers, amplifiers and downtoners).

(doing)
really doing
kind of doing

hardly doing
(not doing)

[Well I **sort of kind of** liked him **to some extent**.]

A large set of attitudinally oriented adverbs are used for grading in this system (e.g. *desperately*, *half-heartedly*, *grimly*, *drastically* etc.); see discussion of attitude in nominal groups below.

g. immediacy
(How soon can they come?)

These systems take the present as point of departure and grade the distance between that point and the completion or inception of another event.

(is doing)	*(is doing)*
immediately	*just done*
soon	*a while ago*
ever	*ages ago*
(will do)	*(done)*

[I'll do it **right away immediately now**.]

h. succession
(How far along are they?)

This system is realised through conjunctions and monitors how far along a particular activity has progressed.

(done)
finally
afterwards
at first
(would do)

[And **finally in the end** it got **wrapped up**.]

5.2 *Nominal Group*

As indicated by Sapir, the relevant nominal group systems deal with quantity and quality. For the nominal group description assumed see Halliday (1985a:159-174).

a. quantity
(How many were there?)

Here we are concerned not with exact measurement and counting, but with ongoing rough and ready assessments of quantity (cf. Sapir 1944/1949:122 "The first thing to realise about grading as a psychological process is that it precedes measurement and counting."). These are realised through the Numerative element in nominal group structure.

(birds)	*(jam)*
many birds	*a lot of jam*
several birds	*some jam*
a few birds	*a little jam*
(no birds)	*(no jam)*

Partitive systems are also relevant here, realised through Pre-Numerative elements with the structural marker of.

(the beer)
most of the beer
half of the beer
a little of the beer
(none of the beer)

[I'd like **a little of** this beer, **just a bit**, **a drop**.]

b. intensity
(**How fit** is he?)

Intensity allows for degrees of quality — size, shape, colour, etc. It is particularly associated with attitudinal Epithets and can also be used to grade Things when these code positive or negative affect.

(fit)	*(an idiot)*
really fit	*such an idiot*
rather fit	*quite an idiot*
somewhat fit	*a bit of an idiot*
(not fit)	*(not an idiot)*

[He was just **such a complete absolute** idiot.]

Note that nominal groups grading non-attitudinal Things are in fact attitudinal: *quite a player* means 'a very good player'; *a bit of a singer means* 'an okay singer', and so on.

Superlatives in general do not imply high intensity: the tallest person in the room need not be very tall. But they do code high intensity when realising an Attribute in an intensive attributive relational clause (Halliday 1985a:112 ff):

You're the greatest!
She's the prettiest little thing!

Intensity is also relevant to manner adverbs, which can perhaps be treated most economically simply as incongruent adjectives (see 4.1.f above) [see Halliday (1985a:319-345) for a discussion of congruent and incongruent expression]:

(desperately)
really desperately
rather desperately
somewhat desperately
(not desperately)

c. position
(**How far** along were they?)

This system is relaised through Pre-Deictic elements and judges position in space.

(first in line)
the front of the line
the middle of the line
the end of the line
(last in line)

[He's at **the front of** the line, **the beginning, at the head** there.]

5.3 Verbal Group (Complex)

Verbal groups are gradable through hypotactic complexes oriented to the degree to which something is underway, appears to be underway or was brought about.

a. fruition — time phase (aspect)
(**How far** along are they?)

This 'aspectual' system grades processes in terms of speakers' assessments of their state of completion (cf. 4.1.h above).

(has done)
finish doing
keep doing
start doing
(not doing)

[He's just **begun to start to get going** with that project.]

b. appearance — reality phase
(How clear are you?)

This 'modal' system permits speakers to judge probability explicitly with respect to their own perception (cf. 5.1a probability above).

(is doing)
turns out to be doing (cf. it turns out we'll win)
looks to be doing (cf. it looks like we'll win)
seems to be doing (cf. it seems like we'll win)
(not doing)

[Well how **I look at** it, they **seem by all appearances** to be winning.]

c. causality
(How much pressure did you have to exert?)

This 'modulation' system measures the degree to which an Agent intervened to bring about the process (cf. 5.1c obligation above; see Halliday 1985a:265).

(did)
make x do
have x do
let x do
(not do)

[**My insisting made** John do it **through sheer pressure**.]

5.4 *Lexis*

While not systematically organised into high-median-low interpersonal values for each experiential meaning, attitude is pervasively coded throughout lexical systems. Poynton 1984 examines grading in names used as vocatives, noting clines such a *Dr Smith, William, Bill, Billy, Billikins, Petal* and so on. Vocation is clearly one very sensitive area; but attitudinal series are common elsewhere:

bad-horrible-appalling
good-great-fantastic
walk-stroll-saunter
cry-scream-howl

acquaintance-friend-lover
problem-mess-fiasco
request-order-demand
etc.

The most prosodic of all attitudinal systems is swearing, which can be realised throughout clause, group and word units:

Jesus that god-damn bastard is un-bloody-believable!

What the hell was he fucking doing down there, the bastard?

Closely related is the lexis of taboo:

penis-prick
breast-tit
urinate-piss
vomit-spew
have intercourse-fuck
perspire-sweat
etc.

And colloquial lexis is marked in many registers; note the use of scare quotes around *blow the whistle* in the ZPG text.

Attitudinal lexis will be noted in the analysis undertaken below, with degree ratings (i.e. high-median-low) assigned subjectively by the author.

For reasons of space, phonological and graphological (including formatting) realisations of interpersonal meaning, though important, will not be considered at all.

In addition interpersonal meanings which are not grammatically gradable in terms of high-median-low values have not been documented (see Labov 1972:378-393 for an more exhaustive treatment of evaluation, in narrrative of personal experience genre; Bolinger 1972 looks comprehensively at degree words in English).

6. Macro-Proposals

Consider the following (constructed) conversation:

1 A. *Hey Mary.*
2 B. — *What?*

3 A. *Can you leave me the pack?*

4 *I can do the shopping.*
5 B. *What do we need?*
6 A. *Fruit, vegies, cat food, you know.*
7 B. *Okay.*

8 A. *Don't forget.*
9 *Sam hasn't got any food.*
10 B. *— Yeah yeah yeah yeah.*

From the point of view of conversational structure this text could be described in terms of three exchanges. Basically it is a proposal and compliance — A's request for the pack and B's compliance (*Can you leave me the pack? — Okay.*) But this core proposal is further enabled in four ways:

a. A first gets B's attention (*Hey Mary. — What?*)

b. B checks to see what shopping A & B need (*What do we need? — Fruit, vegies, cat food, you know.*)
c. A last reminds B not to forget (*Don't forget. — Yeah yeah yeah yeah.*)
d. A motivates both the initial request and the reminder (*Could you leave me the pack? I can do the shopping.* and *Don't forget. Sam hasn't got any food.*)

One way to interpret this is to argue that the basic adjacency pair is supplemented by a number of dependent moves and exchanges each designed to ensure that the request for goods and services is acted upon. Diagrammatically, using Berry's (1981a, 1981b) notation for exchange structure, augmented dynamically along the lines of suggestions by Ventola 1987, the text might be represented as follows:

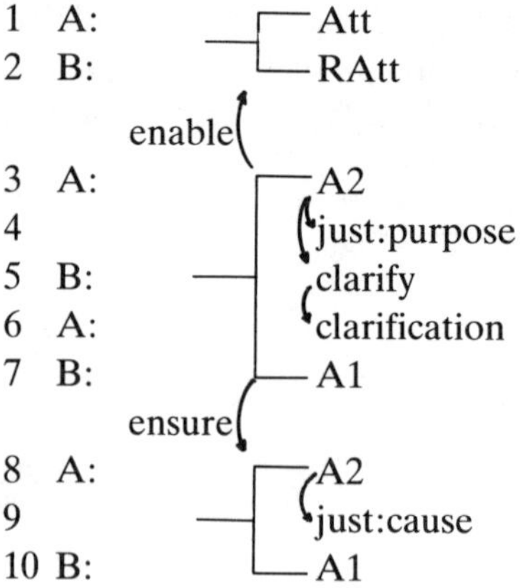

[key: Att = demanding attention; RAtt = responding to demand for attention; A2 = demanding goods and services; just = justification; A1 = complying with demand for goods and services]

[constituency relations: 1 & 2, 3 & 7, 8 & 10; dependency relations: between exchanges — 2 & 3, 7 & 8; between moves — 3 & 4, 4 & 5, 5 & 6, 8 & 9]

This diagram interprets the dialogue in terms of three constituency structures, 1-2, 3-7 and 8-10; 1-2 is dependent on 3-7, enabling the latter, while 8-10 is similarly dependent, but in an ensuring role. In the middle exchange (3-7), there are three dependent moves, justifying and clarifying the request in 3; the final exchange, 8 10, also contains a dependent justifying move.

This diagram illustrates just some of the ways in which a proposal can be elaborated, expanded and enhanced in casual dialogue, displaying some of the structure of the discourse unit exchange underlying the grammatical structure of the clause. It was in fact constructed as a model that might serve as the basis for interpretation of the ZPG text, which is not casual dialogue, but consciously constructed written monologue — a macro-proposal rather than a spoken command.

Inherently, like the model conversation above, the ZPG text is a request — a proposal, demanding goods and services (in this case money). This request is in fact realised (prosodically) several times in the text:

14.2 we urgently need your help
[you should help us as soon as possible]

16. Your support now is critical.
[you should support us now]

18. With your contribution,
[when you contribute]

22. Please make a special contribution today.
[please contribute today]

23.1 Whatever you give -- $25, $50, $100 or as much as you can --
[when you give]

30.3 by completing the enclosed reply form today

In each case the experiential meaning of reader giving money is nominalised: *your help, your support, your contribution, a special contribution, whatever you give* and less directly, *the enclosed reply form*. In terms of the transparency of the proposal, these can perhaps be ranked as follows:

22	imperative	Please make…
16	incongruent modulation	need (= 'should have')
14.2	incongruent modulation	*critical* (= 'should')
30.3	non-finite clause	*by completing…*
23.1	embedded clause	*whatever you give…*
18	prepositional phrase	*with your contribution*

Much of the text is spent justifying these (for a more detailed analysis of the reasoning involved see Mann, Matthiessen & Thompson's RST diagram in this volume):

- 14.2 in order to 14.1 (to use ZPG's UST effectively)
- 16 because 15 (we're stretched to the limit) in light of 17 (it's our best chance ever)
- 18 in order to (arm activists) because 19-21 (we can act locally to get the data to the right officials)
- 22 because 23 (we'll use it immdiately to get information to officials)
- 30 to enable 29 (monitoring the media coverage)

The proposal and justification in the P.S. (29-30) symbolise the 'do this because' structure of 14 to 23, acting as a kind of mood tag. Thus 14-30 can *be taken as* structurally parallel to a tagged imperative: *Do this, won't you?*

The function of these justifications is of course to persuade the reader to comply. The large number of justifications is no doubt due to the monologic nature of the text: predictable objections must be pre-empted whether they would arise in a particular reader's dialogue with the text or not.

Preceding sections of the text, 4-10 and 11-13 can be related to the basic proposal in terms of seeking the reader's attention and elaborating on the goods offered respectively. This allows us to re-interpret the experiential text structure proposed in section 2 above in interpersonal terms as follows:

EXPERIENTIAL	INTERPERSONAL
Involvement	Seek attention (4-10)
Product	Clarify service offered (11-13)
Appeal	Make and justify demands (14-23)
	Reminder (29-30)

And the structure of the text as a whole can be symbolised grammatically with a sentence such as:

> *Mary, leave the pack and I'll do the shopping, fruit, vegies and stuff, okay?*

This symbolises the ZPG text as follows:

Seek attention	*Mary*
Clarify service offered	*fruit, vegies and stuff*
Make demand and justify by offering a service	*leave the pack* *and I'll do the shopping*
Reminder	*okay*

These analogies between text, exchange and clause give a partial account of the way in which the ZPG text acts upon the world. But in order to act successfully it must also react — proposals implicate attitude as outlined above. This raises the question of the use of evaluative meaning in enabling the basic proposal.

7. Evaluation by Degree

A detailed analysis of evaluation in the ZPG text is given clause by clause below. [Clause Themes are in bold face and Subjects underlined, following Halliday (1985a) — starting from the left, clause constituents up to and including the first experiential one are treated as thematic; ellipsed material however has not been filled in and treated as thematic. The text has been divided into ranking clause units appropriate to a clause complex analysis; embedded (non-ranking) clauses are enclosed in double brackets. In addition a very rough transitivity analysis is provided for ranking clauses two layers of interpretation are provided for clauses involving experiential metaphor. All analyses are based on Halliday (1985a).]

As far as possible evaluation is categorised with reference to the systems outlined in section 4 above. To help clarify the categorisation, the place of each item in a high-median-low scale will be exemplified next to its categorisation.

1 ZERO POPULATION GROWTH

2 November 22, 1985

3 Dear Friend of ZPG:

[lexis: *Dear* — low; DEAR-DEAREST-DARLING
lexis: *Friend* — median; COLLEAGUE-FRIEND-LOVER]

4	**At 7:00 a.m. on October 25,**	our phones	started to ring.
	Cir:loc:time	Actor	Process:material

[fruition: *started to* — low; START TO-KEEP ON-FINISH]

5.	**Calls**	jammed	our switchboard	all day.
	Actor	Pro:mat	Goal	Cir:extent

[lexis: *jammed* — high; SPRINKLED-CLUTTERED-JAMMED
quantity: *all day* — high; NOW AND THEN-PART OF-ALL]

6.1	**Staffers**	stayed	late into the night,
	Actor	Pro:mat	Cir:extent

[quantity: *late into the night* — median; A LITTLE-AWHILE-LATE
lexis: *stayed* — median; BEGAN-STAYED-COMPLETED]

6.2	answering	questions
	Pro:beh	Range

6.3	**and**	talking	with reporters from newspapers, radio stations, wire services and TV stations in every part of the country.
		Pro:beh	Receiver

[quantity: *every part* — high; SOME-MANY-EVERY]

7.1	**When**	we	released	the results of ZPG's *1985 Urban Stress Test,*
		Behaver	Pro:beh	Range

7.2	**we**	had	no idea
	Cr	Pro:att/poss	Attr
	Senser	Process:mental........	

[quantity: *no idea* — high; no IDEA-SOME IDEA-KNEW FULL WELL]

7.3	**we**	'd get	such an overwhelming response
	Behaver	Pro:beh	Range

[intensity: *such a* — high; A BIT OF A-QUITE A-SUCH A
lexis: *overwhelming* — high; ACCEPTABLE-POSITIVE-OVERWHELMING]

8.	**Media and public reaction**	has been	nothing short of incredible.
	Carrier	Pro:att	Attribute

[quantity: *nothing short of* — high; KIND OF-QUITE-NOTHING SHORT OF
lexis: *incredible* — high; GOOD-ENCOURAGING-INCREDIBLE]
(para)

9.	**At first,**	**the deluge of calls**	came	mostly
		Actor	Pro:mat	Cir:manner

[succession: *at first* — low; AT FIRST-LATER-FINALLY
quantity: *mostly* — high; PARTLY-GENERALLY-MOSTLY
lexis: *deluge* — high; SPRINKLE-FLOOD-DELUGE

from reporters [[eager to tell the public about Urban Stress test results]] and from outraged public officials [[who were furious that we had "blown the whistle" on conditions in their cities]].
Cir:loc

[inclination: *eager* — median; WILLING-EAGER-DETERMINED
lexis: *outraged* — high; MIFFED-ANGRY-OUTRAGED
lexis: *furious* — high; MIFFED-ANGRY-FURIOUS
lexis: "*blown the whistle*" — high; REVEAL-EXPOSE-BLOW THE WHISTLE ON]

10.	**Now,**	**we**	are hearing	from concerned citizens in
		Beh	Pro:beh	Cir:loc

[succession: *now* — median; NOW-LATER-FINALLY
lexis: *concerned* — low; CONCERNED-TROUBLED-ANGUISHED

all parts of the country [[who want to know what they can do to hold public officials accountable for tackling population-related problems [[that threaten public health and well-being]]]].

[quantity: *all parts* — high; A FEW-SEVERAL-ALL
inclination: *want* — median; BE WILLING-WANT-BE DETERMINED
causality: *hold* — median; LET-HOLD-MAKE
lexis: *accountable* — median; INVOLVED-ACCOUNTABLE-RESPONSIBLE
lexis: *threaten* — median; AFFECT-THREATEN-DAMAGE
lexis: *well-being* — low; WELL-BEING-HEALTH-VIGOUR]
(para)

11.1 ***ZPG's 1985 Urban Stress Test***, ..., is
Token Pro:ident

the nation's first survey [[of how population-linked pressures affect U.S. citizens]].
Value

[fruition: first survey — low; START-KEEP-FINISH (surveying)
lexis: *pressures* — low; PRESSURE-STRESS-PROBLEM
causality: *affect* — low; AFFECT-UPSET-DAMAGE]

11.2 created after months of persistent and exhaustive research
Pro:mat Cir:loc:time

[quantity: *months of* — median; DAYS-MONTHS-YEARS
fruition: *persistent* — median; PRELIMINARY-PERSISTENT-CONCLUSIVE
lexis: *exhaustive* — high; PILOT-SYSTEMATIC-EXHAUSTIVE]

12. **It** ranks 184 urban areas
Actor Pro:mat Goal

on 11 different criteria [[ranging from crowding and birth rates to air quality and toxic wastes]].
Cir:matter

[lexis: crowding — low; CROWDING-CONGESTION-OVER-POPULATION
lexis: toxic — low; TOXIC-POISONOUS-LETHAL]

13. **The Urban Stress Test** translates complex, technical data
Actor Pro:mat Goal
Attributor Carrier

into an easy-to-use *action tool* for concerned citizens, elected officials and opinion leaders.
Cir:loc
Attribute

[lexis: *complex* — low; COMPLEX-DIFFICULT-UNREADABLE
lexis: *technical* — low; TECHNICAL-JARGONISH-UNINTERPRETABLE
lexis: *easy-to use* — low; EASY-TO USE-PERSONALISED-CUSTOMISED
lexis: *concerned* — low; CONCERNED-TROUBLED-ANGUISHED]

14.1 *But* to use it well,
Pro:mat Rg Cir:manner

[lexis: *well* — median; POSITIVELY-WELL-TO GET THE BEST OUT OF IT

14.2	**we**	urgently	need	your help
	Senser	Cir:manner	Pro:ment	Phenomenon
	Carrier		Pro:att/poss	Attribute

[immediacy: *urgently* — high; EVENTUALLY-SOON-URGENTLY
obligation: *need* — median 'should have'; COULD USE-NEED-MUST HAVE
(para)

15.1	***Our small staff***	*is being swamped*
	Goal	Pro:mat

with requests for more information
Actor

[lexis: *small* — low; SMALL-MODEST-NUMEROUS
lexis: *swamped* — high; SPRINKLED-SOAKED-SWAMPED
lexis: *request* — low; REQUEST-CALL-DEMAND

15.2	**and**	**our modest resources**	*are being stretched*
		Goal	*Pro:mat*

to the limit.
Cir:extent

[lexis: *modest* — low; MODEST-LIMITED-LIMITLESS
lexis: *stretched* — median; EXTEND-STRETCH-OVEREXTEND
quantity: *to the limit* — high; SOMEWHAT-SEVERELY-TO THE LIMIT]
(para)

16.	**Your support**	now	is	critical.
	Carrier	Cir:loc	Pro:attr	Attribute

[immediacy: *now* — high; EVENTUALLY-SOMETIME-NOW
obligation: *critical* — median; USEFUL-CRITICAL-ESSENTIAL (cf. *could use-should have-must have*)

17.	**ZPG's 1985 Urban Stress Test**	may be
	Token	Pro:id

our best opportunity ever [[to get the population message heard]].
Value

[probability: *may* — low; MAY-WILL-HAS TO
intensity: *best* — high; RATHER GOOD-QUITE GOOD-BEST
immediacy: *ever* — high; FOR NOW-FOR AWHILE-EVER
causality: *get* — median; LET-GET-ENSURE]
(page, para)

18.	**With your contribution**,	ZPG	can arm
	Cir:manner:means	Actor	Pro:mat

[lexis: arm — median; EQUIP-ARM-FORTIFY

our growing network of local activists	with the materials [[they need to warn community leaders about emerging population-linked stresses *before* they reach crisis stage]].
Goal	Cir:manner:instrument

[lexis: *activist* — median; PARTICIPANT-ACTIVIST-PROTAGONIST
obligation: *need* — median; COULD USE-NEED-MUST HAVE
lexis: *warn* — median; ALERT-WARN-FRIGHTEN
lexis: *stresses* — low; PRESSURE-STRESS-PROBLEM
fruition: *reach* — high; HEAD FOR-APPROACH-REACH
lexis: *crisis* — high; IRRITATION-PROBLEM-CRISIS]
(para)

19.1	**Even though**	**our national government**
		Behaver

continues to ignore	the consequences of uncontrolled population growth,
Pro:beh	Range

[fruition: *continues to* — median; BEGIN TO-CONTINUE TO-END UP
lexis: *uncontrolled* — median; BURGEONING-UNCONTROLLED-RAMPANT]

19.2	**we**	*can act*
	Actor	Pro:mat

19.3	*to take*	*positive action*	*at the local level.*
	Pro:mat	Range	Cir:loc:space

[lexis: *positive* — median; USUFUL-POSITIVE-EFFECTIVE]
(para)

20.	**Every day**	decisions…	are being made
	Cir:extent	Range	Pro:beh

[quantity: *every day* — high; SOME-MANY MOST

by local officials in our communities
Behaver

[[…that could drastically affect the quality of our lives]]

[commitment: *drastically* — high; IN PART-RATHER-DRASTICALLY
causality: *affect* — low; AFFECT-UPSET-DAMAGE]

21.1 **To make** sound choices in planning for people,
Pro:beh Range Cir:loc

[lexis: *sound* — low; SOUND-INSIGHTFUL-WISE]

21.2 **both elected officals and the American public**
Carrier

need the population-stess data [[revealed by our study]].
Pro:poss Attribute

[obligation: *need* — median; COULD USE-NEED-MUST HAVE
lexis: *revealed* — low; REVEAL-EXPOSE-BLOW THE WHISTLE]
(para)

22. **Please** **make** a special contribution
Pro:mat Range

to Zero Population Growth today.
Recipient Cir:loc:time

[lexis: *special* — median; HELPFUL-SPECIAL-GENEROUS]

23.1 **[[Whatever you give]] -- $25, $50, $100 or as much [[as you can]] --**
Range

will be used immediately
Pro:mat Cir:loc:time

[quantity: *whatever* — high; A LITTLE OF-SOME OF-WHATEVER
quantity: *as much as* — high; A LITTLE OF-SOME OF-AS MUCH AS
immediacy: *immediately* — high; EVENTUALLY-LATER-IMMEDIATELY]

23.2 **to put** the Urban Stress Test in the hands of those [[who need it most]].
Pro:mat Goal Cir:loc

[obligation: *need* — median; COULD USE-NEED-MUST HAVE
quantity: *most* — high; A LITTLE-SOMEWHAT-MOST]

24. Sincerely,

[lexis: sincerely — median; LOVE-SINCERELY-YOURS SINCERELY]

25. (handwritten signature)

[lexis: Susan Weber — median; SUE-SUSAN WEBER-MS S WEBER]

26. Susan Weber

[lexis: *Susan Weber* — median; SUE-SUSAN WEBER-MS S WEBER]

27. Executive Director

[lexis: *Executive Director* — high; ASSISTANT DIRECTOR-DIRECTOR-EXECUTIVE DIRECTOR]

28. P.S.

29. **The results of ZPG's 1985 Urban Stress Test**
Range

were reported	as a top news story
Pro:beh	Cir:role

[lexis: *top* — median; LEADING-TOP-FEATURE

by hundreds of newspapers and TV and radio stations from coast to coast.
Behaver

[quantity: *hundreds of* — median; NUMEROUS-HUNDREDS OF-THOUSANDS OF]

30.1	**I**	hope
	Senser	Pro:ment

[inclination: *hope* — median; BE WILLING-HOPE-BE DETERMINED]

30.2	**you**	'll help	us	monitor
	Agent		Behaver	Pro:beh

this remarkable media coverage
Range

[causality: *help* — low; HELP-HAVE-MAKE
lexis: *remarkable* — median; NOTABLE-REMARKABLE-INCREDIBLE]

30.3	**by**	completing	the enclosed reply form.
		Pro:beh	Range

Overall the realisation of attitude throughout the text is fairly evenly distributed — between two and three evaluations per clause. However the distribution of high, median and low values is not even; nor is the distribution by type random. Interestingly enough, very little attitude is realised in either the Subject or Theme:

	THEME		SUBJECT
	textual	topical	
1			
2			
3			
4		*At 7 am on Oct 25*	*our phones*
5		*Calls*	*Calls*
6.1		*Staffers*	*Staffers*
6.2		*(answering)*	
6.3	*and*		
7.1	*When*	*we*	*we*
7.2		*we*	*we*
7.3		*we*	*we*
8		*Media & public reaction*	*Media and…*
9	*at first*	*the deluge of calls*	*the deluge..*
10	*now*	*we*	*we*
11.1		*ZPG's 1985 UST…,*	*ZPG's 1985..*
11.2		*(created)*	
12		*It*	*It*
13		*The Urban Stress Test*	*The Urban…*
14.1	*But*	*(to use)*	
14.2		*we*	*we*
15		*Our small staff*	*Our small…*
16		*Your support*	*Your support*
17		*ZPG's 1985 UST*	*ZPG's 1985..*
18		*With your contribution*	*ZPG*
19.1	*Even though*	*Our national government*	*Our national*
19.2		*we*	*we*
19.3		*(to take)*	
20		*Every day*	*decisions*
21.1		*(To make)*	
21.2		*Both elected officials & the American public*	*Both elected officials &*
22	*Please*	*(make)*	
23.1		*Whatever you give…*	*Whatever…*
23.2		*(to put)*	
24			
25			

26		
27		
28		
29	*The results of ZPG's UST*	*The results*
30.1	*I*	*I*
30.2	*you*	*you*
30.3 *by*	*(completing)*	

As far as the high, median and low values are concerned, the basic pattern is as follows (**only major clauses in the body of the text are considered in the figures given below; segments 1-3 and 24-30, including the P.S. are not included**):

	HIGH	MEDIAN	LOW
Involvement (11 clauses; clauses 4-10)	15	9	4
Product (4 clauses; clauses 11-13)	1	2	9
Appeal (16 clauses; clauses 14-23)	15	15	7
total	**31**	**26**	**20**

Both the Involvement and Appeal stages favor high values over low, with the reverse being true in the Product element. The Involvement stage in particular foregrounds high values, with a 3/1 ratio of these to median ones.

	HIGH	LOW
Involvement	*jammed*	*started to*
	all day	*at first*
	late into the night	*concerned*
	every part	*well-being*
	no idea	
	such an	
	overwhelming	
	nothing short of	
	incredible	
	mostly	
	deluge	
	outraged	
	furious	

	"blown the whistle"	
	all parts	
Product	*exhaustive*	*first*
		pressures
		affect
		crowding
		toxic wastes
		complex
		technical
		easy-to-use
		concerned

The rhetorical strategy here seems to be to react strongly when trying to get the reader to act — first of all to read the text and then to send money. A less subjective pose is adopted to present the product itself — the ZPG's UST. This amplification pattern can be sketched graphically as follows:

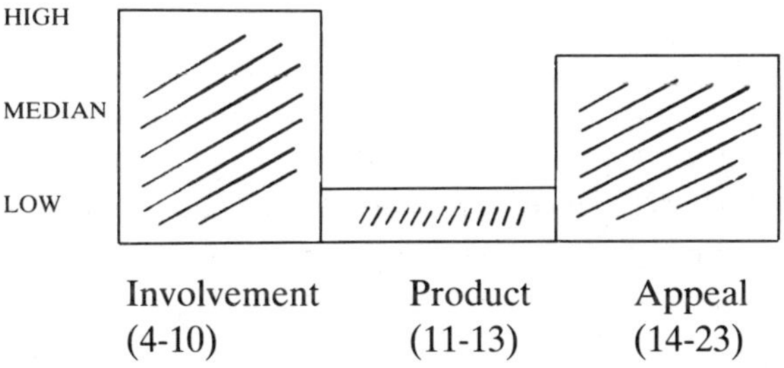

A more detailed breakdown, including type is as follows:

	HIGH		MEDIAN		LOW	
Involvement	quantity	7	lexis	4	lexis	2
	lexis	7	inclination	2	fruition	1
	intensity	1	quantity	1	succession	1
			causality	1		
			succession	1		
Product	lexis	1	quantity	1	lexis	7
			fruition	1	causality	1
					succession	1

Appeal	quantity	4	lexis	8	lexis	5
	immediacy	4	obligation	5	causality	1
	lexis	4	fruition	1	prob..ity	1
	intensity	1	causality	1		
	fruition	1				
	commitment	1				

TOTALS

lexis	**38**
quantity	**13**
obligation	**5**
immediacy	**4**
fruition	**4**
causality	**4**
succession	**3**
inclination	**2**
intensity	**2**
commitment	**1**
probability	**1**

Overall, just under half the evaluation is realised lexically. In interpreting this pattern it is important to take into account the large number of nominalised processes in the text. Once nominalised these are evaluated using nominal group rather than clause or verbal group resources — especially attitudinal Epithets:

such an overwhelming response
persistent and exhaustive research
easy-to-use action tool
modest resources
uncontrolled growth
positive action
sound choices
special contribution
remarkable media coverage

These incongruent processes also appear in attributive relational processes:

The reaction has been nothing short of incredible
your support now is critical

And they themselves appear as participants associated with attitudinal processes:

calls jammed
swamped by requests
threaten public health and well-being

Nominalisation is a distinctive feature of writing (see Halliday 1985a; 1985b on lexical density and grammatical intricacy in spoken and written language) and so one factor influencing the high degree of lexical evaluation may be the number of nominalised processes in the text. On the other hand, one might argue that a large number of processes are so nominalised so that nominal group resources for coding attitude can be brought to bear (the advantage being that attitudinal adjectives are far and away English's largest open class of evaluative items). Some nominalised processes are also quantified:

no idea
months of...research

Quantity is in fact the next largest category of evaluation in the text:

all day, late into the night, every part of the country, no idea, nothing short of incredible, came mostly, all parts of the country, months of...research, to the limit, every day, whatever, as much as, need it most, hundreds of

And this list does not include the following lexical items, with a clear quantitative implication: *swamped, small, stretched, overwhelming, jammed, deluge*. Taken together the maximisers account for just over half the high value evaluations in the text. Rhetorically the argument seems to be: "we're doing as much as we can, so you give as much as you can."

The other distinctive patterns have to do with the association of immediacy (urgently, now, ever, immediately) and obligation (*need, critical, need, need, need*) with the Appeal section. The argument here is that readers should act right away to give money:

we urgently need your help
your support now is critical

And if they do, ZPG will act right away to get the UST results to the people who should have it.

In short then, the reaction in the text is designed to support the action. High values are foregrounded in the Involvement section to attract the reader's attention. Low values are foregrounded in the Product section to lend credibility to the test results. Then median and high values, foregrounding immediacy and obligation, are used to strengthen the Appeal.

8. Interpersonal Structure and Genre

In this paper an attempt was made to analyse the ZPG fund raising text in interpersonal terms. Both the acting and reacting aspects of interpersonal meaning were considered. With respect to action it was suggested that the text could be conceived as a macro-proposal, realised through, and symbolically related to, exchange structure at the level of discourse and imperative mood in grammar:

GENRE	EXCHANGE	CLAUSE
Seek attention	call	vocative
Clarify Service Offered	clarification	elaborating taxis
Make & Justify Demands	command & justification	imperative; enhancing taxis
Reminder	ensurance	mood tag

With respect to reaction it was suggested that the distribution of evaluative meaning through the text was not random. High values were used to seek attention and make and justify demands, while low values were associated with clarifying the service offered. In addition, immediacy and obligation were foregrounded to make and justify demands.

The realisation of both action and reaction was shown to be prosodic rather than particulate. The basic proposal, that the reader send money, was realised no less than 6 times in the text. And reaction was realised 77 times, across a wide range of clause, nominal group and verbal group structures.

One immediate implication of these findings would seem to be that Halliday's (eg. 1978) metafunctional interpretation of clause structure in relation to situation needs to be projected back not simply through register categories but on to the level of genre as well:

GENRE	REGISTER	METAFUNCTION
constituent structure	field	experiential
prosodic structure	tenor	interpersonal
(culminative structure)	mode	textual
(dynamic structure)	?	logical

A second implication may be that as far as interpersonal meaning is concerned text will turn out to be a powerful source of metaphors for interpreting the clause. The non-discrete realisation of interpersonal meaning in the ZPG text is clear. And even more clear is that fact that the text depends critically on this meaning to achieve its ends. From the point of view of genre the meanings and structures associated with action and reaction are not something that can be relegated to pragmatics. They are structured into the text, and to get there they have somewhere to be structured into lexicogrammar. Projecting text onto clause along these lines challenges many formal linguists preoccupation with constituency patterns. Successfully mounting this challenge is long overdue.

References

Berry, M.

1981a "Systemic linguistics and discourse analysis: a multi-layered approach to exchange structure." In M. Coulthard, and M. Montgomery, (eds), *Studies in Discourse Analysis*. London: Routledge & Kegan Paul, 120-145.

1981b "Towards layers of exchange structure for directive exchanges." *Network* 2.23-32.

Bolinger, D.

1972 *Degree Words*. (*Janua Linguarum Series Maior* 53), The Hague: Mouton.

Halliday, M.A.K.

1970 "Functional diversity in language as seen from a consideration of modality and mood in English." *Foundations of Language* 6.3. 322-361. [reprinted in G. Kress (ed.), 1976, *Halliday: system and function in language*. London: Oxford University Press, 1976:189-213.]

1971 "Linguistic function and literary style: An inquiry into the language of William Golding's *The Inheritors*." In S. Chatman, (ed.), *Literary Style: A Symposium*.

London: Oxford University Press, 362-400. [reprinted in M.A.K. Halliday, *Explorations in the Functions of Language*. London: Edward Arnold, 1973:103-143.]

1979 "Modes of meaning and modes of expression: Types of grammatical structure, and their determination by different semantic functions." In D.J. Allerton, E. Carney, and D. Holdcraft, (eds), *Function and Context in Linguistic Analysis: A Festschrift for William Haas*. London: Cambridge Univerity Press, 57-79.

1982 "How is a text like a clause?" In S. Allen, (ed.), *Text Processing: Text Analysis and Generation, Text Typology and Attribution*. Stockholm: Almqvist & Wiskell International, 209-247.

1985a *An Introduction to Functional Grammar*. London: Edward Arnold.

1985b *Spoken and Written Language*. Geelong, Vic.: Deakin University Press. [republished by Oxford University Press, 1989]

Hasan, R.

1977 "Text in the systemic-functional model." In W. Dressler, (ed.), *Current Trends in Textlinguistics*. Berlin: Walter de Gruyter, 228-246.

1979 "On the notion of text." In J.S. Petofi, (ed.), *Text vs. Sentence: Basic Questions of Textlinguistics*. Hamburg: Helmut Buske, 369-390.

1984 "The nursery tale as a genre." *Nottingham Linguistic Circular*. 13,71-102.

Labov, W.

1982 "The transformation of experience in narrative syntax." *Language in the Inner City: Studies in the Black English Vernacular*. Philadelphia: University of Pennsylvania Press, 354-396.

Martin, J.R.

1984a "Language, register and genre." In F. Christie, (ed.), *Children Writing: Reader*. Geelong, Vic.: Deakin University Press, 21-29.

1984b "Functional components in a grammar: A review of deployable recognition criteria." *Nottingham Linguistic Circular* 13,35-70.

1985a "Process and text: two aspects of human semiosis." In J.D. Benson, and W.S. Greaves, (eds), *Systemic Perspectives on Discourse, Vol. 1*. Norwood, N.J.: Ablex, 248-274.

1985b *Factual Writing: Exploring and Challenging Social Reality*. Geelong, Vic.: Deakin University Press. [republished by Oxford University Press 1989]

1986 "Intervening in the process of writing development." In C. Painter, and J.R. Martin, (eds), *Writing to Mean: Teaching Genres Across the Curriculum. Applied Linguistics Association of Australia* (Occasional Papers 9), 11-43.

Matthiessen, C.

1988 "Representational issues in systemic functional grammar." In J.D. Benson, and W.S. Greaves, (eds), *Systemic Functional Approaches to Discourse*. Norwood, NJ: Ablex, 136-175.

Mitchell, T.F.
1957 "The language of buying and selling in Cyrenaica: a situational statement." *Hesperis* 26,31-71. [Reprinted in T.F. Mitchell, *Principles of Firthian Linguistics*. London: Longman, 1975:167-200].

Poynton, C.
1984 "Names as vocatives: forms and functions." *Nottingham Linguistic Circular*. 13,1-34.

1985 *Language and Gender: Making the Difference*. Geelong, Vic.: Deakin University Press. [republished by Oxford University Press, 1989]

Quirk, R., S. Greenbaum, G. Leech, and J. Svartvik
1972 *A Grammar of Contemporary English*. London: Longman.

Sapir, E.
1944 "Grading: a study in senantics." *Philosophy of Science* 11. 93-116. [Reprinted in D.G. Mandelbaum (ed.), *Selected Writings of Edward Sapir in Language, Culture and Personality*. Berkeley: University of California Press, 1949:122-149.

Sinclair, J. McH. and R.M. Coulthard
1975 *Towards an Analysis of Discourse: The English used by teachers and pupils*. London: Oxford University Press.

Ventola, E.
1987 *The Structure of Social Interaction: A Systemic Approach to the Semiotics of Service Encounters*. London: Pinter.

Collocation and Field of Discourse*

James D. Benson and William S. Greaves
Glendon College, York University

In this chapter we use CLOC (Reed 1977, 1984), a computer package which finds collocations (co-occurrences of words in a text), as a means of locating structures which we then parse in terms of systemic functional grammar (Halliday 1985a). These grammatical structures are the realization of register, i.e. semantic choices of three different kinds: ideational, interpersonal, and textual (Halliday 1985a). Register meanings are themselves determined by the components of the context of situation at the semiotic level: field, tenor, and mode of discourse. Ideational meanings realize field, interpersonal meanings realize tenor, and textual meanings realize mode (Halliday 1978: 108-126). Because the lexical end of the lexico-grammatical continuum is sensitive to register, the collocational patterns picked up by CLOC allow us to identify the register of the ZPG letter, i.e. the ideational, interpersonal and textual strands of meaning, and to compare these to meanings in a corpus of 19 other fundraising letters and 1 newspaper opinion piece by an officer of ZPG (Appendix 1).

Our study examines the ZPG letter in two contexts. First, 19 other letters were selected because we recognized them as belonging to the same register as the ZPG letter. The writers were engaged in fundraising on behalf of specific organizations (field); they began by explaining the accomplishments of their organizations, but concluded with a 'pitch' (tenor); they were not speaking, but writing either letters or memoranda to specific addressees (mode). The second context was provided by an opinion

*The authors will be glad to make CLOC available to other academic users at a nominal cost. A machine readable version of the corpus of letters is also available.

piece, which originated from the same organization, as the author was a Past President of Zero Population Growth. The opinion piece was selected because the register was different, i.e. there was only one field, and it was not fundraising; the tenor didn't shift, i.e. the writer remained an expert on his subject from beginning to end, demanding agreement from his audience but not action; and the mode was even more written, i.e. it lacked the slight conversational flavor associated with many letters.

By comparing the the ZPG letter with the corpus, and then with the opinion piece, we are able to show that fundraising is the primary field of the letter. Individual analyses of the ZPG letter and the opinion piece show that there is a single primary field in the opinion piece, and a three-part secondary field in the ZPG letter. Moreover, 'population growth' has different meanings in the ZPG letter and the opinion piece, since it occupies a place in different taxonomies, which can be seen primarily in nominal group structure. Finally, we argue that, in the ZPG letter, the secondary fields provide a context strong enough to make the 'pitch' not seem like a radical shift in field.

The 'pitch' clause in the ZPG letter, 'Please make a special contribution to Zero Population Growth today' illustrates how field, tenor and mode are realized semantically as register, which in turn is realized in lexico-grammar. In terms of ideational meaning, the primary field of fundraising is realized by a Material Process ('make') together with associated Participants, an Actor ('you'), a Range ('a special contribution'), a Beneficiary ('ZPG'), and, finally, a Circumstance ('today'). The Process is realized metaphorically rather than congruently (Halliday 1985a: 319-342), i.e. 'contributing' is not coded directly as a Process (i.e. 'contribute'), but nominalized as 'contribution'. In terms of interpersonal meaning, the tenor is realized by the speech function command ('make') and by a politeness marker ('Please'). In terms of textual meaning, the mode is realized by the relatively high lexical density (Halliday 1985b) of the clause, with 'Please' plus the imperative 'make' as an appropriate point of departure for this particular message.

Because it is the theme of the 'pitch' clause, we have taken 'please' as our own point of departure in the corpus, and have used CLOC to study its collocational patterning there. CLOC works with orthographic words bounded by space or other word separators defined by the user. The user defines a node to be investigated, and the program finds the words that co-occur with the node within a given span. For the purposes of this study, we

Table 1: Wide span (0 by 24) collocates of 'please' in corpus

node	collocate	pair
34 please	16 sincerely	6
34 please	28 children	5
34 please	20 gift	8
34 please	14 send	10
34 please	36 today	14
34 please	39 support	5
34 please	59 $	8
34 please	50 help	8
34 please	9 generous	6
34 please	17 contribution	6

restrict our interest in collocation to words on the lexical end of the lexico-grammatical continuum, and therefore place many words at the 'grammatical' end of the continuum on an exclusion list, among them determiners, pronouns, modal operators, prepositions, and all forms of 'to be' and 'to have'. CLOC examines all words not excluded, and finds the collocates of designated nodes ('please' in this case) within a particular span and with a particular frequency of co-occurrence.

To get a sense of the lexical company 'please' keeps, we asked CLOC to find the lexical collocates of this node in the corpus within a span of 24 words to the right of the node, and to report the co-occurrence if it happened 5 or more times. The results are displayed in Table 1. The second line of the table, for example, tells us that there are 34 tokens of the node 'please' in the corpus, that there are 16 tokens of the collocate 'sincerely', and that these items collocate 6 times within a span of 24 words.

Looking at the other collocates of 'please' in the table, we see that the consistency of register between the ZPG letter and the corpus is obvious. Ideationally, 'gift', 'send', 'support', '$', 'help', and 'generous' go with 'contribution' as integral to fundraising as an activity. 'Children' hints at a Beneficiary, and ZPG's Circumstance 'today' is repeated 36 times, 14 of those in collocation with 'please'. Interpersonally, 'send' and 'help' are commands, and textually, 'sincerely' realizes a feature of a letter.

Since the corpus of letters plus the opinion piece contains lexical words realizing the same register as ZPG, the next question is how these are distributed. We therefore take these collocates of 'Please' and treat them as a list

Table 2: Frequency of fundraising vocabulary in corpus

letter M	children	contribution	generous	gift	help	send	sincerely	support	today	$
letter A	15	0	1	2	5	1	1	2	1	2
letter B	11	1	0	5	2	1	0	1	1	2
letter C	2	4	1	1	1	3	1	3	4	0
letter D	2	3	2	3	12	2	1	5	3	7
letter E	2	1	1	2	1	1	1	5	1	5
letter F	1	1	1	0	1	1	1	0	2	0
letter G	0	2	0	1	4	1	1	0	3	4
letter H	0	1	1	3	0	1	1	1	0	0
letter I	0	1	0	0	2	0	1	1	1	1
letter J	0	1	1	0	7	1	1	8	2	4
letter K	0	2	1	2	6	1	1	1	5	2
letter L	0	2	1	2	3	0	1	2	1	8
letter M	0	3	1	2	5	2	0	0	2	2
letter N	0	0	1	1	2	3	1	1	1	0
letter O	0	0	2	4	7	0	1	1	2	0
text P	0	0	0	4	0	0	0	2	2	12
letter Q	0	0	0	5	0	2	1	4	4	7
letter R	0	0	0	3	1	0	1	1	1	3
letter S	0	0	0	0	2	0	0	1	0	0
letter T	0	0	0	0	0	1	1	6	0	0

of vocabulary items, but first we expand the list to cater to congruency and grammatical metaphor, including, for example, the congruent verb forms ‘give’/‘gives’/‘giving’/‘gave’/‘given’ along with the metaphorical nominalization ‘gift’. CLOC’s index of these items is presented in Table 2.

We can see from Table 2 that with the exception of ‘children’, the vocabulary of the field of fundraising is distributed quite evenly throughout the corpus. We can detect a heavy hand vs. a light touch, given that 9 letters use both ‘contribution’ *and* ‘gift’, whereas 8 letters use ‘contribution’ *or* ‘gift’. In the same vein, letter D contrasts with, say, letter A in using many more tokens of the types of fundraising vocabulary. None of this is particularly surprising, of course, since we included letters in the corpus *because* we judged them to be fundraising letters. But there are three texts which Table 2 shows as somewhat different: letters S and T, which use only 2 and 3 of the 9 available word types, and text P, the opinion piece, which uses only 4 of the 9 available word types.

Table 3: Collocates of 'support' in Letter T

node	collocate	pair
6 support	2 renew	2
6 support	3 annual	3
6 support	4 friend	2
6 support	3 past	2

Table 4: Collocates of 'help' and 'support' in Letter S

node	collocate	pair
2 help	1 grateful	1
2 help	1 relying	1
2 help	1 continued	1
1 support	1 private	1
1 support	1 clubs	1
1 support	1 loyalty	1
1 support	1 made	1

Table 5: Collocates of '$' in Text P ('opinion' piece)

node	collocate	pair
3 given	18 population	2
12 $	8 billion	8
12 $	5 savings	2
12 $	2 japan's	2
12 $	8 percent	2
12 $	2 invested	2
12 $	2 works	2
12 $	3 new	2
12 $	2 worker	2
12 $	4 investment	2
12 $	3 equipment	2

We shall look at each of these texts. Although letter T does not contain 'contribution', 'gift', 'help' or '$', it does use 'support' 6 times, and we can use CLOC again to study the collocational patterning that the word has in the letter. The kind of 'support' this is can be seen in Table 3, which displays its collocates within a span of 4 by 4, and with a frequency of co-occurrence with the node of 2 or more times.

We see that 'support' in this text is squarely within the field of fundraising, with its annual appeals for friends who gave in the past to renew their support. Similarly, the kind of 'help' and 'support' which are involved in letter S can be seen in Table 4, in which the span is 4 by 4, although the frequency of co-occurrence threshold of node and collocate has been lowered to 1 owing to the shortness of the text.

Once again we are undoubtedly in the field of fundraising, in which gratitude for and reliance on the continued help of loyal supporters figures prominently.

This leaves text P, the opinion piece. From the evidence in Table 2 alone, text P looks more like the other fundraising letters than letters S and T, since it has 4 common items, and they have only 3. But what, in fact, do the 2 most frequent items mean in this text? Are the '$' of text P fundraising '$', and is the 'gift' a 'contribution' to a cause? Collocation, again, gives an indication. Table 5 displays the collocates found by CLOC, within a span of 4 by 4, and with a frequency of co-occurrence of node and collocate of 2 or more times.

Clearly the '$' of text P are not fundraising '$', nor does the 'gift' of text P have anything to do with fundraising. Our next step is to see what '$' does mean in text P — in other words, to determine just what field it is realizing.

The opinion piece (i.e. text P) and the ZPG letter do not share the field of fundraising. They are both, however, in some sense 'about' population growth. We ask the question whether the secondary field of the ZPG letter is the same as the primary field of the opinion piece? In order to answer the question, we make an analysis of the two texts in terms of narrow span collocations, i.e. node collocate pairs within a span of 0 by 1 (CLOC looks at no collocates at all on the left, and only the first collocate on the right). We select the nodes by making a list of every lexical word in each text. In the case of the opinion piece, we have limited the output to cases where a collocation occurs at least twice. The results are displayed in Table 6.

Except for 'Canada's immigration' (which is Possessive Deictic Classifier in 'Canada's immigration policy'), and 'invested $' (which is a Material Process Range structure at the clause level), all of the collocations can be parsed as Classifier Thing structures, in which the Classifier 'indicates a

Table 6: Narrow span collocations (0 by 1) of Text P ('opinion' piece) showing primary field of economics

node	collocate	pair
7 canadas	5 immigration	2
5 capital	2 deepening	2
2 growing	18 population	2
5 immigration	3 policy	2
2 invested	12 $	2
2 labor	3 force	2
4 national	5 savings	2
3 new	2 worker	2
8 percapita	2 income	2
18 population	5 growth	3
3 resource	3 base	2
5 savings	2 rate	2
12 $	8 billion	4

particular subclass of the thing in question' (Halliday 1985a: 164). We recognize not only the vocabulary typical of economists but the taxonomy of economists, and consequently we can say that the primary field of the opinion piece is economics. This means that the meaning of 'population growth' is determined by the field (Benson and Greaves 1981); in this text and in this register 'population growth' must be understood in terms of economics (or misunderstood by not being understood in terms of economics).

The situation is quite different when we look at the secondary field of the ZPG letter. Owing to its brevity, we have altered the procedure slightly by treating 'urban-stress-test' as a single lexical item, rather than as 3 separate words, and by reducing the frequency threshold from 2 node collocate pairs to 1. The results are displayed in Table 7.

The collocations which occur 2 or more times are: 'concerned citizens', 'elected officials', 'local officials', 'radio stations', and 'zpg's urban stress test'. The first three Classifier Thing structures (one subclass of 'citizens' and two subclasses of 'officials') fit together as part of a taxonomy of government/politics. The last two structures, Classifier Thing and Possessive Deictic Thing, respectively, do not seem to fit with the first three or with each other. This suggests that there may in fact be three possibly related secondary fields. The collocations which occur only once reinforce the designation of the government/politics field, and suggest two additional

Table 7: Narrow span collocations (0 by 1) of ZPG letter showing secondary fields politics/government, communications/media medical research, and primary field fundraising

node	collocate	pair
2 concerned	2 citizens	2
2 elected	5 officials	2
4 local	5 officials	2
2 action	1 tool	1
2 citizens	2 elected	1
2 day	1 decisions	1
4 local	1 activists	1
4 local	1 level	1
2 make	1 sound	1
5 officials	1 accountable	1
5 public	5 officials	1
5 public	4 need	1
2 radio	3 stations	2
2 calls	1 jammed	1
2 calls	1 came	1
2 day	1 staffers	1
2 media	1 coverage	1
2 newspapers	2 radio	1
2 population	1 message	1
5 public	1 reaction	1
2 reporters	1 eager	1
3 stations	1 wire	1
2 tv	3 stations	1
4 zpg's	7 urbanstresstest	4
2 data	1 revealed	1
2 population	1 growth	1
2 populationlinked	1 pressures	1
2 populationlinked	1 stresses	1
5 public	1 health	1
7 urbanstresstest	3 results	1
7 urbanstresstest	1 created	1
7 urbanstresstest	1 translates	1
2 contribution	4 zpg	1
4 zpg	1 november	1
4 zpg	1 today	1

fields, communications/media and medical research, which are hinted at in 'radio stations' and 'zpg's urban stress test'. We can assign the following Classifer Thing structures to the government/politics field: 'action tool', 'local activists', 'local level, and 'public officials'. There is also a Carrier Relational Possessive Process structure, 'public need', which is a congruent realization of the field. Although they are relevant to this field, we leave the remaining collocations ('citizens elected', 'day decisions', 'make sound', and 'officials accountable') unanalyzed, since they are parts of structures that are not immediately transparent.

Continuing with the one-time collocations, 'radio stations' can now be seen as fitting in with Classifier Thing structures which belong to the field of communciations/media: 'media coverage', 'population message', 'public reaction', and 'tv stations'. In addition, we can include the following Actor Material Process structures as realizations of the field: 'calls jammed', 'calls came'. Again, we leave a few pairs ('day staffers', 'newspapers radio', 'reporters eager', 'stations wire') unanalyzed.

Similarly, other Classifier Thing structures line up with 'zpg's urban stress test' in a third field, medical research: 'population growth', 'population-linked pressures', 'population-linked stresses', 'public health', and 'urban stress test results'. Here, too, we find realizations of the field in the Goal Material Process structures 'data revealed', 'urban stress test created', and the Actor Material Process structure 'urban stress test translates'.

The collocations 'contribution zpg', 'zpg november', and 'zpg today', of course, are realizations of the primary field of fundraising.

In the final analysis, then, 'population growth' is understood quite differently in the ZPG letter and the opinion piece. In ZPG 'population growth' is not part of an economic taxonomy; rather, it is part of an interlocking set of taxonomies from government/politics, communications/media, and medical research. 'Population growth' is a phenomenon that can be studied, and the results of such studies can be communicated to the public which in turn brings this knowledge to bear in the arena of democratic representative institutions. The data of the 'Urban Stress Test Results' (medical research) are the 'action tool' (government/politics) used by 'concerned citizens' (government/politics) to get the 'population message' out (communications/media) to 'elected officials' and the like (government/politics). Among recipients of the ZPG letter, potential donors are assumed to be ideologically and emotionally in tune with these fields and with the way they interact, especially politically. The three secondary fields, then, work together both to assume and to foster a climate of solidarity between the participants in the exchange, within which making a donation will be understood as part of political activity.

The 'pitch' which the potential donors are fed is only the tip of an institutional iceberg. Below the surface there are books on fundraising, seminars on fundraising, consultants specializing in fundraising, and within large institutions there are whole segments of the administrative hierarchy devoted to this activity. These fundraisers create their own taxonomies in which 'population growth', for example might be a Classifer in a 'population growth fundraising campaign'. There are books, reports, and seminars through which the 'science' of extracting money in this way is developed and promoted, but when it comes to actually raising funds, all this is hidden from view. Since fundraising is ultimately a reciprocal activity between sender and receiver of the message, in which the sender's command should cause the receiver to make an offer, any hint of the sophisticated manipulative activity to which the receiver was reacting would be counterproductive; the audience's attention should be firmly drawn to the 'surface' provided by the secondary field.

Since this study treats mainly field, it is not surprising that we have had little to say about genre. Both texts are written by strongly committed people, and both involve persuasion, but in Martin's (1985: 17) terms the genres differ. The genre of the opinion piece is 'Analytical Exposition', the function of which is 'to persuade readers *that* the Thesis is well formulated', the thesis in this case being expressed in the rhetorical question 'Should Canada get bigger or better?'. The genre of the ZPG letter is 'Hortatory Exposition', the function of which is 'to persuade the reader to *do* what the Thesis recommends', the thesis in this case being 'Please make a special contribution to Zero Population Growth today'. Whatever the relation between register and genre may turn out to be, a disputed point in systemic linguistics today, we have shown that field can be isolated as a variable. CLOC, when used with a grammar which is hospitable to the description of discourse, can help to untangle very complex strands of ideational, interpersonal and textual meaning.

Appendix: Should Canada Get Bigger, or Better?

by John Meyers

Over the past year, members of Parliament have been under pressure from constituents to tighten controls on refugees in particular and immigration in general. The refugee controversy has brought to a head the frustration many people feel at Canada's immigration policy and ever-growing population.

The frustration is due to one factor: leadership. There isn't any.

There is no over-all population policy for Canada. Without a target, immigration can't be integrated into a long-term plan. It remains a knee-jerk mechanism manipulated for political reasons. The difference now is that the public has both eyes open.

Canadian leaders are in a quandary because the conditions that gave rise to the country's explosive development no longer exist. Canada's resource base was once considered infinite, but the environment is now declining and cannot sustain the pressure being put on it. The more that is used today, the less there will be for the generations that follow. Or in the more immediate future, "And how did you intend to pay for that pension, sir?"

In the past, the resource base supported a standard of living far beyond that which Canada's manufacturing capabilities alone could produce. Sweat and basic technology were applied to an entirely free treasure chest of resources. There were no management or replacement costs. The assets were simply there to be harvested.

In Canada's development, population growth was a boon because there were large reserves of untapped resources to underwrite initial growth and sustain a high level of use thereafter. Canada's immigration policy is left over from the period when bigger was assumed to be better.

Today, any nation with a growing population faces an enormous capitalization challenge. National savings must not only be applied to improving the lot of the existing population, but must serve to expand the current capital base to accommodate the additional people.

The World Bank refers to these conflicting capital-allocation options as capital widening (expanding) and capital deepening (upgrading). According to its 1984 report on population and economic development, "for incomes to rise, investment needs to grow faster than the labor force, to ensure capital deepening."

Canada cannot continue to divide its modest capital production between accomodating population growth and upgrading the skills of its people and the tools they use.

For 30 years, Canada has had the fastest-growing labor force in the industrial world. The national savings rate is about average but, given the increasing population, it is inadequate. In 1985 Canadians saved $52 billion U.S., which equalled 19 per-cent of their gross domestic product, while U.S. savings were $522.4 billion, or 16.5 per-cent of the GDP. Compare this to Japan's savings of $358 billion (31.7 per-cent of GDP) and West German's $120.5 billion (22 per-cent of GDP).

In the same year, Canada added 240,000 people to its workforce and invested $18 billion U.S. in machinery and equipment, which works out to $75,286 per new worker.

In the United-States, there were 1.9 million more workers, and investment in equipment was $265 billion, or $135,478 for each.

Meanwhile, Japan's investment of $119.8 billion in equipment works out to $334,521 for each of its 35,800 new workers, and France, with a stable population and a savings rate even less than Canada's, increased its work force by only 48,000 but invested $335.2 billion, or a whopping $775,159 per new worker.

Due to the growing population and diluted investment, workers in the Canadian and U.S. manufacturing sector have actually experienced a decline in their real per-capita earnings over the past eight years.

Will borrowing solve the problem? In recent years, the net external liabilities built up by the United-States and Canada have made them the top two largest debtor nations in the world. On a per-capita basis, however, Canada places first (or should that be last?) with a net level seven times that of the United-States.

The key term in any analysis is "per-capita" because it indicates how well the economy is performing for the individual. China, for example, has a larger gross national product than Canada and, of course, more working people. More money, more jobs, but a per-capita income that is 96 per-cent lower than Canada's. By not differentiating between growth and standard of living, Canada is heading toward China's model.

As the population has grown, Canadians have impoverished the soil, stripped the forests and polluted the air. In per-capita terms, the story is quite telling. Between 1950 and 1985, the amount of crop land per-capita fell 45 per-cent, while the per-capita lumber inventory was more than cut in half.

In addition, Canada has been a net energy importer since 1969 and, but for prairie grain production, would be a net food importer. It simply isn't paying attention to environmental and economic fundamentals. For example, given the global nature of the marketplace and the shift of economic power to the most innovative and flexible producers, the size of a country's population is of declining importance. Among the 20 leading nations in terms of per-capita income (excluding oil exporters), Canada is the sixth-largest with its population of more than 25 million. If the United-States is left out, the average population of the top 19 nations is only 24 million.

Canada has basically reached the point that its population should be stable. Given the decline in its natural assets, economic policies based on increased levels of resource exploitation or population growth are counterproductive. The country needs policies that recognize current realities.

To prosper, Canada must get better, not bigger. It must produce products that will do well in both domestic and foreign markets, and this requires focusing on quality, innovation and flexibility.

There has never been a more opportune time for a government to offer leadership with a comprehensive national plan of economic modernization based on the benefits (and the neccessity) of population stabilization and environmental renewal.

More than 65 per-cent of Canadians think the population should grow no larger. Only 25 per-cent think immigration should exceed 50,000 a year (the current level is 120,000). Public support for environmental protection and recovery is at an all-time high.

Change and carry on? Or merely continue in a long decline? As the environment fades, so do the Canadian way of life and its prospects for future generations.

References

Benson, James D. and William S. Greaves
1981 Field of discourse: Theory and application. *Applied Linguistics* 2:45-55.

Halliday, M.A.K.
1978 *Language as Social Semiotic*. London: Edward Arnold.

1985a *An Introduction to Functional Grammar*. London: Edward Arnold.

1985b *Spoken and Written Language*. Victoria: Deakin University Press.

Martin, James R.
1985 *Factual Writing: Exploring and Challenging Social Reality*. Victoria: Deakin University Press.

Reed, Alan
1984 "Anatomy of a text analysis package". *Computer Language* 9 2:89-96.

1977 CLOC: A collocation package. *ALLC Bulletin* 5:168-173.

Since 1990 the following titles have been published or are scheduled for publication in 1992:

6. VERSCHUEREN, Jef (ed.): *Selected Papers from the 1987 International Pragmatics Conference. Vol. I: Pragmatics at Issue. Vol. II: Levels of Linguistic Adaptation. Vol. III: The Pragmatics of Intercultural and International Communication (ed. with Jan Blommaert).* Amsterdam/Philadelphia, 1991.
7. LINDENFELD, Jacqueline: *Speech and Sociability at French Urban Market Places.* Amsterdam/Philadelphia, 1990.
8. YOUNG, Lynne: *Language as Behaviour, Language as Code: A Study of Academic English.* Amsterdam/Philadelphia, 1990.
9. LUKE, Kang-Kwong: *Utterance Particles in Cantonese Conversation.* Amsterdam/Philadelphia, 1990.
10. MURRAY, Denise E.: *Conversation for Action. The computer terminal as medium of communication.* Amsterdam/Philadelphia, 1991.
11. LUONG, Hy V.: *Discursive Practices and Linguistic Meanings. The Vietnamese system of person reference.* Amsterdam/Philadelphia, 1990.
12. ABRAHAM, Werner (ed.): *Discourse Particles. Descriptive and theoretical investigations on the logical, syntactic and pragmatic properties of discourse particles in German.* Amsterdam/Philadelphia, 1991.
13. NUYTS, Jan, A. Machtelt BOLKESTEIN and Co VET (eds): *Layers and Levels of Representation in Language Theory: a functional view.* Amsterdam/Philadelphia, 1990.
14. SCHWARTZ, Ursula: *Young Children's Dyadic Pretend Play.* Amsterdam/Philadelphia, 1991.
15. KOMTER, Martha: *Conflict and Cooperation in Job Interviews.* Amsterdam/Philadelphia, 1991.
16. MANN, William C. and Sandra A. THOMPSON (eds): *Discourse Description: Diverse Linguistic Analyses of a Fund-Raising Text.* Amsterdam/Philadelphia, 1992.
17. PIÉRAUT-LE BONNIEC, Gilberte and Marlene DOLITSKY (eds): *Language Bases ... Discourse Bases.* Amsterdam/Philadelphia, 1991.
18. JOHNSTONE, Barbara: *Repetition in Arabic Discourse. Paradigms, syntagms and the ecology of language.* Amsterdam/Philadelphia, 1991.
19. BAKER, Carolyn D. and Allan LUKE (eds): *Towards a Critical Sociology of Reading Pedagogy. Papers of the XII World Congress on Reading.* Amsterdam/Philadelphia, 1991.
20. NUYTS, Jan: *Aspects of a Cognitive-Pragmatic Theory of Language. On cognition, functionalism, and grammar.* Amsterdam/Philadelphia, 1992.
21. SEARLE, John R. et al.: *(On) Searle on Conversation.* Compiled and introduced by Herman Parret and Jef Verschueren. Amsterdam/Philadelphia, 1992.
22. AUER, Peter and Aldo Di LUZIO (eds): *The Contextualization of Language.* Amsterdam/Philadelphia, 1992. n.y.p.
23. FORTESCUE, Michael, Peter HARDER and Lars KRISTOFFERSEN (eds): *Layered Structure and Reference in a Functional Perspective.* Papers from the Functional Grammar Conference, Copenhagen, 1990. Amsterdam/Philadelphia, 1992. n.y.p.

A full list of titles published in this series is available from the publisher.